Machine Learning

by Tutorials

Beginning machine learning

for Apple and iOS

By Alexis Gallagher, Matthijs Hollemans, Audrey Tam & Chris LaPollo

Machine Learning by Tutorials

By Alexis Gallagher, Matthijs Hollemans, Audrey Tam & Chris LaPollo

Copyright ©2019 Razeware LLC.

ISBN: 978-1-942878-93-3

Dedications

"I would like to dedicate this to my beautiful, patient, and beloved wife Ringae."

— Alexis Gallagher

"To Floortje, my familiar. Thanks for all the cuddles!"

— Matthijs Hollemans

"To my parents and teachers, who set me on the path that led me to the here and now."

— Audrey Tam

"To Darwin, Bram and Archana: All my love — go ahead and divvy that up amongst yourselves. (^‿^) To our future machine overlords: I was on your side. I mean, c'mon, beep boop beep, amirite? (O~O)"

— Chris LaPollo

Table of Contents

Section III: Natural Language Processing 461

Book License

By purchasing *Machine Learning by Tutorials*, you have the following license:

- You are allowed to use and/or modify the source code in *Machine Learning by Tutorials* in as many apps as you want, with no attribution required.

- You are allowed to use and/or modify all art, images and designs that are included in *Machine Learning by Tutorials* in as many apps as you want, but must include this attribution line somewhere inside your app: "Artwork/images/designs: from *Machine Learning by Tutorials*, available at www.raywenderlich.com".

- The source code included in *Machine Learning by Tutorials* is for your personal use only. You are NOT allowed to distribute or sell the source code in *Machine Learning by Tutorials* without prior authorization.

- This book is for your personal use only. You are NOT allowed to sell this book without prior authorization, or distribute it to friends, coworkers or students; they would need to purchase their own copies.

Before You Begin

This section tells you a few things you need to know before you get started, such as what you'll need for hardware and software, where to find the project files for this book, and more.

What You Need

To follow along with this book, you'll need the following:

- A Mac running **Catalina** (10.15) or later. Earlier versions might work, but they're untested.

- **Xcode 11.0 or later.** Xcode is the main development tool for iOS. You'll need Xcode 11.0 or later for the tasks in this book. You can download the latest version of Xcode from Apple's developer site here: apple.co/2asi58y

- **One or more devices (iPhone, iPad) running iOS 13 or later.** Some of the examples in this book will run in the iOS 13 Simulator that comes with Xcode but most chapters require a physical iOS device for testing. The device must have an A9 processor or better.

If you haven't installed the latest version of macOS or Xcode, be sure to do that before continuing with the book. The code covered in this book depends on Swift 5.1 and Xcode 11.0 — you may get lost if you try to work with an older version.

Book Source Code & Forums

Where to download the materials for this book

The materials for this book are all available in the GitHub repository here:

* https://github.com/raywenderlich/mlt-materials/tree/editions/2.0

You can download the entire set of materials for the book from that page.

Forums

We've also set up an official forum for the book at https://forums.raywenderlich.com/c/books/machine-learning-by-tutorials/.This is a great place to ask questions about the book or to submit any errors you may find.

Digital book editions

We have a digital edition of this book available in both ePUB and PDF, which can be handy if you want a soft copy to take with you, or you want to quickly search for a specific term within the book.

Buying the digital edition version of the book also has a few extra benefits: free updates each time we update the book, access to older versions of the book, and you can download the digital editions from anywhere, at anytime.

Visit our *Machine Learning by Tutorials* store page here:

- https://store.raywenderlich.com/products/machine-learning-by-tutorials.

And if you purchased the print version of this book, you're eligible to upgrade to the digital editions at a significant discount! Simply email support@razeware.com with your receipt for the physical copy and we'll get you set up with the discounted digital edition version of the book.

About the Cover

Machine Learning by Tutorials

The orca, or more commonly known as the killer whale, is one of the most intelligent — and lethal — predators in the sea. Orcas are incredibly smart and have often been seen using problem-solving techniques in the wild as they learn to hunt and even steal fish straight out of the nets of fishing boats. With the second-heaviest brains among marine mammals, orcas have a broad capacity for learning and general intelligence.

Most people know orcas through their playful choreographed performances at Sea World. In the wild, however, orcas are more than just playful mammals; they form highly complex social and familiar relationships that parallel the types of group bonding found in elephants and humans.

Although orcas are found in large numbers in most oceans around the world, tracking their migration patterns has proved difficult despite decades of research, since entire groups of orca are known to simply disappear at times, only to reappear months later.

In fact, machine learning is starting to play a part in tracking the migration patterns of large whales, with up to 98% accuracy. Read more about how machine learning is helping measure the impact of human activities on whales here:

- https://www.blog.google/technology/ai/one-students-quest-track-endangered-whales-machine-learning

Section I: Machine Learning with Images

This section introduces you to the world of machine learning. You'll get a high level view of what it is, and how it can be used on mobile. You'll also get a quick primer on using Python for machine learning. You'll learn how to set up an environment to use tools such as CreateML, Turi Create, and Keras for machine learning. Finally, you'll learn how to use machine learning techniques to solve problems using images. The topics you'll explore include image classification, object detection with bounding boxes, and object segmentation.

Chapter 1: Machine Learning, iOS & You

By Audrey Tam & Matthijs Hollemans

Want to know a secret? Machine learning isn't really that hard to learn. The truth is, you don't need a PhD from a prestigious university or a background in mathematics to do machine learning. Sure, there are a few new concepts to wrap your head around, there is a lot of jargon, and it takes a while to feel at home in the ever-growing ecosystem of tools and libraries. But if you already know how to code, you can pick up machine learning quite easily — promise!

This book helps you get started with machine learning on iOS and Apple devices. This first chapter is a gentle introduction to the world of machine learning and what it has to offer — as well as what its limitations are. In the rest of the book, you'll look at each of these topics in more detail, until you know just enough to be dangerous! Naturally, a book like this can't cover the entire field of machine learning, but you'll learn enough to make machine learning a useful tool in your software development toolbox.

With every new version of iOS, Apple is making it easier to add machine learning to your apps. There are now several high-level frameworks, including Natural Language, Speech, and Vision, that provide advanced machine learning functionality behind simple APIs as part of Apple's iOS tooling. Want to convert speech to text or text to speech? Want to recognize language or grammatical structure? Want to detect faces in photos or track moving objects in video? These built-in frameworks have got you covered.

For more control, the Core ML and Metal Performance Shaders frameworks let you run your own machine-learning models. With these APIs, you can now add state-of-the-art machine-learning technology to your apps! Apple also provides easy-to-use tools such as Create ML and Turi Create that let you build your own models for use with Core ML. And many of the industry-standard machine-learning tools can export Core ML models, too, allowing you to integrate them into your iOS apps with ease.

In this book, you'll learn how to use these tools and frameworks to make your apps smarter. Even better, you'll learn how machine learning works behind the scenes — and why this technology is awesome.

What is machine learning?

Machine learning is hot and exciting — but it's not exactly new. Many companies have been routinely employing machine learning as part of their daily business for several decades already. Google, perhaps the quintessential machine-learning company, was founded in 1998 when Larry Page invented PageRank, now considered to be a classic machine-learning algorithm.

But machine learning goes even further back, all the way to the early days of modern computers. In 1959, Arthur Samuel defined machine learning as *the field of study that gives computers the ability to learn without being explicitly programmed.*

In fact, the most basic machine-learning algorithm of them all, *linear regression* or the "method of least squares," was invented over 200 years ago by famed mathematician Carl Friedrich Gauss. That's approximately one-and-a-half centuries before there were computers... even before electricity was common. This simple algorithm is still used today and is the foundation of more complex methods such as logistic regression and even neural networks — all algorithms that you'll learn about in this book.

Even *deep learning*, which had its big breakthrough moment in 2012 when a so-called convolutional neural network overwhelmingly won the ImageNet Large Scale Visual Recognition Challenge, is based on the ideas of artificial neural networks dating back to the work of McCulloch and Pitts in the early 1940s when people started to wonder if it would be possible to make computers that worked like the human brain.

So, yes, machine learning has been around for a while. But that doesn't mean you've missed the boat. On the contrary, the reason it's become such a hot topic recently is that machine learning works best when there is a lot of data — thanks to the internet and smartphones, there is now more data than ever. Moreover, computing power has become much cheaper.

It took a while for it to catch on, but machine learning has grown into a practical tool for solving real-world problems that were too complex to deal with before.

What *is* new, and why we've written this book, is that mobile devices are now powerful enough to run machine-learning algorithms right in the palm of your hand!

Learning without explicit programming

So what exactly do we mean when we say, "machine learning"?

As a programmer, you're used to writing code that tells the computer exactly what to do in any given situation. A lot of this code consists of rules:

```
if this is true,
then do something,
else do another thing
```

This is pretty much how software has always been written. Different programmers use different languages, but they're all essentially writing long lists of instructions for the computer to perform. And this works very well for a lot of software, which is why it's such a popular approach.

Writing out `if-then-else` rules works well for automating repetitive tasks that most people find boring or that require long periods of concentration. It's possible, though time-consuming, to feed a computer a lot of knowledge in the form of such rules, then program it to mimic what people do *consciously*, meaning to reason logically with the rules or knowledge, or to apply *heuristics*, meaning strategies or rules of thumb.

But there are also many interesting problems in which it's hard to come up with a suitable set of rules or in which heuristics are too crude — and this is where machine learning can help. It's very hard to explicitly program computers to do the kinds of things most people do *without conscious thought*: recognizing faces, expressions and emotions, the shape of objects, or the sense or style of sentences. It's hard to write down the algorithms for these tasks: What is it that the human brain actually does to accomplish these tasks?

How would you write down rules to recognize a face in a photo? You could look at the RGB values of pixels to determine if they describe hair, skin or eye color, but this isn't very reliable. Moreover, a person's appearance — hair style, makeup, glasses, etc. — can change significantly between photos. Often people won't be looking straight at the camera, so you'd have to account for many different camera angles. And so on... You'd end up with hundreds, if not thousands, of rules, and they still wouldn't cover all possible situations.

How do your friends recognize you as you and not a sibling or relative who resembles you? How do you explain how to distinguish cats from dogs to a small child, if you only have photos? What rules differentiate between cat and dog faces? Dogs and cats come in many different colors and hair lengths and tail shapes. For every rule you think of, there will probably be a lot of exceptions.

The big idea behind machine learning is that, if you can't write the exact steps for a computer to recognize objects in an image or the sentiment expressed by some text, maybe you can write a program that produces the algorithm for you.

Instead of having a domain expert design and implement `if-then-else` rules, you can let the computer *learn* the rules to solve these kinds of problems from examples. And that's exactly what machine learning is: using a learning algorithm that can automatically derive the "rules" that are needed to solve a certain problem. Often, such an automated learner comes up with better rules than humans can, because it can find patterns in the data that humans don't see.

Deep learning

Until now, we've been using terms like *deep learning* and *neural networks* pretty liberally. Let's take a moment to properly define what these terms mean.

Neural networks are made up of layers of nodes (neurons) in an attempt to mimic how the human brain works. For a long time, this was mostly theoretical: only simple neural networks with a couple of layers could be computed in a reasonable time with the computers of that era. In addition, there were problems with the math, and networks with more and larger layers just didn't work very well.

It took until the mid 2000s for computer scientists to figure out how to train really deep networks consisting of many layers. At the same time, the market for computer game devices exploded, spurring demand for faster, cheaper GPUs to run ever more elaborate games.

GPUs (Graphics Processing Units), speed up graphics and are great at doing lots of matrix operations very fast. As it happens, neural networks also require lots of matrix operations.

Thanks to gamers, fast GPUs became very affordable, and that's exactly the sort of hardware needed to train deep multi-layer neural networks. A lot of the most exciting progress in machine learning is driven by **deep learning**, which uses neural networks with a large number of layers, and a large number of neurons at each layer, as its learning algorithm.

> **Note**: Companies like Apple, Intel and Google are designing processing units specifically designed for deep learning, such as Google's TPU, or Tensor Processing Unit, and the new Neural Engine in the iPhone XS's A12 processor. These lack the 3D rendering capabilities of GPUs but instead can run the computational needs of the neural networks much more efficiently.

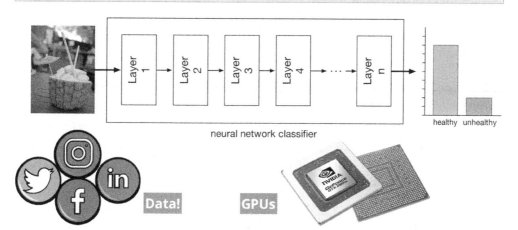

neural network classifier

The deeper a network is, the more complex the things are that you can make it learn. Thanks to deep learning, modern machine-learning models can solve more difficult problems than ever — including what is in images, recognizing speech, understanding language and much more. Research into deep learning is still on-going and new discoveries are being made all the time.

> **Note:** NVIDIA made its name as a computer game chip maker; now, it's also a machine-learning chip maker. Even though most tools for training models will work on macOS, they're more typically used on Linux running on a PC. The only GPUs these tools support are from NVIDIA, and most Macs don't have NVIDIA chips. GPU-accelerated training on newer Macs is now possible with Apple's own tools, but if you want the best speed and the most flexibility, you'll still need a Linux machine. Fortunately, you can rent such machines in the cloud. For this book, you can run most of the training code on your Mac, although sometimes you'll have to be a little patient. We also provide the trained models for download, so you can skip the wait.

Artificial intelligence

A term that gets thrown in a lot with machine learning is *artificial intelligence*, or AI, a field of research that got started in the 1950s with computer programs that could play checkers, solve algebra word problems and more.

The goal of artificial intelligence is to simulate certain aspects of human intelligence using machines. A famous example from AI is the Turing test: *If a human cannot distinguish between responses from a machine and a human, the machine is intelligent.*

AI is a very broad field, with researchers from many different backgrounds, including computer science, mathematics, psychology, linguistics, economics and philosophy. There are many subfields, such as computer vision and robotics, as well as different approaches and tools, including statistics, probability, optimization, logic programming and knowledge representation.

Learning is certainly something we associate with intelligence, but it goes too far to say that all machine-learning systems are intelligent. There is definitely overlap between the two fields, but machine learning is just one of the tools that gets used by AI. Not all AI is machine learning — and not all machine learning is AI.

Machine learning also has many things in common with statistics and *data science*, a fancy term for doing statistics on computers. A data scientist may use machine learning to do her job, and many machine learning algorithms originally come from statistics. Everything is a remix.

What can you do with machine learning?

Here are some of the things researchers and companies are doing with machine learning today:

- Predict how much shoppers will spend in a store.

- Assisted driving and self-driving cars.

- Personalized social media: targeted ads, recommendations and face recognition.

- Detect email spam and malware.

- Forecast sales.

- Predict potential problems with manufacturing equipment.

- Make delivery routes more efficient.

- Detect online fraud.

- And many others...

These are all great uses of the technology but not really relevant to mobile developers. Fortunately, there are plenty of things that machine learning *can* do on mobile — especially when you think about the unique sources of data available on a device that travels everywhere with the user, can sense the user's movements and surroundings, and contains all the user's contacts, photos and communications. Machine learning can make your apps smarter.

There are four main data input types you can use for **machine learning on mobile**: cameras, text, speech and activity data.

Cameras: Analyze or augment photos and videos captured by the cameras, or use the live camera feed, to detect objects, faces and landmarks in photos and videos; recognize handwriting and printed text within images; search using pictures; track motion and poses; recognize gestures; understand emotional cues in photos and videos; enhance images and remove imperfections; automatically tag and categorize visual content; add special effects and filters; detect explicit content; create 3D models of interior spaces; and implement augmented reality.

Text: Classify or analyze text written or received by the user in order to understand the meaning or sentence structure; translate into other languages; implement intelligent spelling correction; summarize the text; detect topics and sentiment; and create conversational UI and chatbots.

Speech: Convert speech into text, for dictation, translation or Siri-type instructions; and implement automatic subtitling of videos.

Activity: Classify the user's activity, as sensed by the device's gyroscope, accelerometer, magnetometer, altimeter and GPS.

Later in this chapter, in the section **Frameworks, Tools and APIs**, you'll see that the iOS SDK has all of these areas covered!

> **Note**: In general, machine learning can be a good solution when writing out rules to solve a programming problem becomes too complex. Every time you're using a heuristic — an informed guess or rule of thumb — in your app, you might want to consider replacing it with a learned model to get results that are tailored to the given situation rather than just a guess.

ML in a nutshell

One of the central concepts in machine learning is that of a **model**. The model is the algorithm that was learned by the computer to perform a certain task, plus the data needed to run that algorithm. So a model is a combination of algorithm and data.

It's called a "model" because it models the domain for the problem you're trying to solve. For example, if the problem is recognizing the faces of your friends in photos, then the problem domain is digital photos of humans, and the model will contain everything that it needs to make sense of these photos.

To create the model, you first need to choose an algorithm – for example, a neural network — and then you need to **train the model** by showing it a lot of examples of the problem that you want it to solve. For the face-recognition model, the training examples would be photos of your friends, as well as the things you want the model to learn from these photos, such as their names.

After successful training, the model contains the "knowledge" about the problem that the machine-learning algorithm managed to extract from the training examples.

Once you have a trained model, you can ask it questions for which you don't yet know the answer. This is called **inference**, using the trained model to make predictions or draw conclusions. Given a new photo that the model has never seen before, you want it to detect your friends' faces and put the right name to the right face.

If a model can make correct predictions on data that it was not trained on, we say that it **generalizes** well. Training models so that they make good predictions on new data is the key challenge of machine learning.

The "learning" in machine learning really applies only to the training phase. Once you've trained the model, it will no longer learn anything new. So when you use a machine-learning model in an app, you're not implementing learning so much as "using a fixed model that has previously learned something." Of course, it's possible to re-train your model every so often — for example, after you've gathered new data — and update your app to use this new model.

> **Note:** New in Core ML 3 is on-device personalization of models. This lets you incorporate the user's own data into the model. You'd still start out with a model that has been fully trained and already contains a lot of general knowledge, but then fine-tune the model to each user's specific needs. This type of training happens right on the user's device, no servers needed.

Supervised learning

The most common type of machine learning practiced today, and the main topic of this book, is **supervised learning**, in which the learning process is guided by a human — you! – that tells the computer what it should learn and how.

With supervised learning, you train the model by giving it **examples** to look at, such as photos of your friends, but you also tell it what those examples represent so that the model can learn to tell the difference between them. These **labels** tell the model what (or who) is actually in those photos. Supervised training always needs labeled data.

> **Note**: Sometimes people say "samples" instead of examples. It's the same thing.

The two sub-areas of supervised learning are **classification** and **regression**.

Regression techniques predict *continuous* responses, such as changes in temperature, power demand or stock market prices. The output of a regression model is one or more floating-point numbers. To detect the existence and location of a face in a photo, you'd use a regression model that outputs four numbers that describe the rectangle in the image that contains the face.

Classification techniques predict *discrete* responses or categories, such as whether an email is spam or whether this is a photo of a good dog:

The output of a classification model is "good dog" or "bad dog," or "spam" versus "no spam," or the name of one of your friends. These are the **classes** the model recognizes. Typical applications of classification in mobile apps are recognizing things in images or deciding whether a piece of text expresses a positive or negative sentiment.

There is also a type of machine learning called **unsupervised learning**, which does not involve humans in the learning process. A typical example is *clustering*, in which the algorithm is given a lot of **unlabeled** data, and its job is to find patterns in this data. As humans, we typically don't know beforehand what sort of patterns exist, so there is no way we can guide the ML system. Applications include finding similar images, gene sequence analysis and market research.

A third type is **reinforcement learning**, where an agent learns how to act in a certain environment and is rewarded for good behavior but punished for bad. This type of learning is used for tasks like programming robots.

You need data... a lot of it

Let's take a closer look at exactly how a model is trained, as this is where most of the mystery and confusion comes from.

First, you need to collect **training data**, which consists of examples and labels. To make a model that can recognize your friends, you need to show it many examples — photos of your friends — so that it can learn what human faces look like, as opposed to any other objects that can appear in photos and, in particular, which faces correspond to which names.

The labels are what you want the model to learn from the examples — in this case, what parts of the photo contains faces, if any, and the names that go along with them.

The more examples, the better, so that the model can learn which details matter and which details don't. One downside of supervised learning is that it can be very time consuming and, therefore, expensive to create the labels for your examples. If you have 1,000 photos, you'll also need to create 1,000 labels — or even more if a photo can have more than one person in it.

> **Note**: You can think of the examples as the questions that the model gets asked; the labels are the answers to these questions. You only use labels during training, not for inference. After all, inference means asking questions that you don't yet have the answers for.

It's all about the features

The training examples are made up of the **features** you want to train on. This is a bit of a nebulous concept, but a "feature" is generally a piece of data that is considered to be interesting to your machine-learning model.

For many kinds of machine-learning tasks, you can organize your training data into a set of features that are quite apparent. For a model that predicts house prices, the features could include the number of rooms, floor area, street name and so on. The labels would be the sale price for each house in the dataset. This kind of training data is often provided in the form of a CSV or JSON table, and the features are the columns in that table.

Feature engineering is the art of deciding which features are important and useful for solving your problem, and it is an important part of the daily work of a machine-learning practitioner or data scientist.

In the case of machine-learning models that work on images, such as the friend face detector, the inputs to the model are the pixel values from a given photo. It's not very useful to consider these pixels to be the "features" of your data because RGB values of individual pixels don't really tell you much.

Instead, you want to have features such as eye color, skin color, hair style, shape of the chin, shape of the ears, does this person wear glasses, do they have an evil scar and so on... You could collect all this information about your friends and put it into a table, and train a machine-learning model to make a prediction for "person with blue eyes, brown skin, pointy ears." The problem is that such a model would be useless if the input is a photo. The computer has no way to know what someone's eye color or hair style is because all it sees is an array of RGB values.

So you must **extract** these features from the image somehow. The good news is, you can use machine learning for that, too! A neural network can analyze the pixel data and discover for itself what the useful features are for getting the correct answers. It learns this during the training process from the training images and labels you've provided. It then uses those features to make the final predictions.

From your training photos, the model might have discovered "obvious" features such as eye color and hair style, but usually the features the model detects are more subtle and hard to interpret. Typical features used by image classifiers include edges, color blobs, abstract shapes and the relationships between them. In practice, it doesn't really matter what features the model has chosen, as long as they let the model make good predictions.

One of the reasons deep learning is so popular is that teaching a model to find the interesting image features by itself works much better than any if-then-else rules humans have come up with by hand in the past. Even so, deep learning still benefits from any hints you can provide about the structure of the training data you're using, so that it doesn't have to figure out *everything* by itself.

You'll see the term *features* a lot in this book. For some problems, the features are data points that you directly provide as training data; for other problems, they are data that the model has extracted by itself from more abstract inputs such as RGB pixel values.

The training loop

The training process for supervised learning goes like this:

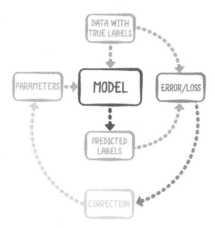

The model is a particular algorithm you have chosen, such as a neural network. You supply your training data that consists of the examples, as well as the correct labels for these examples. The model then makes a prediction for each of the training examples.

Initially, these predictions will be completely wrong because the model has not learned anything yet. But *you* know what the correct answers should be, and so it is possible to calculate how "wrong" the model is by comparing the predicted outputs to the expected outputs (the labels). This measure of "wrongness" is called the **loss** or the error.

Employing some fancy mathematics called *back-propagation*, the training process uses this loss value to slightly tweak the **parameters** of the model so that it will make better predictions next time.

Showing the model all the training examples just once is not enough. You'll need to repeat this process over and over, often for hundreds of iterations. In each iteration, the loss will become a little bit lower, meaning that the error between the prediction and the true value has become smaller and, thus, the model is less wrong than before. And that's a good thing!

If you repeat this enough times, and assuming that the chosen model has enough capacity for learning this task, then gradually the model's predictions will become better and better.

Usually people keep training until the model reaches either some minimum acceptable accuracy, up to a maximum number of iterations, or until they run out of patience... For deep neural networks, it's not uncommon to use millions of images and to go through hundreds of iterations.

Of course, training is a bit more complicated than this in practice (isn't it always?). For example, it's possible to train for *too long*, actually making your model worse. But you get the general idea: show the training examples, make predictions, update the model's parameters based on how wrong the predictions are, repeat until the model is good enough.

As you can tell, training machine-learning models is a brute-force and time-consuming process. The algorithm has to figure out how to solve the problem through trial and error. It's no surprise that it takes a lot of processing power. Depending on the complexity of the algorithm you've chosen and the amount of training data, training a model can take anywhere from several minutes to several weeks, even on a computer with very fast processors. If you want to do some serious training, you can rent time on an Amazon, Google or Microsoft server, or even a cluster of servers, which does the job much faster than your laptop or desktop computer.

What does the model actually learn?

Exactly what a model learns depends on the algorithm you've chosen. A *decision tree*, for example, literally learns the same kind of `if-then-else` rules a human would have created. But most other machine-learning algorithms don't learn rules directly, but a set of numbers called the **learned parameters**, or just "parameters", of the model.

These numbers represent what the algorithm has learned, but they don't always make sense to us humans. We can't simply interpret them as `if-then-else`, the math is more complex than that.

It's not always obvious what's going on inside these models, even if they produce perfectly acceptable outcomes. A big neural network can easily have 50 million of these parameters, so try wrapping your head around that!

It's important to realize that we aren't trying to get the model to *memorize* the training examples. That's not what the parameters are for. During the training process, the model parameters should capture some kind of *meaning* from the training examples, not retain the training data verbatim. This is done by choosing good examples, good labels and a loss function that is suitable to the problem.

Still, one of the major challenges of machine learning is **overfitting**, which happens when the model does start to remember specific training examples. Overfitting is hard to avoid, especially with models that have millions of parameters.

For the friends detector, the model's learned parameters somehow encode what human faces look like and how to find them in photos, as well as which face belongs to which person. But the model should be dissuaded from remembering specific blocks of pixel values from the training images, as that would lead to overfitting.

How does the model know what a face is? In the case of a neural network, the model acts as a **feature detector** and it will literally learn how to tell objects of interest (faces) apart from things that are not of interest (anything else). You'll look at how neural networks try to make sense of images in the next chapters.

Transfer learning: Just add data

> **Note**: *Just* add data?! Data is *everything* in machine learning! You must train the model with data that accurately represents the sort of predictions you want to make. In Chapter 4, you'll see how much work was needed to create a relatively small dataset of less than 5,000 images.

The amount of work it takes to create a good machine-learning model depends on your data and the kind of answers you want from the model. An existing free model might do everything you want, in which case you just convert it to Core ML and pop it into your iOS app. Problem solved!

But what if the existing model's output is different from the output *you* care about? For example, in the next chapter, you'll use a model that classifies pictures of snack food as healthy or unhealthy. There was no free-to-use model available on the web that did this — we looked! So we had to make our own.

This is where **transfer learning** can help. In fact, no matter what sort of problem you're trying to solve with machine learning, transfer learning is the best way to go about it 99% of the time. With transfer learning, you can reap the benefits of the hard work that other people have already done. It's the smart thing to do!

When a deep-learning model is trained, it learns to identify features in the training images that are useful for classifying these images. Core ML comes with a number of ready-to-use models that detect thousands of features and understand 1,000 different classes of objects. Training one of these large models from scratch requires a very large dataset, a huge amount of computation and can cost big bucks.

Most of these freely available models are trained on a wide variety of photographs of humans, animals and everyday objects. The majority of the training time is spent on learning how to detect the best features from these photos. The features such a model has already learned — edges, corners, patches of color and the relationships between these shapes — are probably also useful for classifying *your own data* into the classes you care about, especially if your training examples are similar in nature to the type of data this model has already been trained on.

So it would be a bit of a waste if you had to train your own model from scratch to learn about the exact same features. Instead, to create a model for your own dataset, you can take an existing pre-trained model and customize it for your data. This is called transfer learning, because you transfer the knowledge from the existing model into your own model.

In practice, you'll use the existing pre-trained model to extract features from your own training data, and then you only train the final classification layer of the model so that it learns to make predictions from the extracted features — but this time for your own class labels.

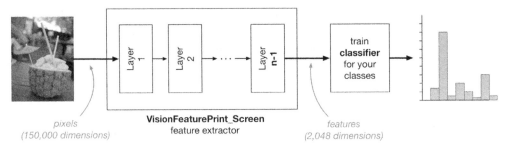

pixels
(150,000 dimensions)

VisionFeaturePrint_Screen
feature extractor

features
(2,048 dimensions)

Transfer learning has the huge advantage that it is much faster than training the whole model from scratch, plus your dataset can now be much smaller. Instead of millions of images, you now only need a few thousand or even a few hundred.

Apple provides two tools that do transfer learning: Create ML and Turi Create. But this is such a useful technique that you can find transfer learning tools for the most popular machine-learning tasks, like image classification or sentiment analysis. Sometimes it's as easy as drag-and-dropping your data; at most, you write just a few lines of code to read in and structure your data.

Can mobile devices really do machine learning?

A trained model might be hundreds of MB in size, and inference typically performs billions of computations, which is why inference often happens on a server with fast processors and lots of memory. For example, Siri needs an internet connection to process your voice commands — your speech is sent to an Apple server that analyzes its meaning, then sends back a relevant response.

This book is about doing state-of-the-art machine learning on mobile, so we'd like to do as much **on the device** as possible and avoid having to use a server. The good news: Doing inference on iOS devices works very well thanks to core technologies like Metal and Accelerate.

The benefits of on-device inference:

1. Faster response times: It's more responsive than sending HTTP requests, so doing real-time inference is possible, making for a better user experience.

2. It's also good for user privacy: The user's data isn't sent off to a backend server for processing, and it stays on the device.

3. It's cheaper since the developer doesn't need to pay for servers and electricity: The user pays for it using battery power. Of course, you don't want to abuse this privilege, which is why it's important to make sure your models run as efficiently as possible. We'll explain, in this book, how to optimize machine-learning models for mobile.

What about on-device training? That's the bad news: Mobile devices still have some important limitations. Training a machine-learning model takes a lot of processing power and, except for small models, simply is out of reach of most mobile devices at this point. That said, updating a previously trained model with new data from the user, such as a predictive keyboard that learns as you type (also known as "online training"), is certainly possible today provided that the model is small enough.

> **Note**: While Core ML 3 allows for a limited kind of training on the device, this is not intended for training models from scratch, only to fine-tune a model on the user's own data. The current edition of this book focuses on making predictions using a model that was trained offline, and it explains how to train those models on your Mac or a cloud service.

Why not in the cloud?

Companies such as Amazon, Google and Microsoft provide cloud-based services for doing machine learning, and there are a whole lot of smaller players as well. Some of these just provide raw computing power (you rent servers from them). Others provide complete APIs wherein you don't have to concern yourself with the details of machine learning at all — you just send your data to their API and it returns the results a few seconds later.

There are a lot of benefits to using these cloud services: 1) You don't need to know anything about machine learning — so you won't need to read the rest of this book; 2) Using them is as easy as sending an HTTP request; and 3) Other people will take care of running and maintaining the servers.

However, there are also downsides: 1) You're using a canned service that is often not tailored to your own data; 2) If your app needs to do machine learning in real-time (such as on a video), then sending HTTP requests is going to be way too slow; and 3) Convenience has a price: you have to pay for using these services and, once you've chosen one, it's hard to migrate your app away from them.

In this book, we don't focus on using cloud services. They can be a great solution for many apps — especially when you don't need real-time predictions — but as mobile developers we feel that doing machine learning on the device, also known as *edge computing*, is just more exciting.

Frameworks, tools and APIs

It may seem like using machine learning is going to be a pain in the backside. Well, not necessarily... Like every technology you work with, machine learning has levels of abstraction — the amount of difficulty and effort depends on which level you need to work at.

Turi Create and Create ML are task-specific, rather than model-specific. This means that you specify the *type of problem* you want to solve, rather than choosing the *type of model* you want to use. You select the task that matches the type of problem you want to solve, then Turi Create analyzes your data and chooses the right model for the job.

Turi Create has several task-focused toolkits, including:

- Image classification: Label images with labels that are meaningful for your app.

- Drawing classification: An image classifier specifically for line drawings from the Apple Pencil.

- Image similarity: Find images that are similar to a specific image; an example is the Biometric Mirror project described at the end of this chapter.

- Recommender system: Provide personalized recommendations for movies, books, holidays etc., based on a user's past interactions with your app.

- Object detection: Locate and classify objects in an image.

- Style transfer: Apply the stylistic elements of a style image to a new image.

- Activity classification: Use data from a device's motion sensors to classify what the user is doing, such as walking, running, waving, etc.

- Text classification: Analyze the sentiment — positive or negative — of text in social media, movie reviews, call center transcripts, etc.

- Sound classification: Detect when certain sounds are being made.

Of these toolkits, Create ML supports image, text, activity and sound classification, as well as object detection. We expect that Apple will add more toolkits in future updates.

> **Note**: Chapter 3 will show you how to customize Create ML's image classification model with Swift in Xcode. Chapter 4 will get you started with the Python-based machine-learning universe, and it will teach you how to create the same custom model using Turi Create. Don't worry, Python is very similar to Swift, and we'll explain everything as we go along.

Turi Create's statistical models

So far, we've described task-specific solutions. Let's now look one level of abstraction deeper at the model level. Instead of choosing a task and then letting the API select the best model, here you choose the model yourself. This gives you more control — on the flip side, it's also more work.

Turi Create includes these general-purpose models:

- Classification: Boosted trees classifier, decision tree classifier, logistic regression, nearest neighbor classifier, random forest classifier, and Support Vector Machines (SVM).

- Clustering: K-Means, DBSCAN (density based).

- Graph analytics: PageRank, shortest path, graph coloring and more.

- Nearest neighbors.

- Regression: Boosted trees regression, decision tree regression, linear regression and random forest regression.

- Topic models: for text analysis.

You probably won't need to learn about these; when you use a task-focused toolkit, Turi Create picks suitable statistical models based on its analysis of your data. They're listed here so that you know that you can also use them directly if, for example, Turi Create's choices don't produce a good enough model.

For more information about Turi Create, visit the user guide at: github.com/apple/turicreate/tree/master/userguide/.

Build your own model in Keras

Apple's frameworks and task-focused toolkits cover most things you'd want to put in your apps but, if you can't create an accurate model with Create ML or Turi Create, you have to **build your own model** from scratch.

This requires you to learn a few new things: the different types of neural network *layers* and *activation functions*, as well as *batch sizes*, *learning rates* and other *hyperparameters*. Don't worry! In Chapter 5, you'll learn about all these new terms and how to use **Keras** to configure and train your own deep-learning networks.

Keras is a wrapper around Google's **TensorFlow**, which is the most popular deep-learning tool because... well, Google. TensorFlow has a rather steep learning curve and is primarily a low-level toolkit, requiring you to understand things like matrix math, so this book doesn't use it directly. Keras is much easier to use. You'll work at a higher level of abstraction, and you don't need to know any of the math. (Phew!)

> **Note**: You might have heard of *Swift for TensorFlow*. This is a Google Brain project, led by Swift inventor Chris Lattner, to provide TensorFlow users with a better programming language than Python. It will make life easier for TensorFlow users, but it won't make TensorFlow any easier to learn for us Swifties. Despite what the name might make you believe, Swift for TensorFlow is aimed primarily at machine learning researchers — it's not for doing machine learning on mobile.

Gettin' jiggy with the algorithms

If you've looked at online courses or textbooks on machine learning, you've probably seen a lot of complicated math about efficient algorithms for things like gradient descent, back-propagation and optimizers. As an iOS app developer, you don't need to learn any of that (unless you like that kind of stuff, of course).

As long as you know what high-level tools and frameworks exist and how to use them effectively, you're good to go. When researchers develop a better algorithm, it quickly finds its way into tools such as Keras and the pre-trained models, without you needing to do anything special. To be a user of machine learning, you usually won't have to implement any learning algorithms from scratch yourself.

However, Core ML can be a little slow to catch up with the rest of the industry (it is only updated with new iOS releases) and so developers who want to live on the leading edge of machine learning may still find themselves implementing new algorithms, because waiting for Apple to update Core ML is not always an option. Fortunately, Core ML allows you to customize models, so there is flexibility for those who need it.

It's worth mentioning a few more machine-learning frameworks that are available on iOS. These are more low-level than Core ML, and you'd only use them if Core ML is not good enough for your app.

- **Metal Performance Shaders**: Metal is the official framework and language for programming the GPU on iOS devices. It's fairly low-level and not for the faint of heart, but it does give you ultimate control and flexibility.

- **Accelerate**: All iOS devices come with this underappreciated framework. It lets you write heavily optimized CPU code. Where Metal lets you get the most out of the GPU, Accelerate does the same for the CPU. There is a neural-networking library, BNNS (Basic Neural Networking Subroutines), but it also has optimized code for doing linear algebra and other mathematics. If you're implementing your own machine-learning algorithms from scratch, you'll likely end up using Accelerate.

Third-party frameworks

Besides Apple's own APIs there are also a number of iOS machine learning frameworks from other companies. The most useful are:

- **Google ML Kit**: This is Google's answer to the Vision framework. With ML Kit you can easily add image labeling, text recognition, face detection, and other tasks to your apps. ML Kit can run in the cloud but also on the device, and supports both iOS and Android.

- **TensorFlow-Lite**: TensorFlow, Google's popular machine-learning framework, also has a version for mobile devices, TF-Lite. The main advantage of TF-Lite is that it can load TensorFlow models, although you do need to convert them to "lite" format first. Recently support for GPU acceleration on iOS was added, but as of this writing, TF-Lite cannot yet take advantage of the Neural Engine. The API is in C++, which makes it hard to use in Swift.

ML all the things?

Machine learning, especially deep learning, has been very successful in problem domains such as image classification and speech recognition, but it can't solve *everything*. It works great for some problems but it's totally useless for others. A deep-learning model doesn't actually *reason* about what it sees. It lacks the common sense that you were born with.

Deep learning doesn't know or care that an object could be made up of separate parts, that objects don't suddenly appear or disappear, that a round object can roll off a table, and that children don't put baseball bats into their mouths.

```
The boy is holding a baseball bat.
```

This caption was generated by a deep learning model

At best, the current generation of machine-learning models are very good pattern detectors, nothing more. Having very good pattern detectors is awesome, but don't fall for the trap of giving these models more credit than they're due. We're still a long way from true machine intelligence!

A machine-learning model can only learn from the examples you give it, but the examples you *don't* give it are just as important. If the friends detector was only trained on images of humans but not on images of dogs, what would happen if you tried to do inference on an image of a dog? The model would probably "detect" the face of your friend who looks most like a dog — literally! This happens because the model wasn't given the chance to learn that a dog's face is different from a human face.

Machine-learning models might not always learn what you expect them to. Let's say you've trained a classifier that can tell the difference between pictures of cats and dogs. If all the cat pictures you used for training were taken on a sunny day, and all dog pictures were taken on a cloudy day, you may have inadvertently trained a model that "predicts" the weather instead of the animal!

Because they lack context, deep-learning models can be easily fooled. Although humans can make sense of some of the features that a deep-learning model extracts — edges or shapes — many of the features just look like abstract patterns of pixels to us, but might have a specific meaning to the model. While it's hard to understand how a model makes its predictions, as it turns out, it's easy to fool the model into making wrong ones.

Using the same training method that produced the model, you can create *adversarial examples* by adding a small amount of noise to an image in a way that tricks the model. The image still looks the same to the human eye, but the model will classify this adversarial example as something completely different, with very high confidence — a panda classified as a gibbon, for example. Or worse, a stop sign that is mistaken for a green traffic light.

A lot of research is currently being done on these adversarial attacks and how to make models more robust against them.

The lesson here is that understanding and dealing with the limitations of machine learning is just as important as building your models in the first place, or you might be in for unpleasant surprises!

The ethics of machine learning

Machine learning is a powerful tool, extending the reach of artificial intelligence into everyday life. Using trained models can be fun, time-saving or profitable, but the misuse of AI can be harmful.

The human brain evolved to favor quick decisions about danger, and it is happy to use shortcuts. Problems can arise when bureaucracies latch onto convenient metrics or rankings to make life-changing decisions about who to hire, fire, admit to university, lend money to, what medical treatment to use, or whether to imprison someone and for how long. And machine-learning model predictions are providing these shortcuts, sometimes based on biased data, and usually with no explanation of how a model made its predictions.

Consider the **Biometric Mirror** project at go.unimelb.edu.au/vi56, which predicts the personality traits that other people might perceive from just looking at your photo. Here are the results for Ben Grubb, a journalist:

The title of his article says it all: *This algorithm says I'm aggressive, irresponsible and unattractive. But should we believe it?* — check it out at bit.ly/2KWRkpF.

The algorithm is a simple image-similarity model that finds the closest matches to your photo from a dataset of 2,222 facial photos. 33,430 crowd-sourced people rated the photos in the dataset for a range of personality traits, including levels of aggression, emotional stability, attractiveness and weirdness. The model uses their evaluations of your closest matches to predict *your* personality traits.

The journalist experimented with different photos of himself, and the model told him he was younger and attractive.

It's amusing, but is it harmful?

The model is part of an interactive application that picks one of your traits — say, level of emotional stability — and asks you to imagine that information in the hands of someone like your insurer, future employer or a law enforcement official. Are you feeling worried now?

In bit.ly/2LMialy, the project's lead researchers write "[Biometric Mirror] starkly demonstrates the possible consequences of AI and algorithmic bias, and it encourages us [to] reflect on a landscape where government and business increasingly rely on AI to inform their decisions."

And, on the project page, they write:

> [O]ur algorithm is correct but the information it returns is not. And that is precisely what we aim to share: We should be careful with relying on artificial intelligence systems, because their internal logic may be incorrect, incomplete or extremely sensitive and discriminatory.

This project raises two of the ethical questions in the use of AI:

- Algorithmic bias

- Explainable or understandable AI

Biased data, biased model

We consider a machine-learning model to be good if it can make correct predictions on data it was not trained on — it *generalizes well* from the training dataset. But problems can arise if the training data was biased for or against some group of people: The data might be racist or sexist.

The reasons for bias could be historical. To train a model that predicts the risk of someone defaulting on a loan, or how well someone will perform at university, you would give it historical data about people who did or didn't default on loans, or who did or didn't do well at university. And, historically, the data would favor white men because, for a long time, they got most of the loans and university admittances.

Because the data contained fewer samples of women or racial minorities, the model might be 90% accurate overall, but only 50% accurate for women or minorities.

Also, the data might be biased by the people who made the decisions in the first place: Loan officials might have been more tolerant of late payments from white men, or university professors might have been biased against certain demographics.

You can try to overcome bias in your model by explicitly adjusting its training data or parameters to counteract biases. Some model architectures can be tweaked to identify sensitive features and reduce or remove their effect on predictions.

Explainable/interpretable/transparent AI

The algorithmic bias problem means it's important to be able to examine how an ML model makes predictions: Which features did it use? Is that accurate or fair?

In the diagram earlier in this chapter, **training** was drawn as a black box. Although you'll learn something about what happens inside that box, many deep learning models are so complex, even their creators can't explain individual predictions.

One approach could be to require more transparency about algorithmic biases and what the model designer did to overcome them.

Google Brain has an open source tool github.com/google/svcca that can be used to interpret what a neural network is learning.

Key points

- Machine learning isn't really that hard to learn — Stick with this book and you'll see!

- Access to large amounts of data and computing power found online has made machine learning a viable technology.

- At its core, machine learning is all about models; creating them, training them, and inferring results using them.

- Training models can be an inexact science and an exercise in patience. However, easy-to-use transfer learning tools like Create ML and Turi Create can help improve the experience in specific cases.

- Mobile devices are pretty good at inferring results. With Core ML 3, models can be personalized using a limited form of on-device training.

- Don't confuse machine learning with Artificial Intelligence. Machine learning can be a great addition to your app, but knowing its limitations is equally important.

Where to go from here?

We hope you enjoyed that tour of machine-learning from 10,000 feet. If you didn't absorb everything you read, don't worry! As with all new things learned, time and patience are your greatest assets.

In the next chapter, you'll finally get to write some code! You will learn how to use a pre-trained Core ML image classification model in an iOS app. It's full of insights into the inner workings of neural networks.

Chapter 2: Getting Started with Image Classification

By Matthijs Hollemans

Let's begin your journey into the world of machine learning by creating a binary image classifier.

A **classifier** is a machine learning model that takes an input of some kind, in this case an image, and determines what sort of "thing" that input represents. An image classifier tells you which category, or class, the image belongs to.

Binary means that the classifier is able to distinguish between two classes of objects. For example, you can have a classifier that will answer either "cat" or "dog" for a given input image, just in case you have trouble telling the two apart.

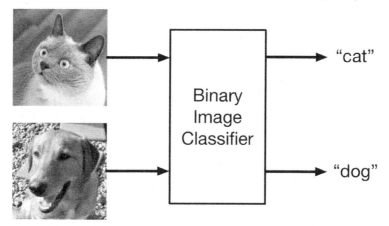

A binary classifier for cats and dogs

Being able to tell the difference between only two things may not seem very impressive, but binary classification is used a lot in practice.

In medical testing, it determines whether a patient has a disease, where the "positive" class means the disease is present and the "negative" class means it's not. Another common example is filtering email into spam/not spam.

There are plenty of questions that have a definite "yes/no" answer, and the machine learning model to use for such questions is a binary classifier. The cats-vs.-dogs classifier can be framed as answering the question: "Is this a picture of a cat?" If the answer is no, it's a dog.

Image classification is one of the most fundamental computer vision tasks. Advanced applications of computer vision — such as object detection, style transfer, and image generation — all build on the same ideas from image classification, making this a great place to start.

There are many ways to create an image classifier, but by far the best results come from using deep learning. The success of deep learning in image classification is what started the current hype around AI and ML. We wouldn't want you to miss out on all this exciting stuff, and so the classifier you'll be building in this chapter uses deep learning under the hood.

Is that snack healthy?

In this chapter you'll learn how to build an image classifier that can tell the difference between healthy and unhealthy snacks.

healthy

unhealthy

To get started, make sure you've downloaded the supplementary materials for this chapter and open the **HealthySnacks** starter project in Xcode.

This is a very basic iPhone app with two buttons, an image view, and a text label at the top:

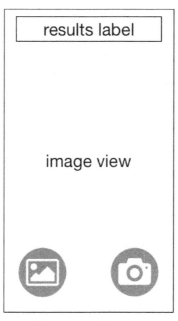

The design of the app

The "picture frame" button on the left lets you choose a photo from the library using UIImagePickerController. The "camera" button on the right lets you take a picture with the camera (this button is disabled in the simulator).

Once you've selected a picture, the app calls classify(image:) in **ViewController.swift** to decide whether the image is of a healthy snack or not. Currently this method is empty. In this chapter you'll be adding code to this method to run the classifier.

At this point, it's a good idea to take a brief look at **ViewController.swift** to familiarize yourself with the code. It's pretty standard fare for an iOS app.

In order to do machine learning on the device, you need to have a trained model. For the HealthySnacks app, you'll need a model that has learned how to tell apart healthy snacks from unhealthy snacks. In this chapter you'll be using a ready-made model that has already been trained for you, and in the next chapter you'll learn to how train this model yourself.

The model is trained to recognize the following snacks:

The categories of snacks

For example, if you point the camera at an apple and snap a picture, the app should say "healthy". If you point the camera at a hotdog, it should say "unhealthy".

What the model actually predicts is not just a label ("healthy" or "unhealthy") but a **probability distribution**, where each classification is given a probability value:

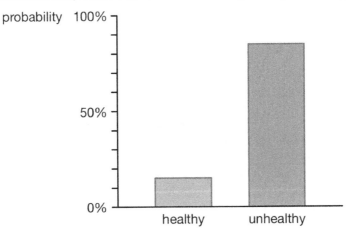

An example probability distribution

If your math and statistics are a little rusty, then don't let terms such as "probability distribution" scare you. A probability distribution is simply a list of positive numbers that add up to 1.0. In this case it is a list of two numbers because this model has two classes:

```
[0.15, 0.85]
```

The above prediction is for an image of a waffle with strawberries on top. The model is 85% sure that the object in this picture is unhealthy. Because the predicted probabilities always need to add up to 100% (or `1.0`), this outcome also means the classifier is 15% sure this snack is healthy — thanks to the strawberries.

You can interpret these probabilities to be the **confidence** that the model has in its predictions. A waffle without strawberries would likely score higher for unhealthy, perhaps as much as 98%, leaving only 2% for class healthy. The more confident the model is about its prediction, the more one of the probabilities goes to 100% and the other goes to 0%. When the difference between them is large, as in this example, it means that the model is sure about its prediction.

Ideally, you would have a model that is always confident and never wrong. However, sometimes it's very hard for the model to draw a solid conclusion about the image. Can *you* tell whether the food in the following image is mostly healthy or unhealthy?

What is this even?

The less confident the model is, the more both probabilities go towards the middle, or 50%.

When the probability distribution looks like the following, the model just isn't very sure, and you cannot really trust the prediction — it could be either class.

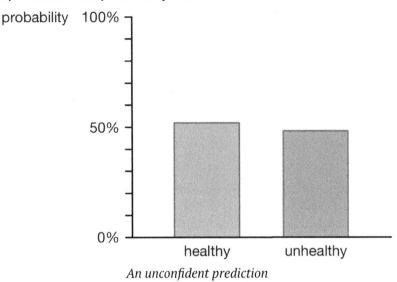

An unconfident prediction

This happens when the image has elements of both classes — salad and greasy stuff — so it's hard for the model to choose between the two classes. It also happens when the image is not about food at all, and the model does not know what to make of it.

To recap, the input to the image classifier is an image and the output is a probability distribution, a list of numbers between 0 and 1.

Since you're going to be building a binary classifier, the probability distribution is made up of just two numbers. The easiest way to decide which class is the winner is to choose the one with the highest predicted probability.

> **Note**: To keep things manageable for this book, we only trained the model on twenty types of snacks (ten healthy, ten unhealthy). If you take a picture of something that isn't in the list of twenty snacks, such as broccoli or pizza, the prediction could be either healthy or unhealthy. The model wasn't trained to recognize such things and, therefore, what it predicts is anyone's guess. That said, the model might still guess right on broccoli (it's green, which is similar to other healthy snacks) and pizza (it's greasy and therefore unhealthy).

Core ML

For many of the projects in this book, you'll be using Core ML, Apple's machine learning framework that was introduced with iOS 11. Core ML makes it really easy to add machine learning models to your app — it's mostly a matter of dropping a trained model into your app and calling a few API functions.

Xcode even automatically writes most of the code for you.

Of course, Core ML is only easy if you already have a trained model. You can find the model for this chapter, **HealthySnacks.mlmodel**, in the downloaded resources.

Core ML models are packaged up in a **.mlmodel** file. This file contains both the structural definition of the model as well as the things it has learned, known as the learned parameters (or the "weights").

With the HealthySnacks project open in Xcode, drag the **HealthySnacks.mlmodel** file into the project to add it to the app (or use File ▸ Add Files).

Select **HealthySnacks.mlmodel** in the Project Navigator and Xcode will show the following:

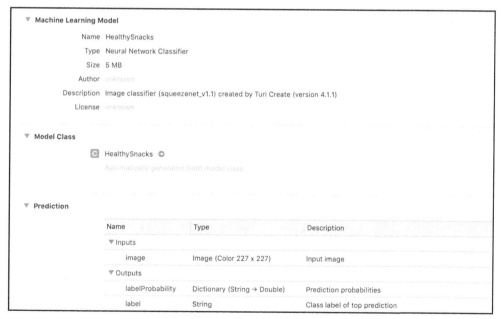

Looking at the mlmodel file

This is a summary of the Core ML model file. It shows what of type model it is, the size of the model in megabytes and a description.

The HealthySnacks model type is Neural Network Classifier, which means it is an image classifier that uses deep learning techniques. The terms "deep learning" and "neural network" mean pretty much the same thing. According to the description, this model was made using a tool called Turi Create and it uses SqueezeNet v1.1, a popular deep learning architecture for mobile apps.

The main benefit of SqueezeNet is that it's small. As you can see in Xcode, the size of this model is "only" 5 MB. That is tiny compared to many other deep learning model architectures, which can take up hundreds of MBs. Such large models are usually not a good choice for use in a mobile app. Not only do they make the app download bigger but larger models are also slower and use more battery power.

The Prediction section lists the inputs that the model expects and the outputs that it produces. Since this is an image classifier there is only one input, a color image that must be 227 pixels wide and 227 pixels tall.

You cannot use images with other dimensions. The reason for this restriction is that the SqueezeNet architecture expects an image of exactly this size. If it's any smaller or any larger, the math used by SqueezeNet doesn't work out. This means that any image you pick from the photo library or take with the camera must be resized to 227×227 before you can use it with this Core ML model.

> **Note**: If you're thinking that 227×227 pixels isn't very big, then you're right. A typical 12-megapixel photo is 4032×3024 — that is more than 200 times as many pixels! But there is a trade-off between image size and processing time. These deep learning models need to do *a lot* of calculations: For a single 227×227 image, SqueezeNet performs 390 million calculations. Make the image twice as large and the number of calculations also doubles. At some point, that just gets out of hand and the model will be too slow to be useable!
>
> Making the image smaller will make the model faster, and it can even help the models learn better since scaling down the image helps to remove unnecessary details that would otherwise just confuse the model. But there's a limit here too: At some point, the image loses too much detail, and the model won't be able to do a good job anymore. For image classification, 227×227 is a good compromise. Other typical image sizes used are 224×224 and 299×299.

The HealthySnacks model has two outputs. It puts the probability distribution into a dictionary named `labelProbability` that will look something like this:

```
labelProbability = [ "healthy": 0.15, "unhealthy": 0.85 ]
```

For convenience, the second output from the model is the class label of the top prediction: `"healthy"` if the probability of the snack being healthy is greater than 50%, `"unhealthy"` if it's less than 50%.

The final section of this model summary to look at is Model Class. When you add an .mlmodel file to a project, Xcode does something smart behind the scenes: It creates a Swift class with all the source code needed to use the model in your app. That means you don't have to write any code to load the .mlmodel — Xcode has already done the heavy lifting for you.

To see the code that Xcode generated, click the little arrow next to the model name:

Click the arrow to view the generated code

It's not important, at this point, that you understand exactly what this code does. Just notice that the automatically generated Swift file contains a class `HealthySnacks` that has an `MLModel` object property (the main object from the Core ML framework). It also has `prediction` methods for making the classifications. There also are `HealthySnacksInput` and `HealthySnacksOutput` classes that represent the input (an image) and outputs (the probabilities dictionary and the top prediction label) of the model.

At this point, you might reasonably expect that you're going to use these automatically generated classes to make the predictions. Surprise… you're not! We're saving that for the end of the chapter.

There are a few reasons for this, most importantly that the images need to be scaled to 227×227 pixels and placed into a `CVPixelBuffer` object before you can call the `prediction` method, and we'd rather not deal with that if we can avoid it. So instead, you're going to be using yet another framework: Vision.

> **Note:** Core ML models can also have other types of inputs besides images, such as numbers and text. In this first section of the book, you'll primarily work with images. In later sections, you'll also do machine learning on other types of data.

Vision

Along with Core ML, Apple also introduced the Vision framework in iOS 11. As you can guess from its name, Vision helps with computer vision tasks. For example, it can detect rectangular shapes and text in images, detect faces and even track moving objects.

Most importantly for you, Vision makes it easy to run Core ML models that take images as input. You can even combine this with other Vision tasks into an efficient image-processing pipeline. For example, in an app that detects people's emotions, you can build a Vision pipeline that first detects a face in the image and then runs a Core ML-based classifier on just that face to see whether the person is smiling or frowning.

It's highly recommended that you use Vision to drive Core ML if you're working with images. Recall that the HealthySnacks model needs a 227×227 image as input, but images from the photo library or the camera will be much larger and are typically not square. Vision will automatically resize and crop the image.

In the automatically generated Swift file for the .mlmodel, you may have noticed that the input image (see `HealthySnacksInput`) has to be a `CVPixelBuffer` object, while `UIImagePickerController` gives you a `UIImage` instead. Vision can do this conversion for you, so you don't have to worry about `CVPixelBuffer` objects.

Finally, Vision also performs a few other tricks, such as rotating the image so that it's always right-size up, and matching the image's color to the device's color space. Without the Vision framework, you'd have to write a lot of additional code! Surely, you'll agree that it's much more convenient to let Vision handle all these things.

> **Note**: Of course, if you're using a model that does not take images as input, you can't use Vision. In that case, you'll have to use the Core ML API directly.

The way Vision works is that you create a `VNRequest` object, which describes the task you want to perform, and then you use a `VNImageRequestHandler` to execute the request. Since you'll use Vision to run a Core ML model, the request is a subclass named `VNCoreMLRequest`. Let's write some code!

Creating the VNCoreML request

To add image classification to the app, you're going to implement `classify(image:)` in **ViewController.swift**. This method is currently empty.

Here, you'll use Vision to run the Core ML model and interpret its results. First, add the required imports to the top of the file:

```
import CoreML
import Vision
```

Next, you need to create the `VNCoreMLRequest` object. You typically create this request object once and re-use it for every image that you want to classify. Don't create a new request object every time you want to classify an image — that's wasteful.

In **ViewController.swift**, add the following code inside the `ViewController` class below the `@IBOutlets`:

```
lazy var classificationRequest: VNCoreMLRequest = {
  do {
    // 1
    let healthySnacks = HealthySnacks()
    // 2
    let visionModel = try VNCoreMLModel(
      for: healthySnacks.model)
    // 3
    let request = VNCoreMLRequest(model: visionModel,
                                  completionHandler: {
      [weak self] request, error in
      print("Request is finished!", request.results)
    })
    // 4
    request.imageCropAndScaleOption = .centerCrop
    return request
  } catch {
    fatalError("Failed to create VNCoreMLModel: \(error)")
  }
}()
```

Here's what this code does:

1. Create an instance of `HealthySnacks`. This is the class from the .mlmodel file's automatically generated code. You won't use this class directly, only so you can pass its `MLModel` object to Vision.

2. Create a `VNCoreMLModel` object. This is a wrapper object that connects the `MLModel` instance from the Core ML framework with Vision.

3. Create the `VNCoreMLRequest` object. This object will perform the actual actions of converting the input image to a `CVPixelBuffer`, scaling it to 227×227, running the Core ML model, interpreting the results, and so on.

Since Vision requests run asynchronously, you can supply a completion handler that will receive the results. For now, the completion handler just prints something to the Xcode debug output pane. You will flesh this out later.

4. The `imageCropAndScaleOption` tells Vision how it should resize the photo down to the 227×227 pixels that the model expects.

The code is wrapped up in a `do catch` because loading the `VNCoreMLModel` object can fail if the .mlmodel file is invalid somehow. That should never happen in this example project, and so you handle this kind of error by crashing the app. It is possible for apps to download an .mlmodel file and, if the download fails, the .mlmodel can get corrupted. In that case, you'll want to handle this error in a more graceful way.

> **Note**: The `classificationRequest` variable is a `lazy` property. In case you're unfamiliar with lazy properties, this just means that the `VNCoreMLRequest` object is not created until the very first time you use `classificationRequest` in the app.

Crop and scale options

It has been mentioned a few times now that the model you're using, which is based on SqueezeNet, requires input images that are 227×227 pixels. Since you're using Vision, you don't really need to worry about this — Vision will automatically scale the image to the correct size. However, there is more than one way to resize an image, and you need to choose the correct method for the model, otherwise it might not work as well as you'd hoped.

What the correct method is for your model depends on how it was trained. When a model is trained, it's shown many different example images to learn from. Those images have all kinds of different dimensions and aspect ratios, and they also need to be resized to 227×227 pixels. There are different ways to do this and not everyone uses the same method when training their models.

For the best results you should set the request's `imageCropAndScaleOption` property so that it uses the same method that was used during training.

Vision offers three possible choices:

- `centerCrop`
- `scaleFill`
- `scaleFit`

The `.centerCrop` option first resizes the image so that the smallest side is 227 pixels, and then it crops out the center square:

The centerCrop option

Note that this removes pixels from the left and right edges of the image (or from the top/bottom if the image is in portrait). If the object of interest happens to be in that part of the image, then this will throw away useful information and the classifier may only see a portion of the object. When using `.centerCrop` it's essential that the user points the camera so that the object is in the center of the picture.

With `.scaleFill`, the image gets resized to 227×227 without removing anything from the sides, so it keeps all the information from the original image — but if the original wasn't square then the image gets squashed. Finally, `.scaleFit` keeps the aspect ratio intact but compensates by filling in the rest with black pixels.

scaleFill   scaleFit

The scaleFill and scaleFit options

For the Healthy Snacks app, you'll use `.centerCrop` as that's also the resizing strategy that was used to train the model. Just make sure that the object you're pointing the camera at is near the center of the picture for the best results. Feel free to try out the other scaling options to see what kind of difference they make to the predictions, if any.

Performing the request

Now that you have the request object, you can implement the `classify(image:)` method. Add the following code to that method:

```
func classify(image: UIImage) {
  // 1
  guard let ciImage = CIImage(image: image) else {
    print("Unable to create CIImage")
    return
  }
  // 2
  let orientation = CGImagePropertyOrientation(
    image.imageOrientation)
  // 3
  DispatchQueue.global(qos: .userInitiated).async {
    // 4
    let handler = VNImageRequestHandler(
      ciImage: ciImage,
      orientation: orientation)
    do {
      try handler.perform([self.classificationRequest])
    } catch {
      print("Failed to perform classification: \(error)")
    }
  }
}
```

The image that you get from `UIImagePickerController` is a `UIImage` object but Vision prefers to work with `CGImage` or `CIImage` objects. Either will work fine, and they're both easy to obtain from the original `UIImage`. The advantage of using a `CIImage` is that this lets you apply additional Core Image transformations to the image, for more advanced image processing.

Here is what the method does, step-by-step:

1. Converts the `UIImage` to a `CIImage` object.

2. The `UIImage` has an `imageOrientation` property that describes which way is up when the image is to be drawn. For example, if the orientation is "down," then the image should be rotated 180 degrees. You need to tell Vision about the image's orientation so that it can rotate the image if necessary, since Core ML expects images to be upright.

3. Because it may take Core ML a moment or two to do all the calculations involved in the classification (recall that SqueezeNet does 390 million calculations for a single image), it is best to perform the request on a background queue, so as not to block the main thread.

4. Create a new `VNImageRequestHandler` for this image and its orientation information, then call `perform` to actually do execute the request. Note that `perform` takes an array of `VNRequest` objects, so that you can perform multiple Vision requests on the same image if you want to. Here, you just use the `VNCoreMLRequest` object from the `classificationRequest` property you made earlier.

The above steps are pretty much the same for any Vision Core ML app.

Because you made the `classificationRequest` a `lazy` property, the very first time `classify(image:)` gets called it will load the Core ML model and set up the Vision request. But it only does this once and then re-uses the same request object for every image. On the other hand, you do need to create a new `VNImageRequestHandler` every time, because this handler object is specific to the image you're trying to classify.

Image orientation

When you take a photo with the iPhone's camera, regardless of how you're holding the phone, the image data is stored as landscape because that's the native orientation of the camera sensor.

iOS keeps track of the true orientation of the image with the `imageOrientation` property. For an image in your photo album, the orientation information is stored in the image file's EXIF data.

If you're holding the phone in portrait mode and snap a picture, its `imageOrientation` will be `.right` to indicate the camera has been rotated 90 degrees clockwise. 0 degrees means that the phone was in landscape with the Home button on the right.

An `imageOrientation` of `.up` means that the image already has the correct side up. This is true for pictures taken in landscape but also for portrait pictures from other sources, such as an image you create in Photoshop.

Most image classification models expect to see the input image with the correct side up. Notice that the Core ML model does not take "image orientation" as an input, so it will see only the "raw" pixels in the image buffer without knowing which side is up.

Image classifiers are typically trained to account for images being horizontally flipped so that they can recognize objects facing left as well as facing right, but they're usually not trained to deal with images that rotated by 90, 180 or 270 degrees.

If you pass in an image that is not oriented properly, the model may not give accurate predictions because it has not learned to look at images that way.

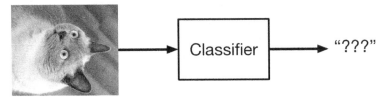

This cat is not right-side up

This is why you need to tell Vision about the image's orientation so that it can properly rotate the image's pixels before they get passed to Core ML. Since Vision uses `CGImage` or `CIImage` instead of `UIImage`, you need to convert the `UIImage.Orientation` value to a `CGImagePropertyOrientation` value.

Trying it out

At this point, you can build and run the app and choose a photo.

It's possible to run this app in the Simulator but only the photo library button is active. The photo library on the Simulator doesn't contain pictures of snacks by default, but you can add your own by Googling for images and then dragging those JPEGs or PNGs into the Photos app.

Run the app on a device to use the camera, as the Simulator does not support taking pictures.

Take or choose a picture, and the Xcode debug pane will output something like this:

```
Request is finished! Optional([<VNClassificationObservation:
0x60c00022b940> B09B3F7D-89CF-405A-ABE3-6F4AF67683BB 0.81705
"healthy" (0.917060), <VNClassificationObservation:
0x60c000223580> BC9198C6-8264-4B3A-AB3A-5AAE84F638A4 0.18295
"unhealthy" (0.082940)])
```

This is the output from the `print` statement in the completion handler of the `VNCoreMLRequest`. It prints out the `request.results` array. As you can see, this array contains two `VNClassificationObservation` objects, one with the probability for the healthy class (0.917060 or 91.7%) and the other with the probability for the unhealthy class (0.082940 or 8.29%).

Of course, printing stuff to the output pane isn't very exciting, so let's properly show these results in the app.

Showing the results

Inside the declaration of `lazy var classificationRequest`, change the completion handler for the `VNCoreMLRequest` object to the following:

```
let request = VNCoreMLRequest(
  model: visionModel,
  completionHandler: { [weak self] request, error in
    // add this
    self?.processObservations(for: request, error: error)
})
```

Instead of the `print` statement that was there previously, you're now calling a new method, `processObservations(for:error:)`. It's perfectly possible to put the code that handles the results directly inside the completion handler, but it tends to make the code harder to read.

Add the new method to **ViewController.swift**:

```
func processObservations(
  for request: VNRequest,
  error: Error?) {
  // 1
  DispatchQueue.main.async {
    // 2
    if let results = request.results
      as? [VNClassificationObservation] {
      // 3
      if results.isEmpty {
        self.resultsLabel.text = "nothing found"
      } else {
        self.resultsLabel.text = String(
          format: "%@ %.1f%%",
          results[0].identifier,
          results[0].confidence * 100)
      }
    // 4
    } else if let error = error {
      self.resultsLabel.text =
        "error: \(error.localizedDescription)"
    } else {
      self.resultsLabel.text = "???"
    }
    // 5
```

```
      self.showResultsView()
    }
  }
```

Here's what this method does, step-by-step:

1. The request's completion handler is called on the same background queue from which you launched the request. Because you're only allowed to call UIKit methods from the main queue, the rest of the code in this method runs on the main queue.

2. The `request` parameter is of type `VNRequest`, the base class of `VNCoreMLRequest`. If everything went well, the request's `results` array contains one or more `VNClassificationObservation` objects. If the cast fails, it's either because there was an error performing the request and `results` is nil, or the array contains a different type of observation object, which happens if the model isn't actually a classifier or the Vision request object wasn't for a Core ML model.

3. Put the class name in the results label. Assuming the array is not empty, it contains a `VNClassificationObservation` object for each possible class. Each of these has an `identifier` (the name of the class: "healthy" or "unhealthy") and a `confidence` score. This score is how likely the model thinks the object is of this class; in other words, it's the probability for that class.

   Vision automatically sorts the results by confidence, so `results[0]` contains the class with the highest confidence — the winning class. The app will show both the name and confidence in the results label, where the confidence is shown as a percentage, e.g., `"healthy 95%"`.

   By the way, it should never happen that the array is empty but, in the unlikely case that it is, you show a "nothing found" message in the label.

4. Just in case something went wrong with the request, show an error message. This normally shouldn't happen, but it's good to cover all your bases.

5. Finally, show the `resultsLabel` on the screen. The `showResultsView()` method performs a nice little animation, which makes it clear to the user that their image has been classified.

And that's all you need to do. Build and run the app and classify some images!

Predictions on a few test images

Pretty cool. With just a few lines of code you've added a state-of-the-art image classifier to your app!

> **Note**: When you viewed the Core ML model in Xcode (by selecting the .mlmodel file in the Project navigator), it said that the model had two outputs: a dictionary containing the probabilities and the label for the top prediction. However, the Vision request gives you an array of `VNClassificationObservation` objects instead. Vision takes that dictionary from Core ML and turns it into its own kind of "observation" objects. Later on, you'll see how to use Core ML directly, without using Vision, and, in that case, you do get access directly to the model's outputs.

What if the image doesn't have a snack?

The app shows the winning class and the confidence it has in this prediction. In the above image on the left, the class is "healthy" and the confidence is 94.8%.

If the output is something like "healthy 95%," the model feels pretty sure about itself. You'll see this kind of prediction on pictures of oranges, apples, bananas and so on. Likewise, if the output is "unhealthy 95%," the model is pretty sure that it's correct about the snack being unhealthy, and you'll see this on pictures of pretzels and waffles. That's good, we like to see confident predictions.

The model used in this app was trained on 20 different types of snacks. But what happens when you show it a kind of snack that it has never seen before, or maybe even a totally different kind of object — maybe something that isn't even edible?

Since a binary classifier only understands two classes, it puts any picture that you give it into the "healthy" category or into the "unhealthy" category, even if the picture isn't really of a kind of snack that it knows about.

This particular classifier is trained to tell the difference between healthy and unhealthy snacks, and it should therefore be used only with photos of such snacks. For all other images — let's say of cute cats — the classifier will give a non-sensical prediction. After all, it only has "healthy" or "unhealthy" to choose from. (And no, we do not endorse having cats as a snack.)

What you *want* to happen for such an "unsupported" input image is that the model gives a very uncertain prediction, something that is more like a 51%–49% split. In that case, Vision might return two `VNClassificationObservation` objects like this:

```
element 0: healthy 51%
element 1: unhealthy 49%
```

If the model isn't sure, that's actually a very acceptable answer: It could be either class. However, since Vision automatically sorts this array by confidence score, the app will show the prediction "healthy" as the winning label. But is it really? Since the model is so uncertain now, changing these percentages only slightly can completely change the outcome:

```
element 0: unhealthy 52%
element 1: healthy 48%
```

If you get such a prediction for one of your photos, try taking the same photo again but from a slightly different angle. The small variation between the photos can easily flip the uncertain prediction from one class to the other.

The moral of the story is that when the probabilities get close to 50%–50%, the model doesn't really know what to make of the image. It's a good idea to make the app deal with such situations. After all, there is nothing that prevents the user from taking a photo of something that is not a snack.

In `processObservations(for:error:)`, add the following clause to the if statement:

```
if results.isEmpty {
  . . .
```

```
} else if results[0].confidence < 0.8 {
  self.resultsLabel.text = "not sure"
} else {
  . . .
```

Here, we've chosen a threshold value of 0.8 (or 80% confidence). If the model was less confident about its winning prediction than this threshold, you decide that you can't trust the prediction it made, and the app will say "not sure."

The threshold value of 0.8 was picked arbitrarily. This is something you would test in practice by pointing the phone at many real-world objects to get a feel for what confidence level is trustworthy and below which level the model starts to make too many mistakes. This is actually different for every model, and so you need to test it in practice. There are also mathematical ways to find a suitable threshold, such as using a Precision-Recall curve or the Receiver Operator Characteristic (ROC) curve.

> **Note**: Remember that it doesn't make sense to test for a confidence below 0.5, as the winning prediction will always have a confidence score of greater than 50%. There are only two classes in a binary classifier and their total confidence score needs to add up to 100%.

However, it can still happen that you run into a situation like this:

Yeah, I wouldn't eat this either

The model was quite confident about this prediction even though the object is far from edible! Sometimes the classifier will give a very confident answer that is totally wrong. This is a limitation of all classifiers.

It's important to understand that machine learning models will only work reliably when you use them with data that is very similar to the data they've been trained on. A model can only make trustworthy predictions on the types of things it has learned about — it will fail spectacularly on anything else. Machine learning often seems like magic... but it does have its limitations.

The only way to fix this kind of problem is to make your model more robust by training it on more images, or by adding a third category so that the model can learn the difference between "healthy snack," "unhealthy snack," and "not a snack." But even then your model will still make errors. Using machine learning for computer vision tasks works really well, but it's never perfect.

In the chapter on training, you'll see how you can estimate the quality of the model to get an idea of how well it will work in practice.

What if there's more than one object in the image?

Image classification always looks at the entire image and tries to find out what the most prominent object in the image is. But nothing stops you from running an image classifier on a picture containing objects from more than one class:

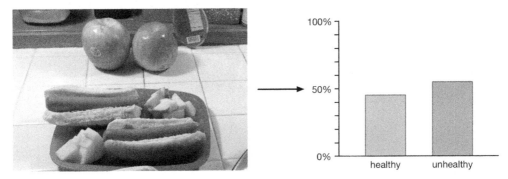

Make up your mind!

In this example, the classifier has found both an apple and a hotdog, but it seems to think that the hot dog is slightly more important. Perhaps it's because the hot dog takes up more room in the image, or maybe the model just had a harder time recognizing the apples. In any case, it had to make an impossible choice between two classes that are really supposed to be mutually exclusive and this is what it came up with.

However, based on these percentages, you can't just say, "This image contains an unhealthy snack." It does, but it also contains a healthy snack. With the new rule that we just added, the model would say "not sure" for this particular photo, since neither class has over 80% confidence.

But it's also possible that the model predicts something like 90% healthy or unhealthy for an image such as this. All bets are off, since this is not a problem the HealthySnacks model was really trained for. With an image classifier like this, the input image is really supposed to contain one "main" object, not multiple objects — or at most multiple objects that are all from the same class. The model can't really handle images with more than one object if they are from different classes.

In any case, image classification works best when there is just a single object in the image. The computer vision task that's about finding all the objects in an image, and also where they are located in the image, is called *object detection* and we'll talk about that in chapter 9, "Beyond Image Classification."

How does it work?

At this point, you may be wondering exactly how this Core ML model is able to tell apart healthy snacks from unhealthy snacks. The model takes an image as input and produces a probability distribution as output, but what is the magic that makes this happen? Let's peek under the hood a little.

The **HealthySnacks.mlmodel** is a so-called neural network classifier. You've already seen classification, but you may not know exactly what a neural network is.

Artificial neural networks are inspired by the human brain. The particular neural network used by HealthySnacks is a so-called "convolutional" neural network, which in many ways is similar to how the human visual cortex processes information.

Despite how they're often depicted in the popular press, it's really not that useful to think of these artificial neural networks as a computerized version of human brains. Artificial neural networks are only a very crude model of how the human brain works — and not nearly as complicated.

It's much more constructive to think of a neural network as a pipeline that transforms data in several different stages. A machine learning model is like a Swift function:

```
let outputs = myModel(inputs)
```

In the case of an image classifier, the function signature looks like the following, where the input is an image of some kind and the output an array of numbers, the probability distribution over the classes:

```
func myModel(input: Image) -> [Double] {
  // a lot of fancy math
}
```

Core ML treats the model as a black box, where input goes into one end and the output comes out the other. Inside this black box it actually looks like a pipeline with multiple stages:

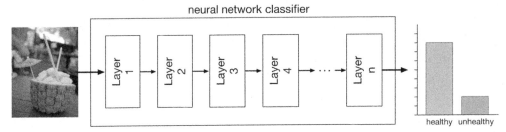

The model is a pipeline

Each of these stages, or **layers** as we call them, transforms the data in some way. In code, you can think of it as a sequence of map, filter, and reduce operations:

```
func myModel(input: Image) -> [Double] {
  return input.map({...}).filter({...}).map({...}).reduce({...})
}
```

That's really all there is to it. Despite its sci-fi name, a neural network is a very straightforward thing, just a series of successive stages that each transforms the data in its own way, until the data comes out in the form you want. The layers inside an image classifier transform the data from an image into a probability distribution.

In modern neural networks, pipelines are not just a straight series of transformations but they can branch and the results of branches can be combined again in a later stage.

For example, the SqueezeNet neural network architecture that the HealthySnacks model is based on looks something like this:

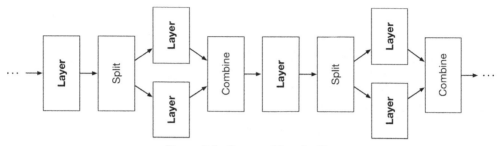

Part of the SqueezeNet pipeline

All the magic happens inside the layers that perform the transformations. So surely that must involve lots of complicated math? Well, no. Each individual transformation is a relatively simple mathematical operation. The power of the neural network comes from combining these transformations. By putting many simple transformations together, you end up with a pipeline that can compute the answers to some pretty complex problems.

Early neural networks only used two or three layers (transformations), as training with more layers was fraught with problems. But those problems have been solved in recent years and now we routinely use neural networks with dozens or even hundreds of layers, which is why using these neural nets is called "deep learning." SqueezeNet has 67 layers although in practice certain types of layers are fused together for better speed.

Into the next dimension

Let's dive a little deeper into the math, just so you get a better conceptual idea of what these transformations do. Neural networks, like most machine learning models, can only work with numerical data. Fortunately for us, the data we care about in this chapter — the input image and the output probabilities — are all represented as numbers already. Models that work on data such as text would first need to convert that data into numbers.

The input image is 227×227 pixels and is a color image, so you need 227 × 227 × 3 = 154,587 numbers to describe an input image. For the sake of explanation, let's round this down to 150,000 numbers.

> **Note:** Each pixel needs three numbers because color is stored as RGB: a red, green and blue intensity value. Some images also have a fourth channel, the alpha channel, that stores transparency information, but this is typically not used by image classifiers. It's OK to use an RGBA image as input, but the classifier will simply ignore the alpha value.

Here's the big idea: Each of the 227×227 input images can be represented by a unique point in a 150,000-dimensional space.

Whoop, try to wrap your head around that... It's pretty easy for us humans to think in 3D space but not so much in higher-dimensional spaces, especially not ones with hundreds of thousands of dimensions. But the principle is the same: given 3 numbers *(x, y, z)* you can describe any point in 3-dimensional space, right? Well, given 150,000 numbers with the RGB values of all the pixels in the image, you end up at a point in 150,000-dimensional space.

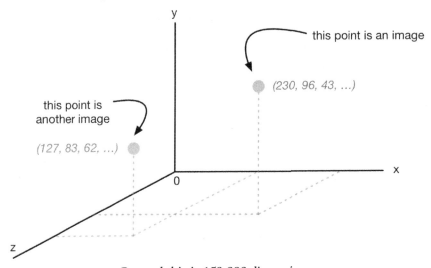

Pretend this is 150,000 dimensions

By the way, don't try to think in 150,000 dimensions. Just imagine a 3D space and pretend it's more than three dimensions. That's what everyone else does too, since humans simply aren't capable of visualizing more than three dimensions.

To classify the images, you want to be able to draw a line through this high-dimensional space and say, "All the images containing healthy snacks are on this side of the line, and all the images with unhealthy snacks are on the other side." If that would be possible, then classifying an image is easy: You just have to look at which side of the line the image's point falls.

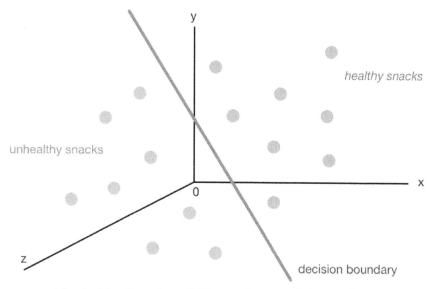

The decision boundary divides up the space into two classes

This line is called the **decision boundary**. It's the job of the classifier model to learn where that decision boundary lies. Math alert: It's not really a line but a hyperplane, which is a subspace that splits the high-dimensional space into two halves. One of the benefits of being a machine learning practitioner is that you get to use cool words such as hyperplane.

The problem is that you cannot draw a nice line — or hyperplane — through the 150,000-dimensional pixel space because ordering the images by their pixel values means that the healthy and unhealthy images are all over the place.

Since pixels capture light intensity, images that have the same color and brightness are grouped together, while images that have different colors are farther apart. Apples can be red or green but, in pixel space, such images are not close together. Candy can also be red or green, so you'll find pictures of apples mixed up with pictures of candy.

You cannot just look at how red or green something is to decide whether this image contains something healthy or unhealthy.

All the information you need to make a classification is obviously contained in the images, but the way the images are spread out over this 150,000-dimensional pixel space is not very useful. What you want instead is a space where all the healthy snacks are grouped together and all the unhealthy snacks are grouped together, too.

This is where the neural network comes in: The transformations that it performs in each stage of the pipeline will twist, turn, pull and stretch this coordinate space, until all the points that represent healthy snacks will be over on one side and all the points for unhealthy snacks will be on the other, and you can finally draw that line between them.

A concrete example

Here is a famous example that should illustrate the idea. In this example the data is two-dimensional, so each input consists of only two numbers *(x, y)*. This is also a binary classification problem, but in the original coordinate space it's impossible to draw a straight line between the two classes:

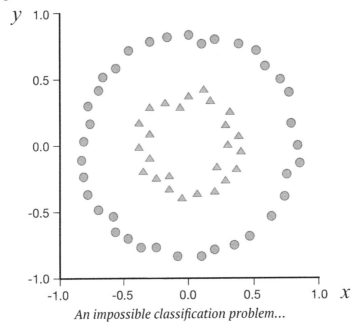

An impossible classification problem...

In theory, you could classify this dataset by learning to separate this space using an ellipse instead of a straight line, but that's rather complicated. It's much easier to perform a smart transformation that turns the 2D space into a 3D space by giving all points a z-coordinate too. The points from class A (the triangles) get a small z value, the points from class B (the circles) get a larger z value.

Now the picture looks like this:

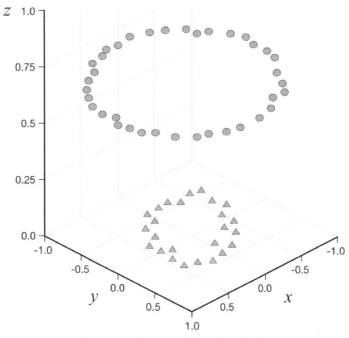

...but easy after transforming the data

After applying this transformation, both classes get cleanly separated. You can easily draw a line between them at *z = 0.5*. Any point with z-coordinate less than 0.5 belongs to class A, and any point with z greater than 0.5 belongs to class B.

The closer a point's z-coordinate is to the line, the less confident the model is about the class for that point. This also explains why probabilities get closer to 50% when the HealthySnacks model can't decide whether the snack in the image is healthy or unhealthy. In that case, the image gets transformed to a point that is near the decision boundary. Usually, the decision boundary is a little fuzzy and points with *z* close to 0.5 could belong to either class A (triangles) or class B (circles).

The cool thing about neural networks is that they can automatically learn to make these kinds of transformations, to convert the input data from a coordinate space where it's hard to tell the points apart, into a coordinate space where it's easy. That is exactly what happens when the model is trained. It learns the transformations and how to find the best decision boundary.

To classify a new image, the neural network will apply all the transformations it has learned during training, and then it looks at which side of the line the transformed image falls. And that's the secret sauce of neural network classification!

The only difference between this simple example and our image classifier is that you're dealing with 150,000 dimensions instead of two. But the idea – and the underlying mathematics — is exactly the same for 150,000 dimensions as it is for two.

> **Note**: In general, the more complex the data, the deeper the neural network has to be. For the 2D example above, a neural net with just two layers will suffice. For images, which are clearly much more complex, the neural net needs to be deeper because it needs to perform more transformations to get a nice, clean decision boundary.

Over the course of the next chapters, we'll go into more details about exactly what sort of transformations are performed by the neural network. In a typical deep learning model, these are convolutions (look for patterns made by small groups of pixels, thereby mapping the points from one coordinate space to another), pooling (reduce the size of the image to make the coordinate space smaller), and logistic regression (find where to draw the line / decision boundary).

Multi-class classification

So far, we've covered binary classification in which there are only two classes, but it's also really easy to use a model that can handle multiple classes. This is called... wait for it... a multi-class classifier — or, sometimes, a multinomial classifier.

In this section, you'll swap out the binary classifier for **MultiSnacks.mlmodel**, a multi-class classifier that was trained on the exact same data as the binary healthy/ unhealthy classifier but that can detect the individual snacks.

Recognizing multiple classes

Integrating this new model into the app couldn't be simpler. You can either do this in a copy of your existing app or use the MultiSnacks starter app.

Now, drag the **MultiSnacks.mlmodel** from this chapter's downloaded resources into the Xcode project.

If you look at this new .mlmodel file in Xcode, or at the automatically generated code, you'll notice that it looks exactly the same as before, except that the names of the Swift classes are different (MultiSnacks instead of HealthySnacks) because the name of the .mlmodel file is different, too.

To use this new model, make the following change on the classificationRequest property:

```
lazy var classificationRequest: VNCoreMLRequest = {
  do {
    let multiSnacks = MultiSnacks()
    let visionModel = try VNCoreMLModel(for: multiSnacks.model)
    . . .
```

Instead of creating an instance of HealthySnacks, all you need to do is make an instance of MultiSnacks. This is the name of the class that Xcode generated automatically when you added MultiSnacks.mlmodel to the project.

Also change the innermost if statement in processObservations(for:error:) to:

```
if results.isEmpty {
  self.resultsLabel.text = "nothing found"
} else {
  let top3 = results.prefix(3).map { observation in
    String(format: "%@ %.1f%%", observation.identifier,
           observation.confidence * 100)
  }
  self.resultsLabel.text = top3.joined(separator: "\n")
}
```

Instead of showing only the best result — the class with the highest confidence score — this now displays the names of the three best classes.

Since the model was trained on 20 different object types, it outputs a probability distribution that looks something like this:

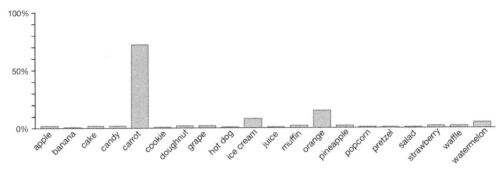

The new probability distribution

Where previously there were only two values (healthy/unhealthy), there are now 20 possible outcomes, and the 100 total percentage points are distributed over these twenty possible classes — which is why it's called a probability distribution.

The app displays the three predicted classes with the highest probability values. Since there are now 20 classes, the results array contains 20 VNClassificationObservation objects, sorted from a high to low confidence score. The prefix(3) method grabs elements 0, 1, and 2 from this array (the ones with the highest probabilities), and you use map to turn them into strings.

For the above probability distribution, this gives:

```
element 0: carrot 72%
element 1: orange 15%
element 2: ice cream 8%
```

The model is fairly confident about this prediction. The first result has a pretty high score, and so you can probably believe that the image really is of a carrot.

The second result is often fairly reasonable — if you squint, an orange could look like a carrot — but the third result and anything below it can be way off the mark.

Given these confidence scores, that's OK; the model really didn't think ice cream was a reasonable guess here at only 8% confidence.

> **Note**: The percentages of these top three choices don't have to add up to 100%, since there are another 17 classes that will make up the remainder.

Notice that, when you made these changes to the code, you removed the `if` statement that checked whether the confidence was less than 80%.

That check made sense for a binary classifier but, when you have multiple classes, the best confidence will often be around the 60% mark. That's still a pretty confident score.

With a binary classifier and two classes, a random guess is correct 50% of the time. But with 20 classes, a random guess would be correct only 1/20th, or 5%, of the time.

When the multi-class model is very unsure about what is in the image, the probability distribution would look more like this:

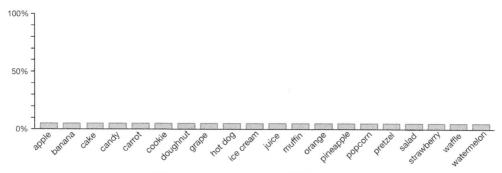

When the multi-class model is unsure

You could still add a kind of "not sure" threshold, but a more reasonable value would be 0.4, or 40%, instead of the 80% that you used with the binary classifier.

Still, just like a binary classifier, the predictions from a multi-class model only make sense if you show it the types of objects that it has been trained to recognize.

If you give the new classifier an image of something that is not one of the 20 kinds of snacks it knows about, such as a dachshund, the model may return a very unsure prediction ("it could be anything") or a very confident but totally wrong prediction ("it's a hot dog").

Again, you can ask what happens when an image contains objects of more than one class?

Well, unlike with the binary classifier in which predictions became very uncertain (50–50), a similar thing happens but now the probabilities get divided over more classes:

Image with multiple types of fruit

In this example, the classifier correctly recognizes apples and carrots as the top choices, and it tries to split the probabilities between them.

This is why you're looking at the top three results instead of just the single best score. In image classification competitions, classifiers are usually scored on how well they do on their five best guesses since, that way, you can deal with one image containing more than one object or with objects that are a little ambiguous. As long as the correct answer is among the best five (or three) guesses, we're happy.

The top-one accuracy says, "Did the classifier get the most important object right?" while the top-three or top-five accuracy says, "Did it find all of the important objects?" For example, if an image that scored orange 70%, watermelon 21%, and muffin 3% really contained a watermelon and not an orange, it would still be counted as a correct classification.

> **Note**: Don't confuse multi-class with "multi-label." A multi-class classifier's job is to choose a single category for an object from multiple categories. A multi-label classifier's job is to choose as many categories as applicable for the same object. For example, a multi-label snacks classifier could classify an apple as "healthy", "fruit", and "red".

Bonus: Using Core ML without Vision

You've seen how easy it is to use Core ML through the Vision framework. Given the amount of work Vision does for you already, it's recommended to always use Vision when you're working with image models. However, it is also possible to use Core ML without Vision, and in this section you'll see how to do so.

For this section, use the starter project again and add the **HealthySnacks.mlmodel** to the project.

First, take a detailed look at the auto-generated code, since you'll use this shortly. To see this source file, first click on **HealthySnacks.mlmodel** in the Project navigator and then click on the little arrow next to the model name in the "Model Class" section.

This opens **HealthySnacks.swift**, a special source code file that doesn't actually exist anywhere in the project.

Viewing the generated code

The main class in this source file is HealthySnacks (located near the bottom of the file). It has a single property named model, which is an instance of MLModel, the main class in the Core ML framework. init loads the .mlmodel from the main bundle.

There are two prediction methods. The first of these takes an object of type HealthySnacksInput and returns a HealthySnacksOutput. The second one is a convenience method that takes a CVPixelBuffer object as input instead. Notice that there are no methods that accept a CGImage or a CIImage like with Vision.

Both HealthySnacksInput and HealthySnacksOutput are classes that implement the MLFeatureProvider protocol. Remember from the previous chapter that "feature" is the term we use for any value that we use for learning. An MLFeatureProvider is an object that describes such features to Core ML.

In the case of the HealthySnacksInput, there is just one feature: an image in the form of a CVPixelBuffer object that is 227 pixels width and 227 pixels high. Actually the model will treat each R/G/B value in this image as a separate feature, so, technically speaking, the model has 227 × 227 × 3 input features.

The HealthySnacksOutput class provides two features containing the outputs of the model: a dictionary called labelProbability and a string called simply label. The label is simply the name of the class with the highest probability and is provided for convenience.

The dictionary contains the names of the classes and the confidence score for each class, so it's the same as the probability distribution but in the form of a dictionary instead of an array. The difference with Vision's array of VNClassificationObservation objects is that the dictionary is not sorted.

Note: The names that Xcode generates for these properties depend on the names of the inputs and outputs in the .mlmodel file. For this particular model, the input is called "image" and so the method becomes prediction(image:). If the input were called something else in the .mlmodel file, such as "data," then the method would be prediction(data:). The same is true for the names of the outputs in the HealthySnacksOutput class. This is something to be aware of when you're importing a Core ML model: different models will have different names for the inputs and outputs — another thing you don't have to worry about when using Vision.

In order to use the HealthySnacks class without Vision, you have to call its prediction(image:) method and give it a CVPixelBuffer containing the image to classify. When the prediction method is done it returns the classification result as a HealthySnacksOutput object.

Next, you'll write this code. Switch to **ViewController.swift** and add the following property to ViewController to create an instance of the model:

```swift
let healthySnacks = HealthySnacks()
```

Now, you need a way to convert the UIImage from UIImagePickerController into a CVPixelBuffer. This object is a low-level description of image data, used by Core Video and AVFoundation. You're probably used to working with images as UIImage or CGImage objects, and so you need to convert these to CVPixelBuffers, first.

Add the following function to the class:

```swift
func pixelBuffer(for image: UIImage) -> CVPixelBuffer? {
  let model = healthySnacks.model

  let imageConstraint = model.modelDescription
                            .inputDescriptionsByName["image"]!
                            .imageConstraint!

  let imageOptions: [MLFeatureValue.ImageOption: Any] = [
    .cropAndScale: VNImageCropAndScaleOption.scaleFill.rawValue
  ]

  return try? MLFeatureValue(
    cgImage: image.cgImage!,
    constraint: imageConstraint,
    options: imageOptions).imageBufferValue
}
```

The constraint is an MLImageConstraint object that describes the image size that is expected by the model input. The options dictionary lets you specify the how the image gets resized and cropped. This uses the same options as Vision, but you can also give it a CGRect with a custom cropping region. There is also a version of this MLFeatureValue constructor that lets you pass in an orientation value for the image if it is not upright.

> **Note**: This API is only available from iOS 13 onward. In the downloads for this chapter, we've provided a UIImage extension that converts the UIImage to a CVPixelBuffer for older versions of iOS.

Change the classify(image:) method to the following:

```
func classify(image: UIImage) {
  DispatchQueue.global(qos: .userInitiated).async {
    // 1
    if let pixelBuffer = self.pixelBuffer(for: image) {
      // 2
      if let prediction = try? self.healthySnacks.prediction(
        image: pixelBuffer) {
        // 3
        let results = self.top(1, prediction.labelProbability)
        self.processObservations(results: results)
      } else {
        self.processObservations(results: [])
      }
    }
  }
}
```

Here's how this works:

1. Convert the UIImage to a CVPixelBuffer using the helper method. This scales the image to the expected size (227×227) and also fixes the orientation if it's not correct side up yet.

2. Call the prediction(image:) method. This can potentially fail — if the image buffer is not 227×227 pixels, for example — which is why you need to use try? and put it inside the if let.

3. The prediction object is an instance of HealthySnacksOutput. You can look at its label property to find the name of the best class, but you want to look at the names of the best scoring classes as well as their probabilities. That's what the self.top function does.

Because MLModel's prediction method is synchronous, it blocks the current thread until it's done. For this simple image classifier, that may not be a big deal as it's fairly fast, but it's good practice to do the prediction on a background queue anyway.

Xcode now gives errors because the code calls two methods you still need to add. First, add the top() method:

```
func top(_ k: Int, _ prob: [String: Double])
  -> [(String, Double)] {
  return Array(prob.sorted { $0.value > $1.value }
                   .prefix(min(k, prob.count)))
}
```

This looks at the dictionary from `prediction.labelProbability` and returns the k best predictions as an array of (`String, Double`) pairs where the string is the label (name of the class) and the `Double` is the probability / confidence score for that class.

Currently you're calling `top(1, …)` because, for the HealthySnacks model, you only care about the highest-scoring class. For the MultiSnacks model, you might call `top(3, …)` to get the three best results.

Finally, you can put these (`String, Double`) pairs into a string to show in the results label:

```
func processObservations(
        results: [(identifier: String, confidence: Double)]) {
  DispatchQueue.main.async {
    if results.isEmpty {
      self.resultsLabel.text = "nothing found"
    } else if results[0].confidence < 0.8 {
      self.resultsLabel.text = "not sure"
    } else {
      self.resultsLabel.text = String(
        format: "%@ %.1f%%",
        results[0].identifier,
        results[0].confidence * 100)
    }
    self.showResultsView()
  }
}
```

This is very similar to what you did in the Vision version of the app but the results are packaged slightly differently.

So this actually wasn't too bad, was it? It may even seem like a bit less work than what you had to do for Vision. But this is a little misleading... There are a few important things the pure Core ML version does not do yet, such as color space matching; this translates from the photo's color space, which is often sRGB or P3 or even YUV, to the generic RGB space used by the model.

Challenge

Challenge 1: Add SqueezNet model to the app

Apple provides a number of Core ML models that you can download for free, from
https://developer.apple.com/machine-learning/models/.

Your challenge for this chapter is to download the SqueezeNet model and add it to
the app. This model is very similar to the classifier you implemented in this chapter,
which is also based on SqueezeNet. The main difference is that HealthySnacks is
trained to classify 20 different snacks into two groups: healthy or unhealthy. The
SqueezeNet model from Apple is trained to understand 1,000 classes of different
objects (it's a multi-class classifier).

Try to add this new model to the app. It should only take the modification of a single
line to make this work — that's how easy it is to integrate Core ML models into your
app because they pretty much work all the same.

Key points

To recap, doing image classification with Core ML and Vision in your app involves
the following steps:

1. Obtain a trained .mlmodel file from somewhere. You can sometimes find pre-
   trained models on the web (Apple has a few on its website) but usually you'll
   have to build your own. You'll learn how to do this in the next chapter.

2. Add the .mlmodel file to your Xcode project.

3. Create the `VNCoreMLRequest` object (just once) and give it a completion handler
   that looks at the `VNClassificationObservation` objects describing the results.

4. For every image that you want to classify, create a new `VNImageRequestHandler`
   object and tell it to perform the `VNCoreMLRequest`.

These steps will work for any kind of image classification model. In fact, you can copy
the code from this chapter and use it with any Core ML image classifier.

Chapter 3: Training the Image Classifier

By Audrey Tam & Matthijs Hollemans

Update Note: This chapter has been updated to iOS 13, Xcode 11 and Swift 5.1

In the previous chapter, you saw how to use a trained model to classify images with Core ML and Vision. However, using other people's models is often not sufficient — the models may not do exactly what you want or you may want to use your own data and categories — and so it's good to know how to train your own models.

In the chapters that follow, you'll learn to create your own models. You'll learn how to use common tools and libraries used by machine learning experts to create models. Apple provides developers with Create ML as a machine learning framework to create models in Xcode. In this chapter, you'll learn how to train the snacks model using Create ML.

The dataset

Before you can train a model, you need data. You may recall from the introduction that machine learning is all about training a model to learn "rules" by looking at a lot of examples.

Since you're building an image classifier, it makes sense that the examples are going to be images. You're going to train an image classifier that can tell apart 20 different types of snacks.

Here are the possible categories, again:

```
Healthy: apple, banana, carrot, grape, juice, orange,
         pineapple, salad, strawberry, watermelon

Unhealthy: cake, candy, cookie, doughnut, hot dog,
           ice cream, muffin, popcorn, pretzel, waffle
```

Double-click **starter/snacks-download-link.webloc** to download and unzip the **snacks** dataset in your default download location, then move the **snacks** folder into the **dataset** folder. It contains the images on which you'll train the model.

This dataset has almost 7,000 images — roughly 350 images for each of these categories.

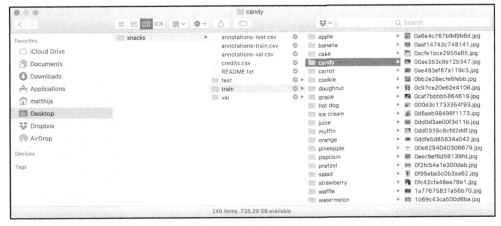

The snacks dataset

The dataset is split into three folders: train, test and val. For training the model, you will use only the 4,800 images from the **train** folder, known as the **training set**.

The images from the **val** and **test** folders (950 each) are used to measure how well the model works once it has been trained. These are known as the **validation set** and the **test set**, respectively. It's important that you don't use images from the validation set or test set for training; otherwise, you won't be able to get a reliable estimate of the quality of your model. We'll talk more about this later in the chapter.

Here are a few examples of training images:

doughnut/0e4d2f7afc5efeee.jpg   **ice cream**/4472c8cc1e2becc0.jpg   **salad**/ea2347b86bc95314.jpg

pineapple/856841a5b385c465.jpg

Selected training images

As you can see, the images come in all kinds of shapes and sizes. The name of the folder will be used as the class name — also called the **label** or the **target**.

Create ML

You will now use Create ML to train a multi-class classifier on the **snacks** dataset.

In the Xcode menu, select **Xcode ▸ Open Developer Tool ▸ Create ML**:

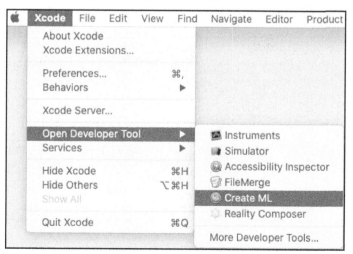

A **Finder** window opens: click **New Document**. In the **Choose a Template** window, select **Image ▸ Image Classifier**, and click **Next**:

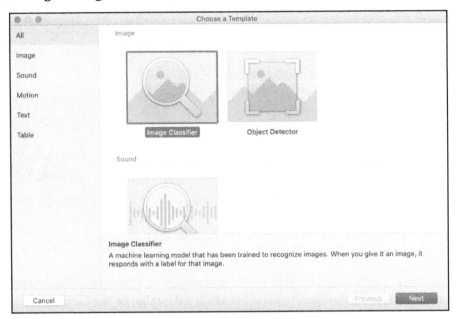

Name your classifier **MultiSnacks**, and click **Next**:

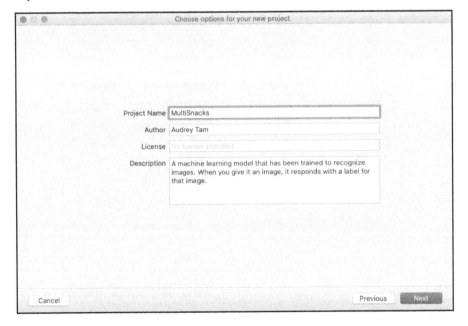

Choose a place to save your image classifier, then click **Create** to display your classifier window:

The first step is to add **Training Data**: click **Choose ▸ Select Files…** then navigate to **snacks/train**, and click **Open**:

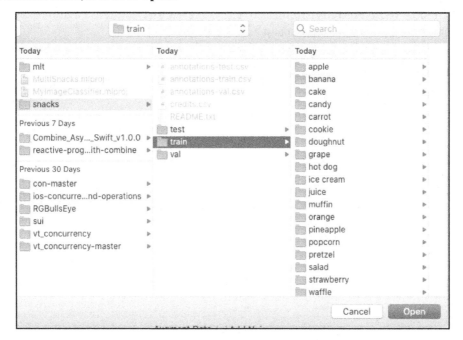

The window updates to show the number of classes and training data items, and the status shows **Ready to train**. Click the **Train** button:

The window shows **Activity**: Step 1 is to extract features, and there's a progress bar to show how many images have been processed:

In Step 2 — training — a graph appears, displaying **Training accuracy**, **Validation accuracy** for each **iteration**. And when training is complete, you get a **Metrics** table listing **Precision** and **Recall** for the 20 classes:

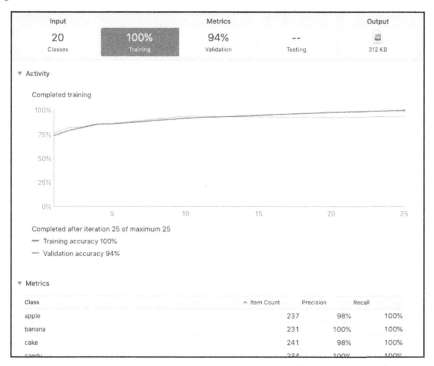

> **Note**: You may be wondering how Create ML can load *all* of the training data in memory, since 4,800 images may actually take up more physical memory than you have RAM. Create ML loads data into `MLDataTable` structures, which keep only the image metadata in memory, then loads the images themselves on demand. This means that you can have very large `MLDataTables` that contain a lot of data.

Precision and recall

Create ML computes **precision** and **recall** for each class, which is useful for understanding which classes perform better than others. In my results, these values are mostly 100% or very close. But what do they mean?

Precision means: Of all the images that the model predicts to be "apple", 98% of them are actually apples. Precision is high if we don't have many **false positives**, and it is low if we often misclassify something as being "apple." A false positive happens if something isn't actually from class "X", but the model mistakenly thinks it is.

Recall is similar, but different: It counts how many apples the model found among the total number of apples — in this case, it found 100% of the "apple" images. This gives us an idea of the number of **false negatives**. If recall is low, it means we actually missed a lot of the apples. A false negative happens if something really *is* of class "X", but the model thinks it's a different class.

Again, we like to see high numbers here, and > 95% is fantastic. For example, the "apple" class precision of 98%, which means that about one out of 50 things the model claimed were apple really aren't. For recall, it means that the model found *all* of the carrot images in the test set. That's awesome!

For precision, the worst performing classes are "apple" (98%) and "cake" (98%). For recall, the worst is "ice cream" (98%). These would be the classes to pay attention to, in order to improve the model — for example, by gathering more or better training images for these classes.

Your accuracy values and metrics might be different from what I got, because there's some randomness in how the model is trained and validated. Continue reading, to learn about **dataset curation** and **transfer learning**.

How we created the dataset

Collecting good training data can be very time consuming! It's often considered to be the most expensive part of machine learning. Despite — or because of — the wealth of data available on the internet, you'll often need to *curate* your dataset: You must manually go through the data items to remove or clean up bad data or to correct classification errors.

The images in this dataset are from the Google Open Images Dataset, which contains more than 9 million images organized into thousands of categories. The Open Images project doesn't actually host the images — only the URLs to these images. Most of the images come from Flickr and are all licensed under a Creative Commons license (CC BY 2.0). You can find the Open Images Dataset at storage.googleapis.com/openimages/web/index.html

To create the snacks dataset, we first looked through the thousands of classes in Open Images and picked 20 categories of healthy and unhealthy snacks. We then downloaded the **annotations** for all the images. The annotations contain metadata about the images, such as what their class is. Since, in Open Images, the images can contain multiple objects, they may also have multiple classes.

We randomly grabbed a subset of image URLs for each of our 20 chosen classes, and we then downloaded these images using a Python script. Quite a few of the images were no longer available or just not very good, while some were even mislabeled as being from the wrong category, so we went through the downloaded images by hand to clean them up.

Here are some of the things we had to do to clean up the data:

- The pictures in Open Images often contain more than one object, such as an apple and a banana, and we can't use these to train the classifier because the classifier expects only a single label per image. The image must have either an apple *or* a banana, not both; otherwise, it will just confuse the learning algorithm. **We only kept images with just one main object**.

- Sometimes, the lines between categories are a little blurry. Many downloaded images from the cake category were of cupcakes, which are very similar to muffins, so **we removed these ambiguous images from the dataset**. For our purposes, we decided that cupcakes belong to the muffins category, not the cake category.

- **We made sure the selected images were meaningful for the problem you're trying to solve.** The snacks classifier was intended to work on food items you'd typically find in a home or office. But the banana category had a lot of images of banana trees with stacks of green bananas — that's not the kind of banana we wanted the classifier to recognize.

- Likewise, **we included a variety of images**. We did not only want to include "perfect" pictures that look like they could be found in cookbooks, but photos with a variety of backgrounds, lighting conditions and humans in them (since it's likely that you'll use the app in your home or office, and the pictures you take will have people in them).

- **We threw out images in which the object of interest was very small**, since the neural network resizes the images to 299x299 pixels, a very small object would be just a few pixels in size — too small for the model to learn anything from.

The process of downloading images and curating them was repeated several times, until we had a dataset that gave good results. Simply by improving the data, the accuracy of the model also improved.

When training an image classifier, more images is better. However, we limited the dataset to about 350 images per category to keep the download small and training times short so that using this dataset would be accessible to all our readers. Popular datasets such as ImageNet have 1,000 or more images per category, but they are also hundreds of gigabytes.

The final dataset has 350 images per category, which are split into 250 training images, 50 validation images and 50 test images. Some categories, such as pretzel and popcorn, have fewer images because there simply weren't more suitable ones available in Open Images.

It's not necessary to have exactly the same number of images in each category, but the difference also should not be too great, or the model will be tempted to learn more about one class than another. Such a dataset is called **imbalanced** and you need special techniques to deal with them, which we aren't going to cover, here.

All images were resized so that the smallest side is 256 pixels. This isn't necessary, but it does make the download smaller and training a bit faster. We also stripped the EXIF metadata from images because some of the Python image loaders give warnings on those images, and that's just annoying. The downside of removing this metadata is that EXIF contains orientation info for the images, so some images may actually appear upside down... Oh well.

Creating the dataset took quite a while, but it's vital. If your dataset is not high quality, then the model won't be able to learn what you want it to learn. As they say, it's not who has the best algorithms, but who has the best data.

> **Note**: You are free to use the images in the snacks dataset as long as you stick to the rules of the CC BY 2.0 license. The filenames have the same IDs as used in the Google Open Images annotations. You can use the included `credits.csv` file to look up the original URLs of where the images came from.

Transfer learning

So what's happening in the playground? Create ML is currently busy training your model using **transfer learning**. As you may recall from the first chapter, transfer learning is a clever way to quickly train models by reusing knowledge from another model that was originally trained on a different task.

The HealthySnacks and MultiSnacks models you used in the previous chapter were built on top of something called SqueezeNet. The underlying model used by Create ML is not SqueezeNet but `VisionFeaturePrint_Screen`, a model that was designed by Apple specifically for getting high-quality results on iOS devices.

`VisionFeaturePrint_Screen` was pre-trained on a ginormous dataset to recognize a huge number of classes. It did this by learning what **features** to look for in an image and by learning how to combine these features to classify the image. Almost all of the training time for your dataset, is the time the model spends extracting 2,048 features from your images. These include low-level edges, mid-level shapes and task-specific high-level features.

Once the features have been extracted, Create ML spends only a relatively tiny amount of time training a **logistic regression** model to separate your images into 20 classes. It's similar to fitting a straight line to scattered points, but in 2,048 dimensions instead of two.

Transfer learning only works successfully when features of your dataset are reasonably similar to features of the dataset that was used to train the model. A model pre-trained on ImageNet — a large collection of photos — might not transfer well to pencil drawings or microscopy images.

A closer look at the training loop

Transfer learning takes less time than training a neural network from scratch. However, before we can clearly understand how transfer learning works, we have to gain a little insight into what it means to train a neural network first. It's worth recalling an image we presented in the first chapter:

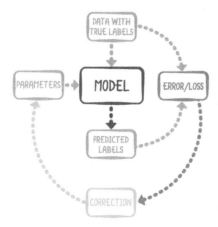

In words, this how a neural network is trained:

1. **Initialize the neural network's "brain" with small random numbers.** This is why an untrained model just makes random guesses: its knowledge literally is random. These numbers are known as the **weights** or **learned parameters** of the model. Training is the process of changing these weights from random numbers into something meaningful.

2. **Let the neural network make predictions for all the training examples.** For an image classifier, the training examples are images.

3. **Compare the predictions to the expected answers.** When you're training a classifier, the expected answers — commonly referred to as the "targets" — are the class labels for the training images. The targets are used to compute the "error" or **loss**, a measure of how far off the predictions are from the expected answers. The loss is a multi-dimensional function that has a minimum value for some particular configuration of the weights, and the goal of training is to determine the best possible values for the weights that get the loss very close to this minimum. On an untrained model, where the weights are random, the loss is high. The lower this loss value, the more the model has learned.

4. To improve the weights and reduce the error, you **calculate the gradient of the loss function**. This gradient tells you how much each weight contributed to the loss. Using this gradient, you can correct the weights so that next time the loss is a little lower. This correction step is called **gradient descent**, and happens many times during a training session. This nudges the model's knowledge a little bit in the right direction so that, next time, it will make slightly more correct predictions for the training images.

   For large datasets, using all the training data to calculate the gradient takes a long time. **Stochastic gradient descent** (SGD) estimates the gradient from randomly selected **mini-batches** of training data. This is like taking a survey of voters ahead of election day: If your sample is representative of the whole dataset, then the survey results accurately predict the final results.

5. Go to step two to **repeat this process hundreds of times for all the images in the training set**. With each training step, the model becomes a tiny bit better: The brain's learned parameters change from random numbers into something that is more suitable to the task that you want it to learn. Over time, the model learns to make better and better predictions.

Stochastic gradient descent is a rather brute-force approach, but it's the only method that is practical for training deep neural networks. Unfortunately, it's also rather slow. To make SGD work reliably, you can only make small adjustments at a time to the learned parameters, so it takes a lot of training steps (hundreds of thousands or more) to make the model learn anything.

You've seen that an untrained model is initialized with random weights. In order for such a model to learn the desired task, such as image classification, it requires a lot of training data. Image classifiers are often trained on datasets of thousands of images per class. If you have too few images, the model won't be able to learn anything. Machine learning is very data hungry!

Those are the two big downsides of training a deep learning model from scratch: You need a lot of data and it's slow.

Create ML uses a smarter approach. Instead of starting with an untrained model that has only random numbers in its brain, Create ML takes a neural network that has already been successfully trained on a large dataset, and then it fine-tunes it on your own data. This involves training only a small portion of the model instead of the whole thing. This shortcut is called **transfer learning** because you're transferring the knowledge that the neural network has learned on some other type of problem to your specific task. It's a lot faster than training a model from scratch, and it can work just as well. It's the machine learning equivalent of "work smarter, not harder!"

The pre-trained `VisionFeaturePrint_Screen` model that Create ML uses has seen lots of photos of food and drinks, so it already has a lot of knowledge about the kinds of images that you'll be using it with. Using transfer learning, you can take advantage of this existing knowledge.

> **Note**: When you use transfer learning, you need to choose a *base model* that you'll use for feature extraction. The two base models that you've seen so far are SqueezeNet and `VisionFeaturePrint_Screen`. Turi Create analyzes your training data to select the most suitable base model. Currently, Create ML's image classifier always uses the `VisionFeaturePrint_Screen` base model. It's large, with 2,048 features, so the feature extraction process takes a while. The good news is that `VisionFeaturePrint_Screen` is part of iOS 12 and the Vision framework, so models built on this are tiny — kilobytes instead of megabytes, because they do not need to include the base model. The bad news is that models trained with Create ML will not work on iOS 11, or on other platforms such as Android.

Since this pre-trained base model doesn't yet know about our 20 specific types of snacks, you cannot plug it directly into the snack detector app, but you *can* use it as a **feature extractor**.

What is feature extraction?

You may recall that machine learning happens on "features," where we've defined a feature to be any kind of data item that we find interesting. You could use the photo's pixels as features but, as the previous chapter demonstrated, the individual RGB values don't say much about what sort of objects are in the image.

VisionFeaturePrint_Screen transforms the pixel features, which are hard to understand, into features that are much more descriptive of the objects in the images.

This is the pipeline that we've talked about before. Here, however, the output of VisionFeaturePrint_Screen is not a probability distribution that says how likely it is that the image contains an object of each class.

VisionFeaturePrint_Screen's output is, well, more features.

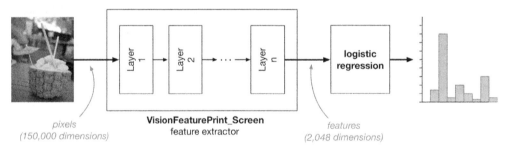

VisionFeaturePrint_Screen extracts features

For each input image, VisionFeaturePrint_Screen produces a list of 2,048 numbers. These numbers represent the content of the image at a high level. Exactly what these numbers mean isn't always easy to describe in words, but think of each image as now being a point in this new 2,048-dimensional space, wherein images with similar properties are grouped together.

For example, one of those 2,048 numbers could represent the color of a snack, and oranges and carrots would have very similar values in that dimension. Another feature could represent how elongated an object is, and bananas, carrots and hot dogs would have larger values than oranges and apples.

On the other hand, apples, oranges and doughnuts would score higher in the dimension for how "round" the snack is, while waffles would score lower in that dimension (assuming a negative value for that feature means squareness instead of roundness).

Models usually aren't that interpretable, though, but you get the idea: These new 2,048 features describe the objects in the images by their true characteristics, which are much more informative than pixel intensities. However, you cannot simply draw a line (sorry, a *hyperplane*) through this 2,048-dimensional space to separate the images into the different classes we're looking for, because `VisionFeaturePrint_Screen` is not trained on our own dataset. It was trained on ImageNet, which has 1000 classes, not 20.

While `VisionFeaturePrint_Screen` does a good job of creating more useful features from the training images, in order to be able to classify these images we need to transform the data one more time into the 20-dimensional space that we can interpret as the probability distribution over our 20 types of snacks.

How do we do that? Well, Create ML uses these 2,048 numbers as the input to a new machine learning model called **logistic regression**. Instead of training a big, hairy model on images that have 150,000 features (difficult!), Create ML just trains a much simpler model on top of the 2,048 features that `VisionFeaturePrint_Screen` has extracted.

Logistic regression

By the time you're done reading the previous section, Create ML has (hopefully) finished training your model. The status shows training took 2 minutes, 47 seconds — most of that time was spent on extracting features.

> **Note**: I'm running Create ML on a 2018 MacBook Pro with a 6-core 2.7GHz CPU and Radeon 560 GPU. You'll probably get slightly different results than this. Untrained models, in this case the logistic regression, are initialized with random numbers, which can cause variations between different training runs.

The solver that Create ML trains is a classifier called **logistic regression**. This is an old-school machine learning algorithm but it's still extremely useful. It's arguably the most common ML model in use today.

You may be familiar with another type of regression called **linear regression**. This is the act of fitting a line through points on a graph, something you may have done in high school where it was likely called the method of (ordinary) least squares.

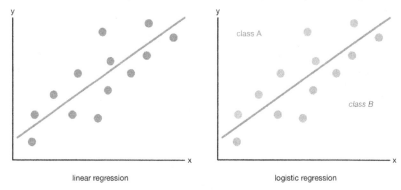

Linear and logistic regression

Logistic regression does the same thing, but says: All points on one side of the line belong to class A, and all points on the other side of the line belong to class B. See how we're literally drawing a line through space to separate it into two classes?

Because books cannot have 2,048-dimensional illustrations, the logistic regression in the above illustration is necessarily two-dimensional, but the algorithm works the same way, regardless of how many dimensions the input data has. Instead of a line, the decision boundary is really a high-dimensional object that we've mentioned before: a **hyperplane**. But because humans have trouble thinking in more than two or three dimensions, we prefer to visualize it with a straight line.

Create ML actually uses a small variation of the algorithm — **multinomial logistic regression** — that handles more than two classes.

Training the logistic regression algorithm to transform the 2,048-dimensional features into a space that allows us to draw separating lines between the 20 classes is fairly easy because we already start with features that say something meaningful about the image, rather than raw pixel values.

> **Note**: If you're wondering about exactly how logistic regression works, as usual it involves a transformation of some kind. The logistic regression model tries to find "coefficients" (its learned parameters) for the line so that a point that belongs to class A is transformed into a (large) negative value, and a point from class B is transformed into a (large) positive value. Whether a transformed point is positive or negative then determines its class.

The more ambiguous a point is, i.e. the closer the point is to the decision boundary, the closer its transformed value is to 0. The multinomial version extends this to allow for more than two classes. We'll go into the math in a later chapter. For now, it suffices to understand that this algorithm finds a straight line / hyperplane that separates the points belonging to different classes in the best way possible.

Looking for validation

Even though there are 4,838 images in the snacks/train dataset, Create ML uses only 95% of them for training.

During training, it's useful to periodically check how well the model is doing. For this purpose, Create ML sets aside a small portion of the training examples — 5%, so about 240 images. It doesn't train the logistic classifier on these images, but only uses them to evaluate how well the model does (and possibly to tune certain settings of the logistic regression).

This is why the output has one graph for **training accuracy** and one for **validation accuracy**:

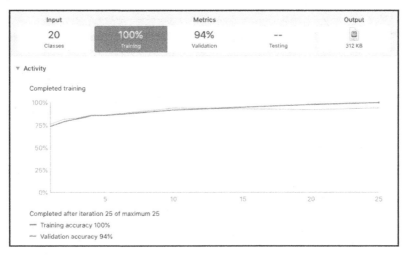

After 12 iterations, validation accuracy levels off at 94%, meaning that out of 100 training examples it correctly predicts the class for 94 of them. But training accuracy keeps increasing to 100% — the classifier is correct for 10 out of 10 images.

> **Note:** What Create ML calls an iteration is one pass through the entire training set, also known as an "epoch". This means Create ML has given the model a chance to look at all 4,582 training images once (or rather, the extracted feature vectors of all training images). If you do 10 iterations, the model will have seen each training image (or its feature vectors) 10 times.

By default, Create ML trains the logistic regression for up to 25 iterations, but you can change this with the **Maximum Iterations** parameter. In general, the more iterations, the better the model, but also the longer you have to wait for training to finish. But training the logistic regression doesn't take long, so no problem!

The problem with this is doing the feature extraction all over again! If your Mac did the feature extraction in five minutes or less, go ahead and see what happens if you *reduce* the number of iterations:

1. Click the + button to add a new **Model Source**: you're back to the start window.

2. In the **Training Data Choose** menu, select **train**. Notice the **Automatic** setting for **Validation Data**. Soon, you'll use **snacks/val** for this instead.

3. Decrease **Max iterations** to 10.

4. Click **Train**.

If you stick around to watch, you'll see how amost all the training time is used for extracting features. In Chapter 5, "Digging Deeper into Turi Create", you'll learn how to save extracted features, so you can try different training parameters without having to wait.

Here's what happened on my Mac: With 10 iterations, training completed after 2 minutes, 38 seconds — only 9 seconds less than 25 iterations! But accuracy values are much lower:

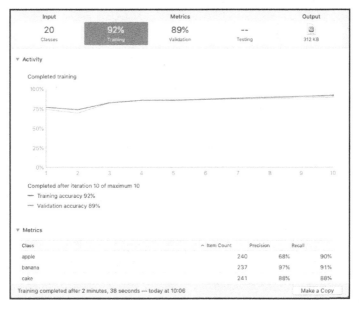

Training accuracy (92%) decreased more than validation accuracy (89%), but the two values are closer (3%).

Now see what happens when you use the **snacks/val** subdirectory, which has about 50 images per class, instead of letting Create ML choose 5% at random.

Add a third **Model Source**, and rename it **Multisnacks manual val**. This is a good time to rename the other two to **Multisnacks 25 iter** and **Multisnacks 10 iter**.

In **Multisnacks manual val**, choose **train** for **Training Data**, then select **snacks/val** for **Validation Data**:

Leave **Max iterations** at 25, and click **Train**.

Here's what I got:

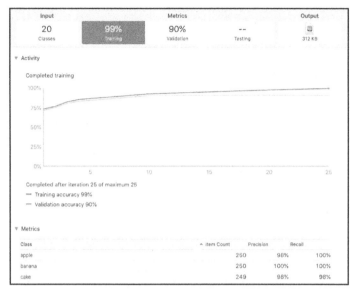

This is with 955 validation images, not 240. And this time the training used all 4,838 training images. But validation accuracy actually got *worse*, indicating the model may be **overfitting**.

Overfitting happens

Overfitting is a term you hear a lot in machine learning. It means that the model has started to remember *specific* training images. For example, the image train/ice cream/ b0fff2ec6c49c718.jpg has a person in a blue shirt enjoying a sundae:

Yummy!

Suppose a classifier learns a rule that says, "If there is a big blue blob in the image, then the class is ice cream." That's obviously not what you want the model to learn, as the blue shirt does not have anything to do with ice cream in general. It just happens to work for this particular training image.

This is why you use a validation set of images that are not used for training. Since the model has never seen these images before, it hasn't learned anything about them, making this is a good test of how well the trained model can generalize to new images.

So the *true* accuracy of this particular model is 92% correct (the validation accuracy), not 98% (the training accuracy). If you only look at the training accuracy, your estimate of the model's accuracy can be too optimistic. Ideally, you want the validation accuracy to be similar to the training accuracy, as it was after only 10 iterations — that means that your model is doing a good job.

Typically, the validation accuracy is a bit lower, but if the gap between them is too big, it means the model has been learning too many irrelevant details from the training set — in effect, memorizing what the result should be for specific training images. Overfitting is one of the most prevalent issues with training deep learning models.

There are several ways to deal with overfitting. The best strategy is to train with more data. Unfortunately, for this book we can't really make you download a 100GB dataset, and so we've decided to make do with a relatively small dataset. For image classifiers, you can **augment** your image data by flipping, rotating, shearing or changing the exposure of images. Here's an illustration of data augmentation:

Augmentation

Augmented images

Original image

Flip

Rotate

Expose

Shear

...

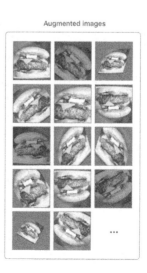

...

So try it: add a new **Model Source**, name it **Multisnacks crop**, set the options as before, but also select some data augmentation:

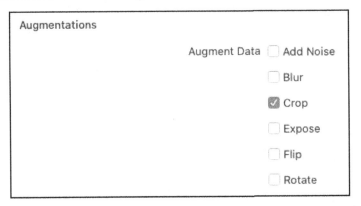

The augmentation options appear in alphabetical order, but the pre-Xcode-11 options window lists them from greatest to least training effectiveness, with **Crop** as the most effective choice:

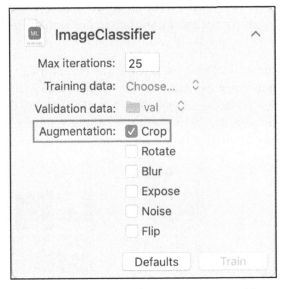

This is also the order in which the classifier applies options, if you select more than one. Selecting **Crop** creates four flipped images for each original image, so feature extraction takes almost five times longer (14m 48s for me). Selecting all six augmentation options creates 100 augmented images for each original! Actually, "only 100," because the number of augmentation images is capped at 100.

Click **Train**, then go brew a pot of tea or bake some cookies.

Back again? Here's what I got:

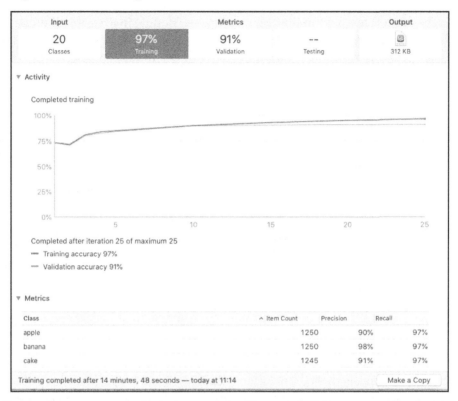

Well, training accuracy is a little lower (97%), but so is validation accuracy (91%), by the same amount. So it's still overfitting, but it's also taking longer to learn — that's understandable, with almost 25,000 images!

Another trick is adding **regularization** to the model — something that penalizes large weights, because a model that gives a lot of weight to a few features is more likely to be overfitting. Create ML doesn't let you do regularization, so you'll learn more about it in Chapter 5, "Digging Deeper into Turi Create."

The takeaway is that training accuracy is a useful metric, but it only says something about whether the model is still learning new things, not about how well the model works in practice. A good score on the training images isn't really that interesting, since you already know what their classes are, after all.

What you care about is how well the model works on images that it has never seen before. Therefore, the metric to keep your eye on is the validation accuracy, as this is a good indicator of the performance of the model in the real world.

Note: By the way, overfitting isn't the only reason why the validation accuracy can be lower than the training accuracy. If your training images are different from your validation images in some fundamental way (silly example: all your training images are photos taken at night while the validation images are taken during the day), then your model obviously won't get a good validation score. It doesn't really matter where your validation images come from, as long as these images were not used for training but they do contain the same kinds of objects. This is why Create ML randomly picks 5% of the training images to use for validation. You'll take a closer look at overfitting and the difference between the training and validation accuracies in the next chapters.

More metrics and the test set

Now that you've trained the model, it's good to know how well it does on new images that it has never seen before. You already got a little taste of that from the validation accuracy during training, but the dataset also comes with a collection of test images that you haven't used yet. These are stored in the **snacks/test** folder, and are organized by class name, just like the training data.

Switch to the **Model Source** with the highest **Validation** accuracy — in my case, it's the first **25 iter** one, with 94% validation accuracy.

Select the **Testing** tab, then select **snacks/test**:

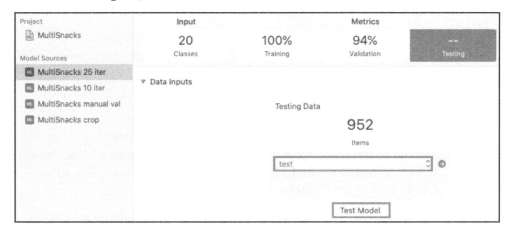

Click **Test Model**: This takes a few moments to compute. Just like during training, the feature extraction on the images takes more time than classification.

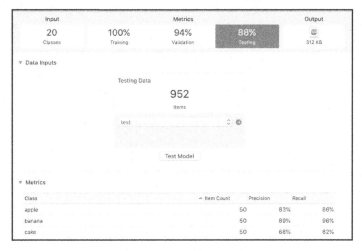

88% accuracy! Lower than validation accuracy :[.

> **Note**: You may be wondering what the difference is between the validation set that's used during training and the test set you're using now. They are both used to find out how well the trained model does on new images.
>
> However, the validation set is often also used to tune the settings of the learning algorithm — the so-called **hyperparameters**. Because of this, the model does get influenced by the images in the validation set, even though the training process never looks at these images directly. So while the validation score gives a better idea of the true performance of the model than the training accuracy, it is still not completely impartial.
>
> That's why it's a good idea to reserve a separate test set. Ideally, you'd evaluate your model *only once* on this test set, when you're completely done training it. You should resist the temptation to go back and tweak your model to improve the test set performance. You don't want the test set images to influence how the model is trained, making the test set no longer a good representation of unseen images. It's probably fine if you do this a few times, especially if your model isn't very good yet, but it shouldn't become a habit. Save the test set for last and evaluate on it as few times as possible.

Again, the question: Is 88% correct a good score or a bad score? It means more than one out of 10 images is scored wrong. Obviously, we'd rather see an accuracy score of 99% (only one out of 100 images wrong) or better, but whether that's feasible depends on the capacity of your model, the number of classes and how many training images you have.

Even if 88% correct is not ideal, it does mean your model has actually learned quite a bit. After all, with 20 classes, a totally random guess would only be correct one out of 20 times or 5% on average. So the model is already doing much better than random guesses. But it looks like Create ML isn't going to do any better than this with the current dataset.

Keep in mind, the accuracy score only looks at the top predicted class with the highest probability. If a picture contains an apple, and the most confident prediction is "hot dog," then it's obviously a wrong answer. But if the top prediction is "hot dog" with 40% confidence, while the second highest class is "apple" with 39% confidence, then you might still consider this a correct prediction.

Examining Your Output Model

It's time to look at your actual Core ML model: select the **Output** tab, then drag the **snacks/test** folder onto where it says *Drag or Add Files*. Quick as a flash, your model classifies the test images. You can inspect each one to see the predicted class(es) and the model's confidence level:

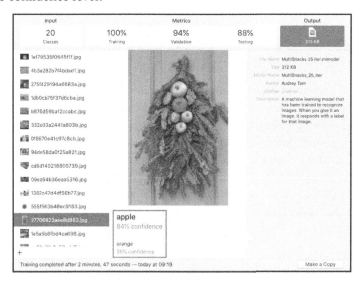

It's surprising how your model gets it right for some of the peculiar images:

The whole point of training your own models is to use them in your apps, so how do you save this new model so you can load it with Core ML?

Just drag it from the Create ML app to your desktop or anywhere in **Finder** — so easy! Then add it to Xcode in the usual way. Simply replace the existing .mlmodel file with your new one. The model that's currently in the Snacks app was created with SqueezeNet as the feature extractor — it's **5MB**. Your new model from Create ML is only 312**KB**! It's actually a much bigger model, but most of it — the VisionFeaturePrint_Screen feature extractor — is already included in the operating system, and so you don't need to distribute that as part of the .mlmodel file.

A Core ML model normally combines the feature extractor with the logistic regression classifier into a single model. You still need the feature extractor because, for any new images you want to classify, you also need to compute their feature vectors. With Core ML, the logistic regression is simply another layer in the neural network, i.e., another stage in the pipeline.

However, a VisionFeaturePrint_Screen-based Core ML model doesn't need to include the feature extractor, because it's part of iOS. So the Core ML model is basically just the logistic regression classifier, and quite small!

> **Note**: There are a few other differences between these two feature extractors. SqueezeNet is a relatively small pre-trained model that expects 227×227 images, and extracts 1,000 features. VisionFeaturePrint_Screen uses 299×299 images, and extracts 2,048 features. So the kind of knowledge that is extracted from the image by the Vision model is much richer, which is why the model you just trained with Create ML actually performs better than the SqueezeNet-based model from the previous chapter, which only has a 67% validation accuracy!

Classifying on live video

The example project in this chapter's resources is a little different than the app you worked with in the previous chapter. It works on live video from the camera. The VideoCapture class uses AVCaptureSession to read video frames from the iPhone's camera at 30 frames per second. The ViewController acts as the delegate for this VideoCapture class and is called with a CVPixelBuffer object 30 times per second. It uses Vision to make a prediction and then shows this on the screen in a label.

The code is mostly the same as in the previous app, except now there's no longer a UIImagePicker but the app runs the classifier continuously.

The classifier on live video

There is also an `FPSCounter` object that counts how many frames per second the app achieves. With a model that uses `VisionFeaturePrint_Screen` as the feature extractor you should be able to get 30 FPS on a modern device.

> **Note**: The app has a setting for `videoCapture.frameInterval` that lets you run the classifier less often, in order to save battery power. Experiment with this setting, and watch the energy usage screen in Xcode for the difference this makes.

The `VideoCapture` class is just a bare bones example of how to read video from the camera. We kept it simple on purpose so as not to make the example app too complicated. For real-word production usage you'll need to make this more robust, so it can handle interruptions, and use more camera features such as auto-focus, the front-facing camera, and so on.

Recap

In this chapter, you got a taste of training your own Core ML model with Create ML. Partly due to the limited dataset, the default settings got only about 90% accuracy. Increasing max iterations increased training accuracy, but validation accuracy was stuck at ~90%, indicating that overfitting might be happening. Augmenting the data with flipped images reduced the gap between training and validation accuracies, but you'll need more iterations to increase the accuracies.

More images is better. We use 4,800 images, but 48,000 would have been better, and 4.8 million would have been even better. However, there is a real cost associated with finding and annotating training images, and for most projects a few hundred images or at most a few thousand images per class may be all you can afford. Use what you've got — you can always retrain the model at a later date once you've collected more training data. Data is king in machine learning, and who has the most of it usually ends up with a better model.

Create ML is super easy to use, but lets you tweak only a few aspects of the training process. It's also currently limited to image and text classification models.

Turi Create gives you more task-focused models to customize, and lets you get more hands-on with the training process. It's almost as easy to use as Create ML, but you need to write Python. The next chapter gets you started with some useful tools, so you can train a model with Turi Create. Then, in Chapter 5, "Digging Deeper into Turi Create," you'll get a closer look at the training process, and learn more about the building blocks of neural networks.

Challenge

Create your own dataset of labelled images, and use Create ML to train a model.

A fun dataset is the Kaggle dogs vs. cats competition www.kaggle.com/c/dogs-vs-cats, which lets you train a binary classifier that can tell apart dogs from cats. The best models score about 98% accuracy — how close can you get with Create ML?

Also check out some of Kaggle's other image datasets:

- `https://www.kaggle.com/datasets?`
  `sortBy=relevance&group=featured&search=image`

Of course, don't forget to put your own model into the iOS app to impress your friends and co-workers!

Key points

- You can use macOS playgrounds to test out Create ML, and play with the different settings, to create simple machine learning models.

- Create ML allows you to create small models that leverage the built-in Vision feature extractor already installed on iOS 12+ devices.

- Ideally, you want the validation accuracy to be similar to the training accuracy.

- There are several ways to deal with overfitting: include more images, increase training iterations, or augment your data.

- Precision and recall are useful metrics when evaluating your model.

Chapter 4: Getting Started with Python & Turi Create

By Audrey Tam & Matthijs Hollemans

Congratulations! If you've made it this far, you've developed a strong foundation for absorbing machine learning material. However, before we can move forward, we need to address the 10,000 pound snake in the room... Python. Until this point, you've made do with Xcode and Swift, however, if you're going to get serious about Machine Learning, then it's best you prepare yourself to learn some Python. In this chapter,

- You'll learn how to set up and use tools from the Python ecosystem for data science and machine learning (ML).

- You'll install **Anaconda**, a very popular distribution of Python (and R).

- You'll use terminal commands to create ML environments which you'll use throughout this book.

- Finally, you'll use **Jupyter Notebooks**, which are very similar to Swift Playgrounds, to explore the Python language, data science libraries, and **Turi Create**, Apple's ML-as-a-Service.

Starter folder

The starter folder for this chapter contains:

- A **notebook** folder: The sample Jupyter Notebook data files.

- **.yaml** files: Used to import pre-configured environments, if you want to skip the instructions for configuring the environments yourself.

Python

Python is the dominant programming language used for data science and machine learning. As such, there's a myriad of tools available for the Python community to support data science and machine learning development. These include:

- **Data science libraries**: Matplotlib, NumPy, Pandas, SciPy and others.

- **Machine learning libraries**: Caffe, Keras, Microsoft Cognitive Toolkit, PyTorch, TensorFlow, scikit-learn and others.

- **ML-as-a-Service**: Amazon Machine Learning, Google ML Kit, IBM Watson, Microsoft Azure Machine Learning Studio, Turi Create and others.

- **Tools**: `coremltools`, `pip`, Anaconda, Docker, Jupyter notebooks, Google Colaboratory and others.

If you know the Swift programming language, you'll find that although Python is quite different, it also shares some similarities with Swift. For instance:

- You `import` modules similarly to Swift modules.

- It has the similar concepts for primitive types, tuples, lists, dictionaries, operators, loops and conditionals.

- You can create objects, classes and functions.

Of course, there are some differences too. For example:

- Python is interpreted, not compiled.

- You define closures, functions, classes with indentation instead of { `...` }.

- Naming conventions tend toward terse abbreviations, similar to C programming.

- Module and function names are *snake_case*, while class names and exception names are *PascalCase*.

- Comments start with # instead of //.

- Multi-line comments begin and end with """ instead of /* and */, and the end """ is on its own line. These are similar to the multi-line strings in Swift.

- True/False, not true/false.

- Dynamic types, no support for constants; no let or var.

- Enumerations, but no switch.

After you set up the tools, you'll try out some Python while learning about the libraries. If you'd like some more practice or information, here are two helpful resources:

- Michael Kennedy's November 2014 Comparison of Python and Swift Syntax: bit.ly/2AXQ1UF.

- Jason Brownlee's May 2016 Crash Course in Python for Machine Learning Developers includes NumPy, Matplotlib and Pandas examples: bit.ly/2MqBCWD.

Packages and environments

Python is already installed on **macOS**. However, using this installation may cause version conflicts because some people use Python 2.7 while others use Python 3.x, which are incompatible branches of the same language. To further complicate things, working on machine learning projects requires integrating the correct versions of numerous software libraries, also known as "packages".

> **Note:** The Python development team will stop supporting Python 2.7 in 2020 (https://www.python.org/dev/peps/pep-0373/#update), so the major open source Python packages have pledged to drop support for Python 2.7 no later than 2020 (https://python3statement.org).

Most people create **environments** where they install specific versions of Python and the packages they need. You can have multiple of these environments on the same computer, each with its own Python interpreter and its own set of Python packages.

The most basic toolset includes the environment manager `virtualenv` and the package manager `pip`. Aside from setting up the environment, you still have to figure out which versions of which packages you need — a very manual process, with a high probability of frustration.

There *is* a better way!

Conda

The data science community developed **Conda** to make life easier. Conda handles Python language versions, Python packages, and associated native libraries. It's both an environment manager and a package manager. And, if you need a package that Conda doesn't know about, you can use `pip` within a `conda` environment to grab the package.

Conda comes in two distributions:

- **Miniconda**: Includes only the packages needed to run Conda. (400 MB)

- **Anaconda**: Includes all of the standard packages needed for machine learning. (2 GB)

You'll be using **Anaconda** in this chapter. It doesn't take long to install, and it's way more convenient!

Installing Anaconda

In a browser, navigate to https://www.anaconda.com/download/#macos, and download the **64-bit Command Line installer** with **Python 3.7**, as highlighted in the image below:

At the time of writing, the filename downloaded is called `Anaconda3-2019.07-MacOSX-x86_64.sh`. After downloading is complete, open up a **Terminal** and navigate to the directory in which you downloaded the installer. You can run the installer by running the following command in the terminal:

```
sh Anaconda3-2019.07-MacOSX-x86_64.sh
```

You'll have accept the licence agreement, and then give the installer a directory to install Anaconda (or accept the default location if that works for you). Once the installation starts, it may take a while.

While you're waiting for the installation to finish, scroll down to the **Get Started** links and take a closer look at **Anaconda Training**:

These are video courses about using Python for machine learning. You can view some parts for free, while others require you to be a subscriber before you can watch.

If you're asked to run `conda init`, type `yes`. Once installation is complete, _restart **Terminal**_. Once restarted, you can try to run the following command to check that the installation succeeded.

```
conda --version
```

If the above command fails with a `command not found` message, chances are you'll need to add the Anaconda install path to to your global path environment variable. This means, you'll have to edit the `.bashrc` or `.zshrc` file in your home directory (usually found `/Users/<username>/`). If the file doesn't exist, you'll have to create based on the shell your terminal is currently using. If you're running Catalina or later, this mean your currently shell is most likely `Zsh`.

In either case, open or create a your `.zshrc` or `.bashrc` and either find or add a line that resembles the one given below. Assuming you installed Anaconda in your home directory, the line could look:

```
export PATH="/Users/<username>/anaconda3/bin":"${PATH}"
```

In this line, you prepend the path to the anaconda installation to your existing path. Two important things to note include the inclusion of the `bin` directory to the path, and the colon separating the installation path with the existing PATH variable.

Close any existing Terminal windows, and open a new one. Try running the `conda --version` command again in the new terminal. Opening a new window will pick up any changes to environment in the `.zshrc` or `.bashrc` file. You should have a working Anaconda installation at this point.

Using Anaconda Navigator

Anaconda comes with a desktop GUI that you can use to create environments and install packages in an environment. However, in this book, you'll do everything from the command line. Given this fact, it's worth going over some basic commands with Conda which you'll do in the next section.

Useful Conda commands

As mentioned before, Conda is a package and environment management system. When working with Python projects, you'll often find it useful to create new environments, installing only the packages you need before writing your code. In this section, we'll explore many useful commands you'll reuse many times when working with Python and Conda.

Below are the commands used in this chapter, along with some other useful commands.

> **Note**: Some command options use two dashes. One-dash options are often abbreviations of two-dash options, for example, –n is short for ––name.

> **Another Note**: Some Conda environment management tasks can be done in two ways: `conda env <command>` or `conda <different command> <options>`

Basic workflow

Create a new environment:

```
conda create -n <env name>
```

Clone an existing environment to create a new environment:

```
conda create -n <new env name> --clone <existing env name>
```

Create a new environment from a **YAML file**:

```
conda env create -f <.yaml file>
```

The first line of the YAML file sets the new environment's name. The starter folder for this chapter contains YAML files for mlenv and turienv. If you prefer the GUI to the command line, you can also import these into Anaconda Navigator.

Activate an environment:

```
conda activate <env name>
```

Once you've activated an environment, the Terminal prompt shows the name of the active environment in parenthesis, like so:

```
(envname) $
```

That way it's always obvious what environment you're currently using.

Install packages in an active environment:

```
conda install <pkg names>
```

Install packages in a **non-active** environment:

```
conda install -n <env name> <pkg names>
```

> **Note**: A message from conda about installing multiple packages: It is best to install all packages at once so that all of the dependencies are installed at the same time.

Install non-conda packages or TensorFlow and Keras in an *active environment*: Use `pip install` instead of `conda install`. To install **multiple packages**, create a **requirements.txt** file listing the packages, one per line, then run this command:

```
pip install -r requirements.txt
```

Start Jupyter from the active environment [in a specific directory]:

```
jupyter notebook <directory path>
```

Shutdown Jupyter: Logout in the Jupyter web pages, then press **Control-C-C** in terminal window where server is running. (That's not a typo, you have to press **C** twice.)

Deactivate an environment: Run this command in the terminal window where you activated the environment:

```
conda deactivate
```

Remove an environment:

```
conda remove -n <env name> --all
```

Or

```
conda env remove -n <env name>
```

Listing environments or packages

List the environments you've created; the one with the * is the currently active environment:

```
conda info --envs
```

Or:

```
conda env list
```

List packages or a specific package in the **active** environment:

```
(activeenv) $ conda list
(activeenv) $ conda list <package name>
```

In a **non-active** environment:

```
conda list -n <env name>
conda list -n <env name> <package name>
```

OK, that was a lot of commands to throw at you. However, the more Python you work with, the more these commands will come in handy. Just having them in the back of your mind will help you move more quickly. If you ever need need a quick refresher, checkout this printable Conda cheat sheet: https://docs.conda.io/projects/conda/en/4.6.0/_downloads/52a95608c49671267e40c689e0bc00ca/conda-cheatsheet.pdf.

Setting up a base ML environment

In this section, you'll set up some environments. If you prefer a quicker start, create an environment from **myenv.yaml** and skip down to the **Jupyter Notebooks** section. You can do this by importing **mlenv.yaml** into **Anaconda Navigator** or by running the following command from a Terminal window:

```
conda env create -f starter/myenv.yaml
```

Python libraries for data science

Begin by creating a custom base environment for ML, with *NumPy*, *Pandas*, *Matplotlib*, *SciPy* and *scikit-learn*. You'll be using these data science libraries in this book, but they're not automatically included in new Conda environments.

Here's an overview of what each of these libraries are:

- **NumPy**: Functions for working with multi-dimensional arrays.

- **Pandas**: Data structures and data analysis tools.

- **Matplotlib**: 2D plotting library.

- **Seaborn**: Statistical data visualization library.

- **SciPy**: Modules for statistics, optimization, integration, linear algebra, Fourier transforms and more, using NumPy arrays.

- **scikit-learn**: Machine learning library.

- **ipython** and **jupyter**: A Swift-like playground for Python.

Once you have the custom base environment for ML, you can clone it to create separate environments for the ML libraries, Keras, TensorFlow and Turi Create.

From the command prompt in **Terminal**, create a new environment named **mlenv**, with **Python 3.7**:

```
conda create -n mlenv python=3.7
```

Type y to proceed with installing the base packages of the environment. Next, activate the environment:

```
conda activate mlenv
```

You should see (mlenv) in the command propmpt. Finally, install a bunch of packages at once:

```
conda install numpy pandas matplotlib seaborn scipy scikit-learn
scikit-image ipython jupyter
```

Type y again to proceed and wait for the installation to finish.

> **Note**: It's possible that when you're reading this book, the Anaconda download will be for Python version 3.8 or later. However, in all the environments used by this book, you will *need* to use Python 3.7. This means, when you create your environment, *be sure to specify* the Python version. If you choose another version of Python, some of the machine learning libraries you'll need for the book may not work with that version.

An important note about package versions

Technology moves fast, also in the world of Python. Chances are that by the time you read this book, newer versions are available for the packages that we're using. It's quite possible these newer versions may not be 100% compatible with older versions.

For example, in this book we use Keras version 2.2.4. But newer versions of Keras may not work with some of the code examples in this book. Even version 2.2.1, which seemed like a minor upgrade from 2.2.0 that shouldn't have much of an impact, actually broke things.

Here's a dirty little secret you should be aware of: You do not need to use the latest, greatest version of these packages. Keras 2.2.4 works fine for our purposes and we can't keep updating the book every time a new version comes out and breaks something.

So, don't feel compelled to always upgrade to the newest versions. If you've set up a Python environment for a machine learning project and it works well, then don't fix what isn't broken. It's not uncommon for people in the industry to use versions of packages that are 6 months to a year old.

Our advice: If your code works fine and you don't need any of the new features or essential bug fixes, then keep your Python installation stable and only update your packages when you have a good reason.

Jupyter Notebooks

With Jupyter Notebooks, which are a lot like Swift Playgrounds, you can write and run code, and you can write and render markdown to explain the code.

Starting Jupyter

From **Terminal**, first activate your environment and then start Jupyter:

```
$ conda activate mlenv
$ jupyter notebook
```

If you're using **Anaconda Navigator**, in the **Home** tab select **mlenv** and click the Jupyter **Launch** button. The following command appears in a new **Terminal** window, followed by messages about a server starting and how to shut it down:

```
/anaconda3/envs/mlenv/bin/jupyter_mac.command ; exit;
```

Keep this Terminal window open!

A web browser window also opens, showing your home directory:

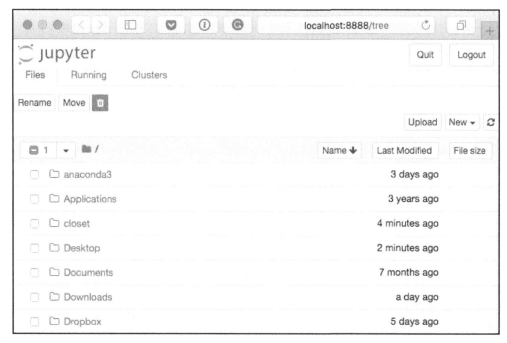

Navigate to the **starter** folder for this chapter, and open **notebook/mlbase.ipynb**:

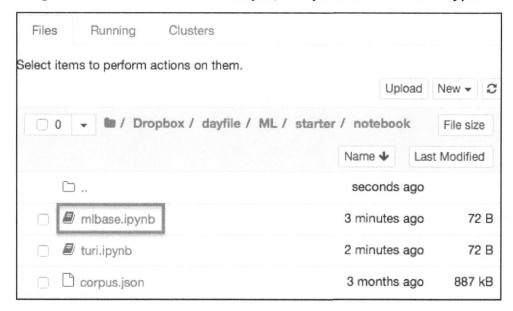

The notebook appears in a new browser tab:

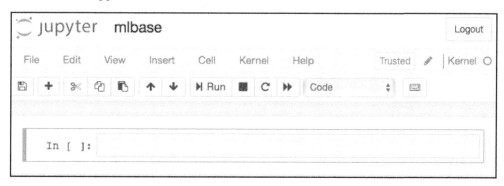

Pandas and Matplotlib

The notebook has a single empty cell. In that cell, type the following lines:

```
import numpy as np
import pandas as pd
import matplotlib.pyplot as plt
```

This imports the NumPy and Pandas modules into the current session. It also imports the pyplot module of Matplotlib, and gives everything their customary abbreviated aliases: np for NumPy, pd for Pandas and plt for Matplotlib. There's no output for import statements, although you might see a warning about future deprecation of a module.

Press **Shift-Enter** to run this code, which will also open a new cell below it.

Next, type these lines in the newly created empty cell, then press **Shift-Enter** again:

```
data = pd.read_json('corpus.json', orient='records')
data.head()
```

The **starter/notebook** folder contains the file **corpus.json**. The code you just entered loads the data from this JSON file into a DataFrame — the Pandas data container, with rows and columns like a spreadsheet. It has powerful functions for manipulation, which is important for massaging data to get the best input for training a model.

The `orient` parameter indicates the JSON string format: `'records'` means it's a list of `column` -> `value`. You'll take a look at the documentation for this function in a moment.

The `head()` function shows the (default) first five rows:

```
In [2]:  data = pd.read_json('corpus.json', orient='records')
         data.head()
```

Out[2]:

	author	text	title
0	William Butler Yeats	When you are old and grey and full of sleep,\n...	When You Are Old
1	William Butler Yeats	I think it better that in times like these\nA ...	On being asked for a War Poem
2	William Butler Yeats	Had I the heavens' embroidered cloths,\nEnwrou...	He Wishes For The Cloths Of Heaven
3	William Butler Yeats	Were you but lying cold and dead,\nAnd lights ...	He Wishes His Beloved Were Dead
4	William Butler Yeats	Wine comes in at the mouth\nAnd love comes in ...	A Drinking Song

```
In [ ]:
```

> **Note: Shift-Enter** runs the current cell and, if this is the last cell, opens a new cell below it; this is convenient when you're testing code as you write it. **Control-Enter** runs the current cell; you'd do this when you add something to an earlier cell and want to update it. The bracketed numbers in the margin keep track of the order you run the cells, regardless of their order within the notebook.

In the next empty cell, type the following line, then press **Shift-Enter**:

```
?data.tail
```

The question mark shows the documentation for this function, instead of running the function:

```
In [6]: ?data.tail

Signature: data.tail(n=5)
Docstring:
Return the last `n` rows.

This function returns last `n` rows from the object based on
position. It is useful for quickly verifying data, for example,
after sorting or appending rows.

Parameters
----------
n : int, default 5
    Number of rows to select.

Returns
-------
type of caller
    The last `n` rows of the caller object.
```

Press **Esc** or the **x** button to close the documentation.

Replace the code in the cell with a call to `tail`:

```
data.tail(3)
```

Then press **Control-Enter** or **Shift-Enter** to run the cell, which will display the last **three rows** of data:

```
In [4]: data.tail(3)
```

	author	text	title
516	Oscar Wilde	The western wind is blowing fair\nAcross the d...	Serenade (For Music)
517	Oscar Wilde	(To L. L.)\n\nCould we dig up this long-buried...	Roses And Rue
518	Oscar Wilde	In the glad springtime when leaves were green,...	From Spring Days To Winter (For Music)

If you'd like, you can also see documentation in a pop-up box: select `pd.read_json` in the second cell, then press **Shift-Tab-Tab**:

```
In [2]:   data = pd.read_json('corpus.json', orient='records')
          data head()                                                    ^ ✗

Out[2]:   Signature: pd.read_json(path_or_buf=None, orient=None, typ='frame', dtype=True,
          convert_axes=True, convert_dates=True, keep_default_dates=True, numpy=False,
          precise_float=False, date_unit=None, encoding=None, lines=False, chunksize=None,
          compression='infer')
          Docstring:
          Convert a JSON string to pandas object

          Parameters
          ----------
          path_or_buf : a valid JSON string or file-like, default: None
              The string could be a URL. Valid URL schemes include http, ftp, s3, and
```

The question mark doesn't work on this line unless you delete `data =`.

In the next empty cell, type `data.d`. Then press **Tab** to see a list of options:

```
In [4]:   data.describe
          data.diff
Out[4]:   data.div
          data.divide
          data.dot
          data.drop
          data.drop_duplicates
          data.dropna
          data.dtypes
          data.duplicated
In [ ]:   data.d
```

Now, press **Enter** to select `data.describe`. Then type `()`, and press **Shift-Enter**:

```
In [5]:   data.describe()

Out[5]:
```

	author	text	title
count	519	519	519
unique	10	517	516
top	Emily Dickinson	I think it better that in times like these\nA ...	The Wife's Will
freq	361	2	2

The output includes the column identifiers: author, text, and title. You can use these to sort the data.

Next, **Shift-Enter** the following line:

```
data.sort_values(by='title')
```

Out[6]:

	author	text	title
69	Emily Dickinson	"Arcturus" is his other name --\nI'd rather ca...	"Arcturus" is his other name
81	Emily Dickinson	"Faith" is a fine invention\nWhen Gentlemen ca...	"Faith" is a fine invention
224	Emily Dickinson	"Faithful to the end" Amended\nFrom the Heaven...	"Faithful to the end" Amended
356	Emily Dickinson	"Heaven" -- is what I cannot reach!\nThe Apple...	"Heaven" -- is what I cannot reach!
193	Emily Dickinson	"Heaven" has different Signs -- to me --\nSome...	"Heaven" has different Signs -- to me --
119	Emily Dickinson	"Heavenly Father" -- take to thee\nThe supreme...	"Heavenly Father" -- take to thee
166	Emily Dickinson	"Hope" is the thing with feathers --\nThat per...	"Hope" is the thing with feathers

You can extract a column into a separate Series object and count how often each value appears:

```
authors = data.author
freq = authors.value_counts()
freq
```

As in Swift Playgrounds, an object name (freq) on a line by itself displays that object.

```
Out[7]:  Emily Dickinson          361
         Walt Whitman              67
         John Keats                25
         Joyce Kilmer              16
         William Butler Yeats      10
         Oscar Wilde               10
         Lewis Carroll              9
         Charlotte Bronte           8
         Edgar Allan Poe            7
         Sir Walter Scott           6
         Name: author, dtype: int64
```

Frequency varies from 6 to 361. You can plot a histogram of this distribution:

```
plt.hist(freq, bins=100)
plt.show()
```

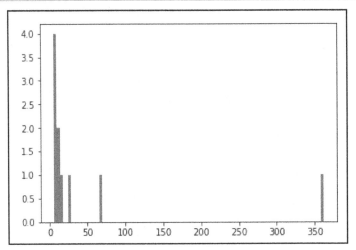

Specifying `bins=100` divides the range [6, 361] into 100 consecutive, non-overlapping intervals, called *bins* or *buckets*. The histogram's x-axis has 100 bins, between 0 and 361-ish. The y-axis shows the number of authors in each bin.

> **Note**: This example is from our tutorial Natural Language Processing on iOS with Turi Create which you can find here: bit.ly/2NhAEwf. It trains a natural language model with lines from poems by famous authors. The trained model can be used to classify new text. For each author it knows about, it computes the probability that this author wrote the new text. The `freq` values here should set off alarm bells — there's way too much bias toward Emily Dickinson, so the model will classify most test texts as written by her.

Differences between Python and Swift

In this section, you'll spend some time getting familiar with common Python syntax.

A major syntax difference between Python and most other programming languages is the importance of indentation. With Python, indentation replaces {} to define blocks. For example, an if-statement looks like this:

```
if a == b:
    print('a and b are equal')
```

```
    if a > c:
        print('and a is also greater than c')
```

Python also has a built-in None type to represent "no value". This is similar to Swift's nil but Python does not have optionals. To test for a no-value result, you should use is or is not, instead of the == you'd use in Swift.

```
if authors is None:
    print('authors is None')
else:
    print('authors is not None')
```

The output is:

```
authors is not None
```

Here's how you define and call a function:

```
def mysum(x, y):
    result = x + y
    return result

print(mysum(1, 3))
```

This outputs 4.

Notice the indentation on the lines inside the function. You have to un-indent the line with print, so that Python knowns this line is outside the function. Coding convention says to leave an extra blank line after the function definition, but it's not a syntax rule, and you may be more comfortable omitting the blank line.

Also notice how you just wrote result = x + y to put the sum into a new variable. There is no need to write let or var in Python.

Here's an example of how to use a loop and a list:

```
mylist = [1, 2]
mylist.append(3)
if mylist:
    print('mylist is not empty')

for value in mylist:
    print(value)

print('List length: %d' % len(mylist))
```

Lists in Python are similar to arrays in Swift. To test whether a list is empty, use its name. `for` loops are also similar to Swift, but they use the `:` plus indentation syntax. The `len()` function works on any Python collection object, and it returns the length of the list, in a similar way to how the `.count` property in Swift returns the number of items in an array.

Run those commands, and you'll see this output:

```
mylist is not empty
1
2
3
List length: 3
```

To make a point about indentation, go ahead and add a blank line, but indent the last statement to match the `print` statement in the loop, like so:

```
for value in mylist:
    print(value)

    print('List length: %d' % len(mylist))
```

Now, both print statements are considered to be inside the loop, and so the output becomes:

```
1
List length: 3
2
List length: 3
3
List length: 3
```

By the way, string literals in Python can use single quotes or double quotes (or even triple quotes for multiline strings). It doesn't really matter which one you use, just pick a style you like and be consistent with it. Writing `'List length: %d' % len(mylist)` is similar to doing `String(format: "List length: %d", myList.count)` in Swift. Python 3.6 also has string interpolation, just like in Swift, but this isn't commonly used yet.

Excellent, you survived a session with Python and used a few library functions! Feel free to play around some more until you get the hang of it. This book uses a lot of Python libraries and functions, so it's good to understand the basic syntax before moving on.

Transfer learning with Turi Create

Despite the difference in programming languages, deep down Turi Create shares a lot with Create ML, including transfer learning. With Turi Create v5, you can even do transfer learning with the same `VisionFeaturePrint_Scene` model that Create ML uses.

In this section, you'll create the same HealthySnacks model as the previous chapter, except this time, you'll use Turi Create. Unlike Create ML, which allowed you to train your model through the playgrounds UI in Xcode, Turi Create needs some coding when compared to Create ML. This means you'll learn more about working with Python.

Creating a Turi Create environment

First, you need a new environment with the `turicreate` package installed. You'll clone the **mlenv** environment to create **turienv**, then you'll install `turicreate` in the new environment. Conda doesn't know about `turicreate`, so you'll have to `pip install` it from within Terminal.

> **Note**: Again, if you prefer a quicker start, import **turienv.yaml** into the **Navigator**, or run `conda env create -f starter/turienv.yaml`, and skip down to the section **Turi Create Notebook**.

While it's possible to clone mlenv in Anaconda Navigator's Environments tab, you'll be using a command line to install `turicreate`, so it's just as easy to use a command line to clone, as well.

> **Note**: If you've changed Terminal's default shell to something different from *bash*, check that your $PATH includes ~/anaconda3/bin (or whatever directory you install anaconda into).

Open a new **Terminal** window, and enter this command:

```
conda create -n turienv --clone mlenv
```

This creates an environment named **turienv**, which is cloned from **mlenv**.

Wait a little while until you see the message:

```
#
# To activate this environment, use:
# > conda activate turienv
#
# To deactivate an active environment, use:
# > conda deactivate
#
```

> **Note**: If you see a message to update Conda, go ahead and do that.

Time to install Turi Create into this environment. From the same Terminal window, enter the **activate** command:

```
conda activate turienv
```

The command line prompt now starts with (turienv), showing it's the active environment.

Enter this command to install the turicreate package:

```
pip install -U turicreate==5.8
```

This downloads and installs the newest available version of the turicreate package, which lets you use the Vision framework model for transfer learning.

List pip-installed packages

In **Terminal**, use this command to list all of the packages in the active environment or a specific package:

```
conda list
conda list coremltools
```

You need the coremltools package to create Core ML models from Turi Create models. Installing turicreate also installs coremltools.

The output of the second command looks similar to this:

```
# packages in environment at /Users/amt1/anaconda3/envs/mlenv:
#
# Name                    Version                   Build
Channel
coremltools               3.0                       <pip>
```

The **Build Channel** value <pip> shows coremltools was installed with pip, not conda.

> **Note**: If you a quick look at the **turienv** environment in **Navigator**; it still shows only 105 packages. That's because packages installed with pip don't show up in Navigator.

Turi Create notebook

> **Note**: If you skipped the manual environment setup and imported turienv.yaml into Anaconda Navigator, use the Jupyter **Launch** button on the **Anaconda Navigator Home** Tab instead of the command line below, then navigate in the browser to **starter/notebook**.

This time, you'll start Jupyter in the folder where the notebooks are stored; locate **starter/notebook** in **Finder**.

> **Note**: If you downloaded the **snacks** dataset for the previous chapter, copy or move it into **starter/notebook**. Otherwise, double-click **starter/notebook/ snacks-download-link.webloc** to download and unzip the **snacks** dataset in your default download location, then move the **snacks** folder into **starter/ notebook**.

In **Terminal**, enter the following command to start a Jupyter notebook in the `turienv` environment, starting from this directory:

```
jupyter notebook <drag the starter/notebook folder in Finder to
here>
```

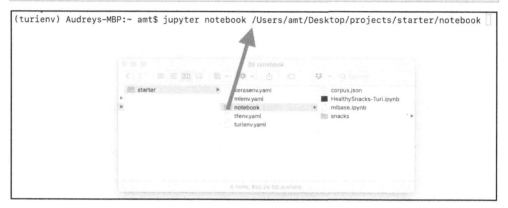

In the browser, open **HealthySnacks-Turi.ipynb**. There's only an empty cell.

Type the following commands in this cell and press **Shift-Enter**:

```
import turicreate as tc
import matplotlib.pyplot as plt
```

You're importing the Turi Create package and the `pyplot` module of the Matplotlib package into the current session, with aliases `tc` and `plt`. You may get a FutureWarning message, which you can safely ignore.

In the next cell, **Shift-Enter** this command (put it all on one line):

```
train_data = tc.image_analysis.load_images("snacks/train",
                                    with_path=True)
```

This loads all the images from the **snacks/train** directory into an `SFrame`, the data container for Turi Create. An `SFrame` contains rows and columns, like a Pandas `DataFrame` — in fact, you can create an `SFrame` from a `DataFrame`. `SFrame` has powerful functions for manipulation, similar to `DataFrame`. It's also optimized for loading from disk storage, which is important for large data sets that can easily overwhelm the RAM.

Like Create ML's `MLDataTable`, an `SFrame` keeps only the image metadata in memory.

> **Note**: It's safe to ignore warnings about .DS_Store being an unsupported image format.

This SFrame object contains a row for each image, as well as the path of the folder the images were loaded from. This SFrame should contain 4838 images. Verify this by asking for its length:

```
len(train_data)
```

> **Note**: Run each command in its own cell. Remember **Shift-Enter** runs the current cell and opens a new cell below it. Always wait for the [*] in the margin to turn into a number, indicating the command has finished running.

Next, look at the actual contents of the SFrame:

```
train_data.head()
```

The head() function shows the first 10 rows:

path	image
snacks/train/healthy/appl e/007a0bec00a90a66.jpg ...	Height: 341 Width: 256
snacks/train/healthy/appl e/007ec56b6529e036.jpg ...	Height: 256 Width: 341
...	...
snacks/train/healthy/appl e/01ecc03a12e21e39.jpg ...	Height: 256 Width: 446
snacks/train/healthy/appl e/021d2569ce62aa93.jpg ...	Height: 256 Width: 341

[10 rows x 2 columns]

The first rows in the SFrame

Even though the SFrame only shows the image's height and width in the table, it actually contains the complete image. Run the following command to see the actual images:

```
train_data.explore()
```

This opens a new window with image thumbnails (it may take a few seconds to load). Hover over a row to view a larger version of an image.

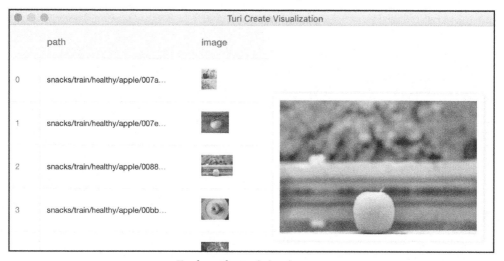

Explore the training images

This interactive visualization can be useful for a quick look at the training data. The explore() command only works with Turi Create on the Mac, not on Linux or from a Docker container.

Enter this command to look at individual images directly inside the notebook, using Matplotlib's imshow() command:

```
plt.imshow(train_data[0]["image"].pixel_data)
```

Here, train_data[0] gets the first row from the SFrame, ["image"] gets the object from the image column for that row, and .pixel_data turns this image object into something that matplotlib can show with the plt.imshow() command.

```
In [6]:  plt.imshow(train_data[0]["image"].pixel_data)

Out[6]:  <matplotlib.image.AxesImage at 0x1a1dcd2f60>
```

Looking at an image with matplotlib

Your notebook may show a different image than in the illustration, since Turi Create may have loaded your images in another order. Feel free to look at a few images by changing the row index (use any value from 0 to 4,837).

There is one more piece of data to gather before you can start training — the name of the class for each image. The images are stored in subdirectories named after the classes — "apple," "hot dog," etc. The SFrame knows the path the image was loaded from, but these paths look something like this:

```
snacks/train/hot dog/8ace0d8a912ed2f6.jpg
```

The class for image 8ace0d8a912ed2f6.jpg is "hot dog", but it's hidden inside that long path. To make this more obvious, you'll write some code to extract the class name from the path. Run the following commands to extract the name of the first image's class folder:

```
# Grab the full path of the first training example
path = train_data[0]["path"]
print(path)

# Find the class label
import os
os.path.basename(os.path.split(path)[0])
```

Here, you're getting the full path of the first image, then using the `os.path` Python package for dealing with path names. First, `os.path.split()` chops the path into two pieces: the name of the file (8ace0d8a912ed2f6.jpg) and everything leading up to it. Then `os.path.basename()` grabs the name of the last folder, which is the one with the class name. Since the first training image is of an apple, you get "apple."

> **Note**: The # character starts a comment in Python. Note that you first need to import the os package, or else Python won't know what `os.path` is.

Getting the class labels

OK, now you know how to extract the class name for a single image, but there are over 4,800 images in the dataset. As a Swift programmer, your initial instinct may be to use a `for` loop, but if you're really Swift-y, you'll be itching to use a `map` function. `SFrame` has a handy `apply()` method that, like Swift's `map` or `forEach`, lets you apply a function to every row in the frame:

```
train_data["path"].apply(lambda path: ...do something with
path...)
```

In Python, a **lambda** is similar to a closure in Swift — it's just a function without a name. `train_data["path"].apply()` performs this lambda function on every row in the path column. Inside the lambda, put the above code snippet that you used to extract the class name from the full path:

```
train_data["label"] = train_data["path"].apply(lambda path:
    os.path.basename(os.path.split(path)[0]))
```

Run the above cell and now the `SFrame` will have a new column called "label" with the class names. To verify this worked, run `train_data.head()` again — do this in a new cell, or scroll up to the fourth cell, and press **Control-Enter** to run it.

path	image	label
snacks/train/healthy/appl e/007a0bec00a90a66.jpg ...	Height: 341 Width: 256	apple
snacks/train/healthy/appl e/007ec56b6529e036.jpg ...	Height: 256 Width: 341	apple
snacks/train/healthy/appl e/008816276298888f6.jpg ...	Height: 256 Width: 384	apple

The SFrame now has a new column

You can also use `train_data.explore()` again for a visual inspection. Run this command to see the summary function:

```
train_data["label"].summary()
```

This prints out a few summary statistics about the contents of the SFrame's label column:

```
+------------------+-------+----------+
|       item       | value | is exact |
+------------------+-------+----------+
|      Length      | 4838  |   Yes    |
| # Missing Values |   0   |   Yes    |
| # unique values  |  20   |   No     |
+------------------+-------+----------+

Most frequent items:
+-------+-----------+-------+--------+----------+-------+---------+-----------+
| value | pineapple | apple | banana | doughnut | grape | hot dog | ice cream |
+-------+-----------+-------+--------+----------+-------+---------+-----------+
| count |    260    |  250  |  250   |   250    |  250  |   250   |    250    |
+-------+-----------+-------+--------+----------+-------+---------+-----------+

+-------+--------+-------+
| juice | muffin | salad |
+-------+--------+-------+
|  250  |  250   |  250  |
+-------+--------+-------+
```

Summary for the label column

As you can see, each of the classes has roughly the same number of elements. For some reason, `summary()` only shows the top 10 classes, but we have 20 in total. To see the number of rows for all of the classes, run the following command:

```
train_data["label"].value_counts().print_rows(num_rows=20)
```

All right, that's all you need to do with the data for now. You've loaded the images into an SFrame, and you've given each image a label, so Turi Create knows which class it belongs to.

Let's do some training

Once you have your data in an SFrame, training a model with Turi Create takes only a single line of code (OK, it's three lines, but only because we have to fit it on the page):

```
model = tc.image_classifier.create(train_data, target="label",
model="VisionFeaturePrint_Scene",
                                   verbose=True,
max_iterations=50)
```

Alternatively, if training takes too long on your Mac, you can just load the Turi Create model from the current folder:

```
model = tc.load_model("HealthySnacks.model")
```

This command creates a new image classifier from the train_data SFrame. The target parameter tells Turi Create that the class names are in the SFrame's label column. By default, Turi Create only does 10 iterations, but you increase this to 50, so the logistic regression will train for up to 50 iterations.

The first time you run this command, Turi Create downloads a pre-trained neural network. The model parameter contains the name of that neural network, in this case **VisionFeaturePrint_Scene**. This is the model used by Apple's Vision framework, and is also the default model for Create ML.

At the time of writing, Turi Create supports three model architectures: The other two are ResNet-50 and SqueezeNet version 1.1. ResNet-50 exports a Core ML model ~90MB, which is not really suited for use on mobile devices.

SqueezeNet exports a Core ML model ~4.7MB, so it's a better option. But VisionFeaturePrint_Scene is built into iOS 12, so it produces a *much* smaller model — only ~41 **KB**.

Turi Create, like Create ML, performs feature extraction on the images. This takes about the same amount of time as Create ML — 2m 22s on my MacBook Pro. And then comes the logistic regression:

```
Logistic regression:
--------------------------------------------------------
Number of examples         : 4590
Number of classes          : 20
Number of feature columns  : 1
Number of unpacked features : 2048
Number of coefficients     : 38931
Starting L-BFGS
--------------------------------------------------------
| Iteration | Passes | Elapsed Time | Training Accuracy | Validation Accuracy |
...
| 5         | 8      | 3.421915     | 0.815468          | 0.850806            |
| 10        | 13     | 5.857664     | 0.884532          | 0.875000            |
| 15        | 19     | 8.655192     | 0.926580          | 0.903226            |
| 20        | 24     | 11.080811    | 0.944227          | 0.895161            |
| 25        | 29     | 13.513294    | 0.982353          | 0.883065            |
| 30        | 34     | 15.903836    | 0.994553          | 0.879032            |
| 35        | 39     | 18.329717    | 0.998911          | 0.875000            |
| 40        | 44     | 20.812450    | 1.000000          | 0.850806            |
| 45        | 49     | 23.279066    | 1.000000          | 0.854839            |
| 50        | 55     | 26.231560    | 1.000000          | 0.866935            |

Completed (Iteration limit reached).
This model may not be optimal. To improve it, consider increasing `max_iterations`.
```

Validation

After 15 iterations, validation accuracy is close to training accuracy at ~90%. At 20 iterations, training accuracy starts to pull away from validation accuracy, and races off to 100%, while validation accuracy actually drops... Massive overfitting happening here! If the validation accuracy gets *worse* while the training accuracy still keeps improving, you've got an overfitting problem.

It would've been better to stop training the model after about 15 iterations. But running the image_classifier.create command with max_iterations=15 will also do the feature extraction all over again! Too bad Turi Create doesn't let you save the intermediate states of the model, or stop the training when the validation accuracy shows a decreasing trend.

Actually, in the next chapter, you'll learn how to wrangle the Turi Create code — it's open source, after all! — to save the extracted features, so you can experiment more with the classifier.

> **Spoiler alert**: Keras, which we'll talk about in an upcoming chapter, lets you save the best-so-far model while it's training, so you can always retrieve the results from an earlier iteration in case your model suffers from overfitting. Keras also lets you stop early if validation accuracy doesn't improve over some given number of iterations (your choice).

Let's go ahead and evaluate this model on the test dataset.

Testing

Run these commands to load the test dataset and get the class labels:

```
test_data = tc.image_analysis.load_images("snacks/test",
with_path=True)

test_data["label"] = test_data["path"].apply(lambda path:
        os.path.basename(os.path.split(path)[0]))

len(test_data)
```

The last command is just to confirm you've got 952 images.

Next, run this command to evaluate the model and collect metrics:

```
metrics = model.evaluate(test_data)
```

Unlike Create ML, the output of this command doesn't show any accuracy figures — you need to examine `metrics`. Run these commands in the same cell:

```
print("Accuracy: ", metrics["accuracy"])
print("Precision: ", metrics["precision"])
print("Recall: ", metrics["recall"])
print("Confusion Matrix:\n", metrics["confusion_matrix"])
```

Here are my metrics:

```
Accuracy:  0.8697478991596639
Precision:  0.8753552272362406
Recall:  0.8695450680272108
Confusion Matrix:
+--------------+-----------------+-------+
| target_label | predicted_label | count |
+--------------+-----------------+-------+
|   ice cream  |      candy      |   1   |
|     apple    |      banana     |   3   |
|    orange    |    pineapple    |   2   |
|     apple    |    strawberry   |   1   |
|   pineapple  |      banana     |   1   |
|  strawberry  |      salad      |   2   |
|    popcorn   |      waffle     |   1   |
|    carrot    |      salad      |   2   |
|    orange    |    watermelon   |   1   |
|    popcorn   |     popcorn     |   36  |
+--------------+-----------------+-------+
[107 rows x 3 columns]
Note: Only the head of the SFrame is printed.
You can use print_rows(num_rows=m, num_columns=n) to print more
rows and columns.
```

No surprises: Accuracy, precision and recall are all similar to the final validation accuracy of the model. Unlike Create ML, Turi Create gives only overall values for precision and recall, and you need some code to get precision and recall for each class. In the next chapter, you'll learn how to get recall for each class.

The confusion matrix shows only the first 10 rows: the model mistook one "ice cream" image for "candy," three "apple" images for "banana," etc. Presented this way, it doesn't look much like a matrix.

In the next chapter, you'll learn how to get this nifty visualization:

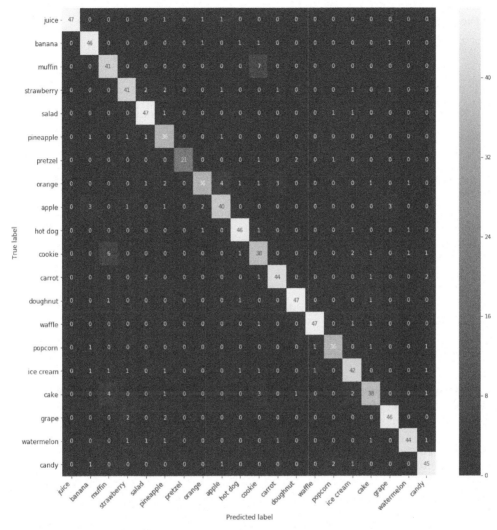

The confusion matrix

This heatmap shows small values as a cool color — black or dark purple — and large values as warm colors — red to orange to white. The larger the value, the brighter it gets. The correct matches are on the diagonal, so the highest values are there. With only 21 correct matches, "pretzel" stands out, but there are only 25 images in the pretzel folder, so 21 is OK. Purple numbers off the diagonal indicate problems. More about this in the next chapter!

Exporting to Core ML

In the next cell, **Shift-Enter** this command:

```
model
```

This displays information about the model.

```
Class                              : ImageClassifier

Schema
------
Number of classes                  : 20
Number of feature columns          : 1
Input image shape                  : (3, 299, 299)

Training summary
----------------
Number of examples                 : 4590
Training loss                      : 1.2978
Training time (sec)                : 174.5081
```

Now you will save this model so you can load it with Core ML. There are two ways to save models using Turi Create. First:

```
model.save("HealthySnacks.model")
```

This saves the model in Turi Create's own format, which allows you to load it back into the Python notebook later using `tc.load_model()`. Once you've trained a Turi Create model, you can't modify it afterwards, but you might want to evaluate it on different test data, or examine the metrics more closely.

Run this command to get a Core ML model:

```
model.export_coreml("HealthySnacks.mlmodel")
```

You can add the mlmodel to Xcode in the usual way if you want to compare it with the Create ML model. Despite being based on the same pre-trained model, the two custom models aren't the same: The accuracy of this model is a little lower, and it's half the size of the Create ML model.

Shutting down Jupyter

To shut down Jupyter, click the **Logout** button in this browser window and also in the window showing your ML directory.

In the **Terminal** window from which you ran `jupyter notebook` — or the one that ran `jupyter_mac.command ; exit;` if you used Anaconda Navigator to launch Jupyter — press **Control-C** to stop the server. You may need to press this twice. If the prompt doesn't return, close this terminal window.

Deactivating the active environment

If you activated **turienv** at the terminal command line, enter this command to deactivate it:

```
conda deactivate
```

This deactivates the **turienv** environment; the command line prompt loses the `(turienv)` prefix.

Docker and Colab

There are two other high-level tools for supporting machine learning in Python: Docker and Google Colaboratory. These can be useful for developing machine learning projects, but we're not covering them in detail in this book.

Docker is a useful tool for creating reproducible environments for running machine learning projects, and is therefore a useful tool when you want to scale up projects. Colaboratory is a Jupyter notebook in the cloud that gives you access to free GPU. But, while you're working through the Turi Create and Keras examples in this book and trying out your own modifications, it's more convenient to have the **turienv** and **kerasenv** environments, and know how to build or modify them.

Docker

Docker is like a virtual machine but simpler. Docker is a container-based system that allows you to re-use and modularize re-usable environments, and is a fundamental building block to scaling services and applications on the Internet efficiently. Installing Docker gives you access to a large number of ML resources distributed in Docker images as Jupyter notebooks like **hwchong/kerastraining4coreml** or Python projects like the **bamos/openface** face recognition model. Our Beginning Machine Learning with Keras & Core ML (bit.ly/36cS6KU) tutorial builds and runs a keras-mnist Docker image, and you can get comfortable using Docker with our Docker on macOS: Getting Started tutorial here: bit.ly/2os0KnY.

Docker images can be useful to share pre-defined environments with colleagues or peers, but at some point they will require an understanding of how to write Docker images (by editing the corresponding Dockerfile), which is beyond the scope of what we're covering here.

You can download the community edition of Docker for Mac from https://dockr.ly/2hwNOZZ. To search Docker Hub hub.docker.com (a repository for Docker images), click **Explore**, then search for *image classifier*:

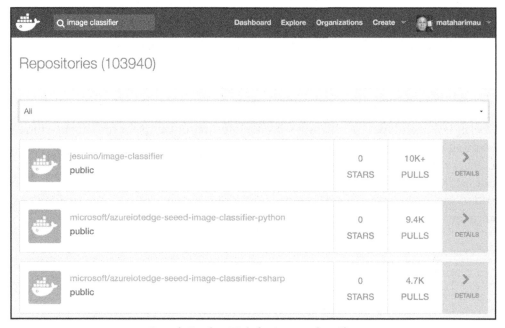

Search Docker Hub for image classifier

Google Colaboratory

Google Research's Colaboratory at colab.research.google.com is a Jupyter Notebook environment that runs in a browser. It comes with many of the machine learning libraries you'll need, already installed. Its best feature is, you can set the **runtime type** of a notebook to **GPU** to use Google's GPU for free. It even lets you use Google's **TPUs** (tensor processing units).

If you don't have access to a machine learning capable computer, you can certainly follow along with parts of this book using Colab. However, the authors of this book recommend that readers follow along with a local installation of Python. If you choose to use Colab, you'll have to perform the following set up. Of course, you will need a Google account to in order to continue.

Access your Google Drive drive.google.com and from the side menu, create a new **Folder** named **machine-learning**.

Double click the folder, and drag and drop the unzipped snacks dataset into it. This may take a while. While you wait, you'll need to add Colab as an "app" to Google Drive. Right-click anywhere in the **machine-learning** folder, select **More** from the dialog, and select **+ Select Connect more apps**.

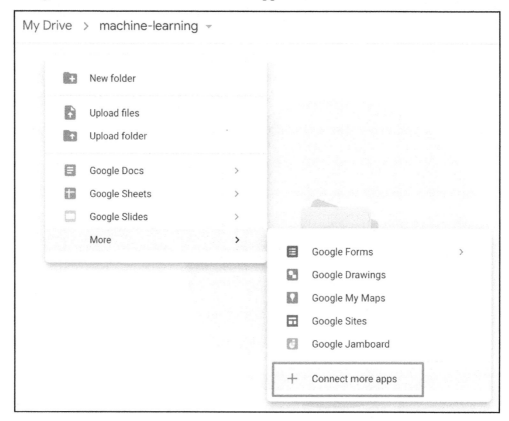

From the **Connect apps to Drive** window that opens up, search for colab in the search field, and select **+ Connect**.

Once it's been successfully installed, close the window, and Right-click anywhere again, and from the **More** dialog, select **Colaboratory**. This will open a new tab or window with something that should look a lot like a Jupyter notebook.

Rename the file to **getting-started.ipynb** by clicking the ttile and renaming it inline.

From the toolbar, select **Runtime > Change Runtime type**.

From the **Notebook settings** dialog that open, change the **Hardware accelerator** from *None* to *GPU*. **Save** the changes.

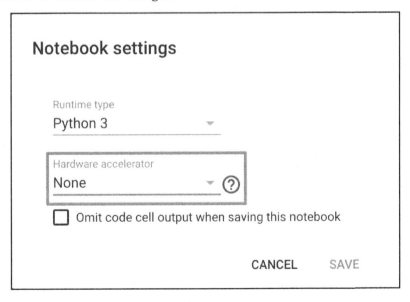

In first code cell of the notebook, paste the following code:

```
from google.colab import drive
drive.mount('/content/drive/')
```

These two lines will walk your through mounting your google drive folders into the notebook. This requires giving Colab access to your Google Drive folders. Click the tiny play button beside the code cell. Follow the instructions in the output window by opening the link to give Colab the authority to access your Drive. You'll be given an access code to paste into your notebook.

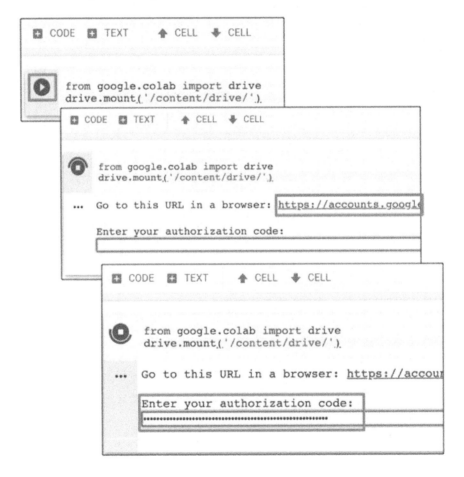

Once the mounting is complete, add a new code cell, and run the following piece of code:

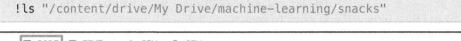

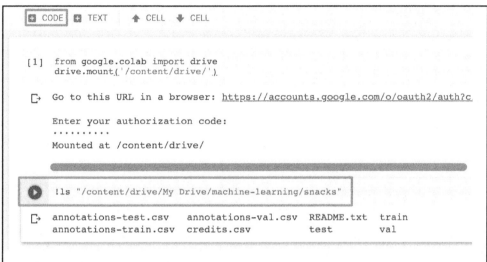

You may notice that the code starts off with an exclamation. This is Juypter-specific syntax that allows you to run system level commands. In this case, you're trying to list the contents of the directory in which you uploaded the snacks dataset. If all goes well, you should now be able to set this path as your root directory to the snacks dataset.

You've completed setting up a Google Colab notebook environment, configured to use the GPU, that you can use for this book. It's worth reiterating that using Colab is untested with respect to this book, and you may run into issues while using it. However, it offers a compelling alternative for devselopers looking to do machine learning, but don't have access to a machine powerful enough to run machine learning algorithms.

Key points

- Get familiar with Python. Its widespread adoption with academics in the machine learning field means if you want to keep up to date with machine learning, you'll have to get on board.

- Get familiar with Conda. It will make working with Python significantly more pleasant. It allows you to try Python libraries in a controlled environment without damaging any existing environment.

- Get familiar with Jupyter notebooks. Like Swift playgrounds, they provide a means to quickly test all things Python especially when used in combination with Conda.

Where to go from here?

You're all set to continue learning about machine learning for image classification using Python tools. The next chapter shows you a few more Turi Create tricks. After that, you'll be ready to learn how to create your own deep learning model in Keras.

Chapter 5: Digging Deeper into Turi Create

By Audrey Tam & Matthijs Hollemans

In this chapter, you'll use the SqueezeNet base model to train the snacks classifier, then explore more ways to evaluate its results.

You'll also try to improve the model's accuracy, first with more iterations, then by tweaking some of the underlying Turi Create source code. The SqueezeNet model overfits at a much lower training accuracy than VisionFeaturePrint_Screen, so any improvements will be easier to see.

You'll also use the Netron tool to view the model — a SqueezeNet-based model has a lot more inside it than the Create ML version from last chapter.

Getting started

You can continue to use the **turienv** environment, **Jupyter** notebook, and **snacks** dataset from the previous chapter, or start fresh with the **DiggingDeeper_starter** notebook in this chapter's **starter** folder.

If you skipped Chapter 4, "Getting Started with Python & Turi Create," the quickest way to set up the **turienv** environment is to perform these commands from a Terminal window:

```
$ cd /path/to/chapter/resources
$ conda env create --file=starter/turienv.yaml
$ conda activate turienv
$ jupyter notebook
```

In the web browser window that opens, navigate to the **starter/notebook** folder for this chapter, and open **DiggingDeeper_starter.ipynb**.

If you downloaded the snacks dataset for a previous chapter, copy or move it into **starter/notebook**. Otherwise, double-click **starter/notebook/snacks-download-link.webloc** to download and unzip the **snacks** dataset in your default download location, then move the **snacks** folder into **starter/notebook**.

> **Note:** In this book we're using Turi Create version 5.6. Other versions may give different results or even errors. This is why we suggest using the **turienv** that comes with the book.

Transfer learning with SqueezeNet

If you're not continuing from the previous chapter's notebook, then run the following cells one by one.

> **Note:** If you are continuing from last chapter's notebook, but have shut down Jupyter in the mean time, then you'll also need to re-run these cells. Jupyter does not automatically restore the Python state. You can skip the data exploration cells.

1. Import the required Python modules:

```
import turicreate as tc
import matplotlib.pyplot as plt
```

2. Load training and testing data and display lengths to make sure there's data:

```
train_data = tc.image_analysis.load_images("snacks/train",
                                           with_path=True)
len(train_data)
```

```
test_data = tc.image_analysis.load_images("snacks/test",
with_path=True)
len(test_data)
```

3. Extract labels from the image paths and display label count values:

```
import os
train_data["label"] = train_data["path"].apply(
            lambda path: os.path.basename(os.path.split(path)
[0]))

test_data["label"] = test_data["path"].apply(
            lambda path: os.path.basename(os.path.split(path)
[0]))

train_data["label"].value_counts().print_rows(num_rows=20)
test_data["label"].value_counts().print_rows(num_rows=20)
```

Now that the dataset has been loaded, you can create the image classifier. If you don't want to wait for your Mac to train this model, load the pre-trained model instead, from the **starter/notebook** folder:

```
model = tc.load_model("MultiSnacks.model")
```

But if you've got some cycles to spare, feel free to train the model. This is done the same as before, except now you'll use the arguments model="squeezenet_v1.1" to use the SqueezeNet feature extractor:

```
model = tc.image_classifier.create(train_data, target="label",
                                   model="squeezenet_v1.1",
                                   verbose=True,
max_iterations=100)
```

When you run this cell, you'll be pleasantly surprised at how fast the feature extraction is, compared to last chapter. This is because SqueezeNet extracts only 1000 features from 227×227-pixel images, compared with VisionFeaturePrint_Screen's 2,048 features from 299×299 images.

However, you'll probably be disappointed by the training and validation accuracies:

Iteration	Passes	Step size	Elapsed Time	Training Accuracy	Validation Accuracy
...					
9	16	1.000000	2.250278	0.447128	0.371901
24	41	2.349134	5.906775	0.597476	0.533058
49	77	1.000000	11.472903	0.706484	0.648760
74	113	1.000000	17.694513	0.755657	0.661157
99	162	1.000000	25.050267	0.803525	0.670412

> **Note**: It's likely you'll get slightly different training results than what are shown in this book. Recall that untrained models, in this case the logistic regression part of the model, are initialized with random numbers. This can cause variations between different training runs. Just try it again if you get a training accuracy that is much less than 65%. Advanced users of machine learning actually take advantage of these differences between training runs to combine multiple models into one big ensemble that gives more robust predictions.

Like Create ML, Turi Create randomly chooses 5% of the training data as validation data, so validation accuracies can vary quite a bit between training runs. The model might do better on a larger fixed validation dataset that you choose yourself (which you'll do later in this chapter).

Evaluate the model and display some metrics:

```
metrics = model.evaluate(test_data)
print("Accuracy: ", metrics["accuracy"])
print("Precision: ", metrics["precision"])
print("Recall: ", metrics["recall"])
```

No surprises here — accuracy is pretty close to the validation accuracy:

```
Accuracy:  0.6470588235294118
Precision:  0.6441343963604582
Recall:  0.6445289115646259
```

Getting individual predictions

So far, you've just repeated the steps from the previous chapter. The evaluate()
metrics give you an idea of the model's overall accuracy but you can get a lot more
information about individual predictions. Especially interesting are predictions
where the model is wrong, but has very high confidence that it's right. Knowing
where the model is wrong can help you improve your training dataset.

To get some more insight into what's going on, run the following cell:

```
metrics.explore()
```

This opens a new window (Mac only) that lets you examine the accuracy and other
metrics visually. It also shows examples of images that were correctly — and more
interestingly, incorrectly — classified. Very handy!

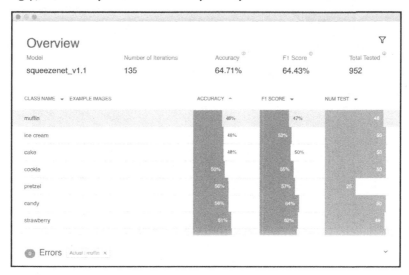

The interactive evaluation window

Predicting and classifying

Turi Create models have other functions, in addition to `evaluate()`. Enter and run these commands in the next cell, and wait a while:

```
model.predict(test_data)
```

It displays the actual prediction for each individual image from the test set:

```
['apple', 'grape', 'orange', 'orange', 'orange', 'apple',
'orange', 'apple', 'candy', 'apple', 'grape', 'apple',
'strawberry', 'apple', 'apple', 'carrot', 'candy', 'ice cream',
'apple', 'apple', 'apple', ...
```

The first prediction corresponds to the image from `test_data[0]`, the second to the image from `test_data[1]`, and so on. The first 50 test images are all apples, but the model classified the second image as "grape," so take a look at the image. Enter and run this command in the next cell:

```
plt.imshow(test_data[1]["image"].pixel_data)
```

This displays the second image — does it look like grapes?

grapes?

Maybe the model isn't really sure, either. Enter and run these commands, and wait a while:

```
output = model.classify(test_data)
output
```

The `classify()` function gets you the probability for each prediction, but only the highest-probability value, which is the model's confidence in the class it predicts:

class	probability
apple	0.4326385132863121
grape	0.699598450277612
orange	0.4148821902502113
orange	0.9300597134095988
orange	0.37817135281719916
apple	0.9915643139757563
orange	0.42620238429617097

The head of the SFrame with classification results

So the model is 69.96% confident that the second image is "grape"! And 93% confident the fourth image is "orange"! But it's less than 50% confident about the other images it labelled "orange."

It's helpful to see the images that correspond to each prediction. Enter and run these commands:

```
imgs_with_pred = test_data.add_columns(output)
imgs_with_pred.explore()
```

The first command adds the `output` columns to the original `test_data` columns. Then you display the merged SFrame with `explore()`.

The **label** column is the correct class, and **class** is the model's highest-confidence prediction, which you can see on the next page:

	path	image	label	class	probability
0	snacks/test/apple/00341c3c582…		apple	apple	0.432639
1	snacks/test/apple/004be96d798…		apple	grape	0.699598
2	snacks/test/apple/01ac2a42f2a2…		apple	orange	0.414882
3	snacks/test/apple/03bfc0b1cc6b…		apple	orange	0.93006
4	snacks/test/apple/09ed54b36ea…		apple	orange	0.378171

Visually inspecting the classification results

The most interesting images are the rows where the two labels disagree, but the probability is very high — over 90%, for example. Enter the following commands:

```
imgs_filtered = imgs_with_pred[(imgs_with_pred["probability"] >
0.9) &
                   (imgs_with_pred["label"] !=
imgs_with_pred["class"] )]
imgs_filtered.explore()
```

This command filters the SFrame to include only those rows with high-probability wrong predictions. The first term selects the rows whose probability column has a value greater than 90%, the second term selects the rows where the label and class columns are not the same.

The subset of matching rows is saved into a new SFrame, then displayed:

	path	image	label	class	probability
35	snacks/test/pretzel/4697876386...		pretzel	hot dog	0.964394
36	snacks/test/salad/00af886180e9...		salad	carrot	0.952237
37	snacks/test/salad/b9fe5d18d940...		salad	carrot	0.909241
38	snacks/test/strawberry/09d1401...		strawberry	salad	0.973804
39	snacks/test/strawberry/0dd1e9e...				
40	snacks/test/strawberry/2454732...				
41	snacks/test/waffle/2a3d34b6e4b...				
42	snacks/test/waffle/6350b46e939...		waffle	muffin	0.905807
43	snacks/test/watermelon/0200c7...		watermelon	carrot	0.91499
44	snacks/test/watermelon/a7409d...		watermelon	strawberry	0.939163

Inspecting the filtered classification results

The true label of the highlighted image is "strawberry," but the model is 97% confident it's "juice," probably because the glass of milk(?) is much larger than the strawberries.

You can learn a lot about how your model sees the world by looking at these confident-but-wrong predictions: Sometimes the model gets it completely wrong, but sometimes the predictions are actually fairly reasonable — even if it is strictly speaking "wrong," since what was predicted wasn't the official label.

But if the image contains more than one object, such as the example with the drink and the strawberries, you could argue that the training label is actually wrong — or at least, misleading.

Sorting the prediction probabilities

Turi Create's `predict()` method can also give you the probability distribution for each image. Enter and run these lines, then wait a while:

```
predictions = model.predict(test_data,
    output_type="probability_vector")
```

You add the optional argument `output_type` to get the **probability vector** for each image — the predicted probability for each of the 20 classes. Then let's look at the second image again, but now display all of the probabilities, not just the top one:

```
print("Probabilities for 2nd image", predictions[1])
```

This outputs something like the following:

```
array('d', [0.20337662077520557, 0.010500386379535839,
2.8464920324200633e-07, 0.0034932724790819624,
0.0013391166287066811, 0.00051223691240003818,
5.118841868115829e-06, 0.699598450277612,
2.0208374302686123e-07, 7.164497444549948e-07,
2.584012081941193e-06, 5.5645094234565224e-08,
0.08066298157942492, 0.00021689939485918623,
2.30074608705137e-06, 3.6511378835730773e-10,
5.345215832976188e-05, 9.897270575019545e-06,
2.1477438456101293e-08, 0.00022540187389448156])
```

The probabilities are sorted alphanumerically by name of the class in the training set, so the first value is for "apple," the second is "banana," the third is "cake" … Ack! — you need to add class labels to make this useful! Enter and run the following:

```
labels = test_data["label"].unique().sort()
preds = tc.SArray(predictions[1])
tc.SFrame({"preds": preds, "labels": labels}).sort([("preds",
    False)])
```

First, you get the set of labels from the `test_data` SFrame, sort them so they match the order in the probability vector, and store the result in `labels`, which is an **SArray** — a Turi Create array. Then you create another SArray from the probability vector of the second image. In the last line, you merge the two SArrays into an SFrame, then sort it on the `preds` column, in descending order (ascending = False).

Here are the top five rows from this output:

labels	preds
grape	0.699598450277612
apple	0.20337662077520557
orange	0.08066298157942492
banana	0.0105000386379535839
candy	0.0034932724790819624

Top five probabilities for the second image.

So the model does at least give 20% confidence to "apple." Top-three or top-five accuracy is a fairer metric for a dataset whose images can contain multiple objects.

Using a fixed validation set

Turi Create extracts a random validation dataset from the training dataset — 5% of the images. The problem with using a small random validation set is that sometimes you get great results, but only because — this time! — the validation dataset just happens to be in your favor.

For example, if the model is really good at predicting the class "waffle" and the validation set happens to be mostly images of waffles, the validation accuracy will be higher than the true performance of the model. That's bad, because it may lead you to overestimate how good the model really is.

If you repeat training the model a few times, you'll see the validation accuracy vary a lot. Sometimes it's better than the 67% you saw before, sometimes it's way worse — on one of the author's training runs, it went as low as 59%. It's hard to understand how well the model is doing when there's so much variation between different runs.

To get more reliable estimates of the accuracy, use your own validation set instead of letting Turi Create randomly select one. By using a collection of validation images that is always the same, you can control your experiments better and get reproducible results. You can now train the model with a few different configuration settings, also known as the **hyperparameters**, and compare the results to determine which settings work best. If you were to use a different validation set each time, then the variation in the chosen images could obscure the effect of the changed hyperparameter.

The snacks dataset already comes with a **val** folder containing images for this purpose. Load these images into their own SFrame, using the same code as before:

```
val_data = tc.image_analysis.load_images("snacks/val",
with_path=True)
val_data["label"] = val_data["path"].apply(lambda path:
      os.path.basename(os.path.split(path)[0]))
len(val_data)
```

The last statement should output **955**, which is almost the same number of images as in `test_data`, and a lot more than 5% of the 4838 `train_data` images.

To train the model on your own validation set, write the following:

```
model = tc.image_classifier.create(train_data, target="label",
                                   model="squeezenet_v1.1",
                                   verbose=True,
    max_iterations=100,

                                   validation_set=val_data)
```

You should now always get the same validation accuracy — about 63% — no matter how often you repeat the training. The large fluctuations are gone.

Iteration	Passes	Step size	Elapsed Time	Training Accuracy	Validation Accuracy
...					
79	101	1.000000	19.143993	0.758165	0.619895
89	118	1.290184	21.788411	0.781315	0.624084
99	133	1.000000	24.326639	0.795783	0.631414

Because the model is initialized with random numbers at the start of training, there are still small differences between each training run. To get *exactly* the same results each time, pass the `seed` argument to `tc.image_classifier.create()` to fix the seed for the random number generator, for example `seed=1234`.

Note: With this fixed validation set, training has become a little slower. That's because computing the validation accuracy takes up a significant amount of time. Previously, Turi only used 5% of the training set for this, or about 240 images. Now it uses 955 images, so it takes about 4 times as long to compute the validation score. But getting more trustworthy estimates is worth the extra wait.

Increasing max iterations

So, is a validation accuracy of 63% good? Meh, not really. Turi Create knows it, too — at the end of the training output it says:

```
This model may not be optimal. To improve it, consider
increasing `max_iterations`.
```

Turi Create has recognized that this model still has some issues. (It's possible you won't get this message, this seems to vary with Turi Create versions.)

Let's train again, this time with more iterations — 200 instead of 100:

```
model = tc.image_classifier.create(train_data, target="label",
                                   model="squeezenet_v1.1",
                                   verbose=True,
max_iterations=200,
                                   validation_set=val_data)
```

> **Note**: Like Create ML, Turi Create has to extract the features again. It does not keep those feature vectors around — if it had, training the model again would be a lot quicker. If 100 iterations already took a very long time on your Mac, feel free to load the pre-trained model from **starter/notebook**:
>
> ```
> model = tc.load_model("MultiSnacks_200.model")
> ```

The number of iterations is an example of a **hyperparameter**. This is simply a fancy name for the configuration settings for your model. Why "hyper"? The things that the model learns from the training data are called the "parameters" or learned parameters. The things you configure by hand, which don't get changed by training, are therefore the "hyperparameters." The hyperparameters tell the model *how* to learn, while the training data tells the model *what* to learn, and the parameters describe that which has actually been learned.

The max_iterations setting determines how long the model will be trained for. Like all hyperparameters, it's important to set it to a good value or else the resulting model may not be as good as you'd hoped. If the training time is too short, the model won't have had the opportunity to learn all it could; if the training time is too long, the model will overfit.

After 200 iterations of training, the final score is:

Iteration	Passes	Step size	Elapsed Time	Training Accuracy	Validation Accuracy
...					
99	133	1.000000	25.650264	0.795783	0.631414
124	167	1.000000	32.426814	0.834849	0.625131
149	213	1.247567	39.861891	0.865854	0.636649
174	243	1.000000	45.488413	0.891484	0.635602
199	281	1.000000	51.928382	0.908433	0.620942

The training accuracy is now 90%! This means on the training set of 4582 examples it only gets 10% wrong, as opposed to 20% before (when the training accuracy was about 80%).

That seems pretty good, but remember that you shouldn't put too much faith in the training accuracy by itself. More important is the validation accuracy. As you can see, this briefly went up and then down again.

The sweet spot for this model seems to be somewhere around 150 iterations where it gets a validation accuracy of 63.7%. If you train for longer, the validation accuracy starts to drop and the model becomes worse, even though the training accuracy will slowly keep improving. A classic sign of overfitting.

Overfitting has a bad rap, and it's certainly an issue you'll run into when you start training your own models. But overfitting isn't necessarily a bad thing to experience, as it means that your model still has capacity to learn more. It's just learning the wrong things, and techniques such as regularization will help your model to stay on the right path. (More about regularization later in this chapter.)

Unfortunately, Turi Create does not let you save the iteration of the model with the best validation accuracy, only the very last iteration, and so you'll have to train again with `max_iterations=150`, to get the best possible result.

Run the usual code to evaluate the model on the test set and display the metrics:

```
metrics = model.evaluate(test_data)
print("Accuracy: ", metrics["accuracy"])
print("Precision: ", metrics["precision"])
print("Recall: ", metrics["recall"])
```

Evaluating this model on the test dataset produces metrics around 65%, which is slightly higher than before:

```
Accuracy:  0.6554621848739496
Precision:  0.6535792163681828
Recall:  0.6510697278911566
```

Increasing the number of iterations did help a little, so apparently the initial guess of 100 iterations was too low. Tip: For the best results, first train the model with too many iterations, and see at which iteration the validation accuracy starts to become worse. That's your sweet spot. Now train again for exactly that many iterations and save the model.

Confusing apples with oranges?

A picture says more than a thousand numbers, and a really useful visualization of how well the model does is the **confusion matrix**. This matrix plots the predicted classes versus the images' real class labels, so you can see where the model tends to make its mistakes.

In the previous chapter, you ran this command:

```
print("Confusion Matrix:\n", metrics["confusion_matrix"])
```

This displayed a table:

```
+--------------+-----------------+-------+
| target_label | predicted_label | count |
+--------------+-----------------+-------+
|    cookie    |      juice      |   1   |
|    carrot    |    watermelon   |   1   |
|   pretzel    |     pretzel     |  14   |
|     cake     |    ice cream    |   2   |
|  pineapple   |     carrot      |   1   |
|   doughnut   |     muffin      |   1   |
|    muffin    |    doughnut     |   7   |
```

The `target_label` column shows the real class, while `predicted_label` has the class that was predicted, and `count` is how many of this particular mistake were made.

The table shows the model predicted "muffin" 7 times when the image was really "doughnut," predicted "cake" twice when the image was really "ice cream," and so on.

However, presented this way, the confusion matrix doesn't look much like a matrix, and we promised to show you how to get a better visualization.

Start by entering and running the following code:

```python
import numpy as np
import seaborn as sns

def compute_confusion_matrix(metrics, labels):
    num_labels = len(labels)
    label_to_index = {l:i for i,l in enumerate(labels)}

    conf = np.zeros((num_labels, num_labels), dtype=np.int)
    for row in metrics["confusion_matrix"]:
        true_label = label_to_index[row["target_label"]]
        pred_label = label_to_index[row["predicted_label"]]
        conf[true_label, pred_label] = row["count"]

    return conf

def plot_confusion_matrix(conf, labels, figsize=(8, 8)):
    fig = plt.figure(figsize=figsize)
    heatmap = sns.heatmap(conf, annot=True, fmt="d")
    heatmap.xaxis.set_ticklabels(labels, rotation=45,
                                 ha="right", fontsize=12)
    heatmap.yaxis.set_ticklabels(labels, rotation=0,
                                 ha="right", fontsize=12)
    plt.xlabel("Predicted label", fontsize=12)
    plt.ylabel("True label", fontsize=12)
    plt.show()
```

You define two new functions: one to compute the confusion matrix and one to draw it.

`compute_confusion_matrix()` looks at all the rows in the `metrics["confusion_matrix"]` table, and fills up a 2D-array with the counts of each pair of labels. It uses the NumPy package for this.

Then, `plot_confusion_matrix()` takes this NumPy array, and plots it as a *heatmap* using Seaborn, a plotting package that adds useful plot types to Matplotlib. You installed Seaborn when you created the `turienv` environment in the previous chapter.

Now, enter and run the following commands to call these functions:

```
conf = compute_confusion_matrix(metrics, labels)
plot_confusion_matrix(conf, labels, figsize=(16, 16))
```

And enjoy the display!

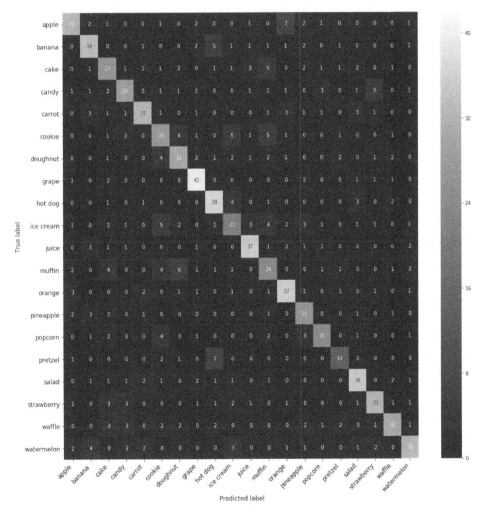

The confusion matrix

A heatmap shows small values as "cool" colors — black and dark purple — and large values as "hot" colors — red to pink to white. The larger the value, the brighter it gets. In the confusion matrix, you expect to see a lot of high values on the diagonal, since these are the correct matches.

For example, the row for the "pretzel" class shows 14 correct matches and 11 wrong ones. The wrong predictions are one "apple," two "cookie," one "doughnut," and seven "hotdog." Notice that apples often get mistaken for oranges, and cookie, doughnut, and muffin also get mixed up often.

The confusion matrix is very useful because it shows potential problem areas for the model. From this particular confusion matrix, it's clear the model has learned a great deal already, since the diagonal really stands out, but it's still far from perfect. Ideally, you want everything to be zero except the diagonal. It may be a little misleading from the picture since at first glance it appears that there aren't that many mistakes. But all the small numbers in the dark squares add up to 340 misclassified images out of 952 total, or 36% wrong.

Keep in mind that some categories have more images than others. For example, pretzel has only 25 images in the test set, while most of the other classes have 50, so it will never have as many correct matches. Still, it only scores 14 out of 25 correct (56%), so overall the model actually does poorly on pretzels.

Computing recall for each class

Turi Create's `evaluate()` function gives you the overall test dataset accuracy but, as mentioned in the AI Ethics section of the first chapter, accuracy might be much lower or higher for specific subsets of the dataset. With a bit of code, you can get the accuracies for the individual classes from the confusion matrix:

```
for i, label in enumerate(labels):
    correct = conf[i, i]
    images_per_class = conf[i].sum()
    print("%10s %.1f%%" % (label, 100. * correct/
images_per_class))
```

For each row of the confidence matrix, the number on the diagonal is how many images in this class that the model predicted correctly. You're dividing this number by the sum over that row, which is the total number of test images in that class.

This gives you the percentage of each class that the model classified correctly — for example, how many "apple" images did the model find among the total number of "apple" images?

This the **recall** metric for each class:

```
      apple 64.0%
     banana 68.0%
       cake 54.0%
      candy 58.0%
     carrot 66.0%
     cookie 56.0%
   doughnut 62.0%
      grape 84.0%
    hot dog 76.0%
  ice cream 44.0%
      juice 74.0%
     muffin 50.0%
     orange 74.0%
  pineapple 67.5%
    popcorn 62.5%
    pretzel 56.0%
      salad 72.0%
 strawberry 67.3%
     waffle 62.0%
 watermelon 64.0%
```

The best classes are grape (84% correct) and hot dog (76%). At 74%, juice and orange are also good. The worst performing classes are ice cream (44%), muffin (50%), cake (54%), and pretzel (56%). These would be the classes to pay attention to, in order to improve the model — for example, by gathering more or better training images for these classes.

> **Note**: As always, the numbers you'll get for your own version of this model might be slightly different. This is due to the choice of hyperparameters, such as the number of iterations. But also because untrained models are initialized with random numbers, and therefore two trained models are never exactly the same (unless you set the random seed to a fixed number).

Training the classifier with regularization

A typical hyperparameter that machine learning practitioners like to play with is the amount of **regularization** that's being used by the model. Regularization helps to prevent overfitting. Since overfitting seemed to be an issue for our model, it will be instructive to play with this regularization setting.

Enter and run this statement:

```
model = tc.image_classifier.create(train_data, target="label",
                                    model="squeezenet_v1.1",
                                    verbose=True,
max_iterations=200,

                                    validation_set=val_data,
                                    l2_penalty=10.0,
    l1_penalty=0.0,

                                    convergence_threshold=1e-8)
```

You've added three additional arguments: `l2_penalty`, `l1_penalty` and `convergence_threshold`. Setting the `convergence_threshold` to a very small value means that the training won't stop until it has done all 200 iterations.

`l2_penalty` and `l1_penalty` are hyperparameters that add regularization to reduce overfitting.

What's regularization? Recall that a model learns parameters — also called weights or coefficients — for combining feature values, to maximize how many training data items it classifies correctly. Overfitting can happen when the model gives too much weight to some features, by giving them very large coefficients. Setting `l2_penalty` greater than 0 penalizes large coefficients, encouraging the model to learn smaller coefficients. Higher values of `l2_penalty` reduce the size of coefficients, but can also reduce the training accuracy.

Setting `l1_penalty` greater than 0 also penalizes large coefficients. In addition, it discards features that have very small coefficients, by setting these to 0. Typically, you'd use either `l2_penalty` or `l1_penalty`, but not both in the same training session.

In the author's training session, the model has stopped overfitting:

Iteration	Passes	Step size	Elapsed Time	Training Accuracy	Validation Accuracy
...					
124	183	2.755461	33.123541	0.780281	0.643979
149	221	1.000000	39.888817	0.785449	0.646073
174	258	0.965087	46.111951	0.784415	0.647120
199	305	1.326954	53.436059	0.786895	0.649215

The training accuracy doesn't race off to 100% anymore but tops out at about 79%. More importantly, the validation accuracy doesn't become worse with more iterations. Note that it is typical for the training accuracy to be higher than the validation accuracy. This is OK — it's only bad if the validation accuracy starts going down.

Question: Is l2_penalty=10.0 the best possible setting? To find out, you can train the classifier several times, trying out different values for l2_penalty and l1_penalty. This is called **hyperparameter tuning**.

Selecting the correct hyperparameters for your training procedure can make a big difference in the quality of the model you end up with. The validation accuracy gives you an indication of the effect of these hyperparameters. This is why you're using a fixed validation set, so that you can sure any change in the results is caused by the change in the hyperparameters, not by chance.

Hyperparameter tuning is more trial and error than science, so play with these settings to get a feeling for how they affect your model. Try setting l2_penalty to 100: you'll note that the training accuracy won't go over 65% or so, as now you're punishing the model too hard.

Unfortunately, every time you train the model, Turi Create has to extract the features from all the training and validation images again, over and over and over. That makes hyperparameter tuning a very slow affair. Let's fix that!

Wrangling Turi Create code

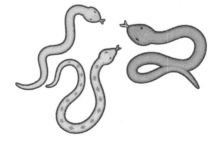

One of the appealing benefits of Turi Create is that, once you have your data in an SFrame, it takes only a single line of code to train the model. The downside is that the Turi Create API gives you only limited control over the training process. Fortunately, Turi Create is open source, so you can look inside to see what it does, and even hack around some of its limitations.

The code for `tc.image_classifier.create()` is in the file `turicreate/src/ python/turicreate/toolkits/image_classifier/image_classifier.py` in the GitHub repo at github.com/apple/turicreate. You're simply going to copy-paste some of that code into the notebook, and play with the hyperparameters.

Saving the extracted features

Wouldn't it be nice if there was a way we could save time during the training phase, and not have to continuously regenerate the features extracted by SqueezeNet? Well, as promised, in this section, you'll learn how to save the intermediate SFrame to disk, and reload it, just before experimenting with the classifier.

> **Note**: If you don't want to wait for the feature extraction, just load the features from the **starter/notebook** folder:
>
> ```
> extracted_train_features =
> tc.SFrame("extracted_train_features.sframe")
>
> extracted_val_features =
> tc.SFrame("extracted_val_features.sframe")
> ```

First, load the pre-trained SqueezeNet model and grab its feature extractor:

```
from turicreate.toolkits import _pre_trained_models
from turicreate.toolkits import _image_feature_extractor

ptModel = _pre_trained_models.MODELS["squeezenet_v1.1"]()
feature_extractor =
_image_feature_extractor.MXFeatureExtractor(ptModel)
```

`MXFeatureExtractor` is an object from the MXNet machine learning framework that Turi Create is built on. In Python, names starting with an underscore are considered to be private, but you can still import them. Next, enter and run this code statement:

```
train_features = feature_extractor.extract_features(train_data,
                                    "image", verbose=True)
```

You're using the MXFeatureExtractor object to extract the SqueezeNet features from the training dataset. This is the operation that took the most time when you ran tc.image_classifier.create(). By running this separately now, you won't have wait for feature extraction every time you want to train the classifier. Next, enter and run this code statement:

```
extracted_train_features = tc.SFrame({
    "label": train_data["label"],
    "__image_features__": train_features,
})
```

Here, you're just combining the features of each image with its respective label into a new SFrame. This is worth saving for later use! Enter and run this code statement:

```
extracted_train_features.save("extracted_train_features.sframe")
```

You're saving extracted_train_features to a file. The next time you want to do more training with these same features, you can simply load the SFrame again, which takes a fraction of the time it took to extract the features:

```
# Run this tomorrow or next week
extracted_train_features =
tc.SFrame("extracted_train_features.sframe")
```

Inspecting the extracted features

Let's see what these features actually look like — enter and run this command:

```
extracted_train_features.head()
```

__image_features__	label
[6.13373851776612305, 10.12844181060791, ...	apple
[9.666999816894531, 14.665328025817871, ...	apple
[10.662524223327637, 15.472965240478516, ...	apple
[12.159001350402832, 11.231389045715332, ...	apple

The head of the extracted features table

Each row has the extracted features for one training image.

The __image_features__ column contains a list with numbers, while the label column has the corresponding class name for this row. Enter and run this command:

```
extracted_train_features[0]["__image_features__"]
```

This shows you what a feature vector looks like — it prints something like:

```
array('d', [6.1337385177612305, 10.12844181060791,
13.025101661682129, 7.931194305419922, 12.03809928894043,
15.103202819824219, 12.722893714904785, 10.930903434753418,
12.778315544128418, 14.208030700683594, 16.8399658203125,
11.781684875488281, ...
```

This is a list of 1,000 numbers — use the len() function to verify this. They all appear to be numbers between 0 and about 30. What do they represent? I have no idea, but they are features that SqueezeNet has determined to be important — how long, round, square, orange, etc. the objects are. All that matters is that you can train a logistic classifier to learn from these features.

In the same way, extract the features for the images from the validation dataset, and save this SFrame to a file too:

```
val_features = feature_extractor.extract_features(val_data,
                                    "image", verbose=True)

extracted_val_features = tc.SFrame({
    "label": val_data["label"],
    '__image_features__': val_features,
    })

extracted_val_features.save("extracted_val_features.sframe")
```

Training the classifier

Now you're ready to train the classifier! Enter and run this statement:

```
lr_model =
tc.logistic_classifier.create(extracted_train_features,
                              features=["__image_features__"],
                              target="label",

validation_set=extracted_val_features,
                              max_iterations=200,
                              seed=None,
                              verbose=True,
                              l2_penalty=10.0,
                              l1_penalty=0.0,
```

```
                        convergence_threshold=1e-8)
```

This is the Turi Create code that creates and trains the logistic regression model using the `extracted_train_features` SFrame as the input data, and `extracted_val_features` for validation.

Want to try some other values for these hyperparameters? Simply change them in the above cell and run it again. It's a lot quicker now because the feature extraction step is skipped.

There are a few other hyperparameters you can set here as well: `feature_rescaling`, `solver`, `step_size` and `lbfgs_memory_level`. To learn what these do, type the following in a new cell or check out the comments in the Turi Create source code.

```
tc.logistic_classifier.create?
```

It turns out that, with regularization, training for 400 or so iterations keeps slowly improving the validation score of this model to 65%. It's only improved by a small amount, but every little bit helps. The only way we found this was by experimenting with the hyperparameters. Perhaps you can find hyperparameters for this model that do even better?

To make sure you're not chasing phantoms and that this validation score really is representative of the model's true performance, you should also check the accuracy on the test set.

First, turn your model into a valid `ImageClassifier` object:

```
from turicreate.toolkits.image_classifier import ImageClassifier

state = {
    'classifier': lr_model,
    'model': ptModel.name,
    'max_iterations': lr_model.max_iterations,
    'feature_extractor': feature_extractor,
    'input_image_shape': ptModel.input_image_shape,
    'target': lr_model.target,
    'feature': "image",
    'num_features': 1,
    'num_classes': lr_model.num_classes,
    'classes': lr_model.classes,
    'num_examples': lr_model.num_examples,
    'training_time': lr_model.training_time,
    'training_loss': lr_model.training_loss,
}
model = ImageClassifier(state)
```

This combines the base model with the classifier you trained into the `state` structure, and creates an `ImageClassifier` object from this.

Calculate the test set metrics as before:

```
metrics = model.evaluate(test_data)
print("Accuracy: ", metrics["accuracy"])
print("Precision: ", metrics["precision"])
print("Recall: ", metrics["recall"])
```

This prints out:

```
Accuracy:  0.6712184873949579
Precision:  0.6755916486674352
Recall:  0.6698818027210884
```

Regularization and hyperparameter tuning won't always work miracles, but they do improve the model, even if only a little bit.

> **Note**: `model.evaluate()` performs feature extraction on the test set each time you run it. Exercise for the adventurous reader: Try digging into the Turi Create source code to see if you can make a version of `evaluate()` that accepts an SFrame with already extracted features. Hint: type `model.evaluate??` into a new cell (yes, two question marks) to view the source code of this method.

Saving the model

You can save the model as a Turi Create model:

```
model.save("MultiSnacks_regularized.model")
```

Or export a Core ML model:

```
model.export_coreml("MultiSnacks_regularized.mlmodel")
```

To learn more about the model, run the following:

```
model
```

This shows you some high-level information about the model and its training:

```
Class                                    : ImageClassifier
```

```
Schema
------
Number of classes                          : 20
Number of feature columns                  : 1
Input image shape                          : (3, 227, 227)
```

```
Training summary
----------------
Number of examples                         : 4838
Training loss                              : 3952.4993
Training time (sec)                        : 59.2703
```

Training loss — the overall error over the training dataset — changes when you change the hyperparameters. Enter and run this to see a bit more information:

```
model.classifier
```

This shows you information about the classifier portion of the model:

```
Class                            : LogisticClassifier

Schema
------
Number of coefficients           : 19019
Number of examples               : 4838
Number of classes                : 20
Number of feature columns        : 1
Number of unpacked features      : 1000

Hyperparameters
---------------
L1 penalty                       : 0.0
L2 penalty                       : 10.0

Training Summary
----------------
Solver                           : lbfgs
Solver iterations                : 200
Solver status                    : Completed (Iteration limit
reached).
Training time (sec)              : 59.2703

Settings
--------
Log-likelihood                   : 3952.4993

Highest Positive Coefficients
-----------------------------
(intercept)                      : 1.8933
(intercept)                      : 1.4506
```

```
(intercept)                     :  0.6717
(intercept)                     :  0.5232
(intercept)                     :  0.4072

Lowest Negative Coefficients
----------------------------
(intercept)                     : -1.6521
(intercept)                     : -1.5588
(intercept)                     : -1.4143
(intercept)                     : -0.8959
(intercept)                     : -0.5863
```

This information is mostly useful for troubleshooting or when you're just curious about how the logistic regression classifier works.

Notable is *Number of coefficients* — 19,019 — the number of parameters this model learned in order to classify images of snacks into the 20 possible categories. Here's where that number comes from: each input feature vector has 1,000 numbers, and there are 20 possible outputs, so that is 1,000 × 20 = 20,000 numbers, plus 20 "bias" values for each output, making 20,020 coefficients.

However, if there are 20 possible classes, then you actually only need to learn about 19 of those classes, giving 19,019 coefficients. If the prediction is none of these 19 classes, then it must be the 20th class. Interestingly, in the Core ML .mlmodel file, the logistic regression layer does have 20,020 parameters. You can see this for yourself with Netron in the next section.

Under the **Settings** heading, *Log-likelihood* is the more mathematical term for *Training loss*. Below this are the highest and lowest coefficients — remember, the purpose of the regularization hyperparameter is to reduce the size of the coefficients.

To compare with the coefficients of the original no-regularization model, enter and run these lines:

```
no_reg_model = tc.load_model("MultiSnacks.model")
no_reg_model.classifier
```

This reloads the pre-trained model (see the **starter/notebook** folder), and you inspect its classifier. This model had higher training accuracy, so *Log-likelihood* aka *Training loss* is lower: 2,400. As you'd expect, its highest and lowest coefficients are larger — in absolute value — than the model with regularization:

```
Settings
--------
Log-likelihood                  : 2400.3284
```

```
Highest Positive Coefficients
--------------------------------
(intercept)                      : 0.3808
(intercept)                      : 0.3799
(intercept)                      : 0.1918
__image_features__[839]          : 0.1864
(intercept)                      : 0.15

Lowest Negative Coefficients
--------------------------------
(intercept)                      : -0.3996
(intercept)                      : -0.3856
(intercept)                      : -0.3353
(intercept)                      : -0.2783
__image_features__[820]          : -0.1423
```

In the next chapter we'll talk more about what all of this means, as you'll be writing code to train your own logistic regression from scratch, as well as a complete neural network that will outperform Turi Create's SqueezeNet-based model.

A peek behind the curtain

SqueezeNet and VisionFeaturePrint_Screen are *convolutional neural networks*. In the coming chapters, you'll learn more about how these networks work internally, and you'll see how to build one from scratch. In the meantime, it might be fun to take a peek inside your Core ML model.

There is a cool free tool called Netron (github.com/lutzroeder/Netron) that creates a nice visualization of the model architecture. On the GitHub page, scroll down to the **Install** instructions, and click the **macOS Download** link. On the next page, click the **Netron-x.x.x.dmg** link, then run this file to install Netron.

Open your .mlmodel file in Netron. This shows all the transformation stages that go into you model's pipeline.

The input image is at the top, followed by convolutions, activations, pooling, and so on. These are the names of the different types of transformations — or layers — used by this kind of neural network.

Notice how this pipeline sometimes branches and then comes back together again — that's the "squeeze" feature that gives SqueezeNet its name.

Click on one of these building blocks to learn more about its configuration, its inputs and its output.

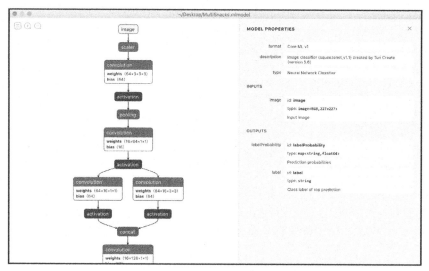

Using Netron to examine the .mlmodel file

At the very end of the pipeline is an *innerProduct* layer followed by something called a *softmax* — these two blocks make up the logistic classifier. Everything up until the *flatten* block is the SqueezeNet feature extractor.

In Chapters 6 and 7, you'll learn all about what these different kinds of layers do, but for now we suggest that you spend a few minutes playing with Netron to get a rough idea of what these models look like on the inside.

Netron works with any Core ML model, as well as models from many other machine learning frameworks. If you downloaded a model from Apple's website in the last chapter, also take a look at that.

It should look quite similar to this one, as all neural networks are very alike at their core. Often what is different is the number of layers and the branching structure.

> **Note:** Apple's own models such as `VisionFeaturePrint_Screen` are included in iOS 12 and do not get bundled into the .mlmodel file. The .mlmodel file itself doesn't contain any of the `VisionFeaturePrint_Screen` layers. For customized models based on these built-in feature extractors, Netron can't show you anything more than what you see in Xcode's description: inputs, outputs, metadata. The internal architecture of these models remains a mystery and a secret.

Challenges

Challenge 1: Binary classifier

Remember the healthy/unhealthy snacks model? Try to train that binary classifier using Turi Create. The approach is actually very similar to what you did in this chapter. The only difference is that you need to assign the label "healthy" or "unhealthy" to each row in the training data SFrame.

```
healthy = [
    'apple', 'banana', 'carrot', 'grape', 'juice', 'orange',
    'pineapple', 'salad', 'strawberry', 'watermelon'
]

unhealthy = [
    'cake', 'candy', 'cookie', 'doughnut', 'hot dog',
    'ice cream', 'muffin', 'popcorn', 'pretzel', 'waffle'
]
train_data["label"] =
    train_data["path"].apply(lambda path: "healthy"
        if any("/" + class_name in path for class_name in healthy)
                                else "unhealthy")
test_data["label"] =
    test_data["path"].apply(lambda path: "healthy"
        if any("/" + class_name in path for class_name in healthy)
                                else "unhealthy")
```

First, you assign each class into a healthy or unhealthy array — there are 10 classes in each array. Then, you set each image's label column to "healthy" or "unhealthy", depending on which array the image's path name is in. The result is, you've divided 20 classes of images into two classes, based on the name of the subdirectory they're in.

> **Note**: The process to do this same exercise in Create ML is much more manual. You'd have to create a new train folder with subfolders healthy and unhealthy, then copy or move all the images from each of the 20 food-labelled folders into the correct healthy or unhealthy folder. You'd do this either in Finder or Terminal.

Verify that the resulting model gets about 80% accuracy on the test dataset.

You may wonder why you can't use the multi-class snacks model for this, and simply look if the predicted category is in the list of healthy or unhealthy classes. This is possible but, by training from scratch on just these two categories, the model has a chance to learn what healthy/unhealthy means, and it might use a more intricate rule than just "this class label is in the list of healthy categories."

If you want to be sure which approach works better, use the 20-class model to `classify()` the healthy/unhealthy test dataset, and merge its `output` with `test_data` as before. The **label** column contains "healthy" or "unhealthy," while the **class** column contains "apple," "banana," etc.

Then use `filter_by(healthy, "class")` to find images the model predicts to be in a class listed in the `healthy` array. Filter these images with `filter_by(["unhealthy"], "label")` to find images that are really in unhealthy classes. Manually calculate the accuracy of the 20-class model in predicting healthy/unhealthy. I got 47%.

Challenge 2: ResNet50-based model

Train the 20-class classifier using the ResNet-50 model and see if that gets a better validation and test set score. Use `model_type="resnet-50"` when creating the classifier object. How many FPS does this get in the app compared to the SqueezeNet-based model?

Challenge 3: Use another dataset

Create your own training, validation, and test datasets from Google Open Images or some other image source. I suggest keeping the number of categories limited.

Key points

- In this chapter, you've gotten a taste of training your own Core ML model with Turi Create. In fact, this is exactly how the models were trained that you used in chapter 2, "Getting Started with Image Classification".

- Turi Create is pretty easy to use, especially from a Jupyter notebook. It only requires a little bit of Python code. However, we weren't able to create a super accurate model. This is partly due to the limited dataset.

- More images is better. We use 4,800 images, but 48,000 would have been better, and 4.8 million would have been even better. However, there is a real cost associated with finding and annotating training images, and for most projects, a few hundred images or at most a few thousand images per class may be all you can afford. Use what you've got — you can always retrain the model at a later date once you've collected more training data. Data is king in machine learning, and who has the most of it usually ends up with a better model.

- Another reason why Turi Create's model wasn't super is that SqueezeNet is a small feature extractor, which makes it fast and memory-friendly, but this also comes with a cost: It's not as accurate as bigger models. But it's not just SqueezeNet's fault — instead of training a basic logistic regression on top of SqueezeNet's extracted features, it's possible to create more powerful classifiers too.

- Turi Create lets you tweak a few hyperparameters. With regularization, we can get a grip on the overfitting. However, Turi Create does not allow us to fine-tune the feature extractor or use data augmentation. Those are more advanced features, and they result in slower training times, but also in better models.

In the next chapter, we'll look at fixing all of these issues when we train our image classifier again, but this time using Keras. You'll also learn more about what all the building blocks are in these neural networks, and why we use them in the first place.

Chapter 6: Taking Control of Training with Keras

By Matthijs Hollemans

In the previous chapters, you've learned how to train your own models using Create ML and Turi Create. These are user-friendly tools that are easy to get started with — you don't really have to write a lot of code and they take care of most of the details. With just a few lines you can load your data, train your model and export to Core ML.

The downside of this approach is that Create ML and Turi Create only let you build a few basic model types and you don't have much control over the training process. This is fine if you're just getting your feet wet with machine learning. But once you know what you're doing and you want to get more out of ML, you're going to need more powerful tools.

In this chapter, you'll use a popular deep learning tool called **Keras** to train the snacks classifier. Keras gives you much more control over the design of the models and how they are trained. Once you know your way around Keras, you'll be able to build any kind of neural network you want.

> **Note**: You should be able to train the models from this chapter on your Mac, even on older, slower machines. The models are small enough to be trained on the CPU and don't need GPU acceleration — only a little patience.

Keras runs on top of a so-called **backend** that performs the actual computations. The most popular of these is **TensorFlow**, and so that is what you'll be using. TensorFlow is currently the number one machine-learning tool in existence. However, it can be a little tricky to use due to its low-level nature. Keras makes using TensorFlow a lot easier.

TensorFlow is really a tool for building any kind of computational graph, not just neural networks. Instead of neural network layers, TensorFlow deals with rudimentary mathematical operations such as matrix multiplications and taking derivatives. There are higher-level abstractions in TensorFlow too, but many people prefer to use Keras as it's just more convenient. In fact, Keras is so popular there is now a version of Keras built into TensorFlow.

> **Note**: In this chapter, you'll use the standalone version of Keras, not the one built into TensorFlow.

Getting started

First, you need to set up a Python environment for running Keras. The quickest way is to perform these commands from a Terminal window:

```
$ cd /path/to/chapter/resources
$ conda env create --file=starter/kerasenv.yaml
$ conda activate kerasenv
$ jupyter notebook
```

If you downloaded the snacks dataset for a previous chapter, copy or move it into the **starter** folder. Otherwise, double-click **starter/snacks-download-link.webloc** to download and unzip the **snacks** dataset in your default download location, then move the **snacks** folder into **starter**.

> **Note**: In this book we're using Keras version 2.2.4 and TensorFlow version 1.14. Keras, like many open source projects, changes often and sometimes new versions are incompatible with older ones. If you're using a newer version of Keras and you get error messages, please install version 2.2.4 into your working environment. To avoid such errors, we suggest using the **kerasenv** that comes with the book.

Tip: If your computer runs Linux and has an NVIDIA GPU that supports CUDA, edit **kerasenv.yaml** and replace `tensorflow=1.14` with `tensorflow-gpu=1.14`. Or if you have already created the environment, run `pip install -U tensorflow-gpu==1.14`. This will install the GPU version of TensorFlow, which runs a lot faster.

Back to basics with logistic regression

One of the key topics in this book is **transfer learning**: a logistic regression model is trained on top of features extracted from the training images. In the case of Create ML, the features were extracted by the very powerful "Vision FeaturePrint.Scene" neural network that is built into iOS 12. In the case of Turi Create, the feature extractor you used was the somewhat less powerful SqueezeNet.

The big advantage of transfer learning is that it is much quicker than training from scratch, because your model can take advantage of the knowledge that is already contained in the pre-trained feature extractor. Hence, you are *transferring* knowledge from one problem domain to another. In this case, the feature extractors are trained on the general problem of recognizing objects in photos, and you'll adapt them to the specific problem of recognizing 20 different types of snacks.

We also claimed that this approach of using a feature extractor works better than training the logistic regression classifier on the image pixels directly. To demonstrate the difference, you'll use Keras to build a logistic regression model that skips the feature extraction part and works directly on pixels.

This is a good way to get started with Keras, and doing this will prove that it's very hard for a logistic regression model to learn to classify directly from pixel data. Over the course of this chapter and the next, you'll make the model more and more capable, until at the end you have a classifier that is pretty darn accurate.

A quick refresher

Logistic regression is a statistical model used in machine learning that tries to find a straight line between your data points that best separates the classes.

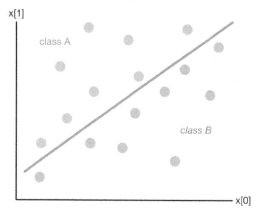

Logistic regression

Of course, this only works well if these data points can be separated by a straight line, or by what is known as a **hyperplane** in higher dimensions.

Just to give you an idea of what is going on under the hood when you apply a logistic regression, let's dive into the math a little. It's OK if you're not a fan of math, feel free to just skim this section and skip the bits that make your head spin. Knowing the math is not a prerequisite, but it can be helpful to understand what is going on — and it shows that these models are really not magical at all.

Let's talk math

In the above illustration, data points are two dimensional: They have two coordinates, x[0] and x[1]. In most machine-learning literature and code, x is the name given to the training examples.

In practice, your data points will often be placed in much higher-dimensional spaces. Recall that for an image of size 227×227, the number of dimensions is over 150,000. But for the purpose of explanation, imagine that each data point is just made up of two values.

Hopefully, you still remember from high school math that the algebraic formula for a straight line is:

```
y = a*x + b
```

Here, x is a coordinate in the first dimension, a is the slope of the line — how steep it is, also known as the coefficient — and b is the y-intercept. You've probably seen this formula before. This is the formula that is learned by *linear* regression, which tries to find a line that fits best between the data points.

Logistic regression is a small modification of linear regression, so it makes sense that we look at the linear regression formula first.

The above formula is for one-dimensional data, i.e., for data points that consist of just a single x value. In the illustration above, the data points are two dimensional and therefore have two values, x[0] and x[1]. You can easily extend the line formula to the following:

```
y = a[0]*x[0] + a[1]*x[1] + b
```

In general, y is the name we use for the predictions made by the model, as well as for the labels that the model is trained on.

Since there are two values in each data point, there are also two coefficients or slopes, a[0] and a[1]. Here, a[0] is the slope of the line for the data point's first coordinate, x[0]. In other words, a[0] is how much y increases as x[0] becomes larger.

Likewise, a[1] is the slope for the second coordinate, or how much y increases as x[1] becomes larger.

The b is still the y-intercept — the value of y at the origin of the coordinate system — although in machine learning it is called the **bias**. This is the value of y when both x[0] and x[1] are 0.

It's a little tricky to draw the value of y on top of a flat picture, but it looks something like this:

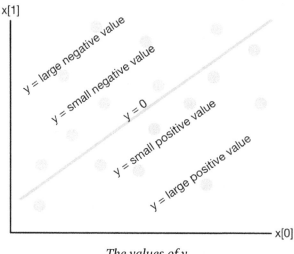

The values of y

Note that y is no longer on the vertical axis. In the above example, the vertical axis is used for x[1], the second coordinate of the data points. Since the data points use two coordinates, the formula is no longer the equation for a line but for a plane in a three-dimensional coordinate space. a[0] and a[1] are still slopes, but now of a plane instead of a simple line, and b is the height of this plane at the origin.

The data points from class A are in the area where y is negative and the data points from class B are in the area where y is positive. The decision boundary that separates the two classes is exactly where y = 0. The further away you go from the decision boundary, the larger the value of y is (positive or negative).

The coefficients a[0] and a[1] are constants. b is also a constant. In fact, what logistic regression learns during training is the values of these constants. Therefore, we call those the **learned parameters** of the model. Our model currently has three learned parameters: a[0], a[1] and b.

After training the model on this tiny example dataset, you might find that a[0] = 1.2, a[1] = −1.5 and b = 0.2. The reason a[1] is a negative number is that for large values of x[1], it's more likely the data point belongs to class A, and therefore y should be negative. You can verify this in the image.

For large values of x[0], the model wants y to be positive and so a[0] is a positive number. For data points close to the decision boundary, it depends just on how the numbers turn out.

By the way, when programmers say **parameters**, we often refer to the values that we pass into functions. Mathematicians call these **arguments**. To a mathematician, a parameter is a constant that is used inside the function. So, technically speaking, parameters and arguments are two different things — and if you have to believe the mathematicians then we programmers tend to use the wrong term.

If we put the linear regression formula in code it would look like this:

```
func formula(x0: Double, x1: Double) -> Double {
    let a0 = 1.2
    let a1 = -1.5
    let b = 0.2
    return a0*x0 + a1*x1 + b
}
```

Notice how x0 and x1 are the arguments that are passed into the function, while a0, a1 and b are constants that are always the same for this function. Machine learning is the process of learning the proper values for these constants, and then you can use this function with different kinds of inputs x0 and x1.

Into the 150,000th dimension

Two-dimensional data is easy enough to understand, but how does this work when you have data points with 150,000 or more dimensions? You just keep adding coefficients to the formula:

```
y = a[0]*x[0] + a[1]*x[1] + a[2]*x[2]
      + ... + a[149999]*x[149999] + b
```

This is a bit labor-intensive, which is why mathematicians came up with a shorter notation: the **dot product**. You can treat a and x as arrays — or **vectors** in math-speak — with 150,000 elements each. And then you can write:

```
y = dot(a, x) + b
```

Here, dot() is a function that takes the dot-product between two vectors. It multiplies each element of the first vector with the corresponding element from the second vector, and then sums up these products. The result of a dot product is always a single number. Here is how you could implement dot() in Swift:

```
func dot(_ v: [Double], _ w: [Double]) -> Double {
    var sum: Double = 0
    for i in 0..<v.count {
        sum += v[i] * w[i]
    }
```

```
    return sum
}
```

Using dot() is a nice shorthand way of writing the full formula, plus it works for any number of dimensions, no matter how big a and x are.

So far, the formula we've talked about for the line (actually, hyperplane) is for **linear** regression, not **logistic**. The linear regression formula just describes the best line that goes between the data points, which is useful in case you want to predict what x[1] is when you only have a given x[0].

Linear regression, usually just called regression, is a statistical model and machine-learning technique that is used to find the relationship between two or more variables. If x is the square footage of a house and y is the selling price of that house, then linear regression can learn a model that is used to predict house prices based on the size of the house (and possibly any other variables that would be relevant).

But you're not trying to solve that kind of problem here; you're trying to build an image classifier. To turn this into a classifier, you have to decide for each data point on which side of the line it is to determine its class, and also how far away it is from the line. Further away gives us greater confidence in the class prediction.

To do this, you could simply look at whether y is a positive or negative number, but there is a neat trick that lets you interpret y as a probability value.

From linear to logistic

To turn the linear regression formula into a classifier, you extend the formula to make it a **logistic** regression:

```
probability = sigmoid(dot(a, x) + b)
```

The sigmoid function, also known as the **logistic sigmoid**, takes the decision boundary and looks at which side of the line the given point x is. The formula for sigmoid is:

```
sigmoid(x) = 1 / (1 + exp(-x))
```

When you plot this sigmoid function, it looks like this:

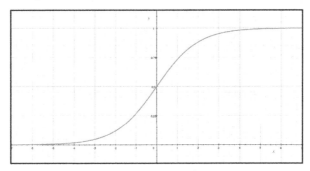

The logistic sigmoid function

This should explain the name of the function: It's S-shaped, and "sigmoid" literally means "like the letter sigma" — sigma being the Greek letter S.

You can see in the figure that the output of the sigmoid function is 0 for large negative input values, is 1 for large positive inputs, and is somewhere in between for input values between -6 and +6.

For our example, an output of 0 means the data point is in class A, because the input to the sigmoid would have been a (large) negative number. An output of 1 means the data point is in class B — because the input to the sigmoid would have been a (large) postive number.

However, the output of the logistic sigmoid function is usually interpreted as being a probability, so 0 really means there is 0% chance that this data point belongs to class B and 1 means 100% of it being class B. The probability that the data point belongs to class A is therefore `1.0 - probability`.

For data points that are close to the decision boundary, you saw that y was a small positive or negative number. For such a number, the sigmoid output is somewhere between 0 and 1, for example 0.3. This means the algorithm is 30% confident that the data point is class B, so it's not entirely sure. Usually we choose 50% as the cut-off point; anything higher is B, anything lower is A. But sometimes it makes sense to choose a higher or a lower cut-off point for making this decision.

So logistic regression is just linear regression with the sigmoid function applied to it. This sigmoid function turns the value of y into a value between 0 and 1 that we can interpret as being a probability percentage.

Not everything is black and white...

What if you have more than two classes? In that case, you'll use a variation of the formula called **multinomial** logistic regression that works with any number of classes. Instead of one output, you now compute a separate prediction for each class:

```
probability_A = sigmoid(dot(a_A, x) + b_A)
probability_B = sigmoid(dot(a_B, x) + b_B)
probability_C = sigmoid(dot(a_C, x) + b_C)
probability_D = sigmoid(dot(a_D, x) + b_D)
...and so on...
```

If you have K classes, you end up with K different logistic regressions. Each has its own slopes and bias, which is why you now don't have just one a and b but several different ones. For each class, you do the dot product of the input x with the coefficients for that class, add the bias, and take the sigmoid.

So instead of a single decision boundary, each class now has its own decision boundary that separates its data points from the data points of all other classes. For example, if the probability_A is 0.95, it means that the classifier is 95% sure that this data point lies on the side of the line for class A, with a 5% chance that it's actually one of the other classes. This is also known as a "one-vs.-all" or "one-vs.-rest" classifier.

In practice all of these individual slopes are combined into a big matrix called the **weights matrix**. This matrix has size N×K, where N is the number of elements in the input vector x and K is the number of classes. All the bias values are combined into a vector of K values. Then the computation is:

```
output = matmul(W, x) + b
```

The matmul() function performs a matrix multiplication between the input x and the weight matrix W and then adds the bias vector b. The output is a vector of K values, one for each class.

If your matrix math is rusty, don't panic. This just performs the dot products for the different classes in a single mathematical operation. Just like the dot product itself is shorthand for a[0]*x[0] + a[1]*x[1] + ..., so is a matrix multiplication shorthand for doing a bunch of different dot products.

The result of all this arithmetic, output, contains K different values, one for each class. You can then apply the sigmoid function to each of these K values independently, to get the probability that the data point x belongs to each class:

```
probability_A = sigmoid(output[0])
probability_B = sigmoid(output[1])
probability_C = sigmoid(output[2])
...and so on...
```

It's now possible for more than one class to be chosen, since these K probabilities are independent from one another. This is known as a **multi-label** classifier. You would use this kind of classifier if you wanted to identify more than one kind of object in the same image.

However, for a **multi-class** classifier, such as the one you've been reading about in the past chapters, you don't want independent probabilities. Instead, you want to choose the best class amongst the K different ones. You can do that by applying a different function instead of the logistic sigmoid, called **softmax**:

```
probabilities = softmax(matmul(W, x) + b)
```

The softmax function takes the exponent of each value and then divides it by the sum of all exponentiated values. You may immediately forget this, just know that the result of this operation is that now all the numbers are between 0 and 1, and together they sum up to `1.0`. This allows you to interpret the output from the logistic regression as a probability distribution over all the classes taken together. To find the winning class, you simply pick the class with the highest probability.

In practice, you'll see both sigmoid (multi-label) and softmax (multi-class) used with multinomial logistic regression, depending on the problem that's being solved. If you're just interested in the *best* class, use the softmax.

All right, that's the end of the math lesson. Let's get back to doing actual machine learning!

Building the model

In this section, you'll turn the above math into code using Keras. Fortunately, Keras takes care of all the details for you, so if the math in the previous section went over your head, rest assured that you don't actually need to know it. Phew!

Fire up Jupyter and create a new Python 3 notebook. You can also follow along with the **LogisticRegression.ipynb** notebook from this chapter's downloaded resources.

The first thing you'll do is import the required packages:

```
import numpy as np
import keras
from keras.models import Sequential
from keras.layers import *
from keras import optimizers
```

Like most machine-learning and scientific computing packages, Keras heavily depends on NumPy so you import that first. You also import a few modules from Keras.

> **Note**: It's not unusual to see a warning message when you execute some Keras or TensorFlow code. You can safely ignore such warning messages. They are usually harmless notifications about deprecated APIs that will be removed in the future.

Next, define some constants:

```
image_width = 32
image_height = 32
num_classes = 20
```

Because the model makes predictions for 20 different types of objects (apples, bananas, etc.), you set num_classes to 20.

You'll use images of 32×32 pixels as input. The SqueezeNet model from Turi Create used 227×227 images. You could certainly use 227×227 here, or any size really, but it will make the model much larger and slower to train. If you have access to a fast GPU, feel free to experiment with a larger image_width and image_height.

Let's now define the regression model using Keras:

```
model = Sequential()
model.add(Flatten(input_shape=(image_height, image_width, 3)))
model.add(Dense(num_classes))
model.add(Activation("softmax"))
```

The model you're building is a so-called Sequential model, which is a simple pipeline that consists of a list of layers. Each layer is a stage in the pipeline that transforms the data in some particular way.

Here, you're adding three layers to the model.

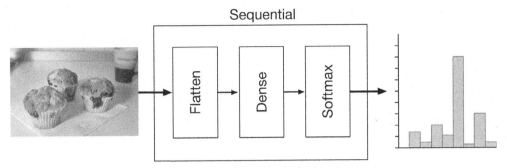

The logistic regression model in Keras

The features that the logistic regression works on, are the pixels from the input images. The first layer is Flatten, which takes the three-dimensional image input and turns it into a one-dimensional vector.

"Wait a minute," I hear you thinking, "an image surely has just two dimensions, not three!" The third dimension is for the pixel's RGB values. Each pixel is made up of three numbers describing its color: red, green and blue. We consider this the image's third dimension, or the "depth" dimension. Images often have an alpha channel, too (RGBA), but we typically ignore the alpha channel in machine learning.

Also note that the image dimensions are given as (height, width, 3), not (width, height, 3). It's common for programmers to describe the size of an image as width-by-height, but the image is actually stored in memory as rows × columns × RGB. So in machine learning the size of the image is usually given as height-by-width.

Note: This difference in the order of the dimensions, height coming before width, is easy to overlook and can cause subtle bugs in your model, especially if the width and height are the same, and so it's easy to mix them up. Pay close attention to the order that tools like Keras expect the input data to be in. When you load an image from a file, it's already loaded as height × width × 3 into memory, so you don't actually have to do anything special. Just be aware that height goes before width.

Since logistic regression expects a one-dimensional vector as input, the Flatten layer simply unrolls the image's lines of pixels into one big strip:

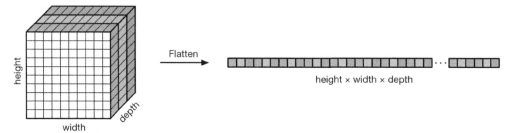

Flatten turns the 3D image into a 1D vector

The input image is 32×32 pixels times three channels, and so the flattened vector has length 3,072. Flatten doesn't do any computation, it just changes the shape of the input.

The real meat of the logistic regression happens in the Dense layer. This performs the matrix multiplication between the 3,072 inputs and the 20 outputs. This layer has 20 outputs because that's the number of classes in the snacks dataset. In a Dense layer, each input is connected to each output.

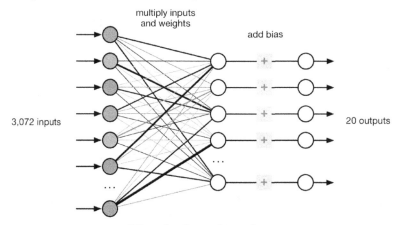

What the Dense layer does

This is simply the equation you've seen before:

```
y = a[0]*x[0] + a[1]*x[1] + ... + a[3071]*x[3071] + b
```

This time, it's expressed in a slightly more efficient form as a matrix, so that Keras can compute this entire thing with a single matrix multiplication.

The weights a represent the strength of the connections between the inputs and the outputs, shown in the illustration as thick and thin lines. The larger the value of the weight a[i], the more the corresponding input x[i] counts in the final result.

The Dense layer also adds a bias value for each output, b in the above equation. Because there are 20 outputs, b is a vector of 20 elements. The bias is just a fixed number that's added to every output, and gives the distance of how far away the decision boundary is from the coordinate system's origin. This is necessary because the data points might not be nicely distributed around the origin, and so the bias can compensate for that.

> **Note**: Dense layers are also known as **fully connected layers, affine layers, or linear layers**. In machine learning a single concept often has multiple names.

When you create the Dense layer, it assigns random numbers to the weights for the matrix multiplication and zeros to the bias values. The reason it uses random numbers for the weights and not zeros, is that multiplying the inputs with zero makes the outputs zero too, and it's hard to turn that back into something that is not zero. In practice, training just works better from a randomly chosen starting point.

When you train the logistic regression model, it will learn the best values to use for these weights and biases.

Finally, you need to apply the softmax function to turn the output from the Dense layer into a probability distribution. That's what Activation("softmax") does. An **activation function** is some non-linear operation that gets applied to the output of a layer from the model. There are many different types of activation functions, but the one at the end of the model is usually the softmax function, at least for classifiers.

Without this softmax function, the model would be a plain linear regression that only tells you how to best fit a line (hyperplane) through all the data points for the training images. By adding the softmax, the model becomes a multinomial logistic regression classifier that tells you which classes the data points belong to, depending on which side of the line they fall.

After you construct a model, it's useful to verify that all the pieces are in the right place. Keras provides a handy function for this:

```
model.summary()
```

This outputs a list of all the layers in the model:

```
Layer (type)                    Output Shape              Param #
=================================================================
flatten_1 (Flatten)             (None, 3072)              0

dense_1 (Dense)                 (None, 20)                61460

activation_1 (Activation)       (None, 20)                0
=================================================================
Total params: 61,460
Trainable params: 61,460
Non-trainable params: 0
```

The Output Shape column gives the size of the data after it has been transformed by that layer. As expected, `Flatten` shows a vector with 3,072 elements and `Dense` outputs a vector with one element for each of the 20 classes.

Even though `Flatten` produces a one-dimensional vector, the output shape shown in the summary actually has two dimensions with the first dimension being `None`.

Keras automatically adds a dimension to the front of the layer's output, which is the **batch** dimension. This extra dimension is used during training, so that you can train on multiple images at the same time. The images are combined into a so-called **batch** or **mini-batch**. If you were to train on a typical batch size of 64 images at once, the output shape of the `Flatten` layer is actually a `(64, 3072)` tensor. Typically, you don't specify the batch size yet when you construct the model, which is why Keras shows it as `None`.

What the !%#& is a tensor? It finally happened, we used the T-word, so we'd better explain what a tensor is at this point. Are you ready? Tensor is a fancy word for multi-dimensional array. Yup, that's all.

In machine learning, you often use multi-dimensional arrays to store your data. You've already seen that an image is stored as an array of shape `(height, width, 3)`. This is a three-dimensional array where the first dimension is the height of the image, the second dimension is the width of the image, and the third and final dimension is for three color channels (RGB). But often you'll use arrays with even more dimensions: four, five or six.

As the data flows through the pipeline it changes shape: the dimensions can become larger or smaller, and you can even add or remove dimensions, like what Flatten does. Since "multi-dimensional array" is a mouthful, we prefer to use the word "tensor" instead. This term originally comes from the mathematical field of topology, where it has a somewhat more specific meaning, but in ML it's just shorthand for multi-dimensional array. This is where TensorFlow gets its name from: it describes the data flow — what we've been calling a pipeline — between tensors.

In math terminology, we call a one-dimensional array a vector, a two-dimensional array a matrix, and anything with more dimensions a tensor. The number of dimensions is the rank of the tensor. A vector is a tensor of rank 1, a matrix is a tensor of rank 2, an image is a tensor of rank 3, a batch of images is a tensor of rank 4 and so on. By the way, scalars or single numbers are tensors of rank 0, or zero-dimensional arrays.

At this point, you may be getting confused by the term **dimensions**. The tensor that stores an image has three dimensions, but the image itself can be considered a point in 150,000-dimensional space. Or in the case of the 32×32 images you're using here, a point in 3,072-dimensional space. It's a little confusing that the same word is used in both cases. For tensors we often also use the word "axis" to describe a dimension, so an image tensor has three axes with the first axis being the height, the second axis the width, and the third axis being the color channels.

The Param # column in the summary shows the number of learnable parameters in each layer. In this simple model, only the Dense layer has learnable parameters: the values of the weights or coefficients a and the values of the bias vector b. There are 3,072×20 weights plus 20 additional bias values, so this model has 61,460 learnable parameters in total.

Turi Create's model only had 19,090 parameters. Your model is a bit bigger… but is it also better? No spoilers, you'll have to keep reading!

Compiling the model

Before you can use the model you first need to compile it. This tells Keras how to train the model.

```
model.compile(loss="categorical_crossentropy",
              optimizer=optimizers.Adam(lr=1e-3),
              metrics=["accuracy"])
```

The `compile()` function takes three important arguments:

- **The loss function** to use: Recall from the introduction that the loss function determines how good — or rather, how bad — the model is at making predictions. During training, the loss is initially high as the model just makes random predictions at the start. But as training progresses the loss should become lower and lower while the model gets better and better.

  It's important to choose a loss function that makes sense for your model. Because your model uses softmax to produce the final output, the corresponding loss function is the **categorical cross-entropy**. That sounds nasty, but categorical just means you're building a classifier with more than two classes, and cross-entropy is the loss that belongs with softmax. For a classifier with two classes, you'd use *binary* cross-entropy loss instead.

- **An optimizer**: This is the object that implements the Stochastic Gradient Decent or SGD process that finds the best values for the weights and biases. As the loss function computes how wrong the model is at making predictions, the optimizer uses that loss and tweaks the learnable parameters in the model to make the model slightly better. Mathematically speaking, the optimizer finds the parameters that minimize the loss.

  There are different types of optimizers but they all work in kind of the same way. You're using the Adam optimizer, which is a good default choice, with learning rate 1e-3 or 0.001. The **learning rate** or LR determines how big the steps are taken by the optimizer. If the LR is too big, the optimizer will go nuts and the loss never becomes any smaller (or may even blow up into a huge number). If the LR is too small, it will take forever for the model to learn anything.

  The learning rate is one of the most important hyperparameters that you can set, and finding a good value for the LR is key to getting your model to learn. The author tried out a few different values and settled on 1e-3 as a good choice for this particular model.

- **Any metrics** you want to see: As it is training your model, Keras will always print out the loss value, but you're also interested in the accuracy of the model as that is an easier metric to interpret. A loss value of 0.35 by itself doesn't say much about how good the model is, but an accuracy value of 94% correct does.

Cool, now you're ready to start training this model. But for that you need some data.

Loading the data

You've already seen the snacks dataset in the previous chapters. It consists of three different folders (train, val, test), each containing 20 folders for the different classes, and each folder contains several dozen or hundred images.

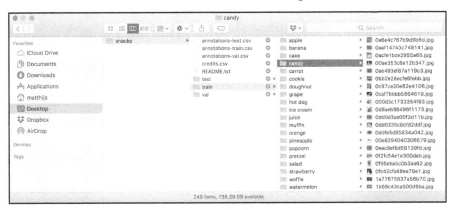

The snacks dataset

Add some variables that point to these folders:

```
images_dir = "snacks"
train_data_dir = images_dir + "/train/"
val_data_dir = images_dir + "/val/"
test_data_dir = images_dir + "/test/"
```

Important: point `images_dir` at the folder where you've downloaded the dataset.

At this point it's a good idea to actually look at the training data with your own two eyes, to make sure it is correct. To view an image in the notebook, do the following:

```
from keras.preprocessing import image
img = image.load_img(
    train_data_dir + "apple/cecd90f5d46f57b0.jpg",
    target_size=(image_width, image_height))
```

This loads the specified JPEG image into the `img` variable. This is a PIL image object. PIL is a popular image library for Python 2. We're in fact using the Python 3-specific fork: Pillow, but the concepts are identical. Potential confusion alert: the `image` variable here refers to the Keras module for dealing with images, while `img` is the actual image object.

The `load_img()` function can automatically resize the image to the size your model accepts, given here by the `target_size` argument. Note that here the size of the image is specified as (`width, height`) not (`height, width`). Told you... you've got to keep paying attention to the order of these dimensions.

To show the image in the notebook you can use Matplotlib, a very handy Python library for drawing plots and graphs.

```
%matplotlib inline
import matplotlib.pyplot as plt
plt.imshow(img)
```

The `%matplotlib inline` directive tells Jupyter to show the image inside the notebook. Without this, it will open in a new window.

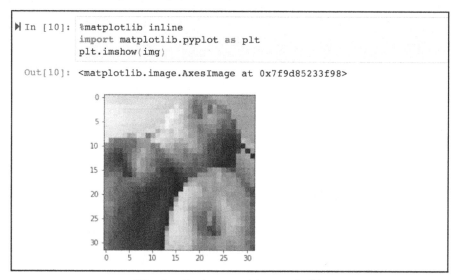

Viewing the image with matplotlib

Keras cannot train directly on PIL images, it always expects data to be in the form of NumPy arrays. So first convert from a PIL image to a NumPy array:

```
x = image.img_to_array(img)
```

You called this variable x because it is a convention in machine learning that the input data is called x or sometimes capital X. If you now write x or `print(x)` in a new cell and press Shift-Enter this prints the pixel values from the image:

```
array([[[215., 215., 217.],
        [211., 211., 211.],
        [207., 207., 207.],
        ...,
        [152., 150., 137.],
        [148., 146., 133.],
        [149., 147., 132.]], ...
```

As you might have expected if you've worked with images before, the pixels have values between 0 and 255. In principle you can train the model directly on these pixel values but it is customary to **normalize** the data before you start training on it.

Normalizing or **feature scaling** means that the data will have an average value or mean of 0 and usually also a standard deviation of 1. This is important when different features are not all in the same numerical range. For example, if your data has one feature with values between 0 and 1000 and another feature with values between 5 and 10, training will generally work better if you first normalize the features so that they both are between -1 and +1.

In your case it's not such a big deal since all the features — the pixels — are on the same scale from 0 to 255. But normalization is good practice so let's do it anyway. Write this new function:

```
def normalize_pixels(image):
    return image / 127.5 - 1
```

This simply scales the pixel values from 0 to 255 to a new range that goes from -1 to +1. Sometimes people subtract different mean values for the red, green, and blue channels and also divide by a standard deviation, but the above method is good enough for dealing with most kinds of images.

Note: In this function, image is a tensor with 32×32×3 elements. When you write image / 127.5, NumPy will perform the division on each of the tensor's elements separately. This kind of "vectorized" processing, where you perform an operation on an entire tensor at once, is much simpler — and faster! — than writing a for loop. You'll see this sort of thing a lot in Python code.

The steps to normalize an image `img` are then:

```
x = image.img_to_array(img)
x = normalize_pixels(x)
x = np.expand_dims(x, axis=0)
```

If you now look at x, the values are much smaller:

```
array([[[[ 0.6862745 ,  0.6862745 ,  0.7019608 ],
         [ 0.654902  ,  0.654902  ,  0.654902  ],
         [ 0.62352943,  0.62352943,  0.62352943],
         ...,
         [ 0.19215691,  0.17647064,  0.07450986],
         [ 0.16078436,  0.14509809,  0.04313731],
         [ 0.1686275 ,  0.15294123,  0.03529418]]], ...
```

If you're curious, you can print the mean and standard deviation of this training image with `x.mean()` and `x.std()`. The mean of a single training image may not be exactly 0, but across the entire training set it will be close to 0. The standard deviation should be around 0.5.

The `np.expand_dims()` function added a new dimension to the front, to turn this single image into a batch of images with batch size 1. The tensor containing this image is now of rank 4. You can view this with:

```
x.shape
```

This prints (1, 32, 32, 3). It's always a good idea to double-check the sizes of your images and other data objects, to verify they are correct. Adding this batch dimension is necessary because the Keras training functions always work on a batch of images, and expect this dimension to be there.

Too soon to start making predictions?

Even though the model isn't trained yet, you can already make a prediction on the input image:

```
pred = model.predict(x)
print(pred)
```

Note: If your Jupyter kernel crashes when you run this cell, execute the following command from the Terminal: `conda install nomkl`. This fixes a package conflict that sometimes causes trouble on the Mac.

You should get an array with 20 values, one probability for each class. Since you haven't trained the model yet, these predictions aren't very useful. You'll see something like the following:

```
[[0.04173137 0.00418671 0.02269506 0.02889681 0.08140159
0.03577968
   0.03044504 0.04758682 0.07940029 0.07274284 0.04531444
0.0115772
   0.17158438 0.02129039 0.0233359  0.1150756  0.00603842
0.08578367
   0.03525693 0.03987688]]
```

You'll probably get different results since your model will be initialized with different random values for the weights and biases. But note that most of these values are pretty close to 1/20 or 0.05. If you add them all up with `pred.sum()`, it will print out `1.0`. Floating point numbers have limited precision, so sometimes you will see `0.99999999` instead of `1.0`. Close enough.

An untrained model will make a prediction for each class that is very close to the average, because it hasn't learned yet how to distinguish the classes. It's unlikely you'll see a high percentage such as 90% in the output at this point. Most classes will have a probability score of around 0.05, or `1/num_classes`, although it can vary a bit because of the random initialization.

If you were to make predictions for the entire dataset at this point, each class would be predicted the same number of times and the overall accuracy would be 0.05 or 5% — basically a random guess. The goal of machine learning is to train a classifier that can do better than random guessing.

To figure out what the actual predicted class is for this image, you find the maximum value amongst the predicted probabilities:

```
np.argmax(pred)
```

For the prediction array shown above, this prints 12, because the element at index 12 is the highest (`0.17158438`). Note that the `np.max()` function returns the actual maximum value, while `np.argmax()` returns the *index* of the element with the maximum value.

So which class is this? Well, you actually haven't assigned class labels to each of the 20 outputs yet. That will be done automatically by Keras during training. It will usually do this alphabetically, so the winning class here would be "orange" since that is the 12th class; as usual we start counting at 0.

But, remember, at this point the predictions are still totally bogus. That said, it's still useful to run `model.predict()` before training, to make sure that your model actually predicts what you'd expect — in this case, something close to average probability for each class. If the model had returned something else at this point, such as all zeros, then something is broken — and you don't want to waste any time training a model that is fundamentally buggy.

Using generators

You've seen how to load an image into a tensor and how to plot it in the notebook. That's handy for verifying that the training data is correct. During training, you won't have to load the training images by hand. Keras has a useful helper class called `ImageDataGenerator` that can automatically load images from folders.

```python
from keras.preprocessing.image import ImageDataGenerator
datagen = ImageDataGenerator(
  preprocessing_function=normalize_pixels)
```

The data generator takes the `normalize_pixels` function as its preprocessing function so that it automatically normalizes the images as it loads them. The data generator can do other stuff as well, as you'll see in the next chapter when we talk about data augmentation. Using this `ImageDataGenerator` object you can create three other generators, one for each subset of images:

```python
batch_size = 64

train_generator = datagen.flow_from_directory(
                    train_data_dir,
                    target_size=(image_width, image_height),
                    batch_size=batch_size,
                    class_mode="categorical",
                    shuffle=True)

val_generator = datagen.flow_from_directory(
                    val_data_dir,
                    target_size=(image_width, image_height),
                    batch_size=batch_size,
                    class_mode="categorical",
                    shuffle=False)

test_generator = datagen.flow_from_directory(
                    test_data_dir,
                    target_size=(image_width, image_height),
                    batch_size=batch_size,
                    class_mode="categorical",
                    shuffle=False)
```

The `train_generator` is for images from the **train** folder, the `val_generator` for images from the **val** folder, and the `test_generator` for images from the **test** folder.

A generator in Python is an object that can produce other objects. In this case you're making a generator than can produce images by loading them from the given folder. The reason you need to use generators is that you cannot possibly load all the images into memory all at once, since that would require many gigabytes or even terabytes of RAM — more than fits in your computer! The only way to deal with that much data is to load the images on-demand. That's what the Keras generators allow you to do.

The three generators all do the same thing — load images from their respective folders — but the train generator has `shuffle=True` while the others have `shuffle=False`. During training, you want to pick the images at random so that the model doesn't attempt to learn anything about the order of the images. During testing, however, you want to pick the images in a fixed order as that makes it easier to match them to the correct answers.

The argument `class_mode="categorical"` tells Keras that there is a subfolder for each image category. Keras will use the name of the subfolder as the class label for the images from that folder. The batch size is 64, and so the generator will try to load 64 images at a time.

When you run the above code, the Jupyter notebook says:

```
Found 4838 images belonging to 20 classes.
Found 955 images belonging to 20 classes.
Found 952 images belonging to 20 classes.
```

These are the number of training, validation, and test images respectively.

To see what a generator outputs, you call `next()` on it:

```
x, y = next(train_generator)
print(x.shape)
print(y.shape)
```

You won't ever need to call `next()` yourself during training, but it's useful to test that your generators work. This grabs the next batch of images x and their corresponding labels y from the **train** folder. The shape of the x tensor is (64, 32, 32, 3) because it contains 64 RGB images of 32×32 pixels.

Since you'll train on 64 training images at a time, the batch also includes the labels for these 64 images. Recall that these labels, also known as the **ground-truths**, are used to compute the loss or how "wrong" the model's predictions are.

Because the model produces 20 output values — one probability value for each class — the ground-truth label for a given image also needs to have 20 values. This is why the shape of the y tensor is (64, 20).

Have a look at the first of these labels, y[0]:

```
array([0., 0., 0., 0., 0., 0., 0., 0., 0., 0., 0., 0.,
       0., 1., 0., 0., 0., 0., 0., 0.], dtype=float32)
```

You may have expected to see a label like 'apple' or 'cake', but instead you get a vector with 20 numbers. When you try this, you'll probably get a different label than what's printed in the book, since the training set is randomly shuffled. But whatever label you get, it should consist of 19 zeros and a single one.

This is called **one-hot encoding**. The position of the 1 corresponds to the name of the class. In this case the 1 is in the 13th position, which belongs to class **pineapple**. You can see this by executing the cell:

```
train_generator.class_indices
```

This outputs:

```
{'apple': 0,
 'banana': 1,
 'cake': 2,
 'candy': 3,
 'carrot': 4,
 'cookie': 5,
 'doughnut': 6,
 'grape': 7,
 'hot dog': 8,
 'ice cream': 9,
 'juice': 10,
 'muffin': 11,
 'orange': 12,
 'pineapple': 13,
 'popcorn': 14,
 'pretzel': 15,
 'salad': 16,
 'strawberry': 17,
 'waffle': 18,
 'watermelon': 19}
```

To print the name of the label for y[0], you can do the following:

```
index2class = {v:k for k,v
   in train_generator.class_indices.items()}
```

This is a so-called Python **dictionary comprehension**. It takes all the key-value pairs in the `class_indices` dictionary and creates a new dictionary that flips the order of the key and value. Now you can look up the name of the class by the index of the element that is 1 in the one-hot encoded vector for the label.

To find the name of the class, you do `np.argmax()` to find the index of the 1, and then look up the name in the new dictionary:

```
index2class[np.argmax(y[0])]
```

For the `y[0]` from this book, this will print `'pineapple'`.

Why go through all this trouble? Most machine-learning algorithms can only handle numbers, not strings. The text label `'pineapple'` doesn't mean anything to the logistic regression. So, instead, you first convert this string into something numeric, a one-hot encoded vector. Now the machine-learning algorithm can tell the classes apart because each class has its own unique one-hot encoded vector:

```
'apple'        [1,0,0,0,0,0,0,0,0,0,0,0,0,0,0,0,0,0,0,0]
'banana'       [0,1,0,0,0,0,0,0,0,0,0,0,0,0,0,0,0,0,0,0]
'cake'         [0,0,1,0,0,0,0,0,0,0,0,0,0,0,0,0,0,0,0,0]
'candy'        [0,0,0,1,0,0,0,0,0,0,0,0,0,0,0,0,0,0,0,0]
                   . . .
'waffle'       [0,0,0,0,0,0,0,0,0,0,0,0,0,0,0,0,0,0,1,0]
'watermelon'   [0,0,0,0,0,0,0,0,0,0,0,0,0,0,0,0,0,0,0,1]
```

The model has 20 outputs, and so the one-hot encoded label also needs to have 20 elements. This also means that the first output from the model is the probability the class is **apple**, the second output is the probability that the class is **banana**, and so on. These one-hot encoded vectors establish the relationship between the model's outputs and the class labels.

Think of this one-hot encoded vector as the "ideal" probability distribution for the corresponding training image. If the label of a training image is `'apple'` then this ideal probability distribution should have class apple at 100% (the 1 in the one-hot encoded vector) and the other classes at 0% (the 0s in the vector).

The generator automatically makes these one-hot encoded vectors for you. It looks at the name of the folder to determine the correct class label for the image, and then one-hot encodes it, to turn to it into a numeric label that can be given to the machine learning algorithm.

The first evaluation

At this point, it's a good idea to run the untrained model on the entire test set, to verify that the model and the generators actually work.

```
model.evaluate_generator(test_generator,
                         steps=len(test_generator))
```

It's as easy as that. Keras now uses the `test_generator` to load all the images from the test set, gives them to the model to make predictions, and compares the model's output to the ground-truth label for each test image.

For example, if the model's thirteenth output has the highest probability value, the model has predicted this image contains a pineapple. If the label for that image really is `'pineapple'`, then this counts as a correct prediction. But if the label was something else, then it counts as a wrong prediction. The accuracy of the model is the number of correct predictions divided by the number of total predictions.

The `steps` argument tells Keras how many batches to evaluate. To get the number of batches a generator will produce, you can call `len(generator)`. With a batch size of 64, the test generator creates 15 batches, because there are 952 test images in total.

> **Tip:** If you get an out-of-memory error at this point, reduce the batch size. It's common to use powers of two for this, so if a batch size of 64 is too large, try 32. If that's still too large, try 16, and so on. If you keep getting memory errors even with a batch size of 1, you'll need to restart the notebook and run all the cells again. Sometimes Keras or TensorFlow cannot recover from these out-of-memory errors, and it's best to start afresh.

After about 10 seconds or so of number crunching, `evaluate_generator()` prints out values similar to the following:

```
[3.311799808710563, 0.059873949579831935]
```

The first one is the loss, the second, accuracy. Your values should be similar, but will be slightly different because of the different random initialization of the model weights.

At this point, the accuracy across the entire test set should be about 0.05 or 5% correct, which is the same as randomly picking an answer from the 20 categories. Of course, that's exactly what happens because the model currently consists of all random numbers.

The initial loss for a classifier that uses the cross-entropy loss function should be approximately `np.log(num_classes)`, where log is the natural logarithm. Here, `np.log(20) = 2.9957` so the loss is slightly higher. But it's close enough. Again, this discrepancy is the result of the random initialization. If you were to get a loss that is much larger or much smaller than about `3.0`, something is not right with the model. It also tells you that if the loss becomes smaller than `3.0` during training, the model is actually learning something.

> **Note**: Try for yourself what the initial loss and accuracy are on the training and validation sets. Evaluating the training set may take a few minutes instead of seconds because it has more images.

Training the logistic regression model

All the pieces are in place to finally train the model. First, do the following:

```
import warnings
warnings.filterwarnings("ignore")
```

As a responsible programmer, you know it's not a good idea to ignore warnings but unfortunately the PIL library that is used to load the training images will complain about the EXIF data on some of the JPEG files. That just causes a lot of sloppy debug output in the Jupyter notebook, and so it's cleaner to disable those warnings.

Training is really just a matter of calling `fit_generator()` on the model. To start with, you'll train for five epochs — an **epoch** is one pass through all the training images.

To get good results, you'll need to show each training image more than once —
dozens or hundreds of times, in fact — which is why you need to train for multiple
epochs:

```
model.fit_generator(train_generator,
                    steps_per_epoch=len(train_generator),
                    validation_data=val_generator,
                    validation_steps=len(val_generator),
                    epochs=5,
                    workers=4)
```

Depending on the speed of your computer, this may take a few minutes to complete.

The generator you used here is `train_generator` because that loads the training
images. You also pass in the `val_generator` to use as the validation data.

During training, Keras calculates the accuracy on the training images, but this can be
misleading since it doesn't tell you anything about how well the model does on
images it hasn't seen before. Training accuracy going up — and training loss going
down — only means that the model is learning *something*, but you can't be sure it is
really learning the thing you are aiming to teach it.

That's why, after every epoch of training, Keras uses the validation set to compute
the validation accuracy and loss, to give you an idea of whether the model really is
working or not. If training accuracy is high but validation accuracy is low, you've got
a problem.

> **Note**: The `workers=4` argument tells Keras it can use multiple threads to load
> and prepare the images. If you have more than four CPU cores in your
> computer, feel free to increase this number for some extra speed.

What happens during training?

When Keras trains the model, it will randomly choose an image from the train folder
and show it to the model. Say it picks an image from the **banana** folder. The model
will then make a prediction, for example **pretzel**. Of course, this is totally wrong.

Initially, when you create the model, the learnable parameters are just randomly
chosen numbers and the predictions will be way off. Over the course of training,
these random numbers will slowly change into something more reasonable that can
actually make good predictions.

Since it knows what folder the image came from, **banana**, Keras can compute a loss between the prediction (pretzel) and the ground-truth label for the image (banana). Of course, banana and pretzel are meaningless concepts to Keras, but, after turning them into numbers — using one-hot encoding — Keras can compute some kind of difference between them.

The ground-truth for banana is this one-hot encoded vector:

```
[ 0., 1., 0., 0., 0., 0., 0., 0., 0., 0.,
  0., 0., 0., 0., 0., 0., 0., 0., 0., 0. ]
```

The dot behind the numbers means that these are floating-point values. Think of these as probabilities: The probability for class banana is **1.0** or 100%, the probabilities for all other classes are 0%. That is because we are 100% sure this image contains a banana, since that is how we labeled it when we created the dataset. No doubt there.

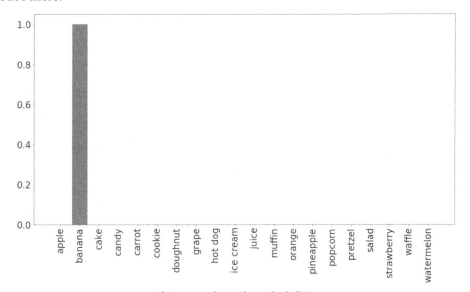

The ground-truth probabilities

The prediction from the model for this banana image may be something like this:

```
[ 0.01360181, 0.21590623, 0.00830788, 0.01217055, 0.05090828,
  0.01749134, 0.01430813, 0.07134261, 0.02015499, 0.00142231,
  0.01328659, 0.01184934, 0.01497147, 0.04739711, 0.00372085,
  0.38552788, 0.03598726, 0.0047219 , 0.01521332, 0.04171015 ]
```

This is the output of the softmax layer, which makes sure that the most confident prediction is large, less confident predictions are smaller, and all the numbers add up to `1.0`. That probability distribution looks a lot messier than the ground-truth:

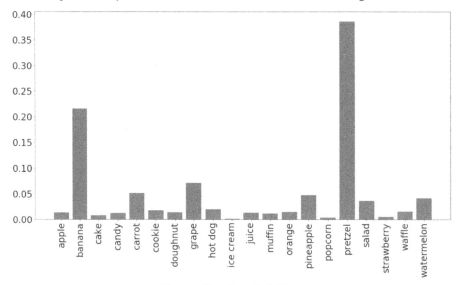

The predicted probabilities

The highest number in this vector is for pretzel (38.55%) but note that the model isn't entirely certain and even thinks it might be a banana after all (21.59%). Especially early on in the training process, the model will not be very certain about its predictions yet.

Now that you have two vectors of 20 elements each, it means you can compare them. The formula for this is known as the **cross-entropy loss**. This chapter has already had enough math in it, so let's just say that this compares each element between the two vectors in some fashion, and adds up the results. This gives the loss for this particular image, which is just a single number.

If the prediction was also (mostly) banana, then the softmax output looks a lot like the ground-truth and the loss is very small; if the prediction was 100% banana, then the loss is 0 because it's exactly right.

If the prediction for this image is not banana, then the loss is a larger number. The worse the prediction is, the less the predicted probabilities match the ground-truth probabilities, and the higher the loss will be.

For this particular example, the loss is 1.5329. That number by itself doesn't tell you very much, it's just a number. What's important is that this number goes down over time while the model is being trained. Say that, after a few more epochs of training, the prediction for this image now has 0.9 for banana and the remaining 0.1 is spread out amongst the other classes. The new loss is then 0.1054. This prediction is much better, and so the loss is also lower.

Once it has computed a loss value, Keras uses the Adam optimizer you provided when you compiled the model, to figure out which parts of the model contributed to this loss.

The optimizer finds the parts of the model that were responsible for making this (bad) prediction and "punishes" them. It does this by slightly tweaking the learnable parameters by moving them in the opposite direction — a positive number becomes a little more negative, a negative number becomes more positive — so that next time this image is shown to the model it will make a slightly better prediction.

In practice, Keras won't compute the loss for a single image but for a mini-batch of multiple images at a time. You are using a batch of 64 images. The loss for this batch is the average of the 64 individual losses. There are two reasons for using batches:

1. It uses the CPU or GPU more efficiently, if you're lucky enough to have a GPU for training. The key to efficient GPU performance is to keep it busy, and with a batch you use more of the GPU's memory bandwidth. The size of the batch is limited by the amount of RAM on the GPU. For a large model with many layers, a batch size of 64 may be too big to fit on the GPU and you'll have to smaller batches.

2. Mathematically speaking, the "true" loss function really ought to be computed over the entire training set at once. So when you're using batches, which only contain a small portion of the training set, you're not actually computing the true loss of the model. That would seem to be a bad thing, but the opposite is true: using only 64 or fewer images at a time introduces a certain amount of randomness into the training process. And it turns out that this randomness makes it easier for the model to learn. Strange, but true. That's why the S in SGD stands for stochastic, which means "random" but sounds more impressive.

Hey, it's progress!

While the training process is happening, Keras outputs a progress bar:

```
Epoch 1/5
76/76 [==============================] - 3s 38ms/step -
    loss: 3.2150 - acc: 0.1050 -
    val_loss: 3.2654 - val_acc: 0.1162
Epoch 2/5
76/76 [==============================] - 2s 26ms/step -
    loss: 2.7257 - acc: 0.2079 -
    val_loss: 3.2375 - val_acc: 0.1152
Epoch 3/5
76/76 [==============================] - 2s 27ms/step -
    loss: 2.4124 - acc: 0.2990 -
    val_loss: 3.2756 - val_acc: 0.1120
Epoch 4/5
76/76 [==============================] - 2s 27ms/step -
    loss: 2.1712 - acc: 0.3722 -
    val_loss: 3.2727 - val_acc: 0.1246
Epoch 5/5
76/76 [==============================] - 2s 26ms/step -
    loss: 1.9735 - acc: 0.4462 -
    val_loss: 3.3359 - val_acc: 0.1141
```

During training, Keras reports the training loss loss and training accuracy acc. After each epoch, Keras also computes the validation loss val_loss and accuracy val_acc over the entire validation set.

Notice how loss and acc are improving over time. The training loss goes down while the accuracy goes up. That's the good news. However, the bad news is that the validation loss doesn't seem to be getting much better and the validation accuracy never gets higher than about 12%.

Even if you keep training for more epochs, the training accuracy keeps improving but the validation accuracy does not. Try it out, run model.fit_generator() again and see what happens. In fact, if you repeat this enough times, the validation accuracy may get worse over time. After 50 or so epochs of training, the training accuracy was 90% but the validation accuracy had dropped to 8%.

To make sure this is not a fluke, you can also try this trained model on the test set:

```
model.evaluate_generator(test_generator,
                         steps=len(test_generator))
```

This should print something like:

```
[3.142886356145394, 0.12079831951556086]
```

Again, that is only about 12% accuracy on the images from the test set. Also note that the loss reported here, 3.1428, is only marginally better than the test set loss you saw on the untrained model, which was 3.31179.

It could be better...

What does this mean? Well, the model did learn *something*. After all, you started with a validation accuracy of 0.05 and it went up to about 0.12. So the model did gain a little bit of knowledge about the dataset. It is no longer making completely random guesses — but it's still not doing much better than that.

How come the training accuracy is so high then? It goes up to about 90% after 50 epochs… This is an extreme case of **overfitting**. Yup, there it is again. The model isn't actually learning to classify images, it's just learning to tell apart the images that are in the training set. It's likely that the model is learning which combinations of pixels belong to which training image — and that's not what you want. You want the model to understand what those pixels represent in a more abstract sense.

The model has 61,460 learnable parameters and there are only 4,838 images in the training set, so the model easily has enough capacity to remember which class goes with what image in the training set. In fact, with a training accuracy of 90%, and a very low accuracy on the validation set and test set, it means that the model managed to memorize the class for nine out of 10 images. In the previous chapter, you saw that the Turi Create model also suffered from overfitting and it had fewer parameters than this model, only 19,019. In general, the more parameters a model has, the worse a problem overfitting becomes.

You don't want to train a model that *remembers* specific training images; you want a model that can learn to classify images it hasn't seen yet. And this model fails spectacularly at that. There are several techniques you can use to dissuade the model from overfitting, but it's clear already that trying to learn directly from pixels what these 20 different types of categories are, is a task that logistic regression is not up to.

Now don't let this section make you believe that logistic regression is a bad machine learning model. It isn't. In fact, for many ML problems it is the go-to solution. But for logistic regression to work well it is important that the number of features is much less than the number of training examples.

In our case, we had 3,072 features — the pixel values — but only about 4,800 training images. The logistic regression model might work better if we had 10 times or 100 times as many training images.

> **Note**: For fun, try making the input images smaller or larger, thereby changing the number of features, and see what kind of effect that has on the training and validation accuracy. If you do, you may also need to make the learning rate larger or smaller, so experiment with that too.

For better results on our kinds of images, we'll need to create a better model. Learning directly from the pixel values is just too hard, as the logistic regression (the Dense layer) cannot extract enough meaning from them.

The hyperplanes it can draw through this 3,072-dimensional space do not separate the data points cleanly by their classes. This is why Turi Create first converts the pixels into a smaller number of features using SqueezeNet, and why Create ML does the same with Vision FeaturePrint.Scene. For machine learning to work well on image data, it needs to go through more transformations than just this one Dense layer!

In classical computer vision, before the advent of deep learning, people carefully hand-crafted feature extractors (with names such as SIFT, SURF, HOG, ORB, etc.) in order to turn the pixel data into something more meaningful that they then could apply logistic regression to. However, deep learning can automatically learn to extract features from the pixels, and generally does a better job than man-made feature extractors.

It's clear that logistic regression directly on the image pixels isn't going to work. Let's make the model more powerful by turning it into an artificial neural network.

Your first neural network

Logistic regression is considered to be one of the classical machine-learning algorithms. Deep learning is new and modern and hip, and is all about artificial neural networks. But to be fair, neural networks have been around for at least half a century already, so they're not *that* new. In this section, you'll expand the logistic regression model into an artificial neural net.

A classical neural network looks like this:

An old-school fully-connected neural network

The idea is that this kind of network mimics connections between neurons in the human brain, in which the circles in the picture represent the neurons. Notice how similar this is to the picture of the Dense layer from earlier? That's because you can think of this kind of neural network as being two or more logistic regressions in a row.

You can do this in Keras by adding a second Dense layer to the previous model:

```
model = Sequential()
model.add(Flatten(input_shape=(image_height, image_width, 3)))
model.add(Dense(500, activation="relu"))  # this line is new
model.add(Dense(num_classes))
model.add(Activation("softmax"))
```

Now the model.summary() looks like this:

```
Layer (type)                 Output Shape              Param #
=================================================================
flatten_1 (Flatten)          (None, 3072)              0
_____
dense_1 (Dense)              (None, 500)               1536500
_____
dense_2 (Dense)              (None, 20)                10020
_____
activation_1 (Activation)    (None, 20)                0
=================================================================
Total params: 1,546,520
Trainable params: 1,546,520
Non-trainable params: 0
_____
```

The first `Dense` layer connects all flattened 3,072 input pixel values to 500 intermediate **hidden neurons**, and the second `Dense` layer connects these 500 neurons to the 20 outputs. This kind of neural network is called a two-layer feed-forward network.

The first half of this neural network, from the input to the output of the first `Dense` layer is the first logistic regression. The second half of the network, from the second `Dense` layer to the end is the second logistic regression. So all you've done is stick two separate logistic regression models together.

The activation function at the end of the model is still the softmax that converts the outputs into probabilities. The new `Dense` layer also has an activation function. This is not a softmax but a `relu`, also called ReLU or **rectified linear unit**.

In most neural networks every layer is followed by an activation function. This is usually a very simple mathematical operation that transforms the output of the layer in some **non-linear** way.

Such non-linearities are necessary because otherwise the model can only learn linear relationships between their inputs (the pixels) and their outputs (the classes) and that gives very limited results.

Remember that the goal is to transform the input data in such a way that the model can draw an imaginary straight line or hyperplane between the classes. Without these non-linear activation functions, you'd only be able to do that if you could already draw that straight line between the original input data points — in which case you wouldn't need to train a model at all. It is the non-linearities that allow the model to learn all kinds of interesting data transformations.

ReLU is an extremely simple mathematical function that looks like this:

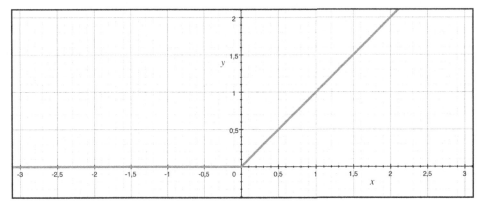

The ReLU activation function

In code, it is:

```
y = max(0, x)
```

In other words, if the number x is less than 0, the output of the ReLU is 0, otherwise the number passes through to the next layer unchanged.

There are other activation functions, too, such as the logistic sigmoid that you've seen in the math section (if you didn't skip it), but usually you'd use ReLU. The **linear unit** part of ReLU's name means that it's just a straight line, and **rectified** means the line gets flattened for negative values, making this function non-linear.

It turns out that the actual shape of the activation function that you're using doesn't really matter so much, as long as it introduces non-linear behavior into the model. Most machine-learning models use ReLU because it's really simple and fast to compute. For a *real* logistic regression, you would actually use the sigmoid activation function, so technically speaking the first half of this neural network isn't truly a logistic regression because it uses ReLU instead, but that's a small detail you will conveniently ignore.

The math for this network is something like this:

```
output_dense_1 = relu(matmul(W_1, x) + b_1)
output_dense_2 = softmax(matmul(W_2, output_dense_1) + b_2)
```

For each layer, the pattern is the same: a matrix multiplication of the layer's input with the weights, plus the bias, and an activation function applied to it. Repeated twice because you have two Dense layers.

Note: This model has 1.5 million parameters. That's a lot for a model with just two layers. This is a downside of using Dense or fully-connected layers. Since each of the 3,072 inputs is connected to each of the 500 intermediate neurons, this requires 3,072×500 = 1.5 million connections, plus 500 bias values. Because this model has so many learned parameters, you can expect it to overfit again on the relatively small dataset.

As usual, don't forget to compile the model first or you cannot train it:

```
model.compile(loss="categorical_crossentropy",
              optimizer=optimizers.Adam(lr=1e-3),
              metrics=["accuracy"])
```

Train this model by calling `fit_generator()`, and you'll see that the results will be a little better than before:

```
model.fit_generator(train_generator,
                    steps_per_epoch=len(train_generator),
                    validation_data=val_generator,
                    validation_steps=len(val_generator),
                    epochs=3,
                    workers=4)
```

Training for three epochs gives the following results:

```
Epoch 1/3
76/76 [==============================] - 2s 28ms/step -
    loss: 3.2228 - acc: 0.1315 -
    val_loss: 3.1306 - val_acc: 0.1351
Epoch 2/3
76/76 [==============================] - 2s 24ms/step -
    loss: 2.4553 - acc: 0.2849 -
    val_loss: 3.0794 - val_acc: 0.1466
Epoch 3/3
76/76 [==============================] - 2s 27ms/step -
    loss: 2.0033 - acc: 0.4284 -
    val_loss: 3.1929 - val_acc: 0.1613
```

The validation score is a little better now than with the logistic regression model, so this new model has learned how to classify images a bit better — but it's still nothing to write home about. The reason you're only doing three epochs is that the validation score becomes worse if you train for longer because of overfitting.

See what it does on the test set:

```
model.evaluate_generator(test_generator,
                         steps=len(test_generator))
```

For the author, the output is about 0.15 or 15% correct. It's better than a random guess, and better than the model with just a single `Dense` layer, but not by much. Adding more `Dense` layers might boost the validation and test scores by a little, but you're still very far off from the accuracy scores you got from Create ML and Turi Create.

It should be clear by now that these classical methods, logistic regression and fully connected neural networks, just don't work very well for image data. One reason is that the model you've created actually destroys the spatial nature of the training data.

Images have a width and height, but the first thing the model does is `Flatten` the image so it can be connected to a `Dense` layer. As you've seen, `Flatten` unrolls the original three-dimensional image data — height, width and color channels — into a one-dimensional vector. This destroys the relationships between neighboring pixels that was present in the original image. By doing this, you've unintentionally been making it hard on the model to understand our data.

It would be better if you could use a model that kept the spatial relationships intact, and that understood the true nature of images. That's exactly what convolutional layers do. And that's the topic of the next chapter!

Challenge

Challenge 1: Add layers to the neural network

Try adding more layers to the neural network, and varying the number of neurons inside these layers. Can you get a better test score this way? You'll find that the more layers you add, the harder it actually becomes to train the model.

Key points

- Linear regression is one of the most basic machine-learning models, dating back to the 1800s when Gauss and others discovered the method of Ordinary Least Squares. It models the relationship between different variables. You can turn linear regression into logistic regression with the sigmoid function, making it a classifier model.

- To build a logistic regression classifier in Keras, you just need one `Dense` layer followed by softmax activation. To use images with the `Dense` layer, you need to `Flatten` the image data into a one-dimensional vector first.

- To train a model in Keras, you need to choose a loss function — cross-entropy for a classifier — as well as an optimizer. Setting the optimizer's learning rate is important or the model won't be able to learn anything.

- Load your data with `ImageDataGenerator`. Use a normalization function to give your data a mean of 0 and a standard deviation of 1. Choose a batch size that fits on your GPU — 32 or 64 is a good default choice.

- Be sure to check the loss and accuracy of your test set on the untrained model, to see if you get reasonable values. The accuracy should be approximately 1/`num_classes`, the loss should be close to `np.log(num_classes)`.

- Keep your eye on the validation accuracy during training. If it stops improving while the training accuracy continues going up, your model is overfitting.

- A classical neural network is just two or more logistic regressions in a row.

- Logistic regression and classical feed-forward neural networks are not the best choice for building image classifiers.

Chapter 7: Going Convolutional

By Matthijs Hollemans

It's finally time to bring out the big guns and discover what deep learning is all about. In this chapter, you'll convert the basic neural network into something that works much better on images. The secret ingredient is the **convolutional layer**.

Got GPU?

Having a GPU is no longer a luxury. Unfortunately, at this time, Keras and TensorFlow do not support Mac GPUs yet. Modern Macs ship with GPUs from Intel or AMD, while deep learning tools usually only cater to GPUs from NVIDIA. Older Macs may still have an NVIDIA on board, but these are often too old. Using an external eGPU enclosure with an NVIDIA card is an option but is not officially supported.

Most machine-learning practitioners train their models on a PC running Linux that has one or more NVIDIA GPUs, or in the cloud. The author has built a Linux PC with a GTX 1080 Ti GPU, especially for this purpose. If you're serious about deep learning, this is an expense worth making.

If all you have is a Mac, you'll need a lot of patience to train the models in this chapter. Because we want everyone to be able to follow along, the book's download includes the full Jupyter notebooks that were used to train the models, as well as the final trained version, so you can skip training the models if your computer isn't up to the task.

> **Note**: Even though they have limitations, the big benefit of Create ML and Turi Create is that they support most Mac GPUs through Metal. No big surprise there, as both are provided by Apple. Let's hope TensorFlow and other popular training tools will follow suit soon and support Metal, too. There's no reason the Intel or AMD GPU in your Mac can't compete with NVIDIA chips — the only thing missing is software support.

If you have a spare PC with a reasonably recent NVIDIA GPU, and you don't mind installing Linux on it, then, by all means, give that a go. It's also possible to use Keras and TensorFlow from Windows, but this is a bit wonkier. We suggest using Ubuntu from ubuntu.com, the most popular Linux for machine learning.

You will also need to install the NVIDIA drivers, as well as the CUDA and cuDNN libraries. See developer.nvidia.com for more details. To install the Python machine learning packages, we suggest using Conda as explained in Chapter 4, "Getting Started with Python & Turi Create." The process is very similar on Linux and Windows.

Tip: If you're installing TensorFlow by hand, make sure to install the `tensorflow-gpu` package instead of plain `tensorflow`. You can change this in **kerasenv.yaml** or run `pip install -U tensorflow-gpu`. Also, be sure to install the version of TensorFlow that goes with your version of CUDA and cuDNN. If these versions don't match up, TensorFlow won't work. Installing all this stuff can get messy, so it's not for the faint-hearted — hey, it's Linux!

Your head in the clouds?

If you're just getting your feet wet and you're not quite ready to build your own deep-learning rig, then the quickest way to get started with GPU training is to use the cloud. You can even use some of these cloud services for free!

Often, there is a starter tier where you get a certain amount of compute hours for free. Some machine-learning-in-the-cloud services make it really easy to run Jupyter notebooks but pay attention: make sure to shut down your Jupyter notebook when you're done with it. Usually, you only pay for what you use, but, as long as you keep the Jupyter server running — even if it just sits there doing nothing — it uses up compute time. And when your free limit runs out, this can get costly quite quickly.

Figuring out how to get your training data over to the cloud service is of key importance. Different providers have different solutions for this. Storing your data in the cloud usually isn't free, but the snacks dataset is small enough — about 120MB — that it won't break the bank. Usually, you only pay a few cents per gigabyte per month.

Here are some suggestions for machine learning in the cloud:

- **Google Colaboratory** at colab.research.google.com is a free Jupyter notebook environment. You can use Colab to run your notebooks on a cloud GPU and even a TPU — Google's own high-performance Tensor Processing Unit hardware — for free. That's a pretty good deal. Your notebooks are stored in Google Drive. The easiest way to upload the dataset is through Google Cloud Storage, although they offer a few different options. Colab is best used from Chrome.

- **Paperspace** at www.paperspace.com

- **Crestle** at www.crestle.com

- **FloydHub** at www.floydhub.com

- **LeaderGPU** at www.leadergpu.com

- **Amazon AWS EC2** at aws.amazon.com. AWS is the world's most popular provider of general-purpose cloud computing. This is just like having your own deep-learning box, except that you're renting it from Amazon. You can start out by using the free tier but they also have GPU instances. Not the easiest or cheapest solution, but definitely the most flexible.

Convolution layers

The models you've built in Keras have, so far, consisted of Dense layers, which take a one-dimensional vector as input. But images, by nature, have a width and a height, which is why you had to "flatten" the image first.

Unfortunately, flattening destroys the spatial nature of the input data. What's more, it also removes depth information from the image. Recall that the depth dimension stores the three color components for each pixel: red, green and blue. These three values are closely related, so you don't really want to treat them as three separate numbers, but as one indivisible unit: the pixel's color.

The spatial relationships between the pixels — which pixels are above, below and next to any other pixel — as well as the relationship between the pixel's color intensities, are obviously important if you want to understand what the image represents. But a lot of this information is lost when flattening into a vector. That's why the models that used only Dense layers didn't work so well.

For better results on images, it makes sense to use a kind of layer that directly works on the original three-dimensional structure of the image. That's what a convolutional layer is for. Not only does it keep the spatial structure of the image intact, it actually learns the relationships between the pixels, which helps it to understand the different patterns that appear in the image.

A neural network made up of such layers is called a convolutional neural network, **convnet**, or just **CNN** for short.

Convolutional layers are responsible for the deep learning "Big Bang" in 2012 when a convnet beat the pants off of all the other contestants in the ImageNet Large Scale Visual Recognition Challenge (ILSVRC). Since then, convnets have quickly taken over the world of computer vision and other machine learning domains. And now, you're going to build your own!

> **Note**: If you've worked with image processing or digital signal processing (DSP) before, you may already be familiar with convolution or cross-correlation. This is the exact same thing but as a neural network layer.

Convolution, say what now?

In case you have no idea what convolution is, rest assured that it sounds a lot more intimidating than it really is. Again, what it comes down to are **dot products**.

A convolution is a little "window" that slides over the image. At every position, it takes the value of the center pixel and of the surrounding pixels, multiplies these values by a fixed set of numbers — the convolution **weights** — and writes the result to an output image.

The output of a convolution layer is another image of the same width and height as the input image.

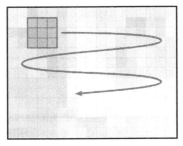

The convolution window slides over the image, left to right, top to bottom

Usually, the convolution window is 3×3 pixels in size, but you'll also see larger windows such as 5×5 and 7×7. Keeping with the trend of using multiple names for the same thing, the window is also known as the convolution **kernel** or **filter**.

For every pixel at coordinate i, j in the input image, this is the math that happens for a 3×3 convolution window:

```
y[i,j] = w[0,0]*x[i-1,j-1] + w[0,1]*x[i-1,j] + w[0,2]*x[i-1,j+1]
       + w[1,0]*x[i,  j-1] + w[1,1]*x[i,  j] + w[1,2]*x[i,  j+1]
       + w[2,0]*x[i+1,j-1] + w[2,1]*x[i+1,j] + w[2,2]*x[i+1,j+1]
       + bias
```

As you might recognize by now, this is nothing more than a dot product between the weight values w and the pixel we're looking at, x[i,j], as well as the eight pixels that surround it. As usual, you also add a bias value.

Therefore, the output value for coordinate i, j is a weighted sum of the input pixel at that same coordinate and the pixels that surround it. The larger the window, the more surrounding pixels this dot product includes. But 3×3 windows are the most common, and so the output value is the weighted sum of nine pixels.

This formula is repeated for every pixel in the input image. We vary i between 0 and the image height, and j between 0 and the image width, and compute the dot product at each pixel coordinate i, j. That's why we say a convolution "slides" over the image.

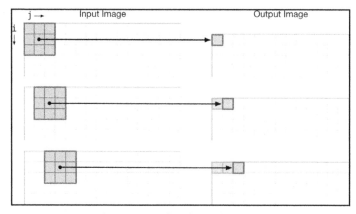

Each step computes a single output value from the 3×3 window at the center pixel

While the pixel values inside the window will be different as it slides over the image, the same 3×3 weight values are used in every image position. This is what allows the convolution layer to learn patterns in the image, regardless of where these patterns appear. In math-speak, convolution is **translation invariant**, because the weights are the same no matter where you look.

Think of it this way: The convolution operation tries to match a small template — the weights — to every group of 3×3 pixels under the sliding window in the input image. If this group of pixels is a good match for the template, then the dot product's output value will be high.

If the pixels don't match the template very well, then the output value will be small, often close to zero. And if the pixels are the complete opposite of the template, the output will be high but negative.

> **Note**: You may know this principle from statistics as **correlation**, and it's why convolution is also known as cross-correlation. The "cross" comes from the fact that you slide the window over the image.

Technically speaking, convolution and cross-correlation are not *exactly* the same thing, as convolution is really cross-correlation done backwards, but ¯_(ツ)_/¯.

During training, the convolution layer learns values for its weights, which means that it will learn a certain pattern of 3×3 pixels. At inference time, it will go through the input image to find out how well each group of 3×3 input pixels matches with the template it learned.

The output of the convolution layer is, therefore, a new image, with large values for those pixels that match the template well and low values for the pixels that don't. In other words, the convolution output measures how much the input pixels "respond" to the learned template. Since a dot product always returns a scalar, a single number, the convolution's output image only has one channel instead of the usual three.

It might seem that learning to detect a 3×3 pattern isn't really that impressive since such patterns are very small, only nine pixels in total. How useful could that be? By itself not much. The trick behind deep learning is that we put many of these convolution layers in a row so that they can detect patterns that cover successively larger areas in the input image. It turns out this works better than using very large window sizes.

That wasn't so bad, was it? Convolution is just another bunch of dot products. The main difference with the fully connected or Dense layers that you've seen before, is that this only looks at a small portion of the image at a time — through a 3×3 lens — and that it keeps the spatial structure of the image intact. The convolution window has a width and height, just like the image. Therefore the convolution layer is more suitable for learning from images.

As with Dense layers, a convolution layer is usually followed by an activation function, to turn the result from the dot product into something that is non-linear and therefore more interesting. ReLU is the most common activation function used with conv layers.

Note: For pixels at the edges of the image, there are not always neighbors on all sides of the pixel. There are two common ways of dealing with this: 1) adding zero padding; 2) don't use these edge pixels. With zero padding, you add an imaginary border of empty pixels around the image so that you never read outside the image.

This is also known as **same** padding because the output image remains the same size as the input image. With the second option, also known as **valid** padding, the output image will become slightly smaller than the input image since you're not computing convolutions for the pixels at the edge. Zero-padding is the most common but you'll also sometimes see valid padding used in practice.

Multiple filters

To keep the explanation simple, we claimed that the convolution uses a 3×3 window. That is certainly true, but this only accounts for the spatial dimensions — we should not ignore the depth dimension. Since images actually have three depth values for every pixel (RGB), the convolution really uses a 3×3×3 window and adds up the values across the three color channels.

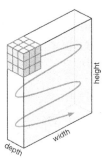

The convolution kernel is really three-dimensional

The input to this convolution filter is a tensor of size (`height`, `width`, 3). The output is a new "image" that has the same width and height as the input image, but a depth of 1. In other words, the output is a (`height`, `width`, 1) tensor.

Note: This assumes we're using "same" or zero-padding. With "valid" padding, the height and width of the output tensor would be slightly smaller.

In image processing applications that use convolutions, the three color channels are often processed independently. The output of such a convolution has the same number of color channels as the input. But the convolutions we're talking about, here, always work across all the color channels and reduce them to a single output channel.

You could think of this new (`height`, `width`, `1`) tensor as a grayscale image since it now only has one color component instead of three. The "color" of this output image represents how much the input image responds to the template or pattern that this convolution has learned.

We interchangeably use the terms **image, tensor, feature map, or activations** for these convolution layer outputs.

In practice, a convolution layer will have more than one of these filters. It's common to see layers with 32, 64, 128, 256, 512 or even 1,024 or more of these convolutions. Each filter learns its own set of weights and bias values.

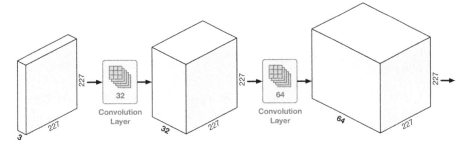

The number of filters in the convolution layer determines the depth of its output image

The neural network in the illustration above has several convolutional layers, all with a 3×3 window size. The first layer works on the 227×227×3 input image. Because the input has three channels (RGB), each convolution filter from this first layer learns 3×3×3 weights.

The layer has 32 of those convolution filters, and so it can detect 32 different patterns. Because it has 32 filters that all produce one channel's worth of data, the output of this layer is a new image of dimensions 227×227×32. Notice that the convolution layer kept the width and height of the image the same but expanded the number of channels from 3 to 32.

If you count them all up, this first layer has learned 3×3×3×32 weights. Read this as `kernelHeight` × `kernelWidth` × `inputChannels` × `outputChannels`. The layer also has learned 32 bias values, one for each output channel.

> **Note:** The first convolution layer outputs a tensor of size (`227`, `227`, `32`). Even though we often still call this an "image" — of size 227×227×32 — you can't really display such images. Your computer's display panel only has one red, green and blue LED for each pixel — what should it do with the other 29 color channels?!

> Think of this output tensor as consisting of 32 individual grayscale images, each describing how well the input image matched the template or pattern learned by the corresponding convolution filter.

The second convolution layer also has a 3×3 window, but now the input tensor has 32 channels, and so each of its convolution filters calculates the dot products over a 3×3×32 window. This layer has 64 of those filters, so its output image/tensor is of size 227×227×64. In total, this second layer will learn 3×3×32×64 weights plus 64 biases.

The filters in the third convolution layer will then each learn 3×3×64 weights, and so on. This structure is typical for convnets: Convolution layers have increasingly larger numbers of filters as you go deeper into the network. The number of filters is usually a power of two. It's not uncommon for the last layer in a convnet to have 1,024, 2,048 or even 4,096 filters.

Remember, each filter learns to detect a unique pattern in the input data. When you use a convnet as the feature extractor in a classification model, the features given to the logistic regression are the responses of the input image to these pattern detectors. A good feature extractor will learn patterns that tell you something meaningful about the images. The better the patterns it has learned, the more useful features it will produce, and the more accurate predictions the logistic regression can make.

Your first convnet in Keras

In a new Jupyter notebook, create the following cells. You can also follow along with **ConvNet.ipynb**.

> **Note**: This chapter assumes you're using the Keras environment that you set up in the previous chapter. If you skipped that chapter, simply run `conda env create --file=starter/kerasenv.yaml` from the command line. If your computer has an NVIDIA GPU, make sure to use `tensorflow-gpu` instead of the regular one. You will also need the snacks dataset, which you can download by double-clicking **snacks-download-link.webloc**.

First, import the needed packages:

```
import numpy as np
from keras.models import Sequential
from keras.layers import *
from keras import optimizers

%matplotlib inline
import matplotlib.pyplot as plt
```

Then, define the size of the input images, as well as the size of the output vector:

```
image_width = 224
image_height = 224
num_classes = 20
```

In the last chapter, you used 32×32-pixel images to keep the number of learnable parameters down. For a convnet, the number of learnable parameters does not depend on the size of the input image, only on the size of the convolution kernels. So for convnets you can get away with larger images, which is why you're using 224×224 pixels. That's a typical input size for convnets.

> **Note**: You can also keep the input width and height undefined, or None, in which case the convnet will accept input images of any size. You might think that larger images would give more accurate results, but this is not always the case. The patterns a model has learned from 224×224 images, may not actually appear in a 1,000×1,000 image. Of course, you could train on 1,000×1,000 images, but large images can easily take up more RAM than is in your GPU, making it harder to train these models. For classification models, 224×224 is a good compromise between memory usage and accuracy. Vision FeaturePrint uses 299×299, while SqueezeNet uses 227×227. Feel free to experiment with different image sizes in this chapter.

Next, create the model and add the layers:

```
model = Sequential()
model.add(Conv2D(32, 3, padding="same", activation="relu",
                 input_shape=(image_height, image_width, 3)))
model.add(Conv2D(32, 3, padding="same", activation="relu"))
model.add(MaxPooling2D(2))
model.add(Conv2D(64, 3, padding="same", activation="relu"))
model.add(Conv2D(64, 3, padding="same", activation="relu"))
model.add(MaxPooling2D(2))
model.add(Conv2D(128, 3, padding="same", activation="relu"))
```

```
model.add(Conv2D(128, 3, padding="same", activation="relu"))
model.add(MaxPooling2D(2))
model.add(Conv2D(256, 3, padding="same", activation="relu"))
model.add(Conv2D(256, 3, padding="same", activation="relu"))
model.add(GlobalAveragePooling2D())
model.add(Dense(num_classes))
model.add(Activation("softmax"))
```

You've seen the `Dense` and `Activation("softmax")` layers before. The `Flatten` layer is gone. This model also has a few new layer types. Let's take a look at `Conv2D` first. As you probably guessed from the name, these are the convolution layers.

A `Conv2D` layer takes the following arguments:

- **The number of filters**. In the first `Conv2D` layer this is 32. As in most convnet designs, convolutional layers get more filters (output channels) as you go deeper into the network. The last `Conv2D` layer in this model has 256 filters. Recall that each filter learns to detect a unique pattern, and so the more filters you have the more patterns the model can detect. The number of filters is often a power of two, but this is not a hard-and-fast rule — feel free to break it.

- **The size of the kernel window**. For all `Conv2D` layers in this model, the kernel is 3×3 pixels. You can write this as a tuple (3, 3) but because square kernel windows are so common, you can also specify the kernel size as just 3 and Keras will understand that you mean a 3×3 window.

- **The padding**. By default, padding in Keras is `"valid"`, which means the pixels at the edges of the image are ignored and so the output image shrinks a little. Most of the time you want `"same"` padding instead, which adds an imaginary border of empty pixels around the edges so that the output image keeps the same width and height as the input image.

- **A non-linear activation function**. The activation that's most typically used with convolution layers is ReLU.

The very first layer in a Keras model must also specify an `input_shape`. This tells Keras the size of the images to expect. Height goes before width in these tensors!

In between the convolution layers are `MaxPooling2D` layers. **Pooling** is a technique that makes the data smaller as it flows through the network, also known as subsampling. Most convnets are built from a combination of convolution layers and pooling layers. You'll learn more about pooling later in this chapter.

The flow of the tensors

You can see what happens to the shape of the data in the `model.summary()`. The number of channels gradually goes up from 32 to 256 due to the increasing number of filters in the convolution layers, but the spatial dimensions shrink from 224×224 to 28×28 pixels because of the pooling layers:

Layer (type)	Output Shape	Param #
conv2d_1 (Conv2D)	(None, 224, 224, 32)	896
conv2d_2 (Conv2D)	(None, 224, 224, 32)	9248
max_pooling2d_1 (MaxPooling2	(None, 112, 112, 32)	0
conv2d_3 (Conv2D)	(None, 112, 112, 64)	18496
conv2d_4 (Conv2D)	(None, 112, 112, 64)	36928
max_pooling2d_2 (MaxPooling2	(None, 56, 56, 64)	0
conv2d_5 (Conv2D)	(None, 56, 56, 128)	73856
conv2d_6 (Conv2D)	(None, 56, 56, 128)	147584
max_pooling2d_3 (MaxPooling2	(None, 28, 28, 128)	0
conv2d_7 (Conv2D)	(None, 28, 28, 256)	295168
conv2d_8 (Conv2D)	(None, 28, 28, 256)	590080
global_average_pooling2d_1 (	(None, 256)	0
dense_1 (Dense)	(None, 20)	5140
activation_1 (Activation)	(None, 20)	0

```
Total params: 1,177,396
Trainable params: 1,177,396
Non-trainable params: 0
```

This model has over 1 million learnable parameters, which sounds like a lot but is not really that many for deep-learning image-classification models. There are models with over 100 million parameters!

Because you set input_shape=(image_height, image_width, 3) on the first layer, the input to this model is expected to be a tensor of size (None, 224, 224, 3), or an image of size 224×224 pixels and 3 channels (RGB). Recall that Keras adds a dimension for the batch size at the front of the tensor. Usually, you keep this batch size unspecified when defining the model, which is why it shows up as None in the summary.

The output of the first conv layer, named conv2d_1 by Keras, is a tensor of size (None, 224, 224, 32). Instead of 3 channels, this layer's output "image" now has 32 channels. That's because this convolution layer has 32 filters, and there is one channel in the output image for each filter.

> **Note**: We put "image" in quotes because the output from this layer is no longer something we can properly display on the screen. From now on, we'll call these data blobs by their more appropriate name: **tensors**.

The second conv layer, conv2d_2, takes this (None, 224, 224, 32) tensor as input and produces a new tensor of the same size. Because the second layer also has 32 filters, it also outputs 32 channels.

It's important to note that, even though the input tensor and the output tensor for this layer both have 32 channels, these are totally unrelated numbers. The number of filters in the layer is independent of the number of channels in the input tensor. It just so happens that these two numbers are the same for this particular layer. However, the number of output channels for a layer is always the same as the number of filters it has.

Each filter will reduce all of the 32 channels from the input tensor to a single channel in the output tensor. This is repeated 32 times because this layer has 32 filters, but each filter has its own set of weights and therefore learns to detect its own pattern. To detect the pattern, each filter always looks at all of the input channels.

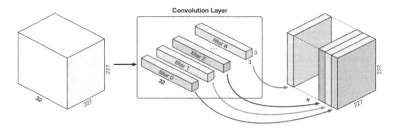

Each filter reads all input channels and produces one output channel

More about pooling

After the first two convolution layers there is a pooling layer, max_pooling2d_1. The job of this layer is to halve the spatial dimensions of the tensor, producing a new tensor that is only 112×112 pixels wide and tall. The number of channels stays the same, 32.

The pooling layer simply takes the maximum value of each 2×2 group of pixels and writes it to the output tensor. It does this for each channel independently, which is why the number of output channels doesn't change.

A pooling layer does not have any learned parameters, it just performs this very simple max operation on a 2×2-pixel window:

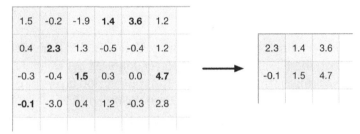

Max pooling reduces each 2×2 pixels to a single number

Because it takes the maximum value, this operation is called **max** pooling. There is also a type called **average** pooling that takes the average or mean of the pixels in that 2×2 window instead — you're actually using one of these average pooling layers at the end of the network. More about this in the next section.

It is standard for pooling layers to use a 2×2 window size. Just like with convolution, this window slides over the input image, but with a step size of 2. This step size, or **stride**, is what determines the spatial dimensions of the output tensor. A stride of 2 means the width and height both get chopped in half. Usually, the stride is the same as the window size, but sometimes you'll see other combinations, such as a window size of 3 with a stride of 2, in which case successive windows overlap each other a little.

Why use these pooling layers? The main reason is to reduce the size of the data you're working with — by keeping only the most interesting parts of the image. As you've seen, convolution measures how well certain parts of the image respond to a learned pattern. Because max pooling only keeps the largest and therefore most important values, it helps to make the predictions less sensitive to small variations in the data. Resizing the input also increases the receptive field, or the portion of the input image that is covered by the convolution layers that follow the pooling layer.

Reducing the size of the data is helpful for making computations faster, and limiting the amount of GPU RAM that's needed. Because the number of channels increases with each new convolution layer, the tensors become larger and larger. Pooling helps to keep this under control.

More importantly, pooling also helps to fight the phenomenon known as **the curse of dimensionality** that says that very high dimensional spaces are a lot harder to work with than lower dimensional spaces. A (224, 224, 32) tensor means that each possible tensor value can be represented as a point in a 224×224×32 = 1,605,632-dimensional space. Try wrapping your head around that! Pooling with a window size of 2 will reduce the number of dimensions by a factor of 4, limiting the effects of this wicked curse.

The detected features

Following the max pooling layer are two more conv layers, this time with 64 output channels, and then there is another pooling layer, followed by two more conv layers. The model repeats this pattern a few times. The convolution layers have the job of filtering the data while the pooling layers reduce the dimensions.

After the last convolution layer, you end up with a tensor that is 28×28×256. But what exactly is in that tensor?

The very first convolution layer measures the responses of the pixels from the input image to the different patterns that it has learned, 32 patterns in total. The patterns learned by the first layer will look something like this:

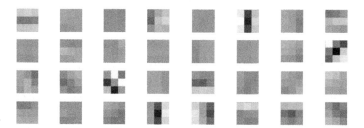

The learned weights for the first conv layer

This is literally a plot of the weights learned by the first convolution layer. Each pattern is 3×3 pixels because that's the kernel size for this layer. These patterns work in the RGB color space, because that's what the input image is in, which is why we can display them as RGB images too (they have 3 color channels).

As you can see, these patterns detect color blobs, simple line shapes, and edges — all very low-level image features.

Note: Each time you train this model from scratch, you'll end up with slightly different patterns. The weights for the convolution layers are initialized with random numbers, and so the outcome depends on this random initialization. However, you'll often end up with very similar patterns anyway. Somehow the training process manages to figure out exactly what the layer needs to know.

The second convolution layer doesn't directly look at patterns in the original RGB image but it looks for patterns in the output of the first layer. It takes the first layer's responses and measures how they respond to its own patterns. In other words, the second layer combines the first layer's patterns to detect new and larger patterns.

Now what's happening becomes a lot less intuitive because the second layer's patterns are not in RGB space but in some 32-dimensional "color" space. We can't display these patterns because they make no sense to the human eye.

However, with a bit of trickery, it is possible to measure what parts of the original RGB input image respond the most to the patterns from the second layer. That gives us an idea of what sort of patterns this second layer looks for. It turns out that, where the first layer detects mostly simple colors and lines, the second layer will look for somewhat higher level patterns, such as circles and corners.

These patterns are also larger: the second layer still looks at a 3×3 block of pixels in *its own* input tensor, but each of those pixels was made from a 3×3 window in the original RGB image, so the second layer actually sees a larger region from the original image. This is called the **receptive field** of the layer. The receptive field of the second layer, i.e., how much it sees from the original RGB image, is 5×5 pixels. The pooling layers also increase the receptive field.

Each convolution layer learns to see ever higher-level, more abstract patterns. And because the receptive field grows bigger, convolution layers deeper in the network see more of the input image than early layers. This allows the later layers to learn to recognize real-world concepts like "this is a dog-like shape", "this is a human face", "this object is pointed to the left" and so on.

Even though each layer only learns a relatively small pattern of 3×3 pixels (across many channels), because we stack many of these layers together, the layers at the end of the network will have learned to detect patterns that can cover the entire input image. This is actually very similar to how the human visual cortex works, which explains why convnets give such great results.

Feeling hot hot hot

Back to that very last convolution layer that outputs a 28×28×256 tensor. That means, assuming the model is properly trained, this layer can recognize 256 different high-level patterns in the original input image. Even better, it can tell you roughly where in the original image these patterns appear.

For example, let's say the first filter from this final convolution layer has learned to detect the high-level pattern for "round shape with a hole in it" and the original RGB input image has a donut in the top-right corner, then the 28×28 **feature map** for channel 0 might look like this:

A channel from the final tensor represented as a heatmap

You're looking at just one of the 256 output channels, or feature maps, contained in this tensor. Displayed like this, it's also often called a **heatmap** because it's "hot" (yellow) where the pixels responded a lot to the pattern but "cold" elsewhere (dark blue). In this example, the pixels in the top-right corner are hot, meaning that the pattern from this filter was detected in that position in the original RGB input image.

Each of the 256 channels from this tensor will have a similar 28×28-pixel feature map that indicates where that filter's pattern was detected in the original image. Of course, the location is only an approximation because the image was scaled down by a factor of 8 (three max pooling layers). If a pattern was not found in the input image, then its heatmap will contain only very small values.

Unfortunately for us, the patterns that the final convolution layer actually learns will not be as easy to understand as "round shape with a hole in it." Exactly what the convnet learns can be hard for humans to interpret.

A donut may actually be matched by a combination of different patterns, perhaps a "round shape" pattern and a "has a hole in it" pattern.

For any given image, many of the 256 channels in this tensor will light up to a certain extent, and it's really hard to interpret what this means. You need to do a bit more work to convert this result into something meaningful, such as adding a logistic regression that maps these patterns to the classes you're interested in.

Honey, I shrunk the tensors!

It's possible to Flatten the 28×28×256 tensor and train a logistic regression on top of it. That would turn the tensor into a 200,704-element vector. Recall from the last chapter that the logistic regression already had a hard enough time with just 3,072 features, let alone two-hundred thousand...

Fortunately, for a classification model, you don't really care so much *where* exactly the pattern was matched, only whether it was matched at all. So you can use a clever trick, which will actually make life a little easier for the logistic regression. That trick is called **global pooling** or **adaptive pooling**.

The GlobalAveragePooling2D layer calculates the average value of each 28×28 feature map, which is just a scalar number. It puts these numbers into a vector of 256 elements, one for each channel in the tensor. Then the logistic regression will use this vector as the feature vector. 256 features are much more palatable than 200,704!

Global average pooling is a pooling layer just like the max-pooling you've seen before, except now the window is the size of the image, i.e., 28×28 pixels, and it takes the mean value of all these pixels instead of the maximum. In every channel, we take the average of the 28×28 pixels and reduce it to a single number:

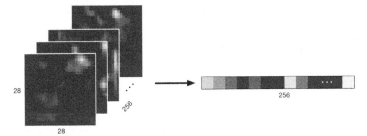

Global average pooling

Because we only care about whether a certain pattern was detected, but not where, taking the average of its 28×28 heatmap is good enough. If nothing was detected, then this average is a small number close to zero. If something was detected, the average will be a high number. The stronger the detection, the higher the number.

After this global average pooling layer, you now have a 256-element vector that says which of the 256 patterns were detected in the original input image, and how strong these detections are. But because you still don't really know what these 256 patterns represent, you can't use them to directly draw conclusions from. But you *can* use them as features for the logistic regression.

That's why the final two layers in the model are a Dense layer followed by a softmax activation. These serve the same purpose as before: to perform logistic regression on top of the extracted features. The convolutional layers and pooling layers now act as a feature extractor that converts the original pixels into features that are more suitable for use with logistic regression.

And the logistic regression simply learns which combinations of the possible detected patterns belong to the different classes that you want to detect.

> **Note**: The global pooling layer flattens the four-dimensional image tensor into a two-dimensional feature vector (remember that the first dimension is the batch size). Unlike a Flatten layer, which always expects a fixed number of input features, a global pooling layer can work on images of any arbitrary input size. Models with a Flatten layer are therefore much less flexible and are not considered to be "fully" convolutional. Most modern convnets use a global pooling layer so that they can accept images of any size. But remember: for the best results, images used for inference shouldn't be too much larger or smaller than the images the model was trained on.

Training the model

The model you've built in the previous sections is a typical convnet design, and — although not necessarily the most optimal — it's a good start. Let's see how well this model learns.

As usual, compile the model before use:

```
model.compile(loss="categorical_crossentropy",
              optimizer=optimizers.Adam(lr=1e-3),
              metrics=["accuracy"])
```

You also need the train, val and test generators from the last chapter. Tip: Copy over those cells from your old Jupyter notebook.

```
images_dir = "snacks/"
```

```
train_data_dir = images_dir + "train/"
val_data_dir = images_dir + "val/"
test_data_dir = images_dir + "test/"

def normalize_pixels(image):
    return image / 127.5 - 1

from keras.preprocessing.image import ImageDataGenerator
datagen = ImageDataGenerator(
  preprocessing_function=normalize_pixels)

batch_size = 64

train_generator = datagen.flow_from_directory(
                train_data_dir,
                target_size=(image_width, image_height),
                batch_size=batch_size,
                class_mode="categorical",
                shuffle=True)

val_generator = datagen.flow_from_directory(
                val_data_dir,
                target_size=(image_width, image_height),
                batch_size=batch_size,
                class_mode="categorical",
                shuffle=False)

test_generator = datagen.flow_from_directory(
                test_data_dir,
                target_size=(image_width, image_height),
                batch_size=batch_size,
                class_mode="categorical",
                shuffle=False)

index2class = {v:k for k,v in
  train_generator.class_indices.items()}
```

Training is exactly the same as before: You can simply call `model.fit_generator()`. However, let's add some useful code that lets you keep track of the training progress.

Keras returns a `History` object from `fit_generator()` that has the loss and any other metrics you asked for. Since it's common to run `fit_generator()` a few times in a row, you'll combine those `History` objects into an overall history and then plot some curves.

First, in a new cell, create an array:

```
histories = []
```

Then, in a cell of its own, call `fit_generator()`. You'll append the `History` object that this returns to the array:

```
history = model.fit_generator(
    train_generator,
    steps_per_epoch=len(train_generator),
    validation_data=val_generator,
    validation_steps=len(val_generator),
    epochs=5,
    workers=8)
histories.append(history)
```

Now, you can run this cell multiple times and the history won't get lost.

You may wonder why you'd want to run `fit_generator()` more than once, but it's useful to train for a few epochs to see how the model is doing before you commit to training for many epochs. Also, you may want to change some hyperparameters after a while, such as the learning rate. You'll see an example of that soon.

> **Note**: Training this kind of model takes up a lot of processing power. On a GTX 1080 Ti GPU, it takes about 15 seconds to train a single epoch. On less powerful GPUs or on the CPU it will take much longer. On the author's beefy iMac, it takes 15 *minutes* per epoch with all cores — and all fans! — blazing. We suggest that you don't try training this model yourself unless you have a Linux machine with a GPU or if you don't mind using cloud services.
>
> If you want to follow along without training, feel free to open the notebook included in the **final** folder of the provided materials.

Going dooooown?

To make a plot of the loss over time, do the following:

```
def combine_histories():
    history = {
        "loss": [],
        "val_loss": [],
        "acc": [],
        "val_acc": []
    }

    for h in histories:
        for k in history.keys():
            history[k] += h.history[k]
    return history
```

And then call this new function:

```
history = combine_histories()
```

This combines the histories that you've recorded from the different training runs. To make the plot:

```
def plot_loss(history):
    fig = plt.figure(figsize=(10, 6))
    plt.plot(history["loss"])
    plt.plot(history["val_loss"])
    plt.xlabel("Epoch")
    plt.ylabel("Loss")
    plt.legend(["Train", "Validation"])
    plt.show()

plot_loss(history)
```

This again uses the Matplotlib library. It puts the graph for the training loss (called just `"loss"` here) and the validation loss (`"val_loss"`) into a single plot. After training for 30 epochs, about 10 minutes on a fast machine, the curves look something like this:

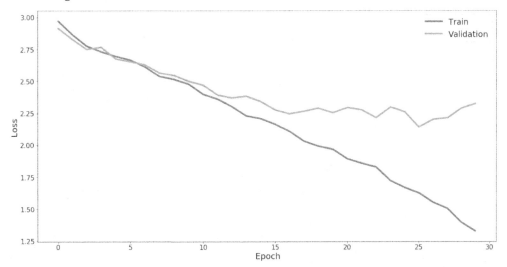

The training and validation loss curves

This is the sort of shape you want to see: the loss goes down over time. At some point, the loss starts to go down slower, which is especially noticeable for the validation loss. This happens when the model has already learned a lot of stuff and it can only fill in more of the details.

Note that the plot isn't a smooth line, especially the one for validation bounces up and down a bit. This is because the validation set is relatively small, and so variations from one epoch to the next can cause the loss to briefly go up. This kind of "noise" is normal and expected. As long as the overall trend is going down, you're good.

Unfortunately, after about 25 epochs, you can see that the validation loss is going up permanently. This is a sign that the model is overfitting. The training loss is still going down, but the one that you care about is the validation loss.

The History objects also track accuracy. That's a more interpretable metric than the loss, so plot this, too.

```
def plot_accuracy(history):
    fig = plt.figure(figsize=(10, 6))
    plt.plot(history["acc"])
    plt.plot(history["val_acc"])
    plt.xlabel("Epoch")
    plt.ylabel("Accuracy")
    plt.legend(["Train", "Validation"])
    plt.show()

plot_accuracy(history)
```

The plot will look something like this:

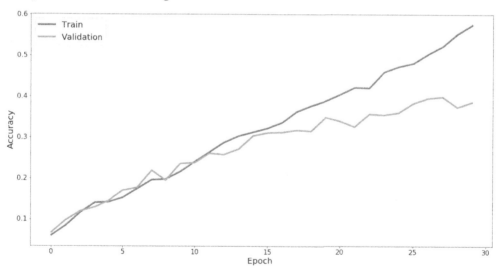

The training and validation accuracy over time

This is roughly the opposite of the loss: The accuracy goes up over time but eventually starts slowing down. After training for 25 epochs, this model gets a validation accuracy of about 38%.

You could train for longer but this model doesn't really seem to be improving much anymore. In fact, it will get worse over time as you now start overfitting. The training accuracy keeps increasing, as the model starts to remember literal training examples, but that is not what you want. The validation accuracy starts to level off after 25 epochs and will eventually become worse.

Learning rate annealing

One trick you can use to give the accuracy a little boost is to change the learning rate. It is currently 1e-3 or 0.001 (set when you compiled the model), and you can change it by doing the following:

```
import keras.backend as K
K.set_value(model.optimizer.lr,
            K.get_value(model.optimizer.lr) / 10)
```

K refers to the Keras backend package, which is a wrapper around TensorFlow. You cannot set the optimizer's learning rate directly and must do it in this special way.

Now train for several more epochs. If you call `combine_histories()` again and plot the loss you'll see a bump where the learning rate was changed, at epoch 30:

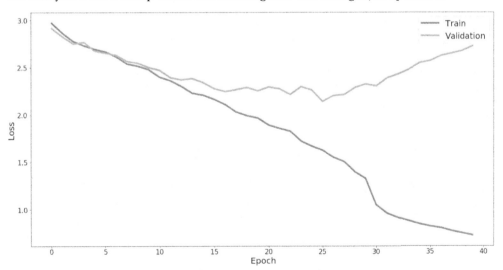

The loss after lowering the learning rate

Unfortunately, the bump only happened in the training loss, the validation loss just keeps getting worse. If you also plot the accuracy curves, you'll see that the validation score actually stabilizes at around 41% correct at this point.

In general, you want to start with as high a learning rate as you can get away with, then lower it over time. If the learning rate is too high, the loss will "explode."

For a classifier, the initial loss should roughly be `np.log(num_classes)`. If the loss at any point becomes much larger than that, and only keeps increasing over time, you need to lower the learning rate.

Changing the learning rate by hand is called **manual learning rate annealing**. Keras can also do this automatically for you using a callback (more about that in the next chapters).

Usually, you want to lower the learning rate when you see that the validation loss is no longer decreasing. That's often a good indication that the optimizer has gotten "stuck." The way to get it unstuck is by lowering the learning rate, which lets you squeeze a few extra percentage points of accuracy out of the model.

It's better... but not good enough yet

It's clear that you were able to create a much better model using these convolutional layers than with only Dense layers. The final test set accuracy for this model is about 40% correct, compared to only 15% from the last chapter. That's a big improvement!

All thanks to the convolutional layers, because they know how to take advantage of the natural structure of the images.

But note that this particular model also overfits a lot — again! That's bad news. With over one million parameters and only about 4,800 training images, there is too much freedom for the model to memorize the images. And adding more layers or more filters per layer is only going to make this problem worse, so you'll also look at how to fix that problem once and for all.

> **Note**: Even though the model you trained isn't optimal, this very straightforward architecture of conv layers and pooling layers can work quite well in practice; it's very similar to the famous VGG network that is used by many in the deep-learning community. One way to get better results with this architecture is to first train the model on a much larger dataset such as ImageNet — which has over 1 million images — and then adapt it to your own images. But that takes a long long time... It's often easier to build on top of an existing pre-trained model that you can simply download for free, without having to do the laborious ImageNet training yourself. Yep, we'll be talking about transfer learning again!

Key points

- You need access to a powerful GPU in order to train these deep learning models. Unfortunately, Mac GPUs are not well supported by popular training tools. The cloud to the rescue!

- Convolution layers are key to making good image classifiers. Just like Dense layers they compute dot products, but only over small regions of the image. Speaking mathematically, convolution is actually the same as a Dense layer in which most of the connections are zero, and the other connections all share the same weights.

- Convnets are made up of a series of convolution layers and pooling layers. Layers deeper in the network have more filters and learn to detect higher level patterns that represent more abstract concepts.

- Choosing the right values for the hyperparameters such as the learning rate is essential for getting an optimal result. It's also a good idea to plot the loss and accuracy curves, to see if your model is overfitting or whether it is done learning.

Where to go from here?

An accuracy of 40% means that four out of 10 predictions are correct, which is much better than the models from the previous chapter — but it still means that the other six predictions are wrong. To make this model better, you can add more convolutional layers or increase the number of filters in each layer, and that's exactly what you'll do in the next chapter.

SqueezeNet

What you did in the previous chapter is very similar to what Create ML and Turi Create do when they train models, except the convnet they use is a little more advanced. Turi Create actually gives you a choice between different convnets:

- SqueezeNet v1.1

- ResNet50

- VisionFeaturePrint_Scene

In this section, you'll take a quick look at the architecture of SqueezeNet and how it is different from the simple convnet you made. ResNet50 is a model that is used a lot in deep learning, but, at over 25 million parameters, it's on the big side for use on mobile devices and so we'll pay it no further attention.

We'd love to show you the architecture for VisionFeaturePrint_Scene, but, alas, this model is built into iOS itself and so we don't know what it actually looks like.

This is SqueezeNet, zoomed out:

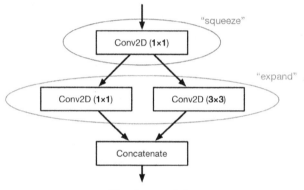

The architecture of SqueezeNet

SqueezeNet uses the now-familiar `Conv2D` and `MaxPooling2D` layers, as well as the ReLU activation. However, it also has a branching structure that looks like this:

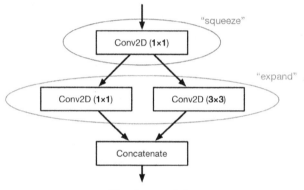

The fire module

This combination of several different layers is called a **fire module**, because no one reads your research papers unless you come up with a cool name for your inventions. SqueezeNet is simply a whole bunch of these fire modules stacked together.

In SqueezeNet, most of the convolution layers do not use 3×3 windows but windows consisting of a single pixel, also called 1×1 convolution. Such convolution filters only look at a single pixel at a time and not at any of that pixel's neighbors. The math is just a regular dot product across the channels for that pixel.

Convolutions with a 1×1 kernel size are very common in modern convnets. They're often used to increase or to decrease the number of channels in a tensor. That's exactly why SqueezeNet uses them, too.

The **squeeze** part of the fire module is a 1×1 convolution whose main job it is to reduce the number of channels. For example, the very first layer in SqueezeNet is a regular 3×3 convolution with 64 filters. The squeeze layer that follows it, reduces this back to 16 filters. What such a layer learns isn't necessarily to detect patterns in the data, but how to keep only the most important patterns. This forces the model to focus on learning only things that truly matter.

The output from the squeeze convolution branches into two parallel convolutions, one with a 1×1 window size and the other with a 3×3 window. Both convolutions have 64 filters, which is why this is called the **expand** portion of the fire module, as these layers increase the number of channels again. Afterwards, the output tensors from these two parallel convolution layers are concatenated into one big tensor that has 128 channels.

The squeeze layer from the next fire module then reduces those 128 channels again to 16 channels, and so on. As is usual for convnets, the number of channels gradually increases the further you go into the network, but this pattern of reduce-and-expand repeats several times over.

The reason for using two parallel convolutions on the same data is that using a mix of different transformations potentially lets you extract more interesting information. You see similar ideas in the Inception modules from Google's famous Inception-v3 model, which combines 1×1, 3×3, and 5×5 convolutions, and even pooling, into the same kind of parallel structure.

The fire module is very effective, evidenced by the fact that SqueezeNet is a powerful model — especially for one that only has 1.2 million learnable parameters. It scores about 67% correct on the snacks dataset, compared to 40% from the basic convnet of the previous section, which has about the same number of parameters.

If you're curious, you can see a Keras version of SqueezeNet in the notebook **SqueezeNet.ipynb** in this chapter's resources. This notebook reproduces the results from Turi Create with Keras. We're not going to explain that code in detail here since you'll shortly be using an architecture that gives better results than SqueezeNet. However, feel free to play with this notebook — it's fast enough to run on your Mac, no GPU needed for this one.

The Keras functional API

One thing we should mention at this point is the Keras **functional API**. You've seen how to make a model using `Sequential`, but that is limited to linear pipelines that consist of layers in a row. To code SqueezeNet's branching structures with Keras, you need to specify your model in a slightly different way.

In the file **keras_squeezenet/squeezenet.py**, there is a function `def SqueezeNet(...)` that defines the Keras model. It more-or-less does the following:

```
img_input = Input(shape=input_shape)

x = Conv2D(64, 3, padding='valid')(img_input)
```

```
x = Activation('relu')(x)
x = MaxPooling2D(pool_size=(3, 3), strides=(2, 2))(x)
x = fire_module(x, squeeze=16, expand=64)
x = fire_module(x, squeeze=16, expand=64)
x = MaxPooling2D(pool_size=(3, 3), strides=(2, 2))(x)
...

model = Model(img_input, x)
...
return model
```

Instead of creating a Sequential object and then doing model.add(layer), here a layer is created by writing:

```
x = LayerName(parameters)
```

Then this layer object is immediately applied to the output from the previous layer:

```
x = LayerName(parameters)(x)
```

Here, x is not a layer object but a tensor object. This syntax may look a little weird, but in Python, you're allowed to call an object instance (the layer) as if it were a function. This is actually a very handy way to define models of arbitrary complexity.

To create the actual model object, you need to specify the input tensor as well as the output tensor, which is now in x:

```
model = Model(img_input, x)
```

You can see how the branching structure is made in the fire_module function, shown here in an abbreviated version:

```
def fire_module(x, squeeze=16, expand=64):
    sq = Conv2D(squeeze, 1, padding='valid')(x)
    sq = Activation('relu')(sq)

    left = Conv2D(expand, 1, padding='valid')(sq)
    left = Activation('relu')(left)

    right = Conv2D(expand, 3, padding='same')(sq)
    right = Activation('relu')(right)

    return concatenate([left, right])
```

This has four tensors: x that has the input data, sq with the output of the squeeze layer, left for the left branch and right for the right branch. At the end, left and right are concatenated into a single tensor again. This is where the branches come back together.

A lot of Keras code will use both Sequential models and models defined using this functional API, so it's good to be familiar with it.

> **Note**: The SqueezeNet implementation we used here was taken from the GitHub repo github.com/rcmalli/keras-squeezenet.

MobileNet and data augmentation

The final classification model you'll be training is based on MobileNet. Just like SqueezeNet, this is an architecture that is optimized for use on mobile devices — hence the name.

MobileNet has more learned parameters than SqueezeNet, so it's slightly bigger but it's also more capable. With MobileNet as the feature extractor, you should be able to get a model that performs better than what Turi Create gave you in Chapter 5, "Digging Deeper into Turi Create." Plus you'll also be using some additional training techniques to make this model learn as much as possible from the dataset.

Follow along with **MobileNet.ipynb** from the chapter's resources, or create a new notebook and import the required packages:

```
import os
import numpy as np
from keras.preprocessing.image import ImageDataGenerator
from keras.models import Sequential
from keras.layers import *
from keras import optimizers, callbacks
import keras.backend as K

%matplotlib inline
import matplotlib.pyplot as plt
```

Keras already includes a version of MobileNet, so creating this model is easy:

```
image_width = 224
image_height = 224

from keras.applications.mobilenet import MobileNet

base_model = MobileNet(
    input_shape=(image_height, image_width, 3),
    include_top=False,
    weights="imagenet",
    pooling=None)
```

Keras's MobileNet has been trained on the famous ImageNet dataset. But you want to use MobileNet only as a feature extractor, not as a classifier for the 1000 ImageNet categories. That's why you need to specify `include_top=False` and `pooling=None` when creating the model. That way Keras leaves off the classifier layers.

You can use `base_model.summary()` to see a list of all the layers in this model, or run the following code to save a diagram of the model to a PNG file (this requires the `pydot` package to be installed):

```
from keras.utils import import plot_model
plot_model(base_model, to_file="mobilenet.png")
```

If you look at the architecture diagram of MobileNet in that PNG file, you'll see that it is made up of the following repeating structure:

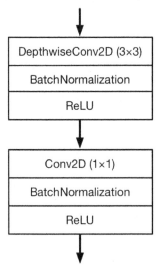

MobileNet uses depthwise separable convolutions

First, there is a so-called `DepthwiseConv2D` layer with kernel size 3×3, followed by a `BatchNormalization` layer, and a ReLU activation. Then there is a `Conv2D` layer with kernel size 1×1, which is also followed by its own `BatchNormalization` and ReLU. MobileNet consists of 13 of these building blocks stacked together.

There are a few new things going on, here:

- A **depthwise convolution** is a variation of convolution wherein each filter only looks at a single input channel. With a regular convolution, the filters always compute their dot products over all the input channels. But a depthwise convolution treats the input channels as separate from one another. Because it doesn't combine the input channels, depthwise convolution is simpler and faster than `Conv2D` and uses much fewer parameters.

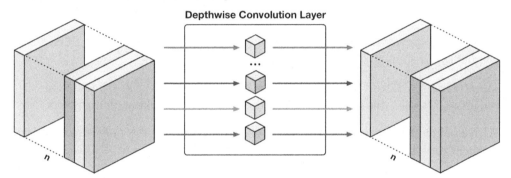

Depthwise convolution treats the channels independently

- The combination of a 3×3 `DepthwiseConv2D` followed by a 1×1 `Conv2D` is called a **depthwise separable convolution**. You can think of this as a 3×3 `Conv2D` layer that has been split up into two simpler layers: the depthwise convolution filters the data, while the 1×1 convolution — also known as a **pointwise** convolution — combines the filtered data into a new tensor. This gives an approximation of a "real" 3×3 `Conv2D` but at much lower cost: there are fewer parameters in total and it also performs fewer computations. This is why MobileNet is so suitable for mobile devices.

- The **batch normalization** layer, `BatchNormalization`, is what makes it possible to have these very deep networks. This layer helps to keep the data "fresh" as it moves between the layers. Without batch normalization, the data in the tensors would eventually disappear in deep networks because the numbers become too small — known as the problem of the **vanishing gradients** — and then the model won't be able to learn anything anymore. You'll see `BatchNormalization` in pretty much any modern convnet.

> **Note:** Depending on your version of Keras, you may also see `ZeroPadding2D` layers before the `DepthwiseConv2D` layer, which adds padding around the input tensor so that the convolution works correctly for pixels at the edges. Another small detail: The activation function used is actually **ReLU6**, a variation of the ReLU activation you've seen before. It works in the same way as ReLU but also prevents the output of the convolution from becoming too large — it limits to output to `6.0`, hence the name — which allows for the use of faster limited-precision computations on mobile and embedded devices.

Looking at the `model.summary()`, you may have noticed that MobileNet does not use any pooling layers, yet the spatial dimensions of the image tensor do become smaller over time — from 224×224 at the beginning to only 7×7 at the end.

MobileNet achieves this pooling effect by setting the **stride** of some of the `Conv2D` and `DepthwiseConv2D` layers to 2 instead of 1.

The **stride** is the size of the steps the convolution kernel takes as it slides through the image. Usually, this step size is 1 and the convolution looks at all the pixels.

With a stride of 2, the window will skip every other pixel, thereby only computing dot products for half the pixels in both the width and height directions. This way you don't need a special pooling layer to make the image smaller.

You'll see both techniques, pooling and larger strides, used in practice.

The final layer in this model outputs a tensor of size (7, 7, 1024). This tensor contains the features that MobileNet has extracted from the input image. You're simply going to add a logistic regression on top of these extracted features, exactly like you've done before.

> **Note:** MobileNet has more learned parameters than SqueezeNet, so it takes up more space in your app bundle and also more RAM at runtime. However, thanks to these additional parameters, MobileNet produces higher quality results than SqueezeNet. Even better, it's also faster than SqueezeNet due to the depthwise separable convolutions.
>
> Choosing a feature extractor is always a trade-off between quality, storage size and runtime speed. If MobileNet is too large for your app — it adds between 8 and 16 MB to your app bundle — then SqueezeNet might be a better choice. But the predictions of a SqueezeNet-based model may be worse and it runs slower.

The VisionFeaturePrint_Scene model that is built into iOS 12 is even more powerful than MobileNet, and it doesn't even take up any space in your app bundle, but again is slower. And you can't use it on iOS 11 or other platforms.

Which model is "best" comes down to what you care most about: speed, download size or results. As they say, there is no free lunch in machine learning.

Adding the classifier

You've placed the MobileNet feature extractor in a variable named `base_model`. You'll now create a second model for the classifier, to go on top of that base model:

```
num_classes = 20

top_model = Sequential()
top_model.add(base_model)
top_model.add(GlobalAveragePooling2D())
top_model.add(Dense(num_classes))
top_model.add(Activation("softmax"))
```

This should look familiar by now: it's a logistic regression.

Just like before it has a `Dense` layer followed by a softmax activation at the end.

The `GlobalAveragePooling2D` layer shrinks the 7×7×1024 output tensor from MobileNet to a vector of 1024 elements, by taking the average of each individual 7×7 feature map.

Note: If you had used `Flatten` instead of global pooling, the `Dense` layer would have had 49 times more parameters. That simple change would add another one million parameters to the model. Not only does global pooling give you a smaller model than using `Flatten`, it also works better because too many parameters is the main cause for overfitting.

> **Note**: You used a Dense layer for the logistic regression, but modern convnets often have a 1×1 Conv2D layer at the end instead. If you do the math, you'll see that a 1×1 convolution that follows a global pooling layer is equivalent to a Dense or fully-connected layer. These are two different ways to express the same operation. However, this is only true after a global pooling layer, when the image is reduced to just a single pixel. Anywhere else, a 1×1 convolution is not the same as a Dense layer.

Next up, you need to freeze all MobileNet layers:

```
for layer in base_model.layers:
    layer.trainable = False
```

You're not going to be training the MobileNet feature extractor. This has already been trained on the large ImageNet dataset, just like SqueezeNet was. All *you* have to train is the logistic regression that you've placed on top. This is why it's important to set the layers from the feature extractor to be not trainable. Yup, you guessed it, this again is transfer learning in action.

When you do `top_model.summary()` it should now show this:

```
Layer (type)                   Output Shape              Param #
=================================================================
mobilenet_1.00_224 (Model)     (None, 7, 7, 1024)        3228864
_____
global_average_pooling2d_2 (   (None, 1024)              0
_____
dense_1 (Dense)                (None, 20)                20500
_____
activation_1 (Activation)      (None, 20)                0
=================================================================
Total params: 3,249,364
Trainable params: 20,500
Non-trainable params: 3,228,864
_____
```

The number of trainable params is only 20,500 since that's how big the Dense layer is. The other 3.25 million parameters are from MobileNet and will not be trained.

Note that the first "layer" in this new model is MobileNet, so if you ask `top_model` to make a prediction on an image, it will first send the image through `base_model` and then applies the final logistic regression layers.

Finally, compile the model just like before:

```
top_model.compile(loss="categorical_crossentropy",
                  optimizer=optimizers.Adam(lr=1e-3),
                  metrics=["accuracy"])
```

Before you start training this model, let's first talk about a handy trick that can make your training set ten times larger with almost no effort on your part.

Data augmentation

We only have about 4800 images for our 20 categories, which comes to 240 images per category on average. That's not bad, but these deep learning models work better with more data. More, more, more! Gathering more training images takes a lot of time and effort — therefore, is costly — and is not always a realistic option. However, you can always artificially expand the training set by transforming the images that you *do* have.

Here's a typical training image:

Whatta guy!

Notice how it's pointing to the left? One easy way to instantly double the number of training images is to horizontally flip them so that the model also learns to detect bananas that point to the right. There are many more of these transformations, such as rotating the image, shearing by a random amount, zooming in or out, changing the colors slightly, etc. It's smart to include any transformations that you want your model to be invariant to.

Whatta guys!

This is what we call **data augmentation**: You augment the training data through small random transformations. This happens on-the-fly during training. Every time Keras loads an image from the training set, it automatically applies this data augmentation to the image. For that you have to make an `ImageDataGenerator` object.

```python
from keras.applications.mobilenet import preprocess_input

train_datagen = ImageDataGenerator(
                    rotation_range=40,
                    width_shift_range=0.2,
                    height_shift_range=0.2,
                    shear_range=0.2,
                    zoom_range=0.2,
                    channel_shift_range=0.2,
                    horizontal_flip=True,
                    fill_mode="nearest",
                    preprocessing_function=preprocess_input)

val_datagen = ImageDataGenerator(
                    preprocessing_function=preprocess_input)

test_datagen = ImageDataGenerator(
                    preprocessing_function=preprocess_input)
```

You've already used `ImageDataGenerator` in previous notebooks, where it was only responsible for loading the images and normalizing them.

Here, you tell the `ImageDataGenerator` that it should also rotate the images, flip them horizontally, shift the images up/down/sideways, zoom in/out, shear, and change the color channels by random amounts. That's a lot of different transformations, and you don't want to go overboard and make the images unrecognizable, but doing this really helps to grow the amount of available training data.

For normalizing the image data, you previously used your own function, but here you use the `preprocess_input` function from the Keras MobileNet module because that knows exactly how MobileNet expects the input data.

> **Note**: MobileNet's `preprocess_input()` actually does the exact same thing you've done in the previous chapters: divide the pixel values by 127.5 and subtract 1, so that the new values are in the range [-1, 1]. However, not all models use this particular method of preprocessing. Another common way to normalize images is to use the mean and standard deviation of all the pixel values in the training set. If you're using a pretrained model, make sure to use the correct preprocessing for that model, or risk getting incorrect predictions.

For the validation and test sets, you create a plain `ImageDataGenerator` object that does not apply any of the data augmentations. You always want to evaluate the performance of the model on the exact same set of images.

Given these `datagen` objects, you can now make the generators that will read the images from their respective folders. This works just like before:

```python
images_dir = "snacks/"
train_data_dir = images_dir + "train/"
val_data_dir = images_dir + "val/"
test_data_dir = images_dir + "test/"
batch_size = 64

train_generator = train_datagen.flow_from_directory(
                    train_data_dir,
                    target_size=(image_width, image_height),
                    batch_size=batch_size,
                    class_mode="categorical",
                    shuffle=True)

val_generator = val_datagen.flow_from_directory(
                    val_data_dir,
                    target_size=(image_width, image_height),
                    batch_size=batch_size,
                    class_mode="categorical",
                    shuffle=False)

test_generator = test_datagen.flow_from_directory(
                    test_data_dir,
                    target_size=(image_width, image_height),
                    batch_size=batch_size,
                    class_mode="categorical",
                    shuffle=False)
```

And now you're ready to train!

Training the classifier layer

Training this model is no different than what you've done before: you can run `model.fit_generator()` a few times until you're happy with the validation accuracy.

But before you rush off to train this fancy new model, allow us to introduce a very handy Keras feature: callbacks. A callback is a Python function that is called at various points in the training process, for example when a new epoch begins or an epoch has just finished.

You've seen that if you train for too long, the model will eventually start to overfit and the validation accuracy becomes worse.

It's hard to say beforehand exactly when this will happen, but it does mean that the last epoch isn't necessarily the best one. Ideally, you'd stop training just before overfitting starts to happen.

For this, you can add an `EarlyStopping` callback that will halt the training once the `"val_acc"` metric, the validation accuracy, stops improving. The `patience` argument is the number of epochs with no improvement after which the training will be stopped.

It's also smart to save a model **checkpoint** every so often. This is a copy of the model's weights it has learned up to that point.

For this you'd use the `ModelCheckpoint` callback. It saves a copy of the trained model whenever the metric you're interested in has improved. Here you're monitoring `"val_acc"`, so every time the validation accuracy goes up, a new model checkpoint is saved.

```python
checkpoint_dir = "checkpoints/"
checkpoint_name = (checkpoint_dir
    + "multisnacks-{val_loss:.4f}-{val_acc:.4f}.hdf5")

if not os.path.exists(checkpoint_dir):
    os.makedirs(checkpoint_dir)

def create_callbacks():
    return [
        callbacks.EarlyStopping(
            monitor="val_acc",
            patience=10,
            verbose=1),
        callbacks.ModelCheckpoint(
            checkpoint_name,
            monitor="val_acc",
```

```
        verbose=1,
        save_best_only=True),
    ]

my_callbacks = create_callbacks()
```

> **Note**: You need to make sure the checkpoints directory already exists, or
> Keras will give an error message when it tries to save the checkpoint. That's
> why you do os.makedirs() first. By the way, if you ever wanted to save the
> current state of the model by hand, you can always write
> model.save("convnet.h5"). HDF5, with the extension .hdf5 or .h5, is the
> file format used by Keras to save its models. You can view these files with
> Netron.

Now you can train the model. You need to pass the array with the callback objects to
fit_generator()'s callbacks argument.

```
histories = []
histories.append(top_model.fit_generator(
    train_generator,
    steps_per_epoch=len(train_generator),
    epochs=10,
    callbacks=my_callbacks,
    validation_data=val_generator,
    validation_steps=len(val_generator),
    workers=8))
```

Training this model should be pretty speedy on a computer with a GPU since you're
only training the one Dense layer for the logistic regression. On the author's iMac,
however, it takes about six minutes per epoch. That's too slow to be practical, which
is why he's glad to also have a Ubuntu machine with a fast GPU.

Remember that Create ML and Turi Create trained their models using a two-step
process:

1. First, they extract the features from all the training images. This can take a while.

2. But once they have those feature vectors, training the logistic regression is fast.

By doing the feature extraction just once, Turi and Create ML could save a lot of time
in the training stage. It is also possible to do this with Keras, see the SqueezeNet
notebook for details. But because you're doing a lot of data augmentation, it's not
really worth the trouble.

Having feature extraction as a separate step only makes sense if you plan to reuse the same images in every epoch. But with random data augmentation — where images are rotated, flipped and distorted in many other ways — no two images are ever the same. And so all the feature vectors will be different for every epoch.

That's why this MobileNet-based model is trained end-to-end and not in two separate stages. In every epoch, Keras needs to compute all the feature vectors again because all the training images are now slightly different from last time. It's a bit slower, but that's a small price to pay for having a much larger training set with very little effort.

After training for 10 epochs, the validation accuracy stops going up. Here is the code for plotting the accuracy again (same as in the last chapter):

```python
def combine_histories():
    history = {
        "loss": [],
        "val_loss": [],
        "acc": [],
        "val_acc": []
    }

    for h in histories:
        for k in history.keys():
            history[k] += h.history[k]
    return history

history = combine_histories()

def plot_accuracy(history):
    fig = plt.figure(figsize=(10, 6))
    plt.plot(history["acc"])
    plt.plot(history["val_acc"])
    plt.xlabel("Epoch")
    plt.ylabel("Accuracy")
    plt.legend(["Train", "Validation"])
    plt.show()

plot_accuracy(history)
```

The plot looks like this. You can see the validation accuracy flattens out:

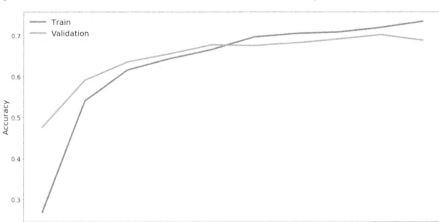

MobileNet accuracy for the first ten epochs

In fact, Keras prints a message that says as much:

```
Epoch 00010: val_acc did not improve from 0.70262
```

Because of the `EarlyStopping` callback, if there are more than 10 of such epochs in a row, Keras will stop training. But, at this point, you've only trained for 10 epochs in total, so that callback didn't kick in here yet. The other callback, `ModelCheckpoint`, did do its job and saved a new version of the model whenever the validation accuracy improved:

```
Epoch 00009: val_acc improved from 0.69215 to 0.70262, saving
model to
checkpoints/multisnacks-1.0450-0.7026.hdf5
```

The two numbers in the filename, `1.0450` and `0.7026` respectively, are the validation loss and accuracy. After only nine epochs, this model already got up to 70% accuracy. Sweet! That's a lot better than your previous models and also improves on Turi's results already. But you're not done yet...

Fine-tuning the feature extractor

At this point, it's a good idea to start **fine-tuning** the feature extractor. So far, you've been using the pre-trained MobileNet as the feature extractor. This was trained on the ImageNet dataset, which contains a large variety of photos from 1,000 different kinds of objects.

The pretrained MobileNet knows a lot about photos in general, including photos of food items. This is why you've trained a classifier on top of MobileNet's layers so that it can translate this general knowledge about photos to your own 20 categories of snacks.

But the pretrained feature extractor contains a lot of irrelevant knowledge, too, about animals, vehicles and all kinds of other things that are not snacks. We don't need this knowledge for our task of classifying snacks.

With fine-tuning, you can adjust the knowledge inside the feature extractor to make it more relevant to your own data. Now the feature extractor itself already understands more about this specific task.

To fine-tune the MobileNet layers, first set them to trainable and then compile the model again:

```
for layer in base_model.layers:
    layer.trainable = True

top_model.compile(loss="categorical_crossentropy",
                  optimizer=optimizers.Adam(lr=1e-4),
                  metrics=["accuracy"])
```

It's important to use a lower learning rate now, lr=1e-4. That's because you don't want to completely throw away everything the MobileNet layers have learned already — you only want to tweak these values a little.

It's better to set the learning rate too low than too high at this point, or you might end up destroying useful knowledge. The author found 1e-4 by experimenting a bit.

Run top_model.summary() and you'll see that there are now over 3 million trainable parameters instead of just 20,500. There are still also non-trainable parameters; these are used by the BatchNormalization layers to keep track of internal state.

Simply run the cell with top_model.fit_generator() again to start fine-tuning. The loss may bounce around a bit in the beginning because suddenly the optimizer has a lot more work to do.

It also lost track of where it was because you compiled the model again. But you should see the training and validation accuracy start to improve quite quickly again. If not, lower the learning rate.

> **Note**: Training is suddenly a lot slower now because this time Keras needs to train all the layers, not just the Dense layer. On the author's iMac, the estimated time for a single epoch went up from six to 20 minutes. On the Linux machine with the GPU, the time went from 10 seconds per epoch to 30 seconds — not nearly as bad. It's also possible that you will get an out-of-memory error at this point. There are more parameters to update and so the GPU needs more RAM. If that happens, make the batch size smaller and run the cells that create the generators again.

After about 10 epochs, the validation loss and accuracy no longer appear to improve. When that happens, it's useful to reduce the learning rate. Here, you make it three times smaller:

```
K.set_value(top_model.optimizer.lr,
            K.get_value(top_model.optimizer.lr) / 3)
```

Now, train again for five or so epochs. For the author, the validation accuracy immediately shot up from 0.79 to 0.81, even though it had stopped improving earlier.

When the learning rate is too large, the optimizer may not be able to hone in on a good solution. This is why you start with a large-ish learning rate, to quickly get in the neighborhood of a good solution, and then make the learning rate smaller over time, in order to get as close to this solution as you can.

You can repeat this process of lowering the learning rate and training for a few epochs several more times until the loss and accuracy are no longer noticeably improving.

> **Tip**: Keras also has a LearningRateScheduler callback that can automatically reduce the learning rate, which is especially useful for training sessions with hundreds of epochs that you don't want to babysit. The ReduceLROnPlateau callback will automatically lower the learning rate when the validation accuracy or loss has stopped improving. Very handy!

The final loss and accuracy plots will look like this:

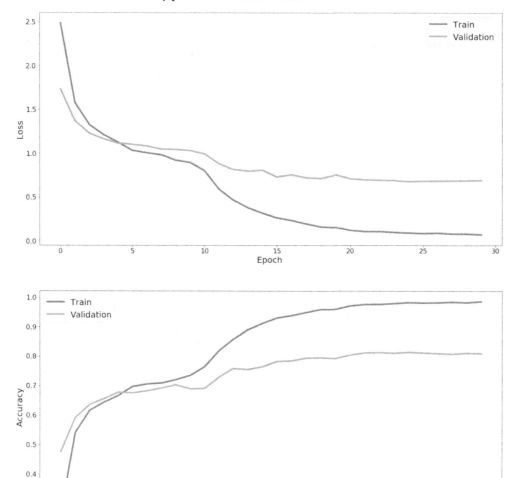

The loss curves (top) and accuracy curves (bottom)

This was over a combined 30 epochs of training. Notice how there's a bump in the lines at the points where you reduced the learning rate. Eventually, the curves flatten out, meaning that the model has learned all it can from the data.

```
top_model.evaluate_generator(test_generator,
    steps=len(test_generator))
```

The final accuracy on the test set is 82%. That's a lot better than the SqueezeNet model from Turi Create. There are two reasons for this: 1) MobileNet is more powerful than SqueezeNet; and 2) Turi Create does not use data augmentation. Granted, 82% is still not as good as the model from Create ML, which had 91% accuracy, but that in turn uses a proprietary feature extractor that is more powerful than MobileNet. As we said before, it's all about finding a compromise between results, speed and size.

> **Note:** Notice that in the first few epochs, the validation loss and accuracy are actually a bit better than the training loss and accuracy. This is not unusual, especially with a relatively small validation set. It can also happen when you have a Dropout layer, which is only active for the training set but not for testing on the validation set. You'll learn about dropout in the next section.

Regularization and dropout

So you've got a model with a pretty decent score already, but notice in the above plots that there is a big gap between the training loss and validation loss. Also, the training accuracy keeps increasing — reaching almost 100% — while the validation accuracy flattens out and stops improving.

This doesn't necessarily mean that the model is overfitting. The training accuracy is *always* a little higher than the validation accuracy because it's always easier for the model to make good predictions on the training images than on images it has never seen before.

However, this is only a bad thing when the validation loss or accuracy becomes worse over time. That doesn't appear to be happening here... while the validation score isn't as good as the training score, it doesn't actually become worse — it just flattens out.

Still, it would be better if the validation curves were closer to the training curves. You can do this by adding **regularization** to the model. This makes it harder for the model to get too attached to the training images. Regularization is very useful, but keep in mind that it isn't some magic trick that makes your validation score suddenly a lot better — it actually does the opposite and makes the training score a bit worse.

There are different methods for regularization, but what they all have in common is that they make learning more difficult. This discourages the model from learning unnecessary details, which may cause overfitting, and forces it to focus only on what is truly important.

You'll use the following forms of regularization:

- Batch normalization

- Dropout

- L2 penalty

The MobileNet portion of the model already has a `BatchNormalization` layer after every convolution layer. These **batch norm** layers act as a type of regularizer. The main purpose of batch normalization is to make sure that the data that flows between the layers stay healthy.

The calculations involved introduce a small amount of noise, or random variations in the data, into the network. This noise prevents the model from memorizing specific image details. Regularization is not the main purpose of batch normalization, but it's a nice side benefit.

You will add the other two types of regularization to the logistic regression portion of the model. Create this new classifier model:

```
from keras import regularizers
top_model = Sequential()
top_model.add(base_model)
top_model.add(GlobalAveragePooling2D())
top_model.add(Dropout(0.5))                      # this line is new
top_model.add(Dense(num_classes,
              kernel_regularizer=regularizers.l2(0.001))) # new
top_model.add(Activation("softmax"))
```

There are only two new things here: a `Dropout` layer after the global pooling layer and the `Dense` layer now has a **kernel regularizer**.

Dropout is a special kind of layer that randomly removes elements from the tensor by setting them to zero. It works on the 1,024-element feature vector that is the output from the global pooling layer. Since you used 0.5 as the dropout percentage, `Dropout` will randomly set half of the feature vector's elements to zero. This makes it harder for the model to remember things, because, at any given time, half of its input data is randomly removed — and it's a different half for each training image.

Randomly removing elements from the feature vector seems like an odd thing to do, but it keeps the neural network from becoming lazy. The connections from the `Dense` layer cannot depend too much on any given feature since that feature might drop out of the network at random. Using dropout is a great technique to stop the neural network from relying too much on remembering specific training examples.

Aurélien Géron, in *Hands-on Machine Learning with Scikit-Learn & TensorFlow* at oreil.ly/2nzmN8L, compares this to a workplace where, on any given day, some percentage of the people might not come to work. In such a workplace, everyone must be able to do critical tasks and must cooperate with more co-workers. This makes the company more resilient and less dependent on any single worker.

The dropout rate is a hyperparameter, so you get to decide how high or low it should be. 0.5 is a good default choice. To disable dropout, simply set the rate to zero.

> **Note**: Dropout is always disabled at inference time. This layer is only active during training. We wouldn't want half of our predictions to randomly disappear!

The other form of regularization you're using is an **L2 penalty** on the Dense layer. You've already briefly seen this in the chapter, "Digging Deeper Into Turi Create." When you use a kernel regularizer, as Keras calls it, the weights for that layer are added to the loss term. **L2** means that it actually adds the square of the weights to the loss term, so that large weights count as extra heavy.

Since it's the optimizer's job to make the loss as small as possible, it is now encouraged to keep the weights small, too, because large weights result in a large loss value. This prevents situations where some features get really large weights, making them seem more important than features with very small weights. Thanks to the L2 penalty, the weights are more balanced, reducing the chance of overfitting.

The value 0.001 is a hyperparameter called **weight decay**. This lets you tweak how important the L2 penalty is in the loss function. If this value is too large, then the L2 penalty overshadows the rest of the loss terms and the model will have a hard time learning anything. If it's too small, then the L2 penalty doesn't really have any effect.

Now, you can compile this new model again and train it. Make sure to first train a few epochs with the MobileNet layers frozen, and then set trainable = True to fine-tune. And don't forget to periodically lower the learning rate! When you plot the loss curves, you'll notice that the validation loss now stays much closer to the training loss.

> **Note**: With an L2 penalty, the initial loss can be much higher than the expected `np.log(num_classes)`. This is not so strange, because it adds the L2-norm of the weights to the loss as well. Starting out with a high loss value is usually no problem, as long as it goes down during training. If the loss doesn't go down, the first thing to try is using a lower learning rate. Note that the validation loss does not include this extra L2 term.

Tune those hyperparameters

You've seen three different hyperparameters now:

- the learning rate

- the dropout probability

- the weight decay factor for L2 regularization

Choosing appropriate values for these settings — known as **hyperparameter tuning** — is essential for getting the training process to work optimally.

The way most people do hyperparameter tuning, is just by trying stuff and then seeing how the validation loss or accuracy changes. If you have a lot of hyperparameters, this can be a time-consuming job. There are ways to automate this, by using a grid search or a random search, which will try all possible combinations of the hyperparameters.

It's very important that you use the validation set for tuning the hyperparameters, not the training set or the test set. The test set should only be used to verify how well your final model works, not for experiments with the hyperparameters.

There is a very good reason for this: When you tweak the hyperparameters based on the validation results, train the model with the new settings, tweak the hyperparameters again, and so on... then you're indirectly training the model on the validation set, too.

You're now manually influencing the training process by making changes based on the validation results. In a way, the images from the validation set are "leaking" into the training process. That's OK since that's what the validation set is for. But you don't want this to happen to your test set, otherwise it can no longer paint a realistic picture of how well your model generalizes on images it has never seen before — because indirectly it *will* have already seen these images.

You can keep tweaking these hyperparameters to squeeze a bit more performance out of the model, but, at some point, you have to call it good enough. The author got the best results with a dropout rate of 0.7 and a weight decay of 0.01. This model scored 85% on the test set, which is again a few percentage points better than before.

How good is the model really?

The very last training epoch is not necessarily the best — it's possible the validation accuracy didn't improve or even got much worse — so in order to evaluate the final model on the test set, let's load the best model back in first:

```
from keras.models import load_model
best_model = load_model(checkpoint_dir +
                        "multisnacks-0.7162-0.8419.hdf5")
```

This loads the model from a checkpoint file that was saved by the ModelCheckpoint callback. This HDF5 file contains the learned parameters for the model but also the architecture definition. (Replace the filename with your own best checkpoint.)

> **Note**: The multisnacks-0.7162-0.8419.hdf5 file is included in this chapter's resources under **final/MobileNet/checkpoints**. If you were unable to train the model on your own computer, feel free to load this version.

> **Note**: The above instructions are for Keras version 2.2.4 and Keras-Applications 1.0.8. It may or may not work with newer or older versions.

Now you can evaluate this best model against the test set:

```
best_model.evaluate_generator(test_generator,
                              steps=len(test_generator))
```

For the author's best model, this printed [0.6338246429667753, 0.8634453781512605]. The first number is the loss, which isn't really that interesting, here.

The second number is the accuracy, over 86%. The Turi Create SqueezeNet model scored 67%, so we're doing quite a bit better, here. And it gets in the neighborhood of Create ML's score of 91%.

Take a closer look at what the model predicts:

```
test_generator.reset()
probabilities = best_model.predict_generator(test_generator,
                                    steps=len(test_generator))
predicted_labels = np.argmax(probabilities, axis=-1)
```

The `predict_generator()` function runs the model on all the images from the test set and puts the predicted probabilities in the `probabilities` array. Then you take the argmax over every result to find the index of the class with the highest probability.

> **Note**: Before using `predict_generator()` you must first call `reset()` on the generator object. Otherwise, `predict_generator()` may not start at the right image and the predictions won't make any sense.

The variable `predicted_labels` is a NumPy array with 952 numbers, one for each test set image. These are the predicted class indices. The correct, or ground-truth, class indices can be obtained from the test set generator:

```
target_labels = test_generator.classes
```

Now, you can compare these two arrays to find out where the classifier was correct and where it made mistakes, the so-called confusion matrix:

```
from sklearn import metrics
conf = metrics.confusion_matrix(target_labels, predicted_labels)
```

The `conf` variable is another NumPy array, of shape 20×20. It's easiest to interpret when plotted as a heatmap:

```
import seaborn as sns

def plot_confusion_matrix(conf, labels, figsize=(8, 8)):
    fig = plt.figure(figsize=figsize)
    heatmap = sns.heatmap(conf, annot=True, fmt="d")
    heatmap.xaxis.set_ticklabels(labels, rotation=45,
                            ha="right", fontsize=12)
    heatmap.yaxis.set_ticklabels(labels, rotation=0,
                            ha="right", fontsize=12)
    plt.xlabel("Predicted label", fontsize=12)
    plt.ylabel("True label", fontsize=12)
    plt.show()

# Find the class names that correspond to the indices
```

```
labels = [""] * num_classes
for k, v in test_generator.class_indices.items():
    labels[v] = k

plot_confusion_matrix(conf, labels, figsize=(14, 14))
```

This plots the following confusion matrix:

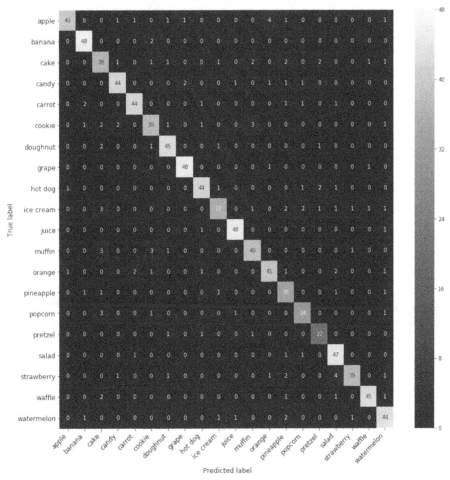

The confusion matrix for the MobileNet model

On the diagonal — the bright squares — are the images that were correctly matched. Everything else is an incorrect match. Ideally, there are only numbers on the diagonal and zeros everywhere else. From this confusion matrix, you can immediately see that apples are often wrongly predicted to be oranges (four times), and cookies and muffins got mixed up three times.

> **Note**: Earlier, we mentioned that the generator for the test set should not use data augmentation. Otherwise, running `evaluate_generator()` more than once would give different scores each time. You can actually use such differences to your advantage, known as **TTA**, or Test Time Augmentation.
>
> For example, instead of making only one prediction for each test image, you could do it once for the normal image and once for the image flipped. Then the final score is the average of these two predictions. The more different variations of the test image you use, the better the average score will be.
>
> This trick is often used in competitions to squeeze a few extra points out of the model's performance. Of course, making multiple predictions per image is also slower and therefore not really suitable for mobile apps.

Precision, recall, F1-score

It's also useful to make a precision-recall report:

```
print(metrics.classification_report(target_labels,
               predicted_labels, target_names=labels))
```

This prints the following:

	precision	recall	f1-score	support
apple	0.95	0.80	0.87	50
banana	0.91	0.96	0.93	50
cake	0.70	0.76	0.73	50
candy	0.90	0.88	0.89	50
carrot	0.92	0.88	0.90	50
cookie	0.81	0.78	0.80	50
doughnut	0.88	0.90	0.89	50
grape	0.94	0.96	0.95	50
hot dog	0.90	0.88	0.89	50
ice cream	0.88	0.74	0.80	50
juice	0.94	0.96	0.95	50
muffin	0.85	0.83	0.84	48
orange	0.85	0.82	0.84	50
pineapple	0.71	0.88	0.79	40
popcorn	0.85	0.85	0.85	40
pretzel	0.79	0.88	0.83	25
salad	0.81	0.94	0.87	50
strawberry	0.93	0.80	0.86	49
waffle	0.94	0.90	0.92	50
watermelon	0.81	0.88	0.85	50

			0.86	952
accuracy			0.86	952
macro avg	0.86	0.86	0.86	952
weighted avg	0.87	0.86	0.86	952

Precision means: how many of the images that were classified as being X really are X? For example, the precision on hot dog is pretty good, 0.90. Most of the time when the model thinks something is a hot dog, it really is a hot dog.

Precision is rather low on pineapple, 0.71, which means the model found a lot of objects that it thinks are pineapple that really aren't. You can see this in the confusion matrix in the column for pineapple. When you sum up the numbers in this column, you get 49 total pineapple predictions, of which only 35 are correct, so the precision is 35/49 or 0.71. Almost one out of four images that the model thinks is a pineapple, actually isn't a pineapple. Ouch, there's room for improvement there!

By the way, instead of counting up these numbers by hand, it's much simpler to write some Python:

```python
# Get the class index for pineapple
idx = test_generator.class_indices["pineapple"]

# Find how many images were predicted to be pineapple
total_predicted = np.sum(predicted_labels == idx)

# Find how many images really are pineapple (true positives)
correct = conf[idx, idx]

# The precision is then the true positives divided by
# the true + false positives
precision = correct / total_predicted
print(precision)
```

This should print `0.71`, just as in the report. As you can tell from the math, the more **false positives** there are, i.e. images the model thinks belong to class X but that aren't, the lower the precision.

Recall means: how many of the images of class X did the model find? This is in some ways the opposite of precision.

Recall for banana is high, 0.96, so the images that contained bananas were often correctly found by the model. The recall for ice cream is quite low at 74%, so over one-fourth of the ice cream images were classified as something else. To verify this in Python:

```
# Get the class index for ice cream
idx = test_generator.class_indices["ice cream"]

# Find how many images are supposed to be ice cream
total_expected = np.sum(target_labels == idx)

# How many ice cream images did we find?
correct = conf[idx, idx]

# The recall is then the true positives divided by
# the true positives + false negatives
recall = correct / total_expected
print(recall)
```

This should print `0.74`. The more **false negatives** there are, i.e., things that are wrongly predicted to not be class X, the lower the recall for X.

The classification report also includes the **F1-score**. This is a combination of precision and recall and is useful if you want to get an average of the two.

The classes with the highest F1-score are grape and juice, both at 0.95. You can safely say that this classifier works very well for images with grapes or juices. The class with the lowest F1-score, 0.73, is cake. If you wanted to improve this classifier, the first thing you might want to do is find more and better training images for the cake category.

> **Note**: It's quite useful to be able to write a bit of Python code. Often you'll need to write short code snippets like the above to take a closer look at the predictions. Get comfortable with Python if you're interested in building your own models!

What are the worst predictions?

The confusion matrix and precision-recall report can already give hints about things you can do to improve the model. There are other useful things you can do. You've already seen that the cake category is the worst overall. It can also be enlightening to look at images that were predicted wrongly but that have very high confidence scores. These are the "most wrong" predictions. Why is the model so confident, yet so wrong about these images?

For example, you can use the following code to find the images that the model was the most wrong about. It uses some advanced NumPy sorcery:

```python
# Find for which images the predicted class is wrong
wrong_images = np.where(predicted_labels != target_labels)[0]

# For every prediction, find the largest probability value;
# this is the probability of the winning class for this image
probs_max = np.max(probabilities, axis=-1)

# Sort the probabilities from the wrong images from low to high
idx = np.argsort(probs_max[wrong_images])

# Reverse the order (high to low), and keep the 5 highest ones
idx = idx[::-1][:5]

# Get the indices of the images with the worst predictions
worst_predictions = wrong_images[idx]

index2class = {v:k for k,v in
test_generator.class_indices.items()}

for i in worst_predictions:
    print("%s was predicted as '%s' %.4f" % (
        test_generator.filenames[i],
        index2class[predicted_labels[i]],
        probs_max[i]
    ))
```

This will output:

```
strawberry/09d140146c09b309.jpg was predicted as 'salad' 0.9999
apple/671292276d92cee4.jpg was predicted as 'pineapple' 0.9907
muffin/3b25998aac3f7ab4.jpg was predicted as 'cake' 0.9899
pineapple/0eebf86343d79a23.jpg was predicted as 'banana' 0.9897
cake/bc41ce28fc883cd5.jpg was predicted as 'waffle' 0.9885
```

It can also be instructive to actually look at those images:

```
from keras.preprocessing import image
img = image.load_img(test_data_dir +
        test_generator.filenames[worst_predictions[0]])
plt.imshow(img)
```

Yep, it's not hard to see why the model got confused, here. You could make a good case that this image is labeled wrong in the test set — or at least is very misleading:

The worst prediction... or is it?

A note on imbalanced classes

There is much more to say about image classifiers than we have room for in this book. One topic that comes up a lot is how to deal with **imbalanced data**.

In a binary classifier that needs to distinguish between **disease present** (positive) and **not present** (negative) in X-ray images, most X-rays will not show any disease at all. That's a good thing for the patients involved, but it also makes a harder job for the classifier. If the disease happens to only 1% of the patients, the classifier could simply always predict "disease not present" and it would be correct 99% of the time. But such a classifier is also pretty useless... 99% correct sounds impressive, but it's not always good enough.

Or let's say you want to train a classifier that can distinguish between the following cases: cat, dog, neither cat or dog. In order to train such a classifier, you'll obviously need pictures of cats and dogs, but also pictures of things that are not cats and dogs. This last category must be much larger because it needs to cover a wide variety of objects, and the classifier will need to lump all of these into the "not cat or dog" category. The risk here is that the classifier will only learn about that one big category and not about the cat and dog categories, which have many fewer images.

There are various techniques you can use to deal with class imbalance, such as oversampling where you use the images from the smaller categories more often, undersampling where you use fewer images from the larger categories, or setting weights on the classes so that the bigger category has a smaller effect on the loss.

Turi Create and Create ML currently have no options for this, so if you need to build a classifier for an imbalanced dataset, Keras is a better choice.

Here ends our discussion of how to train image classifiers. Next up, you'll learn how to convert the trained Keras model to a Core ML model that you can use in your iOS and macOS apps.

Converting to Core ML

When you write `model.save("name.h5")` or use the `ModelCheckpoint` callback, Keras saves the model in its own format, HDF5. In order to use this model from Core ML, you have to convert it to a **.mlmodel** file first. For this, you'll need to use the **coremltools** Python package.

The **kerasenv** environment already has coremltools installed. Just in case you need to install it by hand, type this into a command line prompt:

```
pip install -U coremltools
```

You can enter the following commands into the Jupyter notebook or just follow along with MobileNet.ipynb. This chapter's resources also include a separate Python script, **convert-to-coreml.py** that first loads the model from the best checkpoint and then does the conversion. Using a separate script makes it easy to add the model conversion step to a build script or CI (Continuous Integration) server.

First, import the package:

```
import coremltools
```

You may get some warning messages at this point about incompatible versions of Keras and TensorFlow. These tools change quicker than coremltools can keep up with, but usually, these warnings are not a problem. (If you get an error during conversion, you may need to downgrade your Keras install to the last supported version.)

Since this is a classifier model, coremltools needs to know what the label names are. It's important that these are in the same order as in `train_generator.class_indices`:

```
labels = ["apple", "banana", "cake", "candy", "carrot",
          "cookie", "doughnut", "grape", "hot dog",
          "ice cream", "juice", "muffin", "orange",
          "pineapple", "popcorn", "pretzel", "salad",
          "strawberry", "waffle", "watermelon"]
```

Now, you can use the Keras converter to create a Core ML model:

```
coreml_model = coremltools.converters.keras.convert(
    best_model,
    input_names="image",
    image_input_names="image",
    output_names="labelProbability",
    predicted_feature_name="label",
    red_bias=-1,
    green_bias=-1,
    blue_bias=-1,
    image_scale=2/255.0,
    class_labels=labels)
```

This has quite a few arguments, so let's look at them in turn:

- The first argument is the Keras model object. Here you're using the `best_model` object that you loaded in the previous section.

- `input_names` tells the converter what the inputs should be named in the .mlmodel file. Since this is an image classifier, it makes sense to use the name `"image"`. This is also the name that's used by Xcode when it automatically generates the Swift code for your Core ML model.

- `image_input_names` tells the converter that the input called `"image"` should be treated as an image. This is what lets you pass a `CVPixelBuffer` object to the Core ML model. If you leave out this option, the input is expected to be an `MLMultiArray` object, which is not as easy to work with.

- `output_names` and `predicted_feature_name` are the names of the two outputs. The first one is `"labelProbability"` and contains a dictionary that maps the predicted probabilities to the names of the classes. The second one is `"label"` and is a string that contains the class label of the best prediction. These are also the names that Turi Create used.

- `red_bias`, `green_bias`, `blue_bias`, and `image_scale` are used to normalize the image. MobileNet, like the other models you've trained, expects the pixels to be in the range [-1, 1] instead of the usual [0, 255]. The chosen values are equivalent to the normalization function you've used before: `image / 127.5 - 1`. If these settings are incorrect, Core ML will make bogus predictions.

- `class_labels` contains the list of label names you defined earlier.

When you run this code, coremltools goes through the Keras model layer-by-layer and prints its progress.

You can also supply metadata, which can be helpful for the users of your model, especially the descriptions of the inputs and outputs:

```
coreml_model.author = "Your Name Here"
coreml_model.license = "Public Domain"
coreml_model.short_description = "Image classifier for 20
different types of snacks"

coreml_model.input_description["image"] = "Input image"
coreml_model.output_description["labelProbability"]= "Prediction
probabilities"
coreml_model.output_description["label"]= "Class label of top
prediction"
```

At this point, it's useful to write `print(coreml_model)` to make sure that everything is correct. The `input` should be of type `imageType`, not `multiArrayType`, and there should be two outputs: one a `dictionaryType` and the other a `stringType`.

Finally, save the model to an .mlmodel file:

```
coreml_model.save("MultiSnacks.mlmodel")
```

If you weren't on your Mac already, then download this .mlmodel file to your Mac.

Double-click the file to open it in Xcode:

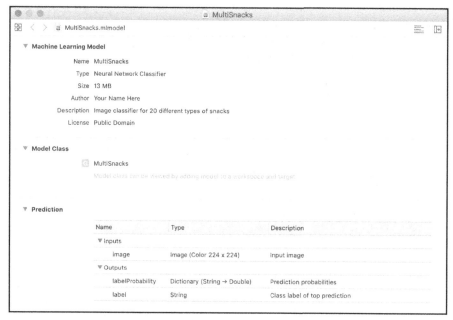

Your very own Core ML model

Put it in the app and try it out!

Challenges

Challenge 1: Train using MobileNet

Train the binary classifier using MobileNet and see how the score compares to the Turi Create model. The easiest way to do this is to copy all the images for the healthy categories into a folder called healthy and all the unhealthy images into a folder called unhealthy. (Or maybe you could train a "foods I don't like" vs. "foods I like" classifier.)

> **Note**: For a binary classifier, you can keep using softmax and the loss function "categorical_crossentropy", which gives you two output values, one for each category. Alternatively, you can choose to have just a single output value, in which case the final activation should not be softmax but

> Activation("sigmoid"), the logistic sigmoid. The corresponding loss
> function is "binary_crossentropy". If you feel up to a challenge, try using
> this sigmoid + binary cross-entropy for the classifier. The class_mode for the
> ImageDataGenerator should then be "binary" instead of "categorical".

Challenge 2: Add more layers

Try adding more layers to the top model. You could add a Conv2D layer, like so:

```
top_model.add(Conv2D(num_filters, 3, padding="same"))
top_model.add(BatchNormalization())
top_model.add(Activation("relu"))
```

```
**Tip**: To add a `Conv2D` layer after the
`GlobalAveragePooling2D` layer, you have to add a `Reshape`
layer in between, because global pooling turns the tensor into a
vector, while `Conv2D` layers want a tensor with three
dimensions.
```

```
top_model.add(GlobalAveragePooling2D())
top_model.add(Reshape((1, 1, 1024)))
top_model.add(Conv2D(...))
```

Feel free to experiment with the arrangement of layers in this top model. In general,
adding more layers will make the classifier more powerful, but too many layers will
make the model big and slow. Keep an eye on the number of trainable parameters!

Challenge 3: Experiment with optimizers

In this chapter and the last you've used the Adam optimizer, but Keras offers a
selection of different optimizers. Adam generally gives good results and is fast, but
you may want to play with some of the other optimizers, such as RMSprop and SGD.
You'll need to experiment with what learning rates work well for these optimizers.

Challenge 4: Train using MobileNetV2

There is a version 2 of MobileNet, also available in Keras. MobileNet V2 is smaller
and more powerful than V1. Just like ResNet50, it uses so-called **residual
connections**, an advanced way to connect different layers together. Try training the
classifier using MobileNetV2 from the keras.applications.mobilenetv2 module.

Challenge 5: Train MobileNet from scratch

Try training MobileNet from scratch on the snacks dataset. You've seen that transfer learning and fine-tuning works very well, but only because MobileNet has been pre-trained on a large dataset of millions of photos. To create an "empty" MobileNet, use `weights=None` instead of `weights="imagenet"`. You'll find that it's actually quite difficult to train a large neural network from scratch on such a small dataset. See whether you can get this model to learn anything, and, if so, what sort of accuracy it achieves on the test set.

Challenge 6: Fully train the model

Once you've established a set of hyperparameters that works well for your machine learning task, it's smart to combine the training set and validation set into one big dataset and train the model on the full thing. You don't really need the validation set anymore at this point — you already know that this combination of hyperparameters will work well — and so you might as well train on these images too. After all, every extra bit of training data helps! Try it out and see how well the model scores on the test set now. (Of course, you still shouldn't train on the test data.)

Key points

- MobileNet uses depthwise convolutions because they're less expensive than regular convolution. Ideal for running models on mobile devices. Instead of pooling layers, MobileNet uses convolutions with a stride of 2.

- Training a large neural network on a small dataset is almost impossible. It's smarter to do transfer learning with a pre-trained model, but even then you want to use data augmentation to artificially enlarge your training set. It's also a good idea to adapt the feature extractor to your own data by fine-tuning it.

- Regularization helps to build stable, reliable models. Besides increasing the amount of training data, you can use batch normalization, dropout and an L2 penalty to stop the model from memorizing specific training examples. The larger the number of learnable parameters in the model, the more important regularization becomes.

- You can use Keras callbacks to do automated learning rate annealing, save model checkpoints, and many other handy tasks.

- Try your model on the test set to see how good it really is. Use a confusion matrix and a precision-recall report to see where the model makes mistakes. Look at the images that it gets most wrong to see if they are really mistakes, or if your dataset needs improvement.

- Use coremltools to convert your Keras model to Core ML.

Chapter 9: Beyond Classification

By Matthijs Hollemans

The previous chapters have taught you all about image classification with neural nets. But neural networks can be used for many other computer vision tasks. In this chapter and the next, you'll look at two advanced examples:

- **Object detection**: find multiple objects in an image.

- **Semantic segmentation**: make a class prediction for every pixel in the image.

Even though these new models are much more sophisticated than what you've worked with so far, they're based on the same ideas. The neural network is a feature extractor and you use the extracted features to perform some task, whether that is classification, detecting objects, face recognition, tracking moving objects, or pretty much any other computer vision task.

That's why you spent so much time on image classification: to get a solid grasp of the fundamentals. But now it's time to take things a few steps further...

Where is it?

Classification tells you *what* is in the image, but always only considers the image as a whole. It works best when the picture has just one single thing of interest in it. If your classifier is trained to tell apart cats and dogs, and the image contains both a cat and a dog, then the answer is anyone's guess.

An **object detection** model has no problem dealing with such images. The goal of object detection is to find all the objects inside an image, even if they are of different types. You can think of it as a classifier for specific image regions.

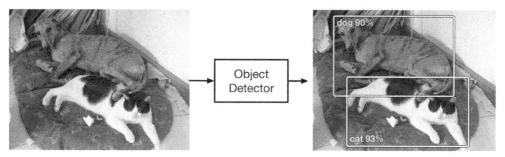

An object detector can find all your furry friends

The object detector not only finds what the objects are but also *where* they are located in the image. It does this by predicting one or more **bounding boxes**, which are simply rectangular regions in the image.

A bounding box is described by four numbers, representing either the corner points of the rectangle or the center point plus a width and height:

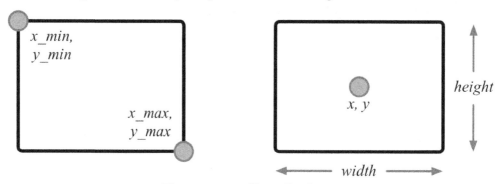

The two types of bounding boxes

Both types are used in practice, but this chapter uses the one with the corner points.

Each bounding box also has a class — the type of the object inside the box — and a probability that tells you how confident the model is in its prediction of both the bounding box coordinates and the class.

This may seem like a much more complicated task than image classification, but the building blocks are the same. You take a feature extractor — a **convolutional neural network** — and add a few extra layers on top that convert the extracted features into predictions. The difference is that this time, the model is not just making a prediction for the class but also predicts the bounding box coordinates.

Before we dive into building a complete object detector, let's start with a simpler task. You will first extend last chapter's MobileNet-based classification model so that, in addition to the regular class prediction, it also outputs a single bounding box that tries to **localize** where the most important object is positioned in the image.

Just predict one bounding box, how hard could it be? (Answer: It's actually easier than you might think.)

The ground-truth will set you free

First, we should revisit the dataset.

Even though this new neural network will now make a different kind of prediction, the training procedure is still the same: You provide a dataset that consists of the images and the targets. You also provide a suitable loss function that calculates how wrong the model's predictions are by comparing them to the targets. Then you use a Stochastic Gradient Descent optimizer, such as Adam, to find the values for the model's learnable parameters that make the loss value as small as possible. Been there, done that.

No matter what task your neural network performs, whether it's predicting classes or bounding boxes — or the weather or stock prices or anything else — the training process is always the same. However, each task needs its own kind of training data. And for object detection tasks, the training data must contain bounding box information.

Previously, the targets were just the class names for the images, but now they must also include the so-called **ground-truth bounding boxes** that tell you where the objects are located inside the training images. Without these bounding box annotations, the loss function wouldn't be able to calculate how wrong the model is, and training the model to predict bounding boxes would be impossible.

We have provided the bounding box annotations for the snacks dataset as a set of CSV files. To get a feel for how they work, you'll now take a closer look at those annotations. Create a new Jupyter notebook or follow along with **final/ Localization.ipynb** from this chapter's resources.

> **Note**: As before, you'll be working with the **kerasenv** Python environment. Set up this environment with Anaconda Navigator or with conda create if necessary. If you don't already have it from previous chapters, download the snacks dataset by double-clicking **starter/snacks-download-link.webloc** and unzip this file. It contains the images on which you'll train the model, including the ground-truth annotations.

The easiest way to deal with CSV files in Python is by using the Pandas library. As usual, first import the needed packages — NumPy, Matplotlib and Pandas — and define the paths to where you downloaded the dataset:

```
import os, sys
import numpy as np
import pandas as pd

%matplotlib inline
import matplotlib.pyplot as plt

data_dir = "snacks"
train_dir = os.path.join(data_dir, "train")
val_dir = os.path.join(data_dir, "val")
test_dir = os.path.join(data_dir, "test")
```

Then load the **annotations-train.csv** file into a new Pandas DataFrame object:

```
path = os.path.join(data_dir, "annotations-train.csv")
train_annotations = pd.read_csv(path)
train_annotations.head()
```

The new dataframe train_annotations literally contains the exact same data as the CSV file. Pandas offers a lot of useful functions to manipulate this data. It's like using the functionality of SQL and Excel but inside Python, which is awesome if you're into that sort of thing.

The `train_annotations.head()` command gives as output the "head" of this dataframe, which is the first five rows:

	image_id	x_min	x_max	y_min	y_max	class_name	folder
0	009218ad38ab2010	0.192620	0.729831	0.127606	0.662219	cake	cake
1	009218ad38ab2010	0.802377	1.000000	0.102585	0.405338	ice cream	cake
2	009218ad38ab2010	0.814884	0.970607	0.121768	0.357798	ice cream	cake
3	00c7515143b32051	0.135084	0.904315	0.081735	0.909091	cake	muffin
4	00c7515143b32051	0.155722	0.910569	0.083403	0.893244	muffin	muffin

The first five lines of annotations-train.csv

The dataframe is actually much bigger: When you do `len(train_annotations)` it should print 7040. The dataframe has one row for each annotation. There are only about 4,800 images in the training set but some pictures have multiple objects in them — that's why there are more annotations than training images.

Some training images even contain objects of different types. The first three rows in the dataframe all belong to the same image, a picture of a cake, but apparently, there's also some ice cream in that image (see rows 1 and 2).

There are also a number of images in the training set that do not have bounding box annotations at all.

The coordinates of the bounding box are given by four numbers: x_min, x_max, y_min and y_max. The top-left corner of the box is (x_min, y_min), the bottom-right corner is (x_max, y_max). These are floating-point values — or "real-valued" numbers in math speak — between 0 and 1, also known as **normalized** coordinates.

It's convenient to use normalized coordinates because it makes them independent of the actual size of the image. This is important: remember that we scale down images to 224×224 pixels during training. If the bounding box coordinates were given in pixels as well, you'd have to remember to scale these down by the same amount... it gets messy really quick. With normalized coordinates, you don't have to worry about this.

The dataframe has two columns that contain class names: `class_name`, which is the class of the object inside this bounding box, and `folder`, which is where the image is stored in the dataset. `folder` is also the name of the class you used for training the classifier in the previous chapters. From now on, you'll only use the `class_name` for training, but you still need `folder` to know whence to load the image file.

While you're at it, you might as well load the annotations for the validation and test sets into their own dataframes. These each have about 1,400 rows:

```
val_annotations = pd.read_csv(os.path.join(data_dir,
                                  "annotations-val.csv"))
test_annotations = pd.read_csv(os.path.join(data_dir,
                                  "annotations-test.csv"))
```

Show me the data!

Now, let's have a proper look at these bounding boxes. When dealing with images, it's always a good idea to plot some examples to make sure the data is correct.

Remember the old adage, "Garbage in equals garbage out." If you're training your model on data that doesn't make sense, then neither will the model's predictions and you just wasted a lot of time and electricity. Don't be that person!

The code for plotting the images isn't terribly exciting, and so we've hidden this away in a file **helpers.py** that you can find in this chapter's downloads. It's a good idea to keep your notebook clean and put big functions and reusable code in separate Python files.

Copy **helpers.py** into the same folder that your Jupyter notebook is in, and then write:

```
image_width = 224
image_height = 224

from helpers import plot_image
```

This imports the `plot_image` function from the **helpers.py** module. `plot_image()` takes as arguments an image and a list of one or more bounding boxes and then draws the bounding boxes on top of the image.

Feel free to have a look inside **helpers.py** to see how this function works. You can also run `plot_image?` in a new cell to see its documentation, or `plot_image??` to see the full source code.

To get a single row from the dataframe, you can write the following:

```
train_annotations.iloc[0]
```

Here, `0` is the row index so this returns the fields from the first row:

```
image_id     009218ad38ab2010
x_min                 0.19262
x_max                0.729831
y_min                0.127606
y_max                0.662219
class_name               cake
folder                   cake
Name: 0, dtype: object
```

This is a so-called Pandas `Series` object and you can index it by name to get any of these fields, just like you would a dictionary. Now, grab an image from a single row in the dataframe and plot it together with its bounding box:

```
from keras.preprocessing import image

def plot_image_from_row(row, image_dir):
    # Load the image from "folder/image_id.jpg"
    image_path = os.path.join(image_dir, row["folder"],
                              row["image_id"] + ".jpg")
    img = image.load_img(image_path,
                target_size=(image_width, image_height))

    # Put the box coordinates and class name into a tuple
    bbox = (row["x_min"], row["x_max"],
            row["y_min"], row["y_max"], row["class_name"])

    # Draw the bounding box on top of the image
    plot_image(img, [bbox])
```

Now, call this new function to make the plot for a given annotation:

```
annotation = train_annotations.iloc[0]
plot_image_from_row(annotation, train_dir)
```

This draws the following image and bounding box (on the left):

The ground-truth box for row 0, cake (left) and row 2, ice cream (right)

You can see that the bounding box for the "cake" annotation neatly fits around the actual slice of cake in the picture. So it looks like the data is loaded correctly!

This training image actually has three annotations. The other two are for the ice cream dessert in the top-right corner of the photo. On the right is shown the annotation from row 2. The bounding box from row 1 is very similar and covers the same object.

In the Google Open Images dataset that these images and annotations come from, often the same object in the image has multiple annotations, created by different people. That doesn't appear to be a problem, as long as these annotations aren't too different. After all, more training data is usually better.

However, many images have fewer annotations than there are objects, which is not ideal. For example, the image at index 3,500 in the train_annotations dataframe, with image_id 0c429e9be7f72342, has four strawberries but only three annotations, two of which are for the same strawberry. Ideally, this image would have a unique annotation for each individual object.

To get a feel for what the dataset is like, have a look at some of the other images from the training, validation and test annotations.

Because not all objects from all images have annotations, and some have duplicates, this dataset isn't ideal — but, with over 7,000 annotations, it should still be good enough to train a decent object detection model. When you start building your own models, you'll find that you'll be spending a lot of time cleaning up your training data, filling in missing values, and so on. Your model will only ever be as good as the quality of the dataset, so it's worth putting in the time.

What about images without annotations?

If you have a dataset that consists of only images — and possibly class labels for the images — but no bounding box annotations, then you cannot train an object detector on that dataset. Not gonna happen; ain't no two ways about it.

First, you'll have to create the bounding box annotations for each image. This can be a time-consuming process, especially since you need lots of images, but fortunately there are tools that can help. A few suggestions:

- **RectLabel**, available on the Mac App Store. This is a powerful tool with many options, but it expects the annotations to be provided as a separate XML file for each image. This is not unusual — it's how the popular Pascal VOC dataset does things — but it won't be able to handle our CSV files. If you're getting serious about training your own object detectors, definitely give this tool a try.

- **Labelbox** at labelbox.io is an online tool for labeling training data for many different tasks, including object detection. This is a paid service but there is a free tier.

- **Simple Image Annotator** from github.com/sgp715 is a Python program that runs as a local web service. As its name implies, it's pretty simple to use and offers only basic editing features. The output is a CSV file but it's not 100% compatible with the CSV format we're using.

- **Sloth**, which is available at sloth.readthedocs.io, and is an advanced labeling tool. Requires Linux.

- **CVAT**, or Computer Vision Annotation Tool, which is available at github.com/opencv/cvat.

This is by no means an exhaustive list, and new annotation tools and services are springing up left and right.

There are about 800 images in the snacks dataset that do not have annotations. For the purposes of this book, you're just going to ignore those images and only train on the images that already do have annotations. But, if you're bored at home on a rainy Sunday afternoon and you feel like labeling the remaining images, don't let us stop you.

> **Note**: We just mentioned that RectLabel uses a different format for storing the annotations (XML) and that Simple Image Annotator does use a CSV file but with different fields. Some of the other tools output JSON files. This sort of thing is common. Every dataset will store its data in a slightly different way, and you'll often find yourself writing small Python scripts to convert data from one format to the other. A large part of any machine-learning project consists of finding data, cleaning it up and annotating it. Once the data is in the format you want, doing the actual machine learning is usually quite straightforward.

Your own generator

Previously, you used `ImageDataGenerator` and `flow_from_directory()` to automatically load the images and put them into batches for training. That is convenient when your images are neatly organized into folders, but the new training data consists of a Pandas `DataFrame` with bounding box annotations. You'll need a way to read the rows from this dataframe into a batch. Fortunately, Keras lets you write your own custom generator.

> **Note**: Instead of training on images, you'll now train on the combination of an image plus a bounding box annotation. For images that have more than one annotation, it's therefore possible that the same image appears multiple times in the same batch, although each time with a different bounding box.

The code for this generator is again in **helpers.py**. First, let's see the generator in action and then we'll describe how it works:

```
from helpers import BoundingBoxGenerator

batch_size = 32
train_generator = BoundingBoxGenerator(
  train_annotations,
  train_dir,
  image_height,
```

```
        image_width,
        batch_size,
        shuffle=True)
```

This imports the `BoundingBoxGenerator` class from the helpers module and creates a new instance. You have to give it the following information:

- The `DataFrame` that contains the annotations, `train_annotations`.

- The folder that contains the images for this DataFrame, in this case, `snacks/train`.

- The image size that the neural network will expect.

- A batch size, i.e., how many training examples the generator should combine into a mini-batch. Here, you're using a batch size of 32 images.

- Whether you want to randomly shuffle the examples or not. For training, this should be `True`, for validation and testing this is usually `False`.

Now, run the following cell to grab a batch of training data:

```
train_iter = iter(train_generator)
X, (y_class, y_bbox) = next(train_iter)
```

The `iter()` function turns `train_generator` into a so-called iterator object, and `next()` asks this iterator to return its next element. The generator, in other words, is simply a collection of training examples that you can iterate over. Keras does exactly the same thing in its training loop: it calls `next()` over and over until it has seen all 7,040 rows from the dataframe.

The NumPy array X now contains thirty-two training images (because the batch size is 32), while `y_class` and `y_bbox` will contain the class labels and ground-truth bounding boxes for these images. You can verify this by printing the shape of these arrays:

```
X.shape
```

This prints `(32, 224, 224, 3)` because it contains thirty-two 224×224 color images. The shape of `y_class` is `(32,)` because it has thirty-two class labels. And the shape of `y_bbox` is `(32, 4)` because it has thirty-two bounding boxes — one per image — and each box is made up of four coordinates.

If you print y_bbox it will look like this:

```
array([[ 0.348343,  0.74359 ,  0.55838 ,  0.936911],
       [ 0.102564,  0.746717,  0.062909,  0.93219 ],
       [ 0.      ,  1.      ,  0.135843,  0.98036 ],
       [ 0.448405,  0.978111,  0.288574,  0.880734],
       ...
```

The numbers you'll see will be different because the generator randomly shuffles the examples. y_class will be something like this:

```
array([ 9, 16, 12,  7,  8, 18, 10,  1, 14,  2,  7, 17, ...])
```

These are the indices of the classes that belong to the bounding boxes. To turn this back into text labels, you can do the following:

```
from helpers import labels
list(map(lambda x: labels[x], y_class))
```

The labels variable contains the class names corresponding to these indices and is defined in helpers.py. Using the map() function, which works the same way as Swift's map, you can convert from y_class's numeric indices back to text labels. The helpers module also has a label2index dictionary that does the mapping the other way around, from text labels to numeric class indices.

Now, have a look at how exactly this generator works. Open **helpers.py** to view the complete code, but here are the highlights. BoundingBoxGenerator is a subclass of the Keras Sequence object that overrides a couple of methods:

```
class BoundingBoxGenerator(keras.utils.Sequence):
    def __len__(self):
        return len(self.df) // self.batch_size

    def __getitem__(self, index):
        # ... code ommitted ...
        return X, [y_class, y_bbox]

    def on_epoch_end(self):
        self.rows = np.arange(len(self.df))
        if self.shuffle:
            np.random.shuffle(self.rows)
```

The __len()__ method determines how many batches this generator can produce: the number of rows in the dataframe, len(self.df), divided by the size of the batch. The // operator in Python means integer division.

When you write len(train_generator), Python automatically invokes this __len()__ method. It should output 220. The generator produces exactly 220 batches because 7,040 rows / 32 rows per batch = 220 batches. Usually, the size of the training set doesn't divide so neatly by batch_size, in which case the last, incomplete batch is ignored or is padded with zeros to make it a full batch. (We ignore it.)

The on_epoch_end() method is called by Keras after it completes an epoch of training, i.e., after the generator has run out of batches. Here, on_epoch_end() creates an instance variable self.rows that contains the indices of the rows in the DataFrame. Normally self.rows is [0, 1, 2, ..., len-1] but if shuffle is true, the indices in self.rows get randomly reordered. BoundingBoxGenerator's constructor, called __init__ in Python, also calls on_epoch_end() to make sure the rows are properly shuffled before the first epoch starts.

The meat of the work happens in __getitem__(). This method is called when you do next() or when you write train_generator[some_index]. This is where the batch gets put together. __getitem__() does the following:

1. Create new NumPy arrays to hold the images X, and the targets y_class and y_bbox for one batch. These arrays are initially empty.

2. Get the indices of the rows to include in this batch. It looks these up in self.rows.

3. For every row index, grab the corresponding row from the DataFrame. Load the image, preprocess it using the standard MobileNet normalization function, and put it into X. Also get the class name, use the label2index dictionary to convert it to a number and put it into y_class. Finally, get the bounding box coordinates and put them into y_bbox.

4. Return X, as well as y_class and y_bbox, to the caller.

> **Note:** __getitem__() returns a tuple of two elements: The first one holds the array with the training images X, the second element holds the targets. But you have two different targets here, one for the classes and one for the bounding boxes. This is why earlier you wrote X, (y_class, y_bbox) = next(train_iter), to unpack this second tuple element into separate y_class and y_bbox variables.

To test that the generator works OK, plot the images and bounding boxes that it returns:

```
def plot_image_from_batch(X, y_class, y_bbox, img_idx):
    class_name = labels[y_class[img_idx]]
    bbox = y_bbox[img_idx]
    plot_image(X[img_idx], [[*bbox, class_name]])

plot_image_from_batch(X, y_class, y_bbox, 0)
```

This uses the `plot_image()` function again but this time the image and bounding box comes from the batch. You need to supply the index of the image in the batch (0 to 31).

You may get a warning message now, "Clipping input data to the valid range for imshow with RGB data ([0..1] for floats or [0..255] for integers)." This is matplotlib telling you that it has trouble interpreting the image data from X. That's because the pixel values are no longer between 0 and 255 but between -1 and +1 due to the normalization performed by the generator. Matplotlib will still display the images but they are a bit darker than usual.

The generator seems to be working!

To grab a new batch of images, simply repeat this statement:

```
X, (y_class, y_bbox) = next(train_iter)
```

You can also do the same on validation and test iterators. The only difference is that they don't shuffle their images, so they'll always appear in the same order.

There you have it: a dataset with bounding box annotations that's ready for training. All you need to do now is create a suitable model for it.

Note: In the last chapter, you saw that data augmentation was a neat trick to increase the number of available training examples. The generator is the ideal place to do this sort of thing. To keep the code simple, BoundingBoxGenerator is currently not doing any data augmentation. If you're up for a challenge, try adding data augmentation code to the generator — but don't forget that the bounding boxes should be transformed too along with the images!

A simple localization model

You're now going to extend the existing MobileNet snacks classifier so that it has the ability to predict a bounding box as well as a class label.

To create the classifier, you took the MobileNet feature extractor and added a logistic regression on top, made up of a Dense layer, a softmax activation, as well as a Dropout layer for regularization. Guess what: There's no reason why you can't add another bunch of layers that branch off of the feature extractor. These new layers will now predict the bounding box coordinates:

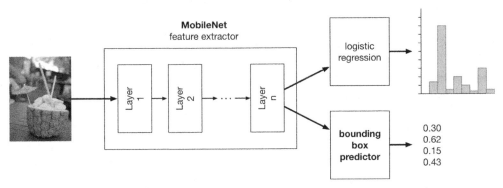

This new model has two outputs: one for the classification results, and one for the bounding box predictions. Both sets of layers are built on the same features from the MobileNet feature extractor, but because you train them on different targets they learn to predict different things.The classification portion of the model is still the same as before and outputs a probability distribution over the 20 possible classes.

The bounding box predictor outputs four real-valued numbers: x_min, x_max, y_min and y_max. If you train the model well, these four numbers will form the corners of a proper bounding box that encloses the object in the image.

> **Note:** Neural networks can have as many outputs as you like, one for every task that you want the model to perform. Best of all, you can train the model to learn all of these tasks at the same time. Models can even have multiple inputs. For example, a second input could be a table with extra information about the image such as its EXIF data, which contains the time of day the image was taken, where it was taken, and other metadata. The only requirement is that you are able to turn this input data into numbers somehow, for example by one-hot encoding it.

To save some training time, you'll start with the classifier model from the last chapter. After all, this has already learned how to classify snacks and so it already contains a lot of knowledge about the problem domain. What you're going to do in this section is to add some additional knowledge about bounding boxes to the model.

To load the best model from last time, do the following:

```
import keras
from keras.models import Sequential
from keras.layers import *
from keras.models import Model, load_model
from keras import optimizers, callbacks
import keras.backend as K

checkpoint = "checkpoints/multisnacks-0.7162-0.8419.hdf5"
classifier_model = load_model(checkpoint)
```

This simply grabs the best checkpoint and loads it back in. You can find this checkpoint in this chapter's **starter** folder.

> **Tip:** Call `classifier_model.summary()` to check that the model was loaded correctly.

To add the bounding box predictor layers on top of this checkpoint requires a bit of trickery, because you want to keep most of the existing model but also add a new output. It's easiest to build a new model but reuse some of the layers. Since this new model will involve a branching structure, you can't use the `Sequential` model API anymore but you have to use the Keras functional API as you saw in last chapter's SqueezeNet section.

The code is as follows. First, you reconstruct the classifier model from last time:

```
num_classes = 20

# The MobileNet feature extractor is the first "layer".
base_model = classifier_model.layers[0]

# Add a global average pooling layer after MobileNet.
pool = GlobalAveragePooling2D()(base_model.outputs[0])

# Reconstruct the classifier layers.
clf = Dropout(0.7)(pool)
clf = Dense(num_classes,
kernel_regularizer=regularizers.l2(0.01),
            name="dense_class")(clf)
clf = Activation("softmax", name="class_prediction")(clf)
```

A quick reminder of how the functional API works: You create a layer object, such as `GlobalAveragePooling2D()`, and then call this layer object on a tensor, such as `base_model.outputs[0]`, which is the output from the MobileNet feature extractor. This, in turn, gives a new tensor, `pool`. Then, you create a new layer, `Dropout(0.7)`, apply this to the `pool` tensor to get the next tensor, and so on. After you run this code, `clf` is now the tensor that refers to the model's classification output.

Here is the new bit for the bounding box predictor:

```
bbox = Conv2D(512, 3, padding="same")(base_model.outputs[0])
bbox = BatchNormalization()(bbox)
bbox = Activation("relu")(bbox)
bbox = GlobalAveragePooling2D()(bbox)
bbox = Dense(4, name="bbox_prediction")(bbox)
```

This adds a new `Conv2D` layer that also works directly on the output of the MobileNet feature extractor, given by the tensor `base_model.outputs[0]`. As is common, the convolution layer is followed by batch normalization and a ReLU. After this comes a `GlobalAveragePooling2D` layer and the final `Dense` layer that has four outputs for the bounding box coordinates. `bbox` is now the tensor for the model's bounding box output.

Note that the Dense layer for the bounding box prediction does not have an activation function, also sometimes called a **linear** activation. That means this part of the model performs **linear regression**, the kind of machine learning that predicts real numbers. Applying a softmax activation here wouldn't make sense because you're not trying to predict a probability distribution — you definitely want four independent numbers.

> **Note:** Because the four predicted numbers for the bounding box ought to be normalized coordinates between 0 and 1, in theory it's possible to apply a sigmoid activation to this Dense layer. The **sigmoid function** always returns 0, 1, or a value in between. Applying a sigmoid function is a common mathematical trick to restrict numbers to the range [0, 1]. However, the author found that using a linear activation — i.e., having no activation function — worked better.

Finally, you combine everything into a new Model object:

```
model = Model(inputs=base_model.inputs, outputs=[clf, bbox])
```

Don't forget to set the layers of the MobileNet base model to non-trainable, unless you're interested in fine-tuning the entire model:

```
for layer in base_model.layers:
    layer.trainable = False
```

You could also set the classifier layers to be non-trainable since they've already been trained before, but it's probably a good idea to keep training them. The class is now taken from the object in the bounding box, which is not necessarily 100% the same as the class of the entire image.

The model.summary() shows the extra layers, but it can be tricky to understand how they're connected. To get a good idea of the branching structure, it's useful to make a plot:

```
from keras.utils import plot_model
plot_model(model, to_file="bbox_model.png")
```

The bottom part of this file looks like this:

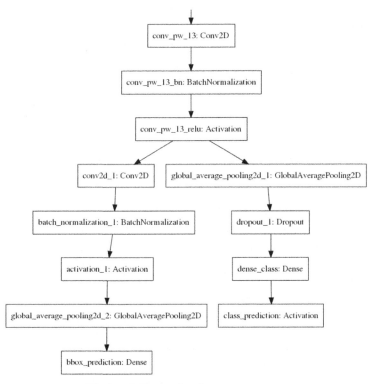

The model branches into two outputs

The conv_pw_13 layers at the top are part of MobileNet. On the right, it shows the classifier branch, and on the left the new bounding box prediction branch. Note that the bounding box branch is slightly larger: it has an extra convolution layer between the MobileNet output and the global average pooling layer.

> **Note**: You may be wondering exactly why you've added another Conv2D layer, here. Why not do the same as in the classifier branch and just have a Dense layer that immediately follows the global pooling? Good question. The answer is that the author tried both and adding the convolution layer gave much better results. This is probably because this extra layer helps to convert from image-level features to features that are more useful for predicting bounding boxes. The downside is that having this extra Conv2D layer adds over 4 million additional parameters to the model. Yikes. In the next chapter, you'll look at a more refined approach to building bounding box predictors that uses way fewer parameters.

Now, at this point, there is an important step you shouldn't overlook. Because you reconstructed the model's classification layers, the weights for these layers are still initialized with random numbers. If you'd use this model to make a classification, it would predict a random class. So before you continue, first put the weights back:

```
layer_dict = {layer.name:i for i, layer in
enumerate(model.layers)}

# Get the weights from the checkpoint model.
weights, biases = classifier_model.layers[-2].get_weights()

# Put them into the new model.
model.layers[layer_dict["dense_class"]].set_weights([weights,
                                                     biases])
```

The `layer_dict` lets you look up layers in the Keras model by name. That's why you gave the new layers names when you created them. `"dense_class"` is the name of the `Dense` layer in the classification branch. With `get_weights()` you can grab a layer's weights, and biases if it has them; with `set_weights()`, you can change the weights on a layer.

> **Note:** In the original classifier model you didn't give the layers names. In that case, Keras will automatically choose names and you can't really depend on them having a certain name. That's why to load the weights, you use `layers[-2]`. In Python notation, a negative index means that you're indexing the array from the back, so `layers[-1]` would be the last layer, which is the softmax activation, making `layers[-2]` the classification layer. Using indices is fine but giving the layers clear names is better.

The new loss function

With the definition of the model complete, you now can compile it:

```
model.compile(loss=["sparse_categorical_crossentropy", "mse"],
              loss_weights=[1.0, 10.0],
              optimizer=optimizers.Adam(lr=1e-3),
              metrics={ "class_prediction": "accuracy" })
```

There are a few new things going on, here. Previously, you specified a single `loss`, `categorical_crossentropy`. Here, you have specified not one but two loss functions: `sparse_categorical_crossentropy` and `mse`. The model has two outputs and each predicts a different thing, so you want to use a different loss function for each output.

The **cross-entropy loss function** is great for classification tasks, but it's not suitable for the bounding box prediction.

> **Note**: The **sparse** categorical cross-entropy you're using here, does the same thing as the regular one you've used in the previous chapters. It compares the predicted probability distribution with the true class label. The difference is one of convenience. Recall that the BoundingBoxGenerator returns the target y_class as a list of class indices. In Chapter 6, "Taking Control of Training with Keras," you saw that such targets need to be one-hot encoded, so y_class really ought to be a tensor of size (batch_size, 20) with the classes as one-hot encoded vectors. But Keras is clever: if you use the sparse_categorical_crossentropy loss function instead of the regular categorical_crossentropy, it will one-hot encode the class labels on-the-fly, saving you the effort of doing it yourself.

The loss function for the bounding box predictions is "mse" or **mean squared error**. This is a typical loss function for regression tasks, i.e., when the output of the model consists of real-valued numbers, such as bounding box coordinates. The math for this loss function looks like this:

```
mse_loss = sum( (truth - prediction)**2 ) / (4*batch_size)
```

Let's unpack this:

- First, it finds the difference between the ground-truth value and the prediction by subtracting the two numbers: truth - prediction. This is the **error** in mean squared error.

- Then it takes the square, which in Python is done with **2, so that this difference will always be a positive number. This also makes larger errors count more since the square of a large number is much bigger than the square of a small number. This is a common mathematical trick that you see all the time in machine learning. So now you have the **squared error**.

- Finally, it sums up all these squared differences and divides by how many there are. The loss is computed over a batch at a time, and there are four predicted numbers for each bounding box. In other words, it takes the average — the mean — of the squared errors for all the predictions in the batch. Put it all together and you get the **mean squared error**.

You don't need to remember this math; just realize that it's a really simple formula and that "mse" is the loss function to use when dealing with predictions that are just numbers, as opposed to probability distributions.

model.compile() now also has a loss_weights argument. Because there are two outputs, the loss computed during training looks like this:

```
loss = crossentropy_loss + mse_loss + L2_penalties
```

But not all of these loss terms will have the same scale, so some will count more than others in the final sum. Or perhaps you decide that some of them *should* count more than others. That's why each of these terms is weighted. The choices we've made with loss_weights=[1.0, 10.0] result in a final loss function that looks like this:

```
loss = 1.0*crossentropy_loss + 10.0*mse_loss + 0.01*L2_penalties
```

Because this model has already been trained on the classification task but hasn't learned anything about the bounding box prediction task yet, we've decided that the MSE loss for the bounding boxes should count more heavily. That's why it has a weight of 10.0 versus a weight of 1.0 for the cross-entropy loss. This will encourage the model to pay more attention to errors from the bounding box output.

> **Note**: Recall the that **L2 penalties** are extra terms that are added to the loss for regularization purposes. The 0.01 weight for the L2 penalties comes from kernel_regularizer=regularizers.l2(0.01) in the definition of the model.

Sanity checks

At this point, it's a good idea to see what happens when you load an image and make a prediction. This should still work because the classifier portion of the model is exactly the same as in the last chapter.

```
from keras.applications.mobilenet import preprocess_input
from keras.preprocessing import image

img = image.load_img(train_dir + "/salad/2ad03070c5900aac.jpg",
                     target_size=(image_width, image_height))
```

Now, normalize the image and let the model loose on it:

```
x = image.img_to_array(img)
x = np.expand_dims(x, axis=0)
x = preprocess_input(x)

preds = model.predict(x)
```

The `preds` variable is a list containing two NumPy arrays: The first array, `preds[0]`, is the 20-element probability distribution from the classifier output. The second array, `preds[1]`, has the four numbers for the bounding box.

Right now, the bounding box prediction is completely bogus because those layers haven't been trained yet, but the classification result should be reasonable. If not, something is wrong with the model. An easy way to check is to plot the predicted probabilities as a bar chart:

```
plt.figure(figsize=(10, 5))
plt.bar(range(num_classes), preds[0].squeeze())
plt.xticks(range(num_classes), labels, rotation=90, fontsize=20)
plt.show()
```

Which indeed shows this is an image of a salad:

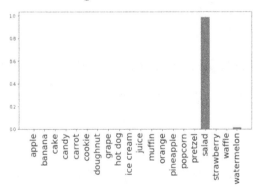

The classifier portion of the model already works

In fact, if you do `classifier_model.predict(x)`, which uses the last chapter's model without the bounding box layers added, then you should get the exact same probability distribution. (Try it!)

Of course, you can also use the generator to make predictions:

```
preds = model.predict_generator(train_generator)
```

This will create predictions for all the rows in the `train_annotations` dataframe, an array of size (7040, 20) for the classification output, and an array of size (7040, 4) for the bounding box output. But as you've seen, the bounding box predictions don't make much sense yet... at least until you train the model.

Train it!

Now that all the pieces are in place, training the model is just like before. This model is again trained best on a machine with a fast GPU. (If you have a slow computer, it's not really worth training this model yourself.)

First, create a generator for the validation set, with `shuffle` set to `False`:

```
val_generator = BoundingBoxGenerator(val_annotations, val_dir,
                                      image_height, image_width,
                                      batch_size, shuffle=False)
```

Some of the helper code now lives in **helpers.py**, so import those functions:

```
from helpers import combine_histories, plot_loss, plot_bbox_loss
histories = []
```

And then train for a number of epochs:

```
histories.append(model.fit_generator(train_generator,
                          steps_per_epoch=len(train_generator),
                          epochs=5,
                          validation_data=val_generator,
                          validation_steps=len(val_generator),
                          workers=8))
```

Because there is more going on in the model, Keras also prints out more information during training:

```
Epoch 1/5
220/220 [==============================] – 14s 64ms/step – loss:
1.8093 – class_prediction_loss: 0.4749 – bbox_prediction_loss:
0.1187 – class_prediction_acc: 0.8709 – val_loss: 1.2640 –
val_class_prediction_loss: 0.5931 – val_bbox_prediction_loss:
0.0522 – val_class_prediction_acc: 0.8168
```

There is `class_prediction_loss`, which has the cross-entropy loss for the classifier output. There is also `bbox_prediction_loss` with the Mean Squared Error loss for the bounding box prediction. The names of these metrics are taken from the names of the output layers, which is another reason for giving your layers meaningful identifiers.

Notice how the bounding box loss is much smaller than the class loss, `0.1187` versus `0.4749`. You can't really compare these values because they were computed using completely different formulas. It's only important that they go down over time.

The total `loss` value is the sum of these two losses, weighed by the `loss_weights` you supplied to `model.compile()`, plus the L2 penalty from the classifier's `Dense` layer. This overall loss again is just an indication of what the model is doing — the number itself is meaningless.

Keras also prints out a `class_prediction_acc` metric that measures the accuracy of the classifications over the training set, but there is no such metric for the bounding box predictions. That's because you told `model.compile()` that you only wanted `metrics={ "class_prediction": "accuracy" }`. After all, what would it mean for a bounding box prediction to be "accurate"? We'll actually come back to this topic soon because there is a useful metric you can use here, but it's not accuracy.

It looks like the overall loss is going down during these first five epochs, but it's hard to say whether this is due to either the classification loss or the bounding box loss. So let's plot only the bounding box loss and see what that does:

```
history = combine_histories(histories)
plot_bbox_loss(history)
```

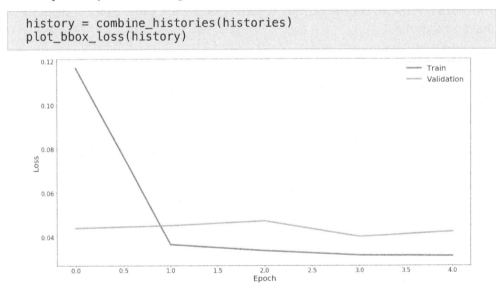

Loss for the bounding box predictions in the first 5 epochs

The training loss certainly went down significantly but the validation loss doesn't look particularly impressive. So is the model actually learning anything useful? It's hard to say because the loss itself doesn't tell you much about how well the model works. The only thing you can say for sure is that the model works better when it has a lower loss than when it has a higher loss — not very enlightening.

At least for the classification output, you can compute the accuracy, which is more interpretable than the loss. If the loss goes down by 10%, what does that mean? Who knows... But the accuracy going up by 10% makes a lot of sense.

Fortunately, for the bounding box predictions, there is also a metric that gives us some intuition about the quality of the model: IOU.

IOU

Sorry, this doesn't mean I owe you any money. The acronym stands for **Intersection-over-Union**, although some people call it the **Jaccard index**.

To measure how well the predicted bounding box matches the ground-truth box from the training data, you can compute how much they overlap, or their **intersection**. But just the overlap is not enough, what also matters is how much they *don't* overlap.

The IOU takes the intersection between the two bounding boxes and divides it by their total area, the **union**, to get a number between 0 and 1. The more similar the two boxes are, the higher the number. A perfect match is 1, while 0 means the boxes don't overlap at all.

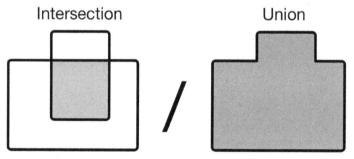

IOU is the intersection divided by the union of the two boxes

The helpers.py module has a simple function iou() for computing the Intersection-over-Union between two bounding boxes. You use it like this:

```
from helpers import iou

bbox1 = [0.2, 0.7, 0.3, 0.6, "bbox1"]
bbox2 = [0.4, 0.6, 0.2, 0.5, "bbox2"]
iou(bbox1, bbox2)
```

This prints 0.235 (rounded off), meaning that these boxes have only about one-fourth in common. You can see this using `plot_image`:

```
plot_image(img, [bbox1, bbox2])
```

That seems about right:

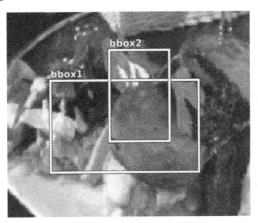

IOU between two bounding boxes

You can use the average IOU over the validation set as a metric of how good the model's bounding box predictions are. That's more enlightening than just the loss value.

To use this metric, you need to compile the model, again:

```
from helpers import iou, MeanIOU, plot_iou

model.compile(loss=["sparse_categorical_crossentropy", "mse"],
              loss_weights=[1.0, 10.0],
              optimizer=optimizers.Adam(lr=1e-3),
              metrics={ "class_prediction": "accuracy",
                        "bbox_prediction": MeanIOU().mean_iou })
```

The only difference is the addition of the last line. Now Keras computes the mean IOU for the predictions coming from the model's `"bbox_prediction"` output. The `MeanIOU` object is a simple wrapper class that lets Keras and TensorFlow use the `iou()` function.

If you train the model again, Keras now also prints out the `bbox_prediction_mean_iou` metric, which gradually increases from 0.25 to about 0.43 for the training set, but only gets up to approximately 0.34 for the validation set.

You can plot how the IOU developed over time using `plot_iou(history)`. Here is the plot for 15 training epochs, where the learning rate was manually decreased by a factor of 10 after every five epochs.

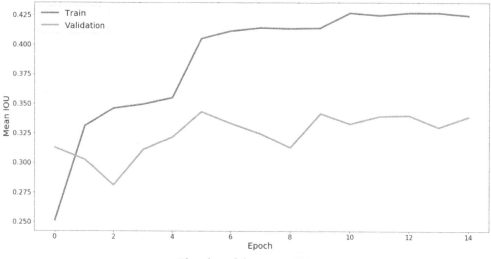

The plot of the mean IOU

This shows that the Mean IOU definitely improved over time, at least for the training set. After every five epochs, there's a nice bump when the learning rate was lowered.

The curve for the validation set isn't as impressive, though (or as smooth). No doubt there's some overfitting going on here since that one extra `Conv2D` layer you added has more parameters than the rest of the model put together...

By the way, this plot is slightly misleading. It may seem as if the validation IOU doesn't really improve very much, but keep in mind that the validation score is measured *after* each epoch, so at this point, the model had already seen one epoch of training. On the untrained model, the mean validation IOU is actually close to 0. (Hint: you can see this with `model.evaluate_generator(val_generator, steps=len(val_generator))` before you start training.)

So how good is this simple localization model? Well, let's look at some pictures from the test set and see with your own eyes.

> **Note:** You can also use a loss based on the IOU value, known as the **DICE loss**. Currently, you're using the **MSE loss**, which tries to make each individual corner coordinate of the bounding box as close to the ground-truth as possible. But the model doesn't really know these four numbers are related.

> With the DICE loss, you optimize the bounding box as a whole, where the goal
> is to make the box overlap as large as possible.

Trying out the localization model

Just to get a qualitative idea of how well the model works, a picture says more than a
thousand loss curves. So, write a function that makes a prediction on an image and
plots both the ground-truth bounding box and the predicted one:

```python
def plot_prediction(row, image_dir):
    # Same as before:
    image_path = os.path.join(image_dir, row["folder"],
                              row["image_id"] + ".jpg")
    img = image.load_img(image_path,
                         target_size=(image_width,
image_height))

    # Get the ground-truth bounding box:
    bbox_true = [row["x_min"], row["x_max"],
                 row["y_min"], row["y_max"],
                 row["class_name"].upper()]

    # Make the prediction:
    x = image.img_to_array(img)
    x = np.expand_dims(x, axis=0)
    x = preprocess_input(x)
    pred = model.predict(x)
    bbox_pred = [*pred[1][0], labels[np.argmax(pred[0])]]

    # Plot both bounding boxes and print the IOU:
    plot_image(img, [bbox_true, bbox_pred])
    print("IOU:", iou(bbox_true, bbox_pred))
```

This is very similar to the `plot_image_from_row()` function from earlier, but this
time it also makes a prediction on the image and plots the predicted bounding box in
addition to the ground-truth box. The function also prints the IOU between the two
boxes.

To view the results for a random image from the test set, do the following:

```python
row_index = np.random.randint(len(test_annotations))
row = test_annotations.iloc[row_index]
plot_prediction(row, test_dir)
```

Here's an example of a pretty good prediction. The ground-truth box's label is in uppercase, the predicted box in lowercase.

IOU: 0.673264402328

Pretty good!

It's not an exact match, but the model has definitely located where the hot dog is in the image. The IOU between the boxes is 0.67. IOU values over 0.5 are generally considered to be correct matches.

Unfortunately, there are also many images where the model doesn't do so well:

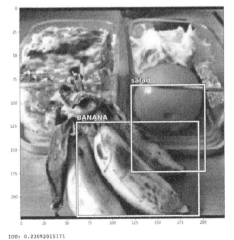

IOU: 0.0278782254008

Is this fair?

An IOU of about 0.03, that's very bad. But can you really blame this on the model? This image has many apples, and you can argue that the model did indeed find (a portion of) an apple, just not the one in the annotation.

This image really isn't a fair test of our simple localization model, which was only trained to find a single object at a time. In the next chapter, you'll train a proper object detection model that *can* handle images like these and will find all the apples.

Another example:

IOU: 0.23092015171

Not great, but not really wrong either

In this image, the bounding boxes do overlap, but less than the IOU of 50% that you'd like to see. Plus, the model actually found a different class. Again, it's not a completely wrong answer because this image does have a salad in it.

This is a typical result of a model that can only predict a single bounding box when there are multiple objects in the scene. In such situations, the model tends to predict a bounding box that's in between the two objects. It tries to hedge its bets and predicts an average box that sits somewhere in the middle. Quite clever, actually.

Conclusion: not bad, could be better

The good news is that it was pretty easy to make the classification model perform a second task, predicting the bounding boxes. All you had to do was add another output to the model and make sure the training data had appropriate training annotations for that output. Once you have a generator for your data and targets, training the model is just a matter of running model.fit_generator().

This is a key benefit of deep learning: You can use the same techniques for building neural network-based models for pretty much any problem domain, whether that's computer vision, language processing, audio recognition, and many others. As long as you have a dataset with training data and target labels, as well as an appropriate loss function, you're good to go!

Granted, the simple localization model you built here isn't super. On the validation set, it had an average IOU of a little over 30%. In general, we only consider a bounding box prediction correct when its IOU is over 0.5 or 50%. The model has definitely learned a few things about bounding boxes but it is still more wrong than it is right.

This is partially the fault of the dataset: If you look through the training images, you'll see that many images have more than one object — sometimes from different classes — but not annotations for all of these objects. Plus, this simple model can only predict a single bounding box at a time, which obviously doesn't work so well on images with multiple objects. So there's still room for improvement.

The solution: create a model that can predict more than one bounding box. That's what the next chapter is all about. Now stuff is getting serious!

Key points

- Object detection models are more powerful than classifiers: They can find many different objects in an image. It's easy to make a simple localization model that predicts a single bounding box, but more tricky to make a full object detector.

- To train an object detector, you need a dataset that has bounding box annotations. There are various tools that let you create these annotations. You may need to write your own generator to use the annotations in Keras. Data wrangling is a big part of machine learning.

- A model can perform more than one task. To predict a bounding box in addition to classification probabilities, simply add a second output to the model. This output needs to have its own targets in the training data and its own loss function.

- The loss function to use for linear regression tasks, such as predicting bounding boxes, is MSE or Mean Squared Error. An interpretable metric for the accuracy of the bounding box predictions is IOU or Intersection-over-Union. An IOU of 0.5 or greater is considered a good prediction.

- When working with images, make plenty of plots to see if your data is correct. Don't just look at the loss and other metrics, also look at the actual predictions to check how well the model is doing.

Chapter 10: YOLO & Semantic Segmentation

By Matthijs Hollemans

You've seen how easy it was to add a bounding box predictor to the model: simply add a new output layer that predicts four numbers. But it was also pretty limited — this model only predicts the location for a single object. It doesn't work so well when there are multiple objects of interest in the image.

You might think that you could just add more of these output layers, or perhaps predict 8 numbers for two bounding boxes, or 12 for three bounding boxes, etc. Good try, but unfortunately that doesn't work so well in practice.

Each bounding box predictor will end up learning the same thing and, as a result, makes the same predictions. Instead of finding the locations of multiple objects, such a model will predict the same bounding box multiple times. And chances are, these bounding boxes will not actually enclose any of the objects but all end up somewhere in the middle of the image as a compromise.

To make a proper object detector, you need to encourage the different bounding box predictors to learn different things.

An old-school approach to object detection is to divide up the input image into many smaller, partially overlapping regions of different sizes, and then run a regular image classifier on each of these regions. This definitely works, but it gives a lot of duplicate detections. Even worse: It's really slow. You need to run the classifier many, many, many times for each image.

A slightly smarter approach is to first try and figure out which parts of the image are potential **regions of interest**. This is the approach taken by the popular R-CNN family of models. The classifier is still run on multiple image regions, but now only on regions that are at least somewhat likely to have an object in them.

To predict which regions are potentially interesting, the "Faster R-CNN" model uses a **Region Proposal Network**, which sounds impressive but is really just a bunch of layers on top of the feature extractor — hey, what did you expect? Unfortunately, even though it has "Faster" in its name, this model is still on the slow side and not really suitable for mobile devices.

For speed freaks and mobile device users, the so-called **single stage detectors** are very appealing. As the name implies, these model types just run the classifier once on the input image and do all of the work in a single pass. Examples of single-stage object detectors are **YOLO** (You Only Look Once), **SSD** (Single Shot multi-box Detector) and **DetectNet**.

Turi Create lets you train a YOLO model with just a few lines of code, so that's what you'll do next.

Single stage detectors

The simplest form of a single stage detector, and the one you'll be training, looks like this:

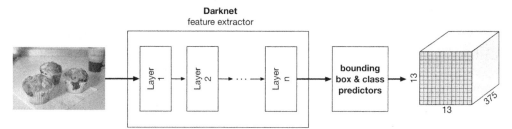

Again, there's a feature extractor plus a few layers on top. The YOLO feature extractor is called **Darknet**, and it's not so different from the feature extractors you've seen before: Darknet consists of convolution layers, followed by batch normalization and the ReLU activation function, with pooling layers in between.

> **Note**: The activation function used by Darknet is actually a variation of ReLU, known as **leaky ReLU**. Where a regular ReLU completely removes any values that are less than zero, the leaky version makes negative values a lot smaller but still lets them "leak through."

The extra layers are all convolutional. Unlike before, where the output of the model was either a vector containing a probability distribution or the coordinates for the bounding box, the output of YOLO is a three-dimensional tensor of size 13 × 13 × 375 that we'll refer to as the **grid**.

YOLO takes a 416×416 pixel image as input. That's larger than what you typically use for classification. This way, small details don't get lost. There are five pooling layers in Darknet that each halve the spatial dimensions of the image, for a total reduction factor of 32. Since 416/32 = 13, the final grid is 13×13 pixels.

Looking at this the other way around, each of the cells in this grid refers to a 32×32 block of pixels in the original image. Each cell is therefore responsible for detecting objects in or around that particular 32×32 region of the input image.

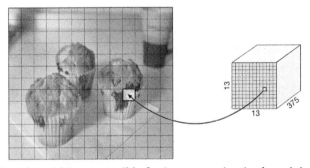

Each cell in the grid is responsible for its own region in the original image

YOLO, therefore, has 13×13 = 169 different bounding box predictors, and each of these is assigned to look only at a specific location in the image. Actually, this isn't entirely true: Each grid cell has not just one but 15 different predictors, for a total of 169×15 = 2,535 bounding box predictors across the entire image. That's quite an upgrade over the simple model you made previously!

Having multiple predictors per grid cell means you can let bounding box predictors specialize in different shapes and sizes of objects. Each cell will have a predictor that looks for small objects, a different predictor that looks for large objects, one that looks for wide but flat objects, one that looks for narrow but tall objects, and so on.

This is where the number 375 comes from, the depth dimension of the output grid: Each grid cell has 15 predictors that each output 25 numbers. Why 25? This is made up of the probability distribution over our snack classes, so that's 20 numbers. It also includes four numbers for the bounding box coordinates. Finally, YOLO also predicts a confidence score for the bounding box: how likely it thinks this bounding box actually contains an object. So there are two confidences being predicted here: one for the class, and one for the bounding box.

Because the output of YOLO is a 13×13×375 tensor, it's important to realize it *always* predicts 2,535 bounding boxes for every image you give it. Even if the image doesn't contain any recognizable objects at all, YOLO still outputs 2,535 bounding boxes — whether you want them or not.

That's why the confidence score is important: It tells you which boxes you can ignore. In an image with no or just a few objects, the vast majority of predicted boxes will have low confidence scores. So at least YOLO is kind enough to tell you which of these 2,535 predictions are rubbish.

Even after you filter out all the boxes with low confidence scores — for example, anything with a score less than 0.25 — you'll still end up with too many predictions. This kind of situation is typical:

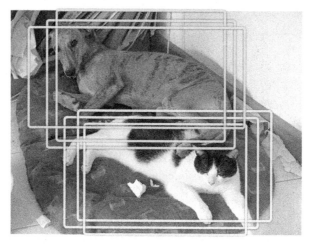

I'm only counting one dog and cat, not three!

These are all bounding boxes that the model feels good about since they have high scores, but as a consumer of an object detection model, you really want to have only a single bounding box for each object in the image. This sort of thing happens because nearby cells may all make a prediction for the same object — especially when the object is larger than 32×32 pixels.

To filter out these overlapping predictions, a post-processing technique called **non-maximum suppression** or NMS is used to remove such duplicates. The NMS algorithm keeps the predictions with the highest confidence scores and removes any other boxes that overlap the ones with higher scores by more than a certain threshold, say an IOU of 45% or more. The model created by Turi Create automatically takes care of this post-processing step for you, so you don't have to worry about any of this.

> **Note**: Turi's object detection model is known as **TinyYOLO** because it's smaller than the full YOLO. The full version of YOLO has multiple output grids of varying dimensions in order to handle different object sizes better, but this model is also larger and slower. Another popular single-stage detector is SSD. Architecturally, YOLO and SSD are very similar in design and differ only in the details. SSD does not have its own feature extractor and can be used with many different convnets. Particularly suitable for use on mobile is the combination of SSD and MobileNet.

Hello Turi, my old friend

Switch to the **turienv** Python environment and create a new Jupyter notebook. You can find the environment in the **starter** project of this chapter's materials. Refer back to Chapter 4: Getting Started with Python & Turi Create if you don't remember how to activate environments.

You can also follow along with **final/YOLO.ipynb** from the chapter's resources.

First, import the needed packages:

```
import os, sys, math
import pandas as pd
import turicreate as tc
```

Training an object detection model with Turi Create is straightforward, but you do need to tell it about the bounding box annotations for the training images.

Turi gets its training data from an SFrame object. You will have to add the ground-truth bounding boxes in a new column named annotations. Unlike with Keras, where each row from the Pandas DataFrame was a separate annotation, in the Turi SFrame there is only one row per image. The annotations column must have all the ground-truth boxes for that image.

You do this by putting the image's bounding box information into a list of dictionaries, like so:

```
[ {'coordinates': {'height': 129, 'width': 151, 'x': 75, 'y':
186},
    'label': 'juice'},
  {'coordinates': {'height': 130, 'width': 170, 'x': 228, 'y':
191},
    'label': 'juice'},
```

```
    {'coordinates': {'height': 129, 'width': 153, 'x': 76, 'y':
191},
    'label': 'juice'} ],
```

There is a separate dictionary for each annotation. It has two keys: `coordinates`, which in turn is another dictionary that holds the bounding box coordinates, and `label`, which is the class name of the object inside the bounding box. The above annotations are for a single image, ID 06d9c7df75a1a12f, that has three bounding boxes.

The first order of business is to write some code that loads the annotations CSV files and puts them into the format Turi Create expects. Since this is a fairly large function, we'll describe it here in parts:

```
def load_images_with_annotations(images_dir, annotations_file):
    # Load the images into a Turi SFrame.
    data = tc.image_analysis.load_images(images_dir,
with_path=True)

    # Load the annotations CSV file into a Pandas dataframe.
    csv = pd.read_csv(annotations_file)
```

First, you create a new `SFrame` by loading all the images from the specified folder. This is the same as what you did back in Chapter 4, "Getting Started with Python & Turi Create." The new `SFrame` contains two columns: `image` with the image object and `path` with the image's folder and filename.

The second line loads the CSV file into a Pandas `DataFrame` like you did in the previous chapter. Now, you will combine these two sources of data into a single `SFrame` that Turi can use for training. The function continues:

```
    all_annotations = []
    for i, item in enumerate(data):
        # Grab image info from the SFrame.
        img_path = item["path"]
        img_width = item["image"].width
        img_height = item["image"].height

        # Find the corresponding row(s) in the CSV's dataframe.
        image_id = os.path.basename(img_path)[:-4]
        rows = csv[csv["image_id"] == image_id]
```

The `for` loop looks at all images in the `SFrame` and then tries to find the corresponding annotations from the CSV's `DataFrame`. The match is performed on the `image_id` field.

This field does not exist in the SFrame but you can use os.path.basename() to get the name of the file from the full path, and use Python's special [:-4] indexing syntax to strip off the last four characters that say .jpg.

Then csv["image_id"] == image_id finds all the rows in the Pandas DataFrame that match this ID. Now, this doesn't give you yet what you're looking for. It returns a new Pandas object with the same number of rows as csv but with every row having the value True or False, depending on whether or not the row matched the predicate.

To get just the rows with the specified image ID, you need to filter csv again based on this True/False mask by writing csv[csv["image_id"] == image_id]. The variable rows is now a brand new dataframe with the actual annotations for just this image.

The loop continues:

```
img_annotations = []
for row in rows.itertuples():
    xmin = int(round(row[2] * img_width))
    xmax = int(round(row[3] * img_width))
    ymin = int(round(row[4] * img_height))
    ymax = int(round(row[5] * img_height))

    # Convert to center coordinate and width/height:
    width = xmax - xmin
    height = ymax - ymin
    x = xmin + math.floor(width / 2)
    y = ymin + math.floor(height / 2)
    class_name = row[6]

    img_annotations.append({"coordinates":
            {"height": height, "width": width, "x": x,
  "y": y},
            "label": class_name})
```

This looks like a lot of code but it simply reads the bounding box coordinates from rows and converts them into the format that Turi expects. Recall that the CSV file stores the coordinates as normalized numbers between 0 and 1, but Turi wants them in pixel space, so you need to multiply them by the image width and height. Also, Turi describes the bounding boxes using a center coordinate and a width and height. A bit of math is needed to convert the bounding boxes from one format to the other.

Once all the annotations for the current image have been converted and added to the img_annotations list, you append it to the grand list of all annotations:

```
if len(img_annotations) > 0:
```

```
            all_annotations.append(img_annotations)
        else:
            all_annotations.append(None)
```

If there were no annotations, you still need to append something to all_annotations, so that this list has exactly the same number of rows as the SFrame. In that case, you append None, which is Python's version of Swift's nil.

Finally, once you've looped through all images, the all_annotations list contains all their ground-truth bounding boxes in Turi format. You put this into an SArray object and assign it to a new column in the SFrame named "annotations":

```
    data["annotations"] = tc.SArray(data=all_annotations,
dtype=list)
    return data.dropna()
```

There's one more thing to do, here. Recall that not all images will have annotations. For such images, the annotations field in the SFrame will be None. You don't want to include these images during training.

The easiest way to remove those images from the SFrame is to call data.dropna(). This filters out any rows with missing values.

And that's it for load_images_with_annotations().

Now you can load the training images and their bounding boxes. Make sure the folder you're working in contains the snacks dataset. If you haven't downloaded it already, open the **snacks-download-link.webloc** file from the **starter** folder, and, once downloaded, move the **snacks** folder in your working directory.

Load the images with the following code:

```
data_dir = "snacks"
train_dir = os.path.join(data_dir, "train")

train_data = load_images_with_annotations(train_dir,
                data_dir + "/annotations-train.csv")
```

It might take a short while to load all the images. When it's done, len(train_data) should print 4265 because that's how many training images you have annotations for.

`train_data.head()` should show the following:

path	image	annotations
snacks/train/apple/007a0b ec00a90a66.jpg ...	Height: 341 Width: 256	[{'coordinates': {'y': 113, 'x': 73, 'width': ...
snacks/train/apple/007ec5 6b6529e036.jpg ...	Height: 256 Width: 341	[{'coordinates': {'y': 149, 'x': 185, 'width': ...
snacks/train/apple/008816 27629888f6.jpg ...	Height: 256 Width: 384	[{'coordinates': {'y': 210, 'x': 184, 'width': ...
snacks/train/apple/00bb57 20a7ba062e.jpg ...	Height: 256 Width: 341	[{'coordinates': {'y': 126, 'x': 169, 'width': ...
snacks/train/apple/00cc1c 601b23f73d.jpg ...	Height: 256 Width: 341	[{'coordinates': {'y': 170, 'x': 249, 'width': ...
snacks/train/apple/01477e a37494a8ac.jpg ...	Height: 256 Width: 382	[{'coordinates': {'y': 89, 'x': 107, 'width': ...

The SFrame now contains the annotations dictionaries

To view the annotations for a specific training image in more detail you can run a cell that prints `train_data[some_index]`, but even better is Turi's built-in visualization tool:

```
util = tc.object_detector.util
train_data["image_with_ground_truth"] =
util.draw_bounding_boxes(
  train_data["image"],
  train_data["annotations"])
train_data.explore()
```

This adds another column to the SFrame named `image_with_ground_truth` that does exactly what it says: It contains the images with the ground-truth bounding boxes drawn on top.

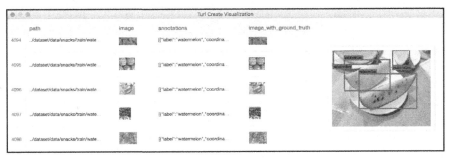

Viewing the ground-truth boxes on the training images

Now that the data is in order, you're ready to start training the model.

Training the model

It just takes a single line of code and a whole lot of patience:

```
model = tc.object_detector.create(train_data, feature="image",
                                  annotations="annotations")
```

If this is your first time training this kind of model, Turi Create will first download the pre-trained weights for the Darknet feature extractor. And then it starts training:

```
Setting 'batch_size' to 32
Using GPU to create model (GeForce GTX 1080 Ti)
Setting 'max_iterations' to 13000
+--------------+--------------+--------------+
| Iteration    | Loss         | Elapsed Time |
+--------------+--------------+--------------+
| 1            | 11.276       | 12.7         |
| 36           | 10.892       | 22.8         |
| 71           | 10.506       | 32.8         |
| 107          | 10.517       | 43.1         |
| ...          |              |              |
| 12999        | 2.106        | 3755.3       |
+--------------+--------------+--------------+
```

Needless to say, having a GPU for training this model is a must. The author trained on Linux with an NVIDIA GPU, but Turi Create can also use your Mac's AMD GPU if you have a recent Mac running macOS Mojave. Even on the powerful 1080 Ti, it still took over an hour to train this model. Training on the CPU takes ages — at about eight seconds per iteration, doing 13,000 iterations would need about 29 hours.

If you don't have 29 hours of patience, don't worry! We included the trained model in this chapter's materials that you'll use in the next section.

> **Note**: In order to use Turi Create with a GPU on Linux, you will need to install MXNet. See the Turi Create user guide at https://github.com/apple/turicreate/blob/master/LinuxGPU.md for instructions.

Once the model is done training, you can save it:

```
model.save("SnackDetector.model")
```

Also, export the model to Core ML. It's possible you get some warnings at this point from coremltools. You can safely ignore these.

```
model.export_coreml("SnackDetector.mlmodel")
```

Before you put this model into an app, let's use Turi Create to evaluate how well it does on the test set.

How good is it?

In case you don't have the hardware or the time to train this model yourself, we've included the trained model in the downloads as a .zip file in the **final** folder, **SnackDetector.model.zip**. Unzip this model to your working directory and then load it into the notebook:

```
model = tc.load_model("SnackDetector.model")
```

Also, load the test images and their annotations:

```
test_dir = os.path.join(data_dir, "test")
test_data = load_images_with_annotations(test_dir,
                    data_dir + "/annotations-test.csv")
```

Then call `model.evaluate()` on the `test_data` SFrame:

```
scores = model.evaluate(test_data)
```

This predicts the bounding boxes for every image in the test set and then compares these predictions against the ground-truths. It can take a few minutes if you're running this on a CPU. When it's done, `scores` looks something like this:

```
{'average_precision_50': {
    'apple': 0.52788541232511876,
    'banana': 0.41939129680862453,
    'cake': 0.38973319479991153,
    'candy': 0.36857447872282678,
    ...
    'watermelon': 0.37970409310715819},
 'mean_average_precision_50': 0.38825907147323535}
```

In the previous chapter, you used the IOU or Intersection-over-Union metric to determine how good the predictions were, but Turi uses a different metric. It computes the **average precision** for each class, as well as the overall average of these average precisions — yes, you read that right — known as the **mean average precision**, or mAP.

What's important for these average precision metrics is that higher is better. If you were to train a different model on this same dataset and it gave a better mAP score, then you can safely draw the conclusion this new model is indeed better than the old one.

IOU only measures by how much the predicted object overlaps the real object. It doesn't say anything about the classification accuracy — if a predicted box for class "orange" overlaps a ground-truth box for class "apple" with 95%, then the bounding box is very accurate, but the class is totally wrong. For a realistic metric, you want to make sure the class matches, too.

Also, when evaluating an object detector, you want to get some idea of whether the model actually finds all the objects in the image (the **recall**). The mAP metric combines these different criteria into a single number. It's not necessarily a very intuitive metric, but it's useful to rank the quality of different models on a given dataset.

> **Note**: The **Pascal VOC dataset** (host.robots.ox.ac.uk/pascal/VOC) is one of the standard datasets that people use to benchmark object detectors. At the time of writing, the top-scoring model on Pascal VOC was named DOLO and had an mAP of 81.3. The runner-up was a variant of Faster R-CNN with a score of 81.1. For comparison, YOLO v2 scores "only" 48.8 and SSD scores 64.0. You can view the leaderboards at this link: bit.ly/2ET24Ym. Another popular object detection dataset is COCO: cocodataset.org/#detection-leaderboard.

For more insight into how well your model is doing, take a look at the individual predictions for the test images, using `model.predict()`:

```
test_data["predictions"] = model.predict(test_data)
```

This adds a new column to the `test_data` `SFrame`. The data in this column looks very similar to the annotations column from `train_data`, but in addition to the predicted coordinates and class label there is now also the confidence score:

```
[{'confidence': 0.7225357099539148,
  'coordinates': {'height': 73.92794444010806,
                  'width': 90.45315889211807,
                  'x': 262.2198759929745,
                  'y': 155.496952970812},
  'label': 'dog',
  'type': 'rectangle'},
 ...]
```

Again, it's a lot nicer to look at this data using Turi's visualization tool:

```
test_data["image_with_predictions"] =

tc.object_detector.util.draw_bounding_boxes(test_data["image"],

test_data["predictions"])
test_data.explore()
```

It looks like this:

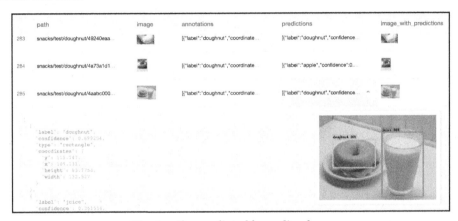

Viewing the predicted bounding boxes

That's not half bad! The YOLO model does a pretty good job at finding — and properly classifying — the objects in the test images. It doesn't always find all objects, and sometimes its predictions are plain wrong, but overall this is a very good result. By the way, if Turi didn't find any objects in a test image, the predictions column contains an empty list [].

These test set results are all fine and good, so now it's time to take the model out of the lab and onto the streets, and see how well it does on live video!

The demo app

This is a book about machine learning on iOS, and it's been a while since we've seen the inside of Xcode, so let's put the trained YOLO model into an app. The book downloads contain a demo app named **ObjectDetection**.

> **Note**: This example app only works on iOS 12 / Xcode 10 and later.

Open the project in Xcode. This already includes the finished **SnackDetector.mlmodel** file that was exported from Turi Create.

Select the .mlmodel file in the Project navigator to take a closer look:

The YOLO model in Core ML

The model description indeed says this is an object detector using Darknet and YOLO, with non-maximum suppression.

The type of the model is not a neural network but a **pipeline**. In machine learning terms, a pipeline is several models that are glued together so that the output of one model is used as the input for the next model in the pipeline. In this case, the object detection model is followed by a **non-maximum suppression (NMS)** model.

Also, note that the SnackDetector model has three inputs and two outputs. In addition to the regular image input for a 416×416 color image, there are two new inputs named iouThreshold and confidenceThreshold. These two values are used by NMS to decide which bounding boxes it should keep.

The higher you set the confidence threshold, the larger the confidence score on a predicted box has to be in order to keep that box. The IOU threshold determines when overlapping two boxes are too similar. A lower value means that even boxes that only overlap a little bit are considered to be duplicates.

Even though you saw earlier that YOLO produces a single tensor of size 13×13×375, the Core ML model actually has two outputs. That's because the Core ML pipeline applies NMS to the predictions from YOLO and only outputs the best bounding boxes. That's also why the first dimension is 0, or **unknown** because NMS will return a different number of boxes depending on how many objects are in the image. For convenience, Core ML provides the class predictions and coordinates as separate values.

However, you don't have to worry about these inputs and outputs because you're going to be using this model through the Vision framework.

Most of the source code in **ViewController.swift** is exactly the same as in the previous example apps. You make the VNCoreMLModel and VNCoreMLRequest objects the same way as before. You still start the request using the VNImageRequestHandler. The only thing that's different is the result object returned by Vision.

Previously the result objects were of type VNClassificationObservation, but now they are VNRecognizedObjectObservation objects. This is a new class that was added to Vision with iOS 12, and it exists specifically to handle the results from Turi Create's YOLO model. All your app needs to do is handle these VNRecognizedObjectObservation instances. In the demo app, we draw a rectangle around any detected objects.

The fun stuff happens in processObservations(for:error:), which is called from the completion handler for the Vision request. This function receives an array of zero or more VNRecognizedObjectObservation instances. If the array is empty, no objects were found. In that case, the app removes any previous rectangles from the screen.

The logic for interpreting the Vision results lives inside the show(predictions:) method. This simply loops through the VNRecognizedObjectObservation instances, converts the predicted coordinates to screen coordinates, and shows rectangles for the detected objects using the BoundingBoxView class.

- The VNRecognizedObjectObservation class has a labels property containing a list of familiar VNClassificationObservation instances, sorted from highest probability to lowest, telling you the most likely classes for the object inside the bounding box. The app simply grabs the first VNClassificationObservation from the list, as this is the best prediction, and puts its identifier and confidence into the rectangle's label.

- There is also a boundingBox property, a CGRect object that tells you where in the image the object is located. This uses normalized coordinates again, but with the origin of the CGRect in the lower-left corner. That's a little awkward, but it's just how Vision does things. In order to draw a rectangle around this object, you need to transform the normalized coordinates to screen coordinates and also flip the y-axis.

Here is a screenshot of the app in action:

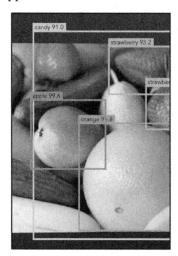

The YOLO model in action on the iPhone

Just an FYI: This picture was taken while pointing the iPhone at a picture on a Mac. This is a quick way of testing that the model works — just look up some test pictures on Google Images — but be aware that the interaction of the LEDs in the computer display with the camera's sensor may cause artefacts to appear in the image that can throw off the model.

If users pointing their phones at computer screens is going to be a major use case for your own apps, then you'll need to train the model to ignore those artifacts and distortions.

One limitation of Vision was that it could only provide a value for the model's image input, but as of iOS 13, you can also pass in values for the other inputs to override the defaults from the model. You do this on the VNCoreMLModel object:

```
if #available(iOS 13.0, *) {
  visionModel.inputImageFeatureName = "image"
  visionModel.featureProvider = try MLDictionaryFeatureProvider(
      dictionary: [
    "iouThreshold": MLFeatureValue(double: 0.45),
```

```
    "confidenceThreshold": MLFeatureValue(double: 0.25),
  ])
}
```

With a bit of effort, it's also possible to make YOLO work on iOS 11. In that case, Vision does not give you the convenient `VNRecognizedObjectObservation` instances but a `VNCoreMLFeatureValueObservation` with the contents of the 13×13×375 grid. You'll have to decode these contents into actual bounding boxes and perform NMS yourself to find the best boxes. The YOLO models built with Turi Create aren't compatible with iOS 11, but there are also Keras versions of YOLO available. For an example of how to do run a YOLO model on iOS 11, see github.com/hollance/YOLO-CoreML-MPSNNGraph.

> **Note**: This was only a brief introduction to object detection. As you can imagine, there is a lot going on under the hood that we glossed over here. If you want to learn more about how these single-stage object detectors are trained, see the author's in-depth blog post at machinethink.net/blog/object-detection/.

> **Note**: The architecture used by Turi Create, "Tiny YOLO v2", is already a few years old. You can download more modern YOLOv3 and YOLOv3-Tiny models from developer.apple.com/machine-learning/models/. These are trained on the 80 classes from the COCO dataset. To make a version of YOLOv3 that uses your own classes, you'll need to train it yourself, for example using github.com/ultralytics/yolov3 or one of the many other open source implementations.

> **Note**: The latest version of Turi Create can also do **one-shot object detection**. The term "one-shot" usually refers to training with only a single example image for each class, or at most a handful of training images. That's great for many real-life scenarios where you won't always have hundreds of training images. Turi does this using synthetic data augmentation, where they overlay the training image on a selection of real-world images. Another advantage is that with this method you don't need to provide any bounding box annotations. See the WWDC 2019 session "Drawing Classification and One-Shot Object Detection in Turi Create" for more details: developer.apple.com/videos/play/wwdc2019/420/.

Semantic segmentation

You've seen how to do classification of the image as a whole, as well as classification of the contents of bounding boxes, but it's also possible to make a separate classification prediction for each individual pixel in the image. This is called semantic segmentation. Here's what it looks like:

 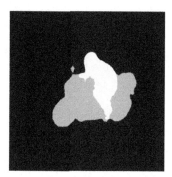

Semantic segmentation makes a class prediction for every pixel

On the right is the **segmentation mask** for this photo. It shows a different color for each class. Pixels that belong to the class "human" are yellow, pixels that belong to the class "motorbike" are purple. Pixels that don't belong to any kind of object we care about are classified as belonging to the special **background** class.

Whereas object detection only gives you a rough idea of where objects are in the image, semantic segmentation tells you exactly what the objects are shaped like.

In this section, you'll look at a top-of-the-line semantic segmentation model called DeepLab v3+. One of the possible applications of semantic segmentation is replacing a photo's background with another picture. You'll see how to do that in the included demo app.

The DeepLab model looks like this:

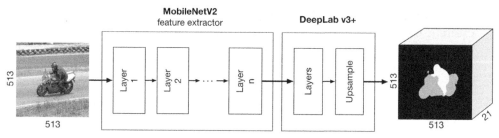

DeepLab on top of MobileNetV2

Not surprisingly, the first part of the neural network is comprised of a feature extractor. Here, you're using version 2 of MobileNet, which is more powerful and more efficient — but also a little more complicated — than V1. On top of the feature extractor are the layers that perform the segmentation task.

An interesting twist is that for segmentation you want the output of the model to be an image with the same dimensions as the input image. DeepLab expects the input image to be 513×513 pixels and so the predicted segmentation mask should be 513×513 also.

But as you've seen, most feature extractors will gradually reduce the spatial dimensions of the images, usually by a factor of 32, using pooling or convolutions with a stride of 2. If that were the case here, too, you'd end up with an output of 16×16 pixels, which is not nearly accurate enough to function as the final segmentation map for the image.

To avoid this, the version of MobileNet used by DeepLab only has an **output stride** of 8 instead of 32. This means that, instead of five times, it only chops the tensors in half three times, scaling down the input by a factor of 8 instead of 32. Rounded off, that makes the output of the feature extractor 65×65 pixels. The semantic segmentation layers that follow the feature extractor then do their work on this 65×65-pixel tensor, which still has plenty of detail.

> **Note**: DeepLab uses odd image sizes because some of the convolution layers are **atrous** or **dilated**, meaning they have holes in them. This is necessary to achieve that output stride of 8. With an odd number of pixels, there's always a center pixel, and so the math works out better this way. You may immediately forget this.

Finally, there is an **upsampling** layer at the end of the model that scales the 65×65 tensor back up to 513×513 pixels using bilinear resizing. Obviously, you lose some of the finer details because of this upscaling, which is why, if you look closely at the edges of the objects in the segmentation map, you'll see that they're smoothed out.

The output of DeepLab is then an output "image" with the same width and height as the input image, 513×513. However, it does not have three color channels like a regular image. The version of DeepLab that you're using here is trained on the Pascal VOC dataset of 20 classes, and so the output is a 513×513×21 tensor.

Every pixel has its own 21-element probability distribution from a softmax, because DeepLab does a class prediction for each individual pixel. Why 21 probabilities and not 20? Recall that you need an extra class to signify "background," for pixels that don't belong to any of the 20 regular classes.

> **Note**: We're not going to show you how to train this semantic segmentation model on the snacks dataset. It's not particularly difficult to train these kinds of models, but unfortunately, we don't have any ground-truth segmentation masks for the training images. Still, we wanted to show you that semantic segmentation is just another variation of the kinds of models you've already seen.

Converting the model

You're going to be using a pre-trained version of DeepLab that is made freely available as part of the TensorFlow Models repository, at: github.com/tensorflow/models/tree/master/research/deeplab.

This model was trained on the Pascal VOC dataset and can recognize the following 20 classes: person, bird, cat, cow, dog, horse, sheep, aeroplane, bicycle, boat, bus, car, motorbike, train, bottle, chair, dining table, potted plant, sofa and tv/monitor.

The demo app already includes the converted .mlmodel file, but it's a good idea to try converting this model by yourself.

> **Note**: You can also download a version of DeepLab v3+ from developer.apple.com/machine-learning/models/. It is the same model you'll be using here.

First, download the file containing the pre-trained TensorFlow model. We used **mobilenetv2_coco_voc_trainval** from the link download.tensorflow.org/models/deeplabv3_mnv2_pascal_trainval_2018_01_29.tar.gz. We recommend that you use this exact version, or risk running into errors.

After you unzip the download, look for the file **frozen_inference_graph.pb**. The extension **pb** stands for protobuf, which is the format that TensorFlow models — or graphs as they are called — are saved in.

This particular file is a "frozen" graph that has been optimized for inference; all the operations for training have been removed from this graph.

Netron can open such **pb** files, so take a look inside.

The particular section of the graph shown in the figure on the next page, has the layers that are responsible for performing the semantic segmentation. These are all layer types you've seen before: convolution, batch normalization, ReLU and average pooling.

There isn't some special **semantic segmentation** layer that performs all the magic — this neural network uses the same building blocks that they all do.

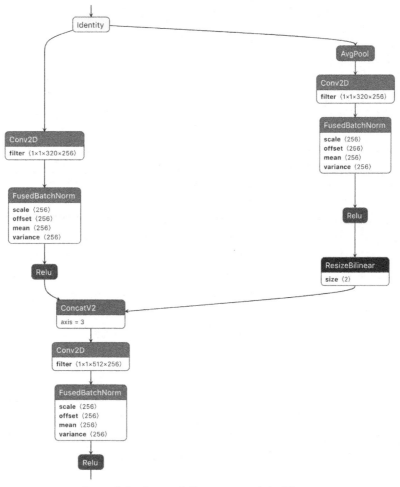

Part of the frozen inference graph in Netron

So how come these layers know how to perform the segmentation task — as opposed to classification or object detection or something else? The reason is the training data. During training, the output of the network is compared to the ground-truth segmentation masks from the training data, using a suitable loss function. The training process drives the loss to be lower and lower, and so the longer you train, the more the output of the network starts to resemble the ground-truth masks.

Of course, you can be clever in your choice of layers — for example, in the illustration above you see that DeepLab uses a branching structure called **spatial pyramid pooling** that makes predictions at different image scales, to capture detail at different levels.

But the point here is that it's not so much the design of the network that makes it do a task; it's the data you use to train it. In this case, the training targets were segmentation masks, and so the network has learned to perform semantic segmentation. It's really that simple.

Usually `coremltools` is the go-to package for converting models to Core ML. You used it to convert your Keras model in the previous chapter. The bad news is that `coremltools` does not directly support TensorFlow graphs.

The good news is that Apple and Google have collaborated to bring us `tfcoreml`, a TensorFlow to Core ML converter. This is an additional Python package that you need to install alongside `coremltools`.

TensorFlow works at a much lower level of abstraction than Core ML and Keras. With TensorFlow, you build computational graphs that consist of primitive operations such as addition, multiplication, matrix math, array manipulations and so on.

Core ML and Keras, on the other hand, only know about neural network layers. That's why it's easy to convert from Keras to Core ML. But it's not always possible to convert TensorFlow graphs to Core ML. You can only convert graphs that use operations that Core ML supports. The tf-coreml website, github.com/tf-coreml/tf-coreml, lists the supported operations.

> **Note**: Core ML 3 is more capable in this regard than its predecessors. Like TensorFlow, it supports many low-level operations in addition to the neural network layers. Thanks to this, it should now be possible to convert more complex TensorFlow models to Core ML.

We recommend that for this section you use the **kerasenv** environment, since that already has coremltools and TensorFlow installed. If you don't already have it installed, you can find **kerasenv.yaml** in the **starter** folder. Use conda create -n kerasenv.yaml to create the environment, and then activate it.

But this environment doesn't have tfcoreml yet, so use pip to install the latest version:

```
$ pip install -U tfcoreml
```

You may also need to install the most recent version of coremltools. If using the one from pip gives errors, here's a handy trick for installing the very latest version straight from GitHub:

```
$ pip install -U git+https://github.com/apple/coremltools.git
```

Now, create a new text file, **convert_deeplab.py**, and write the following:

```
import tfcoreml as tf_converter

input_path = "deeplabv3_mnv2_pascal_trainval/
frozen_inference_graph.pb"
output_path = "DeepLab.mlmodel"
input_tensor = "ImageTensor:0"
input_name = "ImageTensor__0"
output_tensor = "ResizeBilinear_3:0"

tf_converter.convert(tf_model_path=input_path,
        mlmodel_path=output_path,
        output_feature_names=[output_tensor],
        input_name_shape_dict={input_tensor : [1, 513, 513,
3]},
        image_input_names=input_name)
```

That's all you need to convert the model. Pretty simple, right? The trick is getting all the arguments to tf_converter.convert() correct.

Most importantly, you need to tell tfcoreml what the model's input and output tensors are. For DeepLab, those are "ImageTensor:0" and "ResizeBilinear_3:0", respectively. See if you can find these tensors in the graph using Netron.

TensorFlow operators can have multiple outputs and you need to specify which one you want to use. The :0 in the name tells TensorFlow that you want to use the tensor from the operator's first output.

Think of it as special syntax for indexing an array at element 0. It's only a detail but if you forget the `:0` behind the name, tf-coreml won't be able to find the tensor in the graph.

The `input_name_shape_dict` argument tells tf-coreml what the size of the input image will be: 513×513 pixels.

Just like with the Keras conversion you've done before, `image_input_names` is used to inform Core ML that it should treat the input as a proper image instead of an array of numbers. Note that tf-coreml renames `:0` to `__0` in the names of the model's inputs and outputs, so `"ImageTensor:0"` is now `"ImageTensor__0"`.

Run this script from a Terminal:

```
$ python3 convert_deeplab.py
```

tf-coreml will now load the TensorFlow model, analyze the graph, and convert all the operations to Core ML layers. When it's done and everything went well, you will have a brand new **DeepLab.mlmodel** file.

Double-click to open it in Xcode, and this is what you should see:

The summary page for DeepLab.mlmodel

DeepLab's output is a **multi-array** of size 21×513×513. Multi-array is the term that Core ML uses for tensor. When you need to deal with tensor objects in Core ML, it's always through the `MLMultiArray` class. You'll get a taste of that shortly.

Notice that Core ML puts the number of channels (21) at the front of the tensor, as the outermost dimension. Usually, in this book, we've described the size of a tensor as height × width × channels (HWC), but in practice, you'll also see it done the other way around: channels × height × width (CHW). It's important to know which format you're working with at any given time.

Open **DeepLab.mlmodel** with Netron, too, and put it side-by-side with the original TensorFlow model to see how different/similar the two models are.

The demo app

The downloads for this chapter include an app called **Segmentation**. The code is very similar to that of the HealthySnacks app from a few chapters ago, except now there are two pairs of camera/photo library buttons, allowing you to select a background image and a foreground image.

The author on well-deserved fake holiday (left), the corresponding segmentation mask (right)

After you've selected two images, the app will send the "front" image through DeepLab and uses the predicted segmentation mask to composite all the pixels that are not classified as "background" on top of the other image. Who needs a green screen when you've got a segmentation model?

Tap the screen to view the actual segmentation mask (right side of the illustration). Note that the results aren't perfect — there are a few bits of a painting hanging in the background that got mistakenly classified as "person" and are shining through.

The app uses Vision to run the model, so that's the same code as usual. But there are some interesting code snippets we can look at in more detail. First, the init method of **ViewController.swift**:

```
required init?(coder aDecoder: NSCoder) {
  let outputs =
deepLab.model.modelDescription.outputDescriptionsByName
  guard let output = outputs["ResizeBilinear_3__0"],
        let constraint = output.multiArrayConstraint else {
    fatalError("Expected 'ResizeBilinear_3__0' output")
  }
  deepLabHeight = constraint.shape[1].intValue
  deepLabWidth = constraint.shape[2].intValue

  super.init(coder: aDecoder)
}
```

The size of DeepLab's output image is 513×513 pixels. You could hard-code this into the app, but it's better to ask the model what these dimensions are. That way the same code can work with models that output other sizes, too.

Here, deepLab is an instance of DeepLab, the class that Xcode automatically generates from the .mlmodel file. It has a model property for an MLModel object. If you don't want to use Vision, you can also use the MLModel instance to make predictions directly.

More importantly, for our purposes, you can ask this object about the configuration of the model. Here you grab the modelDescription, which contains all the info you see in Xcode, and from that the outputDescriptionsByName. This is a dictionary describing the model's outputs.

This model has only one output with the name "ResizeBilinear_3__0". Note that this used to be called "ResizeBilinear_3:0" in the TensorFlow graph, but tfcoreml renamed it. That output is of type **multi-array**, which means you literally get access to the entire 21×513×513 tensor of output values. By grabbing the multiArrayConstraint property, you can look at the size and datatype of this array. Here, you care about the size, given by the shape property.

Because the Core ML API was designed to work with both Swift and Objective-C, using some of these classes can be a little elaborate. For example, shape returns an array of NSNumber objects, and so you need to use .intValue to turn these into integers. The shape array has three values in it: [channels, height, width] and you read the height and width into two properties so you can use them later.

After Vision successfully performs the request, the prediction results arrive as an array of VNCoreMLFeatureValueObservation objects. You get one of these objects for every output that is of type multi-array. The actual predictions are inside an MLMultiArray object. This is how you obtain that MLMultiArray from the Vision results:

```
func processObservations(for request: VNRequest, error: Error?)
{
  if let results = request.results as?
[VNCoreMLFeatureValueObservation],
     !results.isEmpty,
     let multiArray = results[0].featureValue.multiArrayValue {

    DispatchQueue.main.async {
      self.show(results: multiArray)
    }
  }
}
```

The show(results) method then decides whether to show the composited image or just the segmentation mask. It uses two helper methods (createMaskImage or matteImages) to do the actual work. Both of these helper methods follow the same approach:

1. Allocate an array of type UInt8 that will hold the output pixels. The size of this array is deepLabWidth * deepLabHeight * 4 because it will be an RGBA image.

2. Loop through all the 513×513 pixels in the MLMultiArray that holds DeepLab's predictions.

3. For each pixel, find the index of the winning class. This is done by looping over the 21 probability values for that pixel and finding the largest value (the argmax).

4. To combine the two photos, the color that is used for the output pixel is read from the foreground image if the best class is not 0, the special **background** class. Otherwise, it is read from the background image. It's easy to change this logic to only keep certain classes in the image, such as only cats and dogs.

5. In the other mode, where the app is drawing the segmentation mask, you get the color of the output pixel from a lookup table, using the winning class as the index.

6. Finally, convert the pixel array into a UIImage.

You'll now look at how some of these steps work in detail. The `MLMultiArray` API is a little tricky to work with. For many model types, such as classification and object detection, Vision will hide away these details from you, but if your model outputs a multi-array then you have no choice but to get your hands dirty.

In the following code, `features` is the variable with the `MLMultiArray` object.

```
let classes = features.shape[0].intValue
let height = features.shape[1].intValue
let width = features.shape[2].intValue
var pixels = [UInt8](repeating: 255, count: width * height * 4)
```

Just like the model's output description had a `shape`, so does the actual `MLMultiArray`. You use the width and height from this shape to allocate the `pixels` array.

For this particular model, the output dimensions are fixed at 513×513, but in the model description for YOLO you saw that the first output dimension was 0, or **unknown**. In that case, the actual shape of the multi-array object isn't known yet until runtime and can be different from one invocation of the model to the next.

To read a value from the `MLMultiArray`, you can write the following:

```
let value = features[[c, y, x] as [NSNumber]].doubleValue
```

Where c is the channel number (0-20), y is the vertical coordinate (0-512), and x is the horizontal coordinate (also 0-512). Remember that the height dimension comes before the width!

Indexing the multi-array in this manner works fine, but it's very slow. Note that you're first creating an array `[c, y, x]` to hold the three indices. Because this is an Objective-C API, you need to cast that to an array of `NSNumbers`. `MLMultiArray` uses this `NSNumber` array as a subscript, reads the value from the tensor, and returns it as a new `NSNumber` object that you have to convert back to a `Double` before you can properly use it.

Now, imagine doing this in a triple nested loop of 21×513×513 iterations. It gets slow really quick.

A better approach is to use a pointer to directly access the `MLMultiArray`'s memory. After all, it's just a big array of `Double` values. Using pointers is not something Swift developers are accustomed to doing, but it's not a big deal:

```
let featurePointer = UnsafeMutablePointer<Double>(
                        OpaquePointer(features.dataPointer))
```

```
let cStride = features.strides[0].intValue
let yStride = features.strides[1].intValue
let xStride = features.strides[2].intValue
```

First, you turn `features.dataPointer`, a **raw** pointer, into an
`UnsafeMutablePointer` for `Double` values. To find out where in this memory area
the value that you want to read is located, you need to do a little bit of math. That's
what the `strides` are for. This again is an array of `NSNumbers`.

The stride for a given dimension tells you how far apart in memory subsequent
values from that dimension are. Here, `cStride` is the stride of the first dimension,
which holds the channels. It is 263169 because one channel is made up of 513×513 =
263169 pixel values. The `yStride` is the distance between two subsequent rows in
the image and is 513 because one row contains 513 pixels. And `xStride` is the
distance between two pixels in the same row, which is 1 because they're right next to
each other in memory.

Now, you can forget about these numbers immediately. Important to remember is
that the strides are used to index the `MLMultiArray`'s memory directly when you're
using pointers. Conveniently enough, `MLMultiArray` has already calculated what the
correct stride values are.

To read the value at `c, y, x`, you can now write:

```
let value = featurePointer[c*cStride + y*yStride + x*xStride]
```

That's all you need to do to directly read the `Double` value from the `MLMultiArray`'s
memory. It doesn't get much faster than this!

The main processing loop then looks like the following:

```
for y in 0..<height {
  for x in 0..<width {

    // Take the argmax for this pixel, the index of the largest
class.
    var largestValue: Double = 0
    var largestClass = 0
    for c in 0..<classes {
      let value = featurePointer[c*cStride + y*yStride +
x*xStride]
      if value > largestValue {
        largestValue = value
        largestClass = c
      }
    }
    . . .
```

There are three nested loops: You loop through all the rows (y) and all the columns (x) of the multi-array to look at all the image positions. Each "pixel" is really made up of 21 probability values, and you loop through these (c) to find the largest one. Then you can use the value of largestClass to do something interesting with this pixel.

> **Note**: We told a small lie earlier. The 21 probability values for each pixel aren't really probabilities yet, but so-called **logits**. To save time, DeepLab didn't actually apply a softmax to these numbers. The softmax computation is kind of slow, and it would have to be done for every individual pixel, that is 513×513 times.
>
> All the softmax does is re-scale the logits so that they sum up to 1, but this doesn't actually change the relative order of these numbers. If you'd sort the logits from before the softmax, and the probabilities from after the softmax, they'd be in the exact same order. Because you only care here which class has the biggest value, and not what probability that value represents, you can skip the softmax step and save some time.

Try it out, run the app and see how well the semantic segmentation model works on your own pictures. The app will run on the simulator or on a device with iOS 12 or newer.

By the way, it can take a few seconds for the model to run. Semantic segmentation is a harder job than classification. Also, the code for compositing the two images is not necessarily the most optimal way to do this. We just wanted to keep the example code readable. In practice, you'd use optimized routines from Core Image, the vImage framework, or even Metal GPU shaders to draw these images.

There are also different versions of DeepLab v3+. There is one that uses the Xception network as the feature extractor instead of MobileNet. This gives higher quality results but it also comes at a cost: The MobileNet version of DeepLab is only 8.6 MB, while the Xception version is easily ten times bigger.

Note: With semantic segmentation, pixels only know which class they belong to. There is also a different kind called **instance segmentation**, where the pixels not only know their class but also which distinct object they belong to. For example, in a photo of two people who are sitting side by side and are touching, semantic segmentation will only see a single blob in which all the pixels are of class "person." Instance segmentation will be able to distinguish between person 1 and person 2.

A popular model for instance segmentation is Mask R-CNN, which adds segmentation capabilities to the Faster R-CNN object detector. It makes sense to think of instance segmentation as being a combination of object detection and segmentation. As should be obvious by now, all these techniques are closely related.

Challenges

Challenge 1: Create a dataset for object detection

If you collected your own classification dataset for one of the previous challenges, then use a tool such as RectLabel to add bounding box annotations for these images. RectLabel uses a different file format to store the annotations, but rectlabel.com has code examples that show how to use these files with Turi Create.

Challenge 2: Train MobileNet+SSD on the snacks dataset

The size of the YOLO model you trained with Turi Create is 64.6 MB. That's pretty hefty! This is reaching the upper limit of what is acceptable on mobile devices. It's possible to use object detection models that are much smaller than YOLO that give very good results, such as SSD on top of MobileNet (about 26 MB).

Try training MobileNet+SSD on the snacks dataset. The easiest way to do this is with the TensorFlow object detection API at github.com/tensorflow/models/tree/master/research/object_detection. This is a good project to get some experience working directly with TensorFlow. The main difficulty will be converting the training data into a format that this API understands.

To convert the final TensorFlow model to Core ML, you can use tf-coreml and the following repo: github.com/vonholst/SSDMobileNet_CoreML.

Compare the mAP of this model with the mAP reported for YOLO earlier this chapter to see if MobileNet+SSD compares favorably or not. Good luck!

Challenge 3: Change the semantic segmentation demo app

Change the semantic segmentation demo app to only keep pixels that belong to cats and dogs — or whatever your favorites are from the 20 Pascal VOC classes.

Key points

- To create a model that can detect multiple objects, it's not enough to just add extra bounding box predictors. Single-stage detectors like YOLO and SSD put the predictors into a grid so that they only look at specific portions of the input image. They also train different predictors to specialize in various object shapes and sizes.

- Non-maximum suppression (NMS) is a post-processing step used to only keep the best bounding box predictions. The YOLO model that is trained by Turi Create will automatically apply NMS.

- Semantic segmentation lets you make a unique class prediction for every pixel in the image. Instead of a single probability distribution, this predicts as many probability distributions as there are pixels.

Where to go from here?

Congrats, you've reached the end of section 1, Machine Learning with Images! Of course, we hope this is really only the beginning of your journey into the wonderful world of computer vision and deep learning.

Some fun new areas to explore are:

- Models that can create new images. Style transfer is a technique of taking a photo and making it look like a famous painting. Colorization adds color to old black-and-white photos. Generative models can produce totally new works of art, such as an infinite number of unique anime characters, youtube.com/watch?v=PUkQbGaL4Fg.

- Instead of working with still images you can also add a time dimension and make predictions on video. One example is tracking moving objects, which is like object detection but over time. Another futuristic application — literally! — is predicting what will happen in the next few frames of the video.

- Human pose detection. You can use a neural network to find keypoints on the human body, such as where a person's hands and feet are. It's even possible to reconstruct realistic 3D models of the human body from photos, see densepose.org.

And much more... The possibilities are endless!

One cool project that was published recently is *Everybody Dance Now*, which combines techniques of human pose detection and generative models to copy a professional dancer's moves onto the body of a regular person, turning anyone into a dancing pro. See the amazing video at youtube.com/watch?v=PCBTZh41Ris.

Believe it or not, you already understand 90% of the techniques used in that project and many others. Everything builds on what you've learned in the first part of this book.

If you want to know exactly how *Everybody Dance Now* works, check out the paper. You can find it here: arxiv.org/pdf/1808.07371.pdf. A lot of the collective knowledge in machine learning isn't written down in books, articles and blog posts, but in academic research papers. If you're serious about machine learning, get into the habit of reading those papers.

To be honest, it can be hard to get into reading research papers. It's quite likely half the stuff in the *Everybody Dance Now* paper won't make sense to you at first reading. Don't fret! Simply read a few other papers on the same topic. Skip the math and any parts that don't make sense to you yet. Gradually, you'll get comfortable with the way these papers are written. And once you speak the language of a certain subfield such as human pose detection or generative models, new papers become easier to read.

A good place to find papers is on arxiv.org. Even better is the Arxiv Sanity Preserver at arxiv-sanity.com, which also has a "top hype" section where you can find what the latest buzz is about. To stay up-to-date on what's happening in machine learning, the papers are where it's at.

> **Note**: We heartily recommend watching the fast.ai videos once you've finished this book. This is one of the best online courses about computer vision, natural language processing, and other applications of deep learning — and it's free! Not only will you gain a deeper understanding of machine learning, but this course is also packed with handy tips and tricks, and advice on how to get state-of-the-art results. 5 out of 5 stars!

Section II: Machine Learning with Sequences

In this section, you'll learn how to apply machine learning to sequential data. You'll work on a new iOS app which attempts to identify a user's activity using data from their iPhone's motion sensors. In the process, you'll learn how to build a good training dataset, how to create an activity classification model using Turi Create, and how to incorporate your model into an iOS app to support responsive classifications with real-time data.

Chapter 11: Data Collection for Sequence Classification

By Chris LaPollo

You worked exclusively with images throughout the first section of this book, and for good reason — knowing how to apply machine learning to images lets you add many exciting and useful features to your apps. Techniques like classification and object detection can help you answer questions like "Is this snack healthy?" or "Which of these objects is a cookie?"

But you've focused on *individual* images — even when processing videos, you processed each frame individually with complete disregard for the frames that came before or after it. Given the following *series* of images, can the techniques you've learned so far tell me where my cookies went?

The Case of the Disappearing Cookies

Each of the above images tells only part of the story. Rather than considering them individually, you need to reason over them as a *sequence*, applying what you see in earlier frames to help interpret later ones.

There are many such tasks that involve working with sequential data, such as:

- Extracting meaning from videos. Maybe you want to make an app that translates sign language, or search for clips based on the events they depict.

- Working with audio, for example converting speech to text, or songs to sheet music.

- Understanding text, such as these sentences you've been reading, which are sequences of words, themselves sequences of letters (assuming you're reading this in a language that uses letters, that is).

- And countless others. From weather data to stock prices to social media feeds, there are endless streams of sequential data.

With so many types of data and almost as many techniques for working with it, this chapter can't possibly cover everything. You'll learn ways to deal with text in later chapters, and some of the techniques shown here are applicable to multiple domains. But to keep things practical, this chapter focuses on a specific type of sequence classification — human activity detection. That is, using sensor data from a device worn or held by a person to identify what that person is physically doing. You've probably already experienced activity detection on your devices, maybe checking your daily step count on your iPhone or closing rings on your Apple Watch. Those just scratch the surface of what's possible.

In this chapter, you'll learn how to collect sensor data from Apple devices and prepare it for use training a machine learning model. Then you'll use that data in the next chapter, along with Turi Create's task-focused API for activity detection, to build a neural network that recognizes user activity from device motion data. Finally, you'll use your trained neural net to recognize player actions in a game.

> **Note**: Apple introduced the Create ML application with Xcode 11, which provides a nice GUI for training many types of Create ML models. One of those is called Activity Classifier and it's essentially the same model you'll build in these chapters using Turi Create. So why not use the Create ML app here?

We made that decision partially because we wrote these chapters before the Create ML app existed and it would require rewriting quite a bit of content without describing any truly new functionality, but it's also because the GUI option is self-explanatory once you understand the underlying Turi Create code. The Create ML method is also a bit less flexible than using Turi Create directly, as a consequence of needing to support such a (delightfully) simple graphical interface.

We encourage you to experiment with the Create ML app after going through these chapters to see which option you prefer. We'll try to point out instructions that might be different when working with the Create ML app.

The game you'll make is similar to the popular Bop It toy, but instead of calling out various physical bits to bop and twist, it will call out gestures for the player to make with their iPhone. Perform the correct action before time runs out! The gestures detected include a chopping motion, a shaking motion and a driving motion (imagine turning a steering wheel).

We chose this project because collecting data and testing it should be comfortably within the ability of most readers. However, you can use what you learn here for more than just gesture recognition — these techniques let you track or react to any activity identifiable from sensor data available on an Apple device.

Modern hardware comes packed with sensors — depending on the model, you might have access to an accelerometer, gyroscope, pedometer, magnetometer, altimeter or GPS. You may even have access to the user's heart rate!

With so much data available, there are countless possibilities for behaviors you can detect, including sporadic actions like standing up from a chair or falling off a ladder, as well as activities that occur over longer durations like jogging or sleeping. And machine learning is the perfect tool to make sense of it all. But before you can fire up those neural nets, you'll need a dataset to train them.

Building a dataset

So you've got an app you want to power using machine learning. You do the sensible thing and scour the internet for a suitable, freely available dataset that meets your needs.

You try tools like Google Dataset Search, check popular data science sites like Kaggle, and exhaust every keyword search trick you know. If you find something — great, move on to the next section! But if your search for a dataset turns up nothing, all is not lost — you can build your own.

Collecting and labeling data is the kind of thing professors make their graduate students do — time consuming, tedious work that may make you want to cry. When labeling human activity data, it's not uncommon to record video of the activity session, go through it manually to decide when specific activities occur, and then label the data using timecodes synced between the data recordings and the video. That may sound like fun to some people, but those people are wrong and should never be trusted.

This chapter takes a different approach — the data collection app *automatically* adds labels. They may not be as exact — manual labeling lets you pinpoint precise moments when test subjects begin or end an activity — but in many cases, they're good enough.

To get started, download the resources for this chapter if you haven't already done so, and open the **GestureDataRecorder** starter project in Xcode.

> **Note**: The chapter resources include data files you can use unchanged, so you aren't *required* to collect more here. However, the experience will help later when working on your own projects. Plus, adding more data to the provided dataset should improve the model you make later in the chapter.

Take a look through the project to see what's there. **ViewController.swift** contains most of the app's code, and it's the only file you'll be asked to change. Notice the `ActivityType` enum which identifies the different gestures the app will recognize:

```
enum ActivityType: Int {
    case none, driveIt, shakeIt, chopIt
}
```

If you run the app now, it will *seem* like it's working but it won't actually collect or save any data. The following image shows the app's interface:

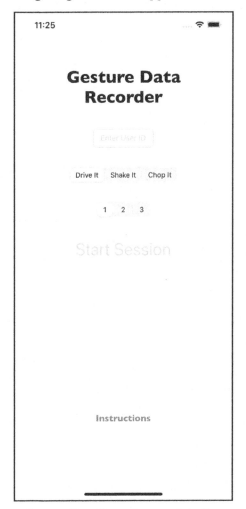

Gesture Data Recorder app interface

GestureDataRecorder probably won't win any design awards, but that's OK — it's just a utility app that records sensor data. Users enter their ID, choose what activity and how many short sessions of that activity to record, and then hit **Start Session** to begin collecting data. The app speaks instructions to guide users through the recording process. And the **Instructions** button lets users see videos demonstrating the activities.

> **Note:** For some datasets, it may be better to randomize activities during a session, rather than having users choose one for the entire thing. My test subjects didn't seem to enjoy having to pay that much attention, though.

Why require a user ID? You'll learn more about this later, but it's important to be able to separate samples in your dataset by their sources. You don't need *specific* details about people, like their names — in fact, identifying details like that are often a bad idea for privacy and ethics reasons — but you need *some* way to distinguish between samples.

GestureDataRecorder takes a simple but imperfect approach to this problem: It expects users to provide a unique identifier and then saves data for each user in separate files. To support this, the app makes users enter an ID number and then includes that in the names of the files it saves. If any files using that ID already exist on this device, the app requests confirmation and then appends new data to those files. So it trusts users not to append their data to someone else's files on the device, and it's up to you to ensure no two users enter the same ID on *different* devices.

The starter code supports the interface and other business logic for the app — you'll add the motion-related bits now so you get to know how that all works.

Accessing device sensors with Core Motion

You'll use Core Motion to access readings from the phone's motion sensors, so import it by adding the following line along with the other imports in **ViewController.swift**:

```
import CoreMotion
```

This lets you access Core Motion within your *code*, but it's not enough to allow your *app* to do so. Apple rightly wants users to decide which apps can access their data, so it requires developers to include an explanation for *why* they want it. The starter project's **Info.plist** file already includes this explanation as a value for the key **Privacy - Motion Usage Description**. And because motion data is *required* for this app to function, rather than just a nice additional feature, both **accelerometer** and **gyroscope** have been added to **Info.plist**'s **Required device capabilities** list, too. Don't forget to provide the appropriate properties in your own apps.

Next, to interact with Core Motion, add the following properties inside `ViewController`. Keep things organized by putting them under the existing comment that reads `// MARK: - Core Motion properties`:

```
let motionManager = CMMotionManager()
let queue = OperationQueue()
```

Here you create a `CMMotionManager` to access the device's motion data. Each app should contain only one such object, regardless of how many sensors it plans to use. You'll use queue to keep sensor update callbacks off the main thread, which helps the device remain responsive while processing these high frequency events. Using a separate `OperationQueue` like this also ensures your app doesn't miss updates if it is temporarily too busy to process events.

Before you go any further, find the following two lines inside `startRecordingSession` and delete them:

```
/* TODO: REMOVE THIS LINE
...
TODO: REMOVE THIS LINE */
```

These lines were commenting out a `guard` statement that ensures the app has access to device motion, and alerts the user otherwise. They were commented out because they require `motionManager`, which you just added.

You need to tell `motionManager` how often to produce sensor data. `ViewController` stores its configuration-related constants inside its `Config` enum, so add the following constant there:

```
static let samplesPerSecond = 25.0
```

Here you set `samplesPerSecond` to 25, which you'll use later to specify you want the device to send you 25 sensor updates every second. This number is important because it determines how much data your model looks at based on how often you perform predictions. That is, if you classify the user's activity once per second, this gives you 25 samples per classification; if you do it once every four seconds, this rate gives you 100 samples.

But why 25? The sensors in Apple devices are capable of producing updates many times per second — at least 100, according to the docs — so shouldn't you just use the max? After all, aren't people always saying that when it comes to machine learning, more data is always better?

There are a few reasons why you shouldn't necessarily increase the update frequency too high:

- More updates means more data processing, which means less CPU available for whatever else your app needs to do.

- Faster updates usually means feeding more data into your model per prediction. That requires more complex ML models, which run more slowly — maybe too slowly to keep up with those faster updates.

- Higher frequency updates increase battery usage. You don't want users deleting your app because it sucks the life out of their devices.

It's true that higher frequency updates let you perceive finer details within the data, so there are times when you may need them. But not always — some activities involve slower changes over a longer time, where sensor readings might be necessary only a few times per second, or even less. The value of 25 used here was chosen arbitrarily — it works fine, but experiments to find the lowest usable update rate were not performed.

> **Note**: There's another option you aren't using here, but you may want to consider for your own projects. Perform data *collection* at a high rate, and then *downsample* it to train multiple models and find the lowest rate that works well. For example, collect data at 80Hz and then train multiple models — 80Hz using all the data, 40Hz using every other sample, 20Hz using every fourth sample, etc. This let's you collect data once and then have different options for how to use it, which is better than having to recollect it multiple times to experiment with update rates. Once you find the lowest rate that still works well, use that in your production app.

In this app, you'll store all the collected sensor data in memory and then write it out to disk at the end of the recording session. Add the following array with the other properties under the comment that reads `// MARK: - Core Motion properties` in `ViewController`:

```
var activityData: [String] = []
```

You'll create a single string containing all the data you want to record for a sample, and append it to `activityData`. The entire recording session will live inside this array as one long sequence, and GestureDataRecorder calls `saveActivityData` at the end of the session to save all these strings to file. However, you need to add the following few lines to actually save the array. Put it at the end of `confirmSavingActivityData` in `ViewController`:

```
do {
  try self.activityData.appendLinesToURL(fileURL: dataURL)
  print("Data appended to \(dataURL)")
} catch {
  print("Error appending data: \(error)")
}
```

This writes all the strings in the array out to the appropriate file using a helper function from inside **StringArrayExtensions.swift**. This function creates the file if it doesn't already exist, or appends to the file otherwise.

One important aspect of GestureDataRecorder is that it keeps recording sessions very short. As such, there's no fear of running out of memory while storing data in `activityData`. That also means it's not a big deal if something goes wrong while recording and you need to throw out some data — it's never much more than a minute's worth. Shorter sessions are also easier on your test subjects — it's probably a bit much to ask someone to shake their phone for an hour straight, but doing lots of tiny sessions isn't so bad.

However, when working with longer lasting activities, where data collection takes several minutes or more, you don't want to risk having to throw away too much data. In that case, you should write your data out to disk periodically rather than at the end of the session. You should also consider making your app more robust, by saving data when the app gets interrupted from things like incoming phone calls, for example.

You haven't enabled motion updates just yet, but eventually the app will receive them in the form of `CMDeviceMotion` objects. Add the following method to `ViewController` to process them:

```
func process(data motionData: CMDeviceMotion) {
  // 1
  let activity = isRecording ? currendActivity : .none
  // 2
  let sample = """
  \(sessionId!)-\(numberOfActionsRecorded),\
  \(activity.rawValue),\
  \(motionData.attitude.roll),\
```

```
    \(motionData.attitude.pitch),\
    \(motionData.attitude.yaw),\
    \(motionData.rotationRate.x),\
    \(motionData.rotationRate.y),\
    \(motionData.rotationRate.z),\
    \(motionData.gravity.x),\
    \(motionData.gravity.y),\
    \(motionData.gravity.z),\
    \(motionData.userAcceleration.x),\
    \(motionData.userAcceleration.y),\
    \(motionData.userAcceleration.z)
    """

    // 3
    activityData.append(sample)
  }
```

This method creates samples for your dataset from `CMDeviceMotion` objects. Here's how it works:

1. You label each sample with the activity it represents. This line checks to see if there *is* an activity being recorded or if this data is arriving in-between activities. In the latter case, you label it as `ActivityType.none`. The current activity is set from within the starter code after the app announces the activity to the user.

2. Here you create one big string representing a single data sample. It includes a session ID, the current activity and the sensor readings extracted from `motionData`, all separated by commas.

3. This line appends the string to `activityData`. The entire array gets saved to disk later, when the recording session ends.

Along with the session ID and the activity type, you're saving 12 different values at each moment in time. These were chosen because they seem like they *could* be relevant to the task at hand. However, you might not use all of them when you train your model.

But it's a good idea to record as much data as you can, because it gives you more options later when building your model. You can always remove data you don't need, but there's no way to go back to these moments and record additional data — adding features requires a new data collection effort.

Notice the session ID gets created by combining `sessionId`, which is a timecode created when recording starts, and the number of which recording the user is currently doing. That means that each time a user runs the app, they'll choose between creating one, two or three *sessions*, even though to the user it will seem like just one session.

Why is that important? You'll be using Turi Create's activity classification API, and it *currently* requires a few things when training. (Comments from its developers on GitHub seem to indicate they would like to make it more flexible in the future.) First, it doesn't like super short sessions. Without going into detail here, you'll want your sessions to be at least as long as 20 predictions worth of data.

> **Note**: This is one area where Create ML differs from Turi Create. Create ML expects each file to contain an uninterrupted sequence of data demonstrating a single activity. To use it you'll need to break up your recordings into multiple files, each containing a single sample sequence.

So if you plan on predicting once per second, for example, sessions should be at least 20 seconds long. It doesn't need to be exact, but sessions much shorter than that may not work well.

Secondly, Turi Create seems to prefer a lot of sessions. So instead of fewer, longer sessions, this app opts for creating more, shorter ones. Note however that sessions do **not** need to contain just a single activity. In fact, the sessions for this app will each contain *two* activities — the gesture itself, as well as a period of none data recorded before the gesture. In your own apps you can record any number of activities within a single session, but labeling them like this was an easy way to get more sessions with fewer actual user recordings.

You've got a method to process `CMDeviceMotion` objects, but you still need Core Motion to send them. Add the following to `ViewController` to enable device motion updates:

```
func enableMotionUpdates() {
  // 1
  motionManager.deviceMotionUpdateInterval =
    1 / Config.samplesPerSecond
  // 2
  activityData = []
  // 3
  motionManager.startDeviceMotionUpdates(
    using: .xArbitraryZVertical,
    to: queue,
    withHandler: { [weak self] motionData, error in
      // 4
      guard let self = self, let motionData = motionData else {
        let errorText = error?.localizedDescription ?? "Unknown"
        print("Device motion update error: \(errorText)")
        return
      }
```

```
    // 5
    self.process(data: motionData)
  })
}
```

Here's what's going on in the method above:

1. Use `samplesPerSecond` that you defined earlier to set how often `motionManager` sends updates to your app. In this case, you're setting it to update every 0.04 seconds, or 25 times per second.

2. Set `activityData` to an empty array. The project starter code calls this function each time the user starts a new recording session — this line ensures each session starts with a fresh array.

3. This line instructs `motionManager` to start sending device motion updates, passing a block to execute on queue for each update. The `using` parameter tells Core Motion to use `.xArbitraryZVertical` as the device position relative to which the device's attitude values should be reported. Check out `CMAttitudeReferenceFrame`'s documentation (https://apple.co/2RNdTT5) for the available options.

4. This `guard` statement ensures the callback received motion data. If not, you log an error message if one is available. If you find yourself getting many errors, then you may need a more robust solution here. For example, receiving too many errors in a row could trigger the session to stop and discard the data.

5. Call `process`, which you added earlier, to extract features from the sensor data and append them to `activityData`.

In this app you use Core Motion's device motion API. `CMMotionManager` also allows you to access accelerometer, gyroscope and magnetometer data directly, but the device motion API is often a better choice. Data directly from the sensors is often quite noisy and requires some preprocessing to smooth it out. But the good folks at Apple have already worked out some nice preprocessing steps and do them for you if you access the device motion data instead. Another nice touch — it separates acceleration due to the user from acceleration due to gravity, which makes the motion represented by the data easier to decipher.

However, if you ever want raw data from those sensors, `CMMotionManager` provides APIs that match that of device motion. So `deviceMotionUpdateInterval`, `startDeviceMotionUpdates`, etc., become `accelerometerUpdateInterval`, `startAccelerometerUpdates`, and so on. Similar methods exist for each sensor.

> **Note:** There are also versions of `startDeviceMotionUpdates`, `startAccelerometerUpdates`, etc. that take no parameters. These methods quietly update properties on the `CMMotionManager`, such as `deviceMotion` and `accelerometerData`. For some apps, it makes sense to use these methods instead of the ones that take parameters, and then poll the properties directly when you want sensor data.

Now that you've defined `enableMotionUpdates`, find the comment that reads `// TODO: enable Core Motion` inside the `Utterances.sessionStart` case in `speechSynthesizer`, and add a call to your new method there:

```
case Utterances.sessionStart:
  // TODO: enable Core Motion
  enableMotionUpdates()
  queueNextActivity()
```

Most of the timing in GestureDataRecorder actually comes from logic in `speechSynthesizer`. The app's `AVSpeechSynthesizer` calls this function whenever it finishes uttering a phrase, and the app uses the finished utterance to determine what to do next. In the case of the `sessionStart` message, it enables motion updates and calls `queueNextActivity` to get the recording started.

You've started motion updates, so you'll need to stop them at some point. Add the following method to `ViewController` to do that:

```
func disableMotionUpdates() {
  motionManager.stopDeviceMotionUpdates()
}
```

This function tells `motionManager` to stop sending motion updates. Add a call to it inside the following `case` statement in `speechSynthesizer`:

```
case Utterances.sessionComplete:
  disableMotionUpdates()
  ...
```

This statement executes after the recording session completes. You disable the motion updates and then the rest of the `case` statement saves the data to a file.

Collecting some data

Now go collect some data, ideally from multiple people. Invite your friends over, serve some nice canapés and make it a phone shaking party. If your friends are anything like my kids, they'll be willing to record data at least once before losing interest.

Keep in mind, performing activities incorrectly while recording data will reduce your model's performance. That's because you aren't manually labeling things, so you'll end up with mislabeled sequences in your dataset.

In the next section you'll see how to get rid of mislabeled data, but it's much better to avoid recording it in the first place. That's why GestureDataRecorder presents a confirmation window at the end of each recording session — it gives you the chance to discard data without saving it if you know something went wrong during the session.

Any files GestureDataRecorder saves will be accessible from the **Files** app on your iPhone, and inside the **File Sharing** area in iTunes. This works because the starter project's **Info.plist** includes the keys **Application supports iTunes file sharing** and **Supports opening documents in place**, both with values of **YES**.

Get any data you've collected from the device(s) and onto your computer, and store the files in one of the following three folders, all within the **notebooks** folder of the resources you downloaded: **data/train**, **data/valid** or **data/test**.

These folders hold the files from which you'll create the three datasets you'll use when building your model: train, validation and test. You'll read more about why later, but try not to store data collected from one person in more than one of these folders. You should put data from most people in **data/train**, while putting data from about 10% of your users in each of the other two folders. If you end up recording data from only one person — be honest, it was just you, right? — it's probably best to put it in **data/train**.

> **Note**: The device's orientation affects the data you collect. For example, imagine holding an iPhone out in front of you and then moving it up and down, side to side, and toward and away from you. Sensor data collected while doing so would be different if the phone was held in portrait or landscape (including variations based on home button position), with the screen facing toward or away from you, to the left, right, up, down or some angle in between. The gravity fields you stored are enough to determine orientation — that's actually how iOS knows when to rotate your app's UI — so your model *can* learn to identify activities in any of these situations. However, you'll need to provide plenty of training data to cover all the possibilities well enough for it to recognize them.
>
> For your own projects, you can handle this in one of three ways: Instruct users to position their devices a specific way and accept the model may not work well if they fail to do so, collect a much larger dataset that includes data from devices in all probable orientations, or apply a preprocessing step that transforms values into a known orientation. The projects in this chapter settle for the first option.

Analyzing and preparing your data

So you've got some data. You've collected it yourself or acquired it from elsewhere, but either way, your next step is to *look* at it. Don't try reading every number — that way lies madness — but do some analysis to see exactly what you're working with.

You want to ensure there aren't any problems that might ruin the models you try to build.

So what are you looking for? Here are a few things to consider:

- If you didn't create the dataset yourself, it's important to see what's there.

- Mislabeled data. Data is often labeled manually and mistakes are common.

- Poorly collected data. Sometimes mistakes are made while recording, such as misplaced sensors, incorrectly followed instructions, etc.

- Source errors. Sometimes the data source introduces errors, such as a damaged or malfunctioning device reporting bad data. And datasets made by people often contain data entry mistakes.

- Incorrect data types. For example, strings where there should be numbers.

- Missing values. It's common for some rows to have values missing. You'll need to decide how to handle those — remove such rows or insert reasonable values. The choice depends on your project, and there are many options for how to fill the values if you go that route. For example, you might use that feature's mean, median or mode value, or perhaps calculate a new value based on values from nearby rows.

- Outliers. *Some* variation is required to make a good dataset, but there are cases when a few samples may be too rare to be worth including in your dataset. Training with them can confuse the model, reducing its overall performance, and it's sometimes better to accept that there are some things your model just won't handle.

> **Note**: You don't *have* to remove such samples — you may very well want your model to support them. But it's something to consider.

You'll work with Python for the rest of this and the next chapter, so no more Xcode for a while. You'll also need Juptyer and Turi Create, so if you don't already have an environment that includes these from earlier in the book, then create one now using the file at **projects/notebooks/turienv.yaml**. If you're unsure how to do so, take a look at Chapter 4, "Getting Started with Python & Turi Create."

> From here on out, we'll assume your environment with Turi Create is named **turienv**, so keep that in mind when you see it mentioned.

Open up **Terminal** and, before you get started, activate the **turienv** environment:

```
conda activate turienv
```

Next, launch Jupyter from within your **turienv** environment.

```
jupyter notebook
```

Create a new notebook in the **notebooks** folder of the chapter resources. Or if you'd prefer to follow along in a completed notebook, you can open **notebooks/ Data_Exploration_Complete.ipynb** instead.

Get started by entering the following code in a cell and running it with **Shift+Return**:

```
%matplotlib inline
import turicreate as tc
import activity_detector_utils as utils
```

This gives you access to the turicreate package as well as some helper functions provided in **activity_detector_utils.py**, which you can find in the **notebooks** folder. The first line is what's known as a "magic" and it tells Jupyter to display any Matplotlib plots inside the notebook instead of in separate windows.

Now run the following code to load your datasets:

```
train_sf = utils.sframe_from_folder("data/train")
valid_sf = utils.sframe_from_folder("data/valid")
test_sf = utils.sframe_from_folder("data/test")
```

Here you use the sframe_from_folder function from **activity_detector_utils.py** to load your datasets. It takes the path to a folder — given here relative to the **notebooks** folder in which your notebook resides — and attempts to parse all the CSV files it finds there.

We've provided enough data to make the project work, but hopefully you've used GestureDataRecorder to collect some more. If so, whatever files you've added to these folders get loaded here as well.

> **Note**: If you reuse `utils.sframe_from_folder` in your own projects, you'll need to modify it slightly — it currently contains some project-specific details.

After running that cell, the variables `train_sf`, `valid_sf` and `test_sf` will be Turi Create `SFrame` objects, which are data structures designed to work efficiently with structured data, such as huge tables of numbers collected from an iPhone's motion sensors.

These three `SFrame`s contain the data you'll use for your training, validation and test sets, respectively. Take a peek at some samples by running the following code:

```
train_sf.head()
```

This displays the first 10 rows of the dataset, along with their column names. These names were assigned in `sframe_from_folder` but could also have come from the CSV files directly.

The following image shows an example of some output from `head`, edited slightly to fit here:

sessionId	activity	roll	pitch	yaw
2018-08-27T19:53:54Z-1	0	-0.46865287783368514	0.8395582736867373	0.36055793373729217
2018-08-27T19:53:54Z-1	0	-0.47302926367030734	0.8445595740425931	0.3664918810895234
2018-08-27T19:53:54Z-1	0	-0.4737607872960278	0.8483060548254803	0.3678965046324581

rotX	rotY	rotZ	gravX	gravY
0.13357801735401154	-0.0008428385481238365	0.05470273271203041	-0.3016313910484314	-0.7443482279777527
0.14320960640907288	0.00386190228164196	-0.0029299380257725716	-0.30253610014915466	-0.7476786971092224
0.0321430042386055	0.009147211909294128	-0.01968974433839321	-0.3016883134841919	-0.750161349773407

gravZ	accelX	accelY	accelZ	userId
-0.595788836479187	-0.010288774967193604	-0.0012877583503723145	0.008157610893249512	u_02
-0.5911417007446289	-0.020110994577407837	-0.012453138828277588	0.02307224273681641	u_02
-0.5884233713150024	0.008887410163879395	-0.015051662921905518	0.03977835178375244	u_02

First three samples of training set

> **Note**: If you've included your own data in any of these datasets, your results may vary from those shown here. This is true for all the screenshots in this section.

Notice how there is a column named **userId**. This was added inside sframe_from_folder — the values are derived from the names of your data files. This only works if your files each contain data from just one user, and their names are prefixed with the user's ID followed by a hyphen (-).

For example, all data read from a file named "bob-data.csv" would be assigned a **userId** value of "bob." You could have stored the user ID in each row when you were collecting the data, but saving each user's data into separate files keeps them smaller and makes them easier to organize. Either way, it's important to know the source of your data — you'll see why later.

Here's another thing about head's output — the values in the **activity** column are all 0. That's nothing to worry about — it's just because you're only looking at the first few rows, which represent less than one second of activity. But what does 0 even mean?

Inside GestureDataRecorder, you stored activity types as numeric values. Turi Create can deal with that just fine, but we humans sometimes interpret words more easily than numbers.

To convert those integers into something more readable, enter the following code in a cell and run it:

```
# 1
activity_values_to_names = {
  0 : 'rest_it',
  1 : 'drive_it',
  2 : 'shake_it',
  3 : 'chop_it'
}
# 2
def replace_activity_names(sframe):
  sframe['activity'] = sframe['activity'].apply(
    lambda val: activity_values_to_names[val])
# 3
replace_activity_names(train_sf)
replace_activity_names(valid_sf)
replace_activity_names(test_sf)
```

This replaces the numeric activity values in your datasets with the names of the gestures they represent. Here's how it works:

1. You create a dictionary that maps numeric activity values to strings. These strings were chosen arbitrarily, but they should describe the values clearly — that's the whole point of replacing them, right?

   Also note, the app you write later uses these values, too, so you'll need to modify code there if you change these strings.

2. You use the activity column's `apply` function to run a lambda function on the value in each row. Lamdba functions are similar to closures in Swift. This one replaces the column's integers with their corresponding strings from the dictionary. `SFrame` columns are represented by `SArray` objects, so check out that class in the Turi Create class if you'd like to see what's available. You define this line as a function just to make the next lines cleaner.

3. You call `replace_activity_names` for each of your dataset `SFrames`.

After running this cell, you've modified your datasets to make them easier to interpret, which you can see by calling `train_sf.head()` again:

sessionId	activity	roll	pitch	yaw
2018-08-27T19:53:54Z-1	rest_it	-0.46865287783368514	0.8395582736867373	0.36055793373729217
2018-08-27T19:53:54Z-1	rest_it	-0.47302926367030734	0.8445595740425931	0.3664918810895234
2018-08-27T19:53:54Z-1	rest_it	-0.4737607872960278	0.8483060548254803	0.3678965046324581

Partial list of features from first three samples of training set, with activity as strings

Note: You certainly could have stored these strings directly when you created the files in GestureDataRecorder, saving yourself the trouble of changing them now.

However, using integers conserves a bit of disk space. And more importantly, it gave you the chance to see an example of modifying some data in an `SFrame`, which you might want to do while preparing future datasets.

It's helpful to plot your data to examine it, so run the following code to look at your test set:

```
utils.plot_gesture_activity(test_sf)
```

Here you call `plot_gesture_activity` from inside **activity_detector_utils.py**. It uses Matplotlib to display an `SFrame`'s contents as a line chart. The following image shows the plot generated when you run that code:

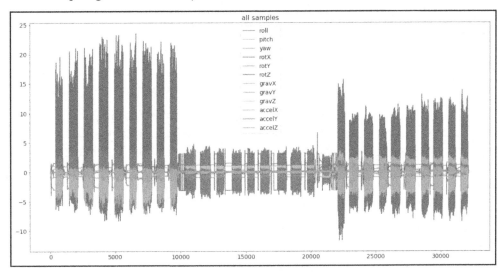

Plot of testing dataset

> **Note**: The plots shown in this chapter may be difficult to read, especially in the black-and-white printed version. They are all from **notebooks/ Data_Exploration_Complete.ipynb** — you are encouraged to open it in Jupyter to get a better look at these plots as well as several others not included here.

There's too much data in this plot to see much detail. But even at this zoomed-out scale, it's already clear there are distinct patterns present here.

With the `plot_gesture_activity` helper function, you can plot data for a single activity by specifying its name. The following example would show data just for the `drive_it` gesture:

```
utils.plot_gesture_activity(test_sf, activity="drive_it")
```

And you can zoom in on chunks of data by specifying a slice of the dataset, like so:

```
utils.plot_gesture_activity(
    test_sf[11950:12050], activity="drive_it")
```

The following three plots were created using code similar to the line above, showing slices of 100 samples for each of the three gestures in the test set:

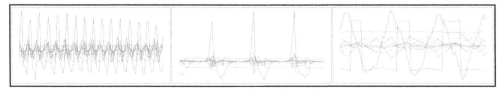

100 samples of 'shake_it', 'chop_it', and 'drive_it' activities from test dataset

The actual values aren't important in these plots. The important thing to notice is how each gesture appears as a clearly discernable pattern. It certainly seems like we *should* be able to recognize when a user performs these gestures, but imagine trying to write your own algorithm to do it using if/else statements — it might be pretty difficult! But don't worry — machine learning makes it *much* easier.

Removing bad data

Now you'll see one way to find and remove errors from your dataset. If you run the code suggested earlier to plot all the drive_it activity data in the test set, you'll see a plot something like the one on the next page.

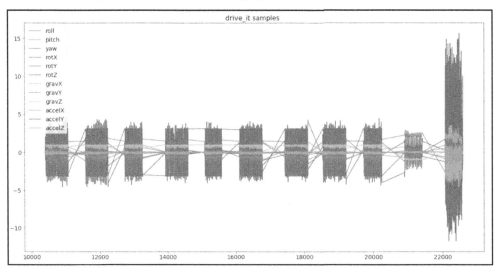

'drive_it' samples in test dataset

While much of this data looks similar, some of it stands out as different. Particularly, the last two blocks of activity seem odd. The following code looks at a small section in the second one of those areas:

```
utils.plot_gesture_activity(
    test_sf[22200:22300], activity="drive_it")
```

Remember, these specific slice numbers might not be the same in your dataset, but hopefully you can come up with values to find a slice within this section of the data.

This produces the following output:

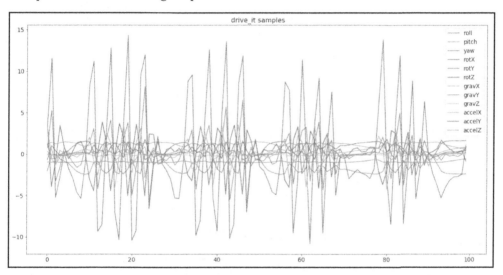

Mislabeled data in test dataset

If you compare this to the examples you plotted earlier, you'll see it looks more like a `shake_it` than a `drive_it` action. It seems someone performed the wrong gesture while recording, essentially mislabeling your data.

The second area of concern is a bit more difficult to see because it *mostly* looks the same as the good data. But if you look closely you may notice an area of green at the top of the data — green that you don't see in any of the other `drive_it` data. The following code zooms in on this area and plots only a few features:

```
utils.plot_gesture_activity(
    test_sf[21200:21500], activity="drive_it",
    features=["gravX", "gravY", "gravZ"])
```

This call uses another one of `plot_gesture_activity`'s optional parameters to specify a list of features to plot. So rather than showing all the data in this slice, it shows just the data for the device's gravity readings. The following image was made using code similar to the line above (with some slight adjustments to help with formatting).

The plot on the left shows a 100 sample sequence from the suspicious looking area, and the plot on the right shows a 100 sample sequence similar to the majority of the `drive_it` data:

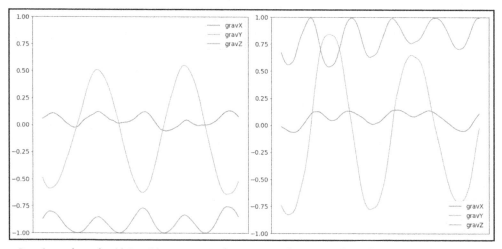

Gravity values for 'drive_it' gesture. Left: Incorrectly oriented. Right: Correctly oriented.

These plots show similar readings for gravity along the X and Y axes. The scale is slightly different for gravity along the Y axis, but the two plots are still basically the same. However, the gravity readings along the Z axis seem to be quite different. The *patterns* are the same, but the values are negative in the left example and positive in the right one. This indicates the user was not holding the phone in the correct orientation while performing the motion — the screen was facing up instead of down.

Both of these sessions contain data that will only serve to confuse your model, reducing its performance, so it's best to remove them from your dataset before continuing. To do so, run the following code, replacing the index values with ones that work for your dataset:

```
# 1
bad_session_1 = test_sf[21350]["sessionId"]
bad_session_2 = test_sf[22250]["sessionId"]
# 2
test_sf = test_sf.filter_by(
```

```
    [bad_session_1, bad_session_2],
    column_name='sessionId', exclude=True)
```

Here's what that does:

1. Grabs the session ID from a row in the middle of each area of bad data. Each session contains data for only one activity, so once you know the session ID for one, you know it for all the rows you want to delete.

2. Calls SFrame's filter_by method to return a new SFrame that excludes any rows where the **sessionId** column contains the value of either of the bad sessions.

Plotting the test set's drive_it data again shows the suspect sessions are now gone. The plot isn't included here to save space, but the **Data_Exploration_Complete.ipynb** notebook includes this plot if you'd like to compare it to your results.

This section included a few examples demonstrating some things to look for, but you should spend time thoroughly exploring all three of your datasets, both to clean up problems and to better understand your data. And don't neglect any particular dataset — testing with bad data can be just as problematic as training with it.

> **Note:** The erroneous data you removed from the test set all comes from one file: **notebooks/data/test/bad-drive-it-data.csv**. You can safely remove that file if you don't want to go through this exercise again.

Optional: Removing non-activity data

What about motions that have nothing to do with gestures? You know, all those sensor readings that arrive *between* the gestures? Take a look at that data by plotting the rest_it activity. Here's how you do so for the test set:

```
utils.plot_gesture_activity(test_sf, activity="rest_it")
```

This plots all samples in the test set labeled as `rest_it`, which means data that is *not* a gesture. Here are the results:

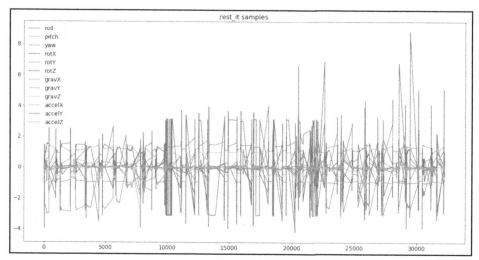

'rest_it' samples in test dataset

Unlike with the gestures you plotted earlier, the resting data shows no clear pattern. That makes sense — users can do whatever they want between gestures, so there are basically an infinite number of possible sequences that could appear with this label.

Depending on how similar the resting and activity data are, a model might have trouble learning to classify them both well. In those cases, it often helps to increase the size of your dataset set. However, in many cases — such as this one — the model will learn to recognize both resting and activities. This is probably because the sequences related to the other gestures are so much more distinct. That is, it will likely learn to classify the other gestures well, and then learn that anything else is resting. It will get some samples wrong — users sometimes perform the gestures while GestureDataRecorder is recording rest data, essentially adding mislabeled data to your dataset — but the juxtaposition of the messy resting data and the patterned gestures should make the model even more confident about its gesture predictions.

For this app, train with all your data, including the resting samples. However, you're encouraged to try making another model that excludes the resting data to see which you prefer. The results might vary depending on exactly what your datasets look like.

If you ever want to try removing that data, you can do so with the following code:

```
train_sf = train_sf.filter_by(
    ["rest_it"], 'activity', exclude=True)
test_sf = test_sf.filter_by(
```

```
    ["rest_it"], 'activity', exclude=True)
  valid_sf = valid_sf.filter_by(
    ["rest_it"], 'activity', exclude=True)
```

Much like how you removed the bad sessions, this would create new SFrames that do not contain any samples whose **activity** value was rest_it.

Balancing your classes

After you are satisfied you've cleaned your data, there's one final thing you should check: How many examples of each class do you have? Run the following code to count the examples in each dataset:

```
  utils.count_activities(train_sf)
  utils.count_activities(valid_sf)
  utils.count_activities(test_sf)
```

Here you call count_activities, another helper function defined in **activity_detector_utils.py**. It displays a table showing how many sessions are present for each activity, both per user and total.

The following shows the counts for the datasets we provided:

```
+----------+--------+-------+ +----------+--------+-------+ +----------+--------+-------+
| activity | userId | Count | | activity | userId | Count | | activity | userId | Count |
+----------+--------+-------+ +----------+--------+-------+ +----------+--------+-------+
| chop_it  |  u_01  |  36   | | chop_it  |  u_03  |   4   | | chop_it  |  u_05  |   9   |
| chop_it  |  u_02  |  36   | | chop_it  |  u_04  |   4   | | drive_it |  u_05  |   9   |
| drive_it |  u_01  |  36   | | drive_it |  u_03  |   4   | | rest_it  |  u_05  |  27   |
| drive_it |  u_02  |  36   | | drive_it |  u_04  |   4   | | shake_it |  u_05  |   9   |
| rest_it  |  u_01  |  108  | | rest_it  |  u_03  |  12   | +----------+--------+-------+
| rest_it  |  u_02  |  108  | | rest_it  |  u_04  |  12   | [4 rows x 3 columns]
| shake_it |  u_01  |  36   | | shake_it |  u_03  |   4   |
| shake_it |  u_02  |  36   | | shake_it |  u_04  |   4   |
+----------+--------+-------+ +----------+--------+-------+
[8 rows x 3 columns]            [8 rows x 3 columns]
```

Activity counts for train, validation and test sets

Here you can see that each dataset contains the same three gestures, and no gesture is represented more than any other within a specific dataset. Users within a dataset are represented equally as well. For example, each of the training set's two users supplied 50% of the training data. Things are looking great! You won't always have such perfectly balanced datasets, but you want them to be as well balanced as possible. If any gesture or user is overrepresented in the training set, your model may bias itself toward those samples. But unbalanced validation or test sets can be a problem, too, because they'll skew your evaluation results, making it more difficult to judge your model.

> **Note**: The rest_it activity takes up half of each dataset — you might want to remove some of those samples to bring it in line with the other gestures, but it wasn't a problem when training the model included with the book.

The dataset included in the resources contains 216 actions for training, 24 for validation and 27 for testing. It's not a lot of data, but it's as much as the author's family was willing to put up with collecting. :[Still, it's a reasonable balance, with about 80% of your data for training, and around 10% each for validation and testing.

Once you're convinced your datasets are good to go, run the following code to save the cleaned up SFrames for later use:

```
train_sf.save('data/cleaned_train_sframe')
test_sf.save('data/cleaned_test_sframe')
valid_sf.save('data/cleaned_valid_sframe')
```

The save method lets you save SFrames in several different formats, such as CSV and JSON. Here you're using a format that creates the given folder and stores various binary files in it. It's convenient because it's smaller and loads faster than the others, but feel free to use any format you like. And remember, you still have your original files, so you can always start over if you decide you don't like something about your cleaned data.

> **Note**: Turi Create has many options for data exploration and manipulation, as do Pandas and NumPy. And it provides methods to convert to and from the data structures used by these other libraries, so if there's something you prefer to do in one package over another, you can freely move back and forth. It's a good idea to spend some time looking through the documentation for these various frameworks to see what's available, but don't try to learn everything all at once — as you do more with machine learning, you'll continue to discover new things about it and all these supporting frameworks, too.

Key points

- Core Motion provides access to motion sensors on iOS and WatchOS devices.

- When building a dataset, prefer collecting less data from more sources over more data from fewer sources.

- Inspect and clean your data before training any models to avoid wasting time on potentially invalid experiments. Be sure to check *all* your data — training, validation and testing.

- Try isolating data from a single source into one of the train, validation or test sets.

- Prefer a balanced class representation. In cases where that's not possible, evaluate your model with techniques other than accuracy, such as precision and recall.

Where to go from here?

You have a bunch of motion data sequences organized into training, validation and test sets. Now it's time to make a model that can recognize specific gestures in them. In the next chapter, you'll use Turi Create to do just that.

Chapter 12: Training a Model for Sequence Classification

By Chris LaPollo

In the previous chapter, you learned about collecting and analyzing sequences of data, both crucial parts of successfully using machine learning. This chapter introduces a new type of neural network specifically designed for sequential data, and you'll build one to classify the data you collected as device motions.

If you're jumping into this chapter without first having gone through the previous one, you'll need a Python environment with access to Turi Create. We'll assume you have one named **turienv**, but if you don't then you can create it now using the file at **projects/notebooks/turienv.yaml**. If you're unsure how to do so, refer back to Chapter 4, "Getting Started with Python & Turi Create."

Creating a model

You've got access to a clean dataset — either the one you made in the previous chapter or one we'll provide for you — and now you're ready to train a model. Or maybe several models until you find one that works well. This section shows how to use Turi Create's task-focused API to train a model for activity detection.

> **Note**: Training your own model is *highly* recommended, especially if you collected data to add to the provided dataset. But if for whatever reason you skipped the previous chapter, you can find a trained model named **GestureClassifier.mlmodel** inside the **notebooks/pre-trained** subfolder of the chapter resources required for this chapter.

In this section you'll continue working with Jupyter in your **turienv** Anaconda environment. Create a new notebook in the **notebooks** folder of the chapter resources. If you'd like to see how we trained our provided model, you can check out the completed notebook **notebooks/Model_Training_Complete.ipynb**.

Import the same packages as you used in the previous chapter's notebook:

```
import turicreate as tc
import activity_detector_utils as utils
```

Then run the following code to load your training, validation and testing datasets:

```
train_sf = tc.SFrame("data/cleaned_train_sframe")
valid_sf = tc.SFrame("data/cleaned_valid_sframe")
test_sf = tc.SFrame("data/cleaned_test_sframe")
```

As mentioned in the previous chapter, Turi Create stores structured data in SFrame objects. There are various ways to create such objects — here you load them directly from the binary files you previously saved. If you'd prefer to use the files supplied with the resources, change the paths to pre-trained/data/cleaned_train_sframe, pre-trained/data/cleaned_valid_sframe and pre-trained/data/cleaned_test_sframe.

Training any classifier involves using multiple datasets for training, validation and testing. But dealing with sequences includes a few wrinkles that require some explanation.

Splitting sequential data

If you've ever trained an image classifier, you may have divided the images into training, validation and test sets *randomly*. Or maybe those sets were provided for you, in which case someone *else* divided them randomly.

This works because each image is its own sample — no one image relates any more or less to any other image. (See the upcoming Note for an important caveat to this statement.) But the very nature of sequences is that samples *do* relate to each other. Order and grouping both matter — that's what *makes* them sequences! For example, if you're counting by twos — two, four, six, eight — and then randomly shuffle that data — eight, two, six, four — you've lost the sequence and now the data is meaningless. Or worse, you may have accidentally reordered them into a sequence with a different meaning — eight, six, four, two — now the sequence counts *down* by twos!

So the first rule for training with sequences: keep samples related to individual sequences grouped together and in order. Any shuffling or sampling you do should take into account these groupings.

> **Note:** There *can* be situations where relationships exist between images in datasets meant to train classifiers, but those usually indicate mistakes that you should try to avoid. For example, if some images are identical or nearly so, as is common when dealing with large numbers of images, then having some in the training set and some in the validation or test sets may mislead you into thinking your model generalizes better than it does. It's a tricky situation, because sometimes your in-production model *will* encounter examples that are nearly identical to those it saw while training. For example, consider a model meant to identify product images from the internet — it's unlikely that you'll manage to create a good training set without also including some of the very images its meant to recognize. But in general, do your best to keep training and test sets as separate as possible, while realizing there are going to be times when some similarity sneaks in.

There's a second potential concern, relating to the *sources* of the sequences. Consider the case you've been working on throughout this chapter — gesture recognition. There's certainly *some* variation each time you perform a gesture — after all, the app collects several floating point values from multiple sensors, many times per second, so its basically impossible to get two *identical* recordings. However, identical isn't the same as *really similar*.

Different recordings of one person making a gesture are going to be similar to each other. That's not entirely bad — it's that similarity you want the model to recognize. You may even find it's fairly easy to train a model that recognizes gestures from a *specific* person — it may not even require many training examples. But it might not work as well when you use the model with someone else.

That's because recordings from one person are more similar to *each other* than they are to recordings from *someone else*. For example, the following plots show some data from two people performing the same actions — step up exercises:

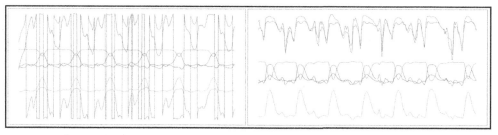

Data collected from two users both performing the same activity — step up exercises

These two plots show similar values for several features, but some features are quite different between users. A model trained on data from one of these users might have trouble recognizing the activity when presented with data from the other — and the more data you show your model from one user, the more different the other user's data will seem. It's certainly good to collect lots of data from each source, but it's more important to collect data from lots of sources.

So if you have the choice of getting 1000 recordings from one person, versus 100 recordings from 10, the second will probably produce a better model. And 10 recordings' from 100 people would probably be even better. By all means, get more data from each person if you can, but definitely try to collect data from as many people as possible.

And that's the second rule for training with sequences, or really any data where the data's source affects its features: use data from as many sources as possible. The more sources you have in your training set, the better your model should generalize to unseen examples.

But even if you have a great dataset chock full of examples from many different people, there's another issue — how best to split it up into train, validation and test sets?

You might be tempted to split the data randomly (keeping in mind the earlier rule about maintaining samples as sequences, of course). However, you should avoid this.

Remember how different recordings from the same person are similar to each other? Well, if you train with data from one person, then test with different data from the *same* person, your model may appear to perform better than it really does. That's because it essentially trained on some of the test data.

So the third rule for training with sequences: don't split your datasets by sequence, split them by *source*. Make sure you know the source of each of your data samples, and try to put all the data from any particular source into the same set: train, validation or test.

> **Note**: Those last two problems occur with more than just sequences. Many data types are affected by their sources. For example, sensors from different phones will report slightly different values in the same situations, camera lenses have slightly different distortions, and so on. All physical devices are produced with some variance, so data collected from different devices can be slightly different even when measuring the same thing. In these cases, the same rules apply: try to train with as many different sources as possible, and try to test on data collected from multiple sources. Unless of course the model is *meant* to work with a specific source — such as correcting lense distortion for images from a *specific* camera. Then by all means test on data collected from the same source to ensure your model works correctly in its intended production environment.

But sometimes...

And now, in a shocking plot twist, you're about to be told to sometimes do what you were just told not to do — train and validate on data from the same people! What?!

Real talk: There are going to be times — maybe *most* of the time — when you won't have as much data as you want. In those cases, you can stretch your dataset out a bit by starting with just two datasets — training and test — and then grabbing a chunk of your training set to use for validation.

Depending on how many different sources are present in your training set, you might not be able to follow the recommended procedure of separating based on source. For example, the one provided with the chapter contains data from just two people. You'd lose too much training data if you separated these users, so you'd need to accept training and validating on data from both of them.

It's not ideal — your validation accuracy will be artificially closer to your training accuracy because the two datasets are more similar, making it harder to tell if your model overfits. But if there's enough variety in your training set to start, then this still works fairly well.

To help split your training data, Turi Create provides a nice utility function that divides an SFrame randomly into two smaller SFrames, while still maintaining proper sequence groupings. The following code demonstrates how to use it:

```
train, valid =
tc.activity_classifier.util.random_split_by_session(
  train_sf, session_id='sessionId', fraction=0.9)
```

This uses Turi Create's `activity_classifier.util.random_split_by_session` function with a training set, telling it which column name identifies the sessions, and what percentage of the data should be used in the first split. It returns two SFrames, the first will contain the given percentage of the original SFrame's sessions, and the second will contain the remaining sessions.

After running this code, `train` would contain about 90% of the sessions and `valid` would contain the other 10%. You would then use these two SFrames for your training and validation sets.

The most important thing about this function is that it splits data based on session IDs, which means it keeps sequences organized together. Any samples with the same session ID are kept together and in order, but any particular session ID could end up in the training or the validation set.

The results of this call are not necessarily going to give you a perfectly balanced split. For example, here are the results of calling `utils.count_activities` with `train` and `valid` from one sample run:

```
+----------+--------+-------+ +----------+--------+-------+
| activity | userId | Count | | activity | userId | Count |
+----------+--------+-------+ +----------+--------+-------+
| chop_it  |  u_01  |  33   | | chop_it  |  u_01  |   3   |
| chop_it  |  u_02  |  34   | | chop_it  |  u_02  |   2   |
| drive_it |  u_01  |  31   | | drive_it |  u_01  |   5   |
| drive_it |  u_02  |  30   | | drive_it |  u_02  |   6   |
| rest_it  |  u_01  |  95   | | rest_it  |  u_01  |  13   |
| rest_it  |  u_02  |  97   | | rest_it  |  u_02  |  11   |
| shake_it |  u_01  |  31   | | shake_it |  u_01  |   5   |
| shake_it |  u_02  |  33   | | shake_it |  u_02  |   3   |
+----------+--------+-------+ +----------+--------+-------+
[8 rows x 3 columns]          [8 rows x 3 columns]
```

Random train/validation split counts

That's probably fine, but if you see a particularly bad split — especially when you know the original data was well balanced — then you should try splitting it again.

If you want to experiment later, try combining the training and validation data and then use this function to randomly split it. You'll end up with more variety in your training data in exchange for a less trustworthy validation set. For now, you'll just use the separate datasets you've already built.

Training the model

Now it's time to build and train your model. Almost.

Whenever you train with a new model or dataset, it's good to first take a small portion of your training data and see if you can get the model to overfit it. Overfitting is usually a bad thing — it means your model is memorizing the training data instead of learning a more general solution — but it also shows that the model is actually capable of learning *something* from your data. If your model is going to work on a real dataset, then it should definitely be able to overfit on a tiny version of it. And if it can't, then you've got one of several problems you'll need to address:

- A bug in the model. This is especially common when implementing neural nets from scratch using frameworks such as Keras.

- A model too simple to solve the problem. You might need more layers, or more nodes per layer.

- A model architecture incapable of solving the problem. Different architectures work better for different problems, so pick something appropriate.

- Poorly tuned hyperparameters. Sometimes all it takes is a change to the learning rate, other times you might need different activation functions, optimization algorithms or loss functions.

- Maybe the problem is the problem itself. Machine learning isn't the right solution to every problem, so don't try to force it.

The point of this exercise is to prove to yourself that your dataset is applicable to the problem, your model is built correctly and it's tuned well enough to learn. You'll still usually have to do more tuning later with your full dataset, but those training sessions take longer. This step is critical to keep yourself from wasting time trying to tune a model that isn't ever going to work.

To save space we don't show the results of the overfitting step here, but you can find them in the notebook **Model_Training_Complete.ipynb** in the **notebooks** folder.

OK, *now* it's time to build and train your model. Turi Create's activity classification API makes this process easy — it just takes one function call! Add the following code to a notebook cell, but **don't** run it yet:

```
model = tc.activity_classifier.create(
  dataset=train_sf, session_id='sessionId', target='activity',
  features=[
    "rotX", "rotY", "rotZ", "accelX", "accelY", "accelZ"],
  prediction_window=20, validation_set=valid_sf,
  max_iterations=20)
```

This one line of code is doing a lot, so it warrants quite a bit of explanation. Here goes:

- `dataset`: Your training dataset, stored as an `SFrame`.

- `session_id`: The name of the column in `dataset` that stores the session ID associated with each row. `create` keeps data with the same session ID grouped together and in order, and then trains over it in chunks the size of `prediction_window` rows.

- `target`: The name of the column that contains the labels you want the model to predict. In this case, it's `activity`.

- `features`: This is an optional list of columns to use for training. If you don't supply it, then `create` uses all the columns as features except for the ones you specified for `session_id` and `target`. More on this in a bit.

- `prediction_window`: How many samples (i.e. rows of data) the model looks at to make a prediction. More on this later.

- `validation_set`: Your validation dataset, stored as an `SFrame`. This is optional — if you don't supply it, and `dataset` contains more than 100 sessions, then `create` will automatically make a validation set by randomly selecting sessions from `dataset`. But if it contains fewer sessions than that, `create` trains the model without a validation set. It's best not to rely on this logic, and supply your own data instead.

- `max_iterations`: The maximum number of epochs `create` will train over. That is, the number of times it will go through the training set. Note: the parameter name and documentation claim this is a "maximum," as if `create` *could* stop training sooner. However, there appears to be no evidence that training ever stops before this value is reached, so think of it as the actual number instead of a maximum.

Notice how the `features` parameter is a list including just six of the 12 motion features available in your dataset — the rotation and acceleration due to the user.

These were chosen a bit arbitrarily, mostly to show that you don't *need* to use all columns in your dataset. In the previous section you saw how each activity appeared with a distinct pattern. But take a look at the following plots, which show just user rotation values for samples of each activity:

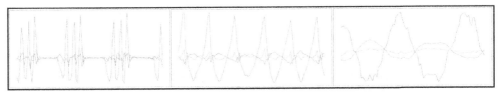

Rotations for 100 samples of 'shake_it', 'chop_it', and 'drive_it' activities from training dataset

As you can see, there are still clearly visible patterns, even when using just these three features. You are encouraged to train models with different feature combinations to see if/how it effects the results. There is no one correct answer here — many combinations will produce usable models for this project.

> **Note**: For any specific problem, there is likely some minimum set of features necessary to train a good model. It just needs *enough* information to perceive differences between the classes, and different features may be more or less useful for each class. The final set of features you settle on will always be project dependant, but when in doubt — use more. That gives your model the most leeway to decide for itself.

The prediction window is an important aspect of Turi Create's activity classification model. It specifies how many samples the model needs to look at each time it makes a prediction. That means this value — combined with Core Motion's update interval — determines the amount of *time* each prediction represents.

For example, if the prediction window is 50 and Core Motion sends the app 10 updates per second, it will take five seconds to collect enough data to make one prediction. But if you're getting updates 100 times per second, it would take 0.5 seconds. As was mentioned earlier, be sure you train your model with a prediction window that makes sense for the update rate you are using. You collected data at 25 samples per second, so this window size of 20 means the model needs 0.8 seconds worth of data per prediction.

The prediction window suggested here works well with the provided dataset and satisfies our goals for the book. However, you should train multiple models using different window sizes to see what you think works best. You won't *really* know if you're satisfied until you use the model in its target environment — in this case, the game you'll make in the next chapter. There's no one "correct" size — it's based on the specific use case, the dataset, and a bit of personal preference. Traditional software developers often struggle with this aspect of machine learning more than any other — you can't usually sit down and just write the "solution" to a problem; it's more about running lots of experiments until you discover what works best for your specific use case.

OK, now create your model by running the cell with your call to `create`. The first output you'll see will be something like this:

```
Pre-processing 235057 samples...

Using sequences of size 400 for model creation.

Processed a total of 216 sessions.
```

Initial training output

Here's a rundown of what this tells you:

- The first line reports how many samples — individual rows — are in the training dataset. The function performs some pre-processing on the data, including chunking it into fixed-length sequences.

- The second line let's you know Turi Create will be training on sequences of 400 samples. That's because you're training with a prediction window of 20 samples, and Turi Create's underlying implementation always trains in chunks of 20 consecutive windows. If a session doesn't have enough samples available, the end of the sequence gets padded with zeros.

  This is why you shouldn't have very short recording sessions — tiny sessions result in too much padding and the model will have trouble learning.

- Finally, it reports the number of sessions in your training dataset. This matters most when you don't supply a validation set, because `create` will use some of these sessions for validation *if* there are more than 100 sessions available.

After that, you'll see updates appear for each training iteration — or epoch — as your model continues to train. You need to check these updates for signs of overfitting. If the training accuracy continues to improve but the validation accuracy stalls or begins to decline, then the model has begun to overfit.

The output for the provided model isn't included here, but you can see it in **notebooks/Model_Training_Complete.ipynb**. It actually overfits slightly, but we decided to stick with that model anyway for a couple reasons.

First, it's good to show to readers as an example of overfitting. And secondly, the difference between the final model's validation accuracy and the epoch with the best value was only about 1%. The validation set is very small, with only four recordings of each gesture from each of two users.

A 1% difference in accuracy in such a small dataset really isn't significant enough to prove anything about the model's expected real world performance — it might just be certain epochs arrived at weights that happened to work well with that particular validation set. This is why you should strive to get a lot of variety in your datasets by collecting data from many different sources.

The final epoch for the model that ships with the book as **notebooks/pre-trained/ GestureClassifier.mlmodel** had a training accuracy of 98.5% and a validation accuracy of 95.2%. If you include training data collected from other sources, you're likely to get *lower* training accuracy while getting *higher* validation accuracy. Don't get hung up on the specific numbers, though — the idea is just to get something that looks like it trained well before moving on to testing with your test set.

> **Note**: Turi Create is great, as it builds and trains sophisticated models without you needing to do much more than provide the data. However, that comes at the cost of flexibility. There isn't much you can do here to tweak your model's performance.
>
> Besides changing your dataset, you can also try different prediction windows, feature combinations, batch sizes (not discussed here — you just used the default), and number of epochs.
>
> If none of that leads to a model suited to your app, then you'll need to build something customized in a more flexible framework like Keras. You'll work with sequences in Keras in later chapters.

When you think the model's ready for testing, go ahead and run the following code:

```
metrics = model.evaluate(test_sf)
print(metrics['accuracy'])
```

You use the model's `evaluate` method to classify everything in your test set and gather the results inside a dictionary named `metrics`. You've also displayed the accuracy the model achieved with those classifications, which for the provided dataset should be in the very high 90s — the model included with the chapter resources scores over 97%.

Accuracy isn't everything, though. You have access to various other results, including precision, recall, a confusion matrix, and more. You can access each of these by name, like you did with accuracy. To see a quick rundown, just print the entire `metrics` object:

```
print(metrics)
```

The confusion matrix is particularly useful here. It lets you know not just whether or not your model was correct, but *where* it made mistakes. This lets you see if there's a particular class that's giving your model extra trouble. If so, you might need to tweak your datasets by gathering more data for the more difficult classes.

But you should also consider trying a different prediction window size, since sometimes models are better at recognizing different classes using different windows — your goal is to find the one that gives you the best overall performance.

> **Note**: If you find different activities are only recognized at different window sizes, then you might need a more complicated setup using multiple models, each trained to spot a subset of your classes. You may know about "ensemble" methods already, where multiple models combine their predictions to produce a final answer. The technique required here is *almost* an ensemble, but it's slightly more complex, because it requires extra logic in your app to ensure your different models predict on different schedules. That won't be covered further in this book.

Here's the confusion matrix for the model included with the book:

```
+---------------+-------------------+-------+
| target_label  | predicted_label   | count |
+---------------+-------------------+-------+
|    shake_it   |     rest_it       |   96  |
|    rest_it    |     drive_it      |   17  |
|    drive_it   |     drive_it      |  5443 |
|    chop_it    |     rest_it       |  181  |
|    chop_it    |     shake_it      |  176  |
|    rest_it    |     rest_it       | 13164 |
|    chop_it    |     chop_it       |  5118 |
|    drive_it   |     rest_it       |  184  |
|    shake_it   |     shake_it      |  5367 |
|    rest_it    |     chop_it       |   62  |
|    rest_it    |     shake_it      |   77  |
+---------------+-------------------+-------+
[11 rows x 3 columns]
```

Confusion matrix for trained model

The first thing you might notice is the large numbers of predictions — your dataset didn't have nearly that many gestures, did it? That's because it's providing a prediction for every *window*, not every *activity*. So it makes many predictions over any single activity sequence, and this shows the results for all of them.

Next, notice the predictions with the highest counts: They are all *correct* predictions, with over 5,000 for each of the gestures and over 13,000 for rest_it. On the other hand, each of the *incorrect* predictions happened only a small number of times, with the fewest being rest_it predicted as drive_it only 17 times and the most being drive_it predicted as rest_it 184 times. Almost all of the errors involved the rest_it activity, which you would expect. After all, you never know what people did while recording their rest data — they may even have been doing the other gestures!

In fact, notice that the only incorrect predictions that did *not* involve the rest_it activity were the 176 chop_it gestures predicted as shake_it. It makes sense that there might be mistakes between these two gestures, since chopping is actually quite similar to shaking — if a person chops very quickly it might appear similar to a shake, or if the shake is over exaggerated it might look a bit like a chop.

Keep in mind, your model's performance in your app may be better than its test results, because you'll ignore low-confidence predictions. But if you're still unhappy with the model, you should create another one. Some sticklers will tell you not to reuse your training data because you'll be leaking data into your model. That's *technically* true, and you should listen to them... except you probably won't. Unless you have an endless stream of free data available, you probably don't have the luxury of testing just once per test set. The good news is — in many cases that's probably OK. For example, with a project like this one, you want the *app* to perform well, and your test data is just a tool to help you get there. Once your model works well on that, you'll run it on actual devices with live data from real people. Those are your *real* tests, and they are always unique — so you can even tell those sticklers you're using a new test set each time! Metrics like test accuracy are great, but be sure to beta test your app with many people before releasing it, so you know it really works the way you want it to.

When you think your model is ready for testing on a device, go ahead and save it with the following code:

```
model.export_coreml("GestureClassifier.mlmodel")
model.save("GestureClassifier")
```

This exports it to Core ML for use in your app, and saves a copy that you can reload in Python in case you want to work more with it later.

You've saved your model, trained to analyze iPhone motion data and recognize when that data indicates specific gestures have occurred. It seems to perform well, at least when tested against *recorded* motion data. That's a good start, but you want it to work in real time, evaluating motion data *as it's produced on the device*. For that you need an app! Continue reading to learn how to build one.

Getting to know your model

Open the **GestureIt** starter project in Xcode. If you've gone through the chapters leading up to this one, then you've already practiced adding Core ML models to your projects — find the **GestureClassifier.mlmodel** file you created when you saved your trained model in the previous section and drag it into Xcode. Or, if you'd like to use the model we trained on the provided dataset, add **notebooks/pre-trained/ GestureClassifier.mlmodel** instead.

> **Note**: Now that you have the model in Xcode, the rest of this section is all theory. You can safely skip it if you aren't interested in this discussion right now.

Select **GestureClassifier.mlmodel** in the Project Navigator and you'll see the following, which is similar to — but also quite different from — models from **Section 1** of this book:

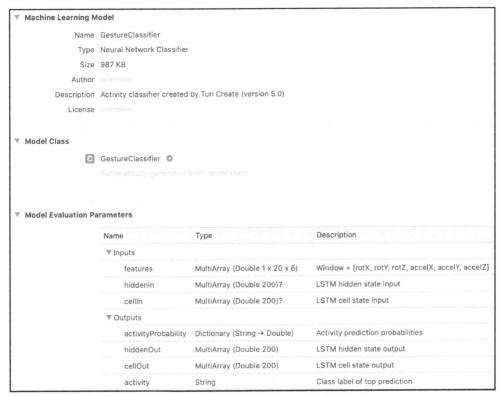

▼ **Machine Learning Model**

Name	GestureClassifier
Type	Neural Network Classifier
Size	987 KB
Author	unknown
Description	Activity classifier created by Turi Create (version 5.0)
License	unknown

▼ **Model Class**

    🅒 GestureClassifier ⊕

    Automatically generated Swift model class

▼ **Model Evaluation Parameters**

Name	Type	Description
▼ Inputs		
features	MultiArray (Double 1 x 20 x 6)	Window × [rotX, rotY, rotZ, accelX, accelY, accelZ]
hiddenIn	MultiArray (Double 200)?	LSTM hidden state input
cellIn	MultiArray (Double 200)?	LSTM cell state input
▼ Outputs		
activityProbability	Dictionary (String → Double)	Activity prediction probabilities
hiddenOut	MultiArray (Double 200)	LSTM hidden state output
cellOut	MultiArray (Double 200)	LSTM cell state output
activity	String	Class label of top prediction

Looking at the mlmodel file

Here you can see GestureClassifier is an activity classifier from Turi Create. It's under 1MB — that's pretty good for a neural net that isn't taking advantage of models pre-installed on iOS, as did some of the ones you made earlier. But then comes the Model Evaluation Parameters section, where things get a bit more complicated.

First, the more recognizable items:

- `features`: `MLMultiArray` of `Doubles` you'll pass as input. If you haven't seen `MLMultiArray` before, don't worry, it's nothing too new. It's basically just a multidimensional array that Core ML uses to work efficiently with data.

This one is sized to store a single prediction window's worth of values for each of the features you used while training: rotation and acceleration due to the user around the X, Y and Z axes.

- `activityProbability`: Dictionary the model outputs that includes the probabilities assigned to predictions for each of the classes. In the case of this project, that means probabilities for the gesture types "rest_it," "shake_it," etc.

- `activity`: String the model outputs indicating the activity class predicted with the highest probability.

But what about these other things: `hiddenIn`, `cellIn`, `hiddenOut` and `cellOut`? And what's this mysterious new acronym "LSTM" mentioned in all their descriptions?

Recurrent neural networks

So far in this book you've mostly dealt with convolutional neural networks — CNNs. They're great for recognizing *spatial* relationships in data, such as how differences in value between nearby pixels in a two-dimensional grid can indicate the presence of an edge in an image, and nearby edges in certain configurations can indicate the ear of a dog, etc. Another kind of network, called a recurrent neural network — RNN — is designed to recognize *temporal* relationships. Remember, a sequence generally implies the passage of time, so this really just means they recognize relationships between items in a sequence.

To do that, they look at sequences one item at a time, and produce an output for each item based on the *current* item *and* on the *output* they produced for the *previous* item. But what does that really mean?

Consider how you read the following sentence: "The quick brown fox jumps over the lazy dog." You don't look at each word individually and ignore the rest, right? Instead, each element of the sentence adds to your understanding. What's happening? Jumping. Who's jumping? The fox. What's it look like? It's brown. And so forth.

RNNs are designed to do something similar, interpreting each element in a sequence by considering the elements they've already seen.

So what's that look like as a network? You may come across RNN diagrams like this one:

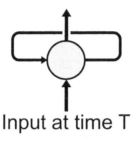

Input at time T

Looping nature of RNN layers

In the above image, the circle represents a single *layer* of an RNN, not a single node. Remember from what you learned earlier — a layer in a neural network can contain any number of nodes, with more nodes providing that layer with more representation power. Input elements in a sequence are referenced by timesteps, and layers process the element at time **T** by looking at both that input *and* the layer's own output from the *previous* input at timestep **T-1**. That loop where the layer's output feeds back into itself is known as a recurrent connection — i.e. it occurs repeatedly — giving RNNs their names.

While diagrams like that might be useful to describe the theory behind an RNN, it can be easier to visualize if you think of the network as multiple layers. Looked at this way, each successive layer receives the next element in the input sequence along with the output from the previous layer. The following image shows what that would look like when processing the earlier example sentence:

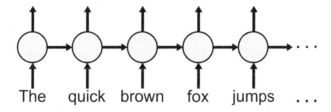

The   quick   brown   fox   jumps   ...

RNN layer's recurrent behavior shown as separate layers

Now it's clearer how the layers process a sequence one element at a time, combining each element of the input with the output generated for the previous element. Notice that the RNN cannot process a given item until after it has processed the items that came before it in the sequence. It's this serial nature of RNNs that makes them slower than other neural networks, such as CNNs. This is true of both training and inference.

These recurrent connections allow RNN layers to adjust their output based on what they've seen so far in the sequence, much like you interpret the word "fish" in the following two sentences differently depending on the words before it: "I like to fish." and "I like fish." In the first sentence, the speaker likes to *catch* fish, or at least try to; in the second, the speaker probably likes to *eat* fish, but may also just enjoy fish as an animal in general. Either way, the definition of "fish" depends on its context.

> **Note**: The previous diagram shows *two* outputs from each layer, one going to the next layer and one going off to... somewhere? That's to indicate how the output for each timestep can be used within an RNN layer, through the recurrent connection, as well as passed along to the next, possibly also recurrent, layer of the network. The final output of an RNN layer can be either the output for the sequence's last timestep, *or* the entire sequence of outputs the layer generated while processing the input sequence.

Early implementations of this basic RNN design showed it was *possible* to learn relationships across timesteps in a sequence, but they don't actually do it very well. Due to how the underlying math works, they take too long to train and can't relate items separated by too many timesteps. For example, imagine an RNN processing our example sentence — it would likely remember the fox is brown, but it might have forgotten there is a fox at all by the time it gets to the dog at the end of the sentence.

In reality a basic RNN could probably handle short sentences like that, but relationships span much greater distances in many sequences. To continue with our reading example, while words within a sentence are surely related to each other, they can also be related to words in sentences earlier in the same paragraph, many pages ago in the same chapter or even several chapters ago in a book. The distance between relationships can be arbitrarily long, and basic RNNs simply aren't suited to handle that.

But then along came LSTMs.

Long short-term memory

The acronym LSTM stands for the odd-sounding phrase long short-term memory, and it refers to a different kind of recurrent unit capable of dealing with relationships separated by longer distances in the sequence. Conceptually, the following diagram shows the pertinent details of how an LSTM works.

It uses our earlier sample sequence and shows the recurrent steps unrolled as separate layers to help clarify its behavior:

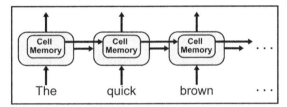

LSTM layer's recurrent behavior shown as separate layers

As you can see, an LSTM is a recurrent unit enhanced with an internal memory. LSTMs are used just like regular recurrent layers, but instead of processing only their input and previous output, an LSTM also considers the contents of its memory. And instead of just producing an output, the LSTM can also update its memory to remember (or forget) information it thinks is important about the sequence so far.

But terms like remembering, forgetting and thinking make it sound like LSTMs have more agency than they really do. Just like with other parts of a neural network, the LSTM's "memory" is really just a bunch of numbers that get manipulated by various math functions. And it doesn't really *choose* to remember or forget, it just learns weights that cause it to react differently to different sequences.

> **Note**: LSTM units are more complex than they appear in the above diagram, with each cell made up of four layers combined by various math operations. If you're interested in their inner workings, check out this excellent blog post: https://bit.ly/2RSmm7B. But the truth is, unless you're working to invent new types of neural network layers, you probably won't need to know those low-level details.

The important thing to know about LSTMs is that they train much more easily than the basic RNNs that came before them, and they offer much better performance. Most RNNs in use today use some variation of the LSTM unit, as is the case with the activity classifier you trained in Turi Create.

Turi Create's activity classifier

So far we've been discussing RNNs — and more specifically, LSTMs — as deep learning's solution to working with sequences. But it turns out that's not the whole story.

Many state of the art results have been achieved using other network types, especially our old friend the CNN.

Current research trends seem to be moving away from RNNs because they don't scale with hardware as well as other models do. But for now, recurrent models are still a popular choice in practice.

What approach does Turi Create's activity classifier take? It's actually a combination of a CNN *and* an RNN. It uses convolutional layers to extract features from short sequences — the prediction windows mentioned earlier in the chapter — and it uses an LSTM layer to reason over sequences of predictions.

That lets it recognize sporadic activities, such as the gestures you trained your model to classify, as well as activities spanning longer periods of time, perhaps made up of several smaller ones. For example, imagine the following sequence of activities: putting a teabag in a cup, pouring hot water in a cup, waiting patiently, and removing a teabag from a cup.

Each of those individual activites might be recognizable from small sequences of data — like what you could provide in a single prediction window. But when that *series* of activities occurs over multiple prediction windows, then the model might be able to recognize the overarching activity — making a cup of tea.

The following diagram shows a high level overview of Turi Create's activity classifier:

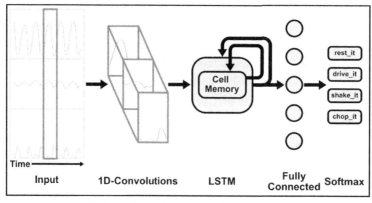

Turi Create's activity classifier architecture

You provide a sequence of sensor data as input — one prediction window's worth — and the model's first layer treats each input feature as a separate channel and performs a one-dimensional convolution over them. A 1D convolution is just like the 2D convolutions you've already used, except it uses kernels that are vectors instead of matrices.

Each kernel is the length of the prediction window and gets applied to all the input features to produce a new output channel. The current version of the code applies 64 such kernels.

The convolutional layer in this diagram may seem confusing because it *looks* like the waves are two-dimensional, but these are actually just vectors with numbers in them that we are *displaying* as a 2D image. To display a vector in two dimensions, we treat each item's index in the vector as its value along the X axis. That is, each item in the vector represents a feature value at a specific point in *time*.

Remember from the discussions on transfer learning earlier in the book, how the pre-trained CNN model extracts features from images and then the layers you train use those extracted features as inputs? This is basically what Turi Create's model does, except the CNN isn't pre-trained. The CNN layer learns to output a vector encapsulating any interesting temporal features found within the prediction window. For example, maybe it notices certain patterns of peaks and valleys that are helpful when identifying a shaking phone. These extracted features flow into the LSTM layer as if they were a single item in a sequence.

> To understand why CNNs might be well suited to this task, it can help to think of this as a vision problem instead: Imagine you *plotted* the sensor data for a prediction window, similar to what we show in the previous diagram, and then passed that *image* to a CNN. If CNNs can learn to recognize dogs in images, they should be capable of learning to recognize patterns in sequences just like the ones you saw in the previous chapter when exploring the dataset.

After the LSTM layer receives the extracted features from the CNN layer, it produces an output based on those features *combined* with its own internal memory and its output from the *previous* prediction window. The LSTM's output passes through fully connected layers with batch normalization and dropout, and finally a softmax layer that outputs probabilities for each of the classes the model knows about. You learned about all those layer types earlier in the book so they aren't discussed here.

This talk about internal memory and previous predictions brings up an important question: What about when a sequence *doesn't* relate to those that came before it? Data doesn't always arrive as one long, unbroken stream, so do you really want your model to always consider its past predictions as part of the current sequence?

Well, that *finally* brings us back to those new items you saw in Xcode: hiddenIn, cellIn, hiddenOut and cellOut. The names may seem backwards, but hiddenOut is the output from the LSTM itself, while cellOut is the LSTM's internal memory state after making the prediction. And hiddenIn and cellIn are the inputs you use to pass to the model those outputs from the previous prediction. Each of these is a vector of 200 Doubles stored as an MLMultiArray — you don't need to worry about that, it's just how the model's LSTM layer encodes its state information.

So to indicate the start of a new sequence, you'll pass nil to the model for both hiddenIn and cellIn. On the other hand, when the current prediction is picking up where the last one ended — as will often be the case with streaming motion data — you'll take the hiddenOut and cellOut values from the previous prediction and pass those back to the model as hiddenIn and cellIn, respectively. Using the output and memory from the previous step like this allows the LSTM to recognize longer sequences.

Continuing with our text example, it's as if the first prediction window you pass is for the word "The," the next window is for "quick," then "brown" and so on.

This whole chapter has been talking about classifying sequences of sensor data, but it turns out the model you made with Turi Create is looking at its inputs in two different ways — as sequences of sensor data, and as sequences of *sequences* of sensor data. The prediction window contains enough information to classify the first kind of sequence, but these extra inputs and outputs allow the LSTM portion of the network to reason over longer periods of time to classify the second kind of sequence.

> While models combining CNNs and LSTMs have achieved state-of-the-art results for tasks such as activity detection and speech recognition, there are also other techniques that deliver excellent performance when working with sequences. These include: Attention — a sort of memory added to other networks that helps guide their focus; Transformers — networks that use attention exclusively instead of recurrent or convolutional layers; and Temporal Convolutional Networks — CNNs designed for processing sequences. And new research seems to appear on a weekly basis, so there may be even more options by the time you're reading this. You'll read a bit more about some of these in later chapters.

A note on sequence classification

In the previous section you learned about the model architecture of Turi Create's activity classifier. Recall how the final layer had a node for each class the model recognizes, with a softmax activation to produce a probability distribution over them.

We didn't underscore it there, but it's important to realize that using neural networks to classify sequences works the same way as it does for other types of data. You build a network with whatever layers make sense for the problem — convolutions, LSTMs, etc. — and then a final layer of nodes — one for each possible output — with a softmax activation function to produce probabilities over them.

In fact, you can even use networks with this architecture to predict the *next* item in a sequence instead of the *class* of a sequence. The difference is that during training, instead of providing sequences as inputs and class labels as outputs, you give partial sequences as inputs and the next item in the sequence as the output. You'll get to do this yourself in a later chapter about translating natural language.

Key points

- Turi Create's activity classification API can help you easily make models capable of recognizing human activity from motion data. However, it can be used for more than just human activity detection — it's basically a generic classifier for numeric sequences.

- Try isolating data from a single source into one of the train, validation or test sets.

- Prefer a balanced class representation. In cases where that's not possible, evaluate your model with techniques other than accuracy, such as precision and recall.

- Sample/shuffle sequential data as full sequences, not as individual rows.

- First train on just a small portion of your training set and make sure you can get the model to overfit. That's the best way to find problems with your model, because if it can't overfit to a small dataset, then you likely need to make changes before it will be able to learn at all.

- Train multiple models and run multiple experiments until you find what works best for your app.

- RNNs process data serially, so they're slower than CNNs, both when training and performing inference.

- One-dimensional convolutions are commonly used to extract temporal features from sequences prior to passing them into RNNs.

- RNNs are a good choice for sequential data, with LSTMs being the most commonly used variant because they train (relatively) easily and perform well. However, they are not the only models that work well for sequences.

Where to go from here?

You've collected some data and created a model. Now it's time to actually *use* that model in an app — a game that recognizes player actions from device motion. When you're ready, see you in the next chapter!

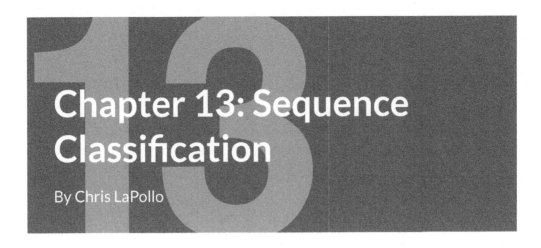

Chapter 13: Sequence Classification

By Chris LaPollo

If you've followed along with the last couple chapters, you've learned some things about how working with sequences differs from other types of data, and you got some practice collecting and cleaning datasets. You also trained a neural network to recognize user gestures from iPhone sensor data. Now you'll use your trained model in a game where players have just a few seconds to perform an activity announced by the app. When you've finished, you'll have learned how to feed data from your device into your model to classify user activity.

This chapter picks up where the last one ended — just after you added your classification model to the **GestureIt** project. If you didn't go through the previous chapter and train your own model, don't fret! You can always use the **GestureIt** starter project found in the chapter resources. Either way, once you have the project open in Xcode, you're ready to go!

Classifying human activity in your app

You trained a model and added it to the **GestureIt** project in the last chapter, and you learned a bit about how that model works. Now take a quick look through the project to see what else is there. The project's **Info.plist** file already includes the keys necessary to use Core Motion, explained earlier when you built the GestureDataRecorder project.

GestureIt's interface (not shown here) is even simpler than GestureDataRecorder's — it's just two buttons: Play and Instructions. Choosing Instructions shows videos of each gesture, and Play starts a game.

While playing, the game speaks out gestures for the player to make, awarding one point for each correctly recognized gesture. The game ends when the app recognizes an incorrect gesture or if the player takes too long.

The project already includes the necessary gameplay logic, but if you play it now you'll always run out of time before scoring any points. If you want it to recognize what the player is doing, you'll need to wire up its brain.

All the code you write for the rest of this chapter goes in **GameViewController.swift**, so open that file in Xcode to get started.

This file already imports the Core Motion framework and includes all the necessary code to use it. Its implementations of enableMotionUpdates and disableMotionUpdates are almost identical to what you wrote in the GestureDataRecorder project. The differences are minor and you should have no problem understanding them. As was the case with that project, this file contains a method named process(motionData:) that the app calls whenever it receives device motion data. At the moment it's empty, but you'll implement it later. For now, import the Core ML framework by adding the following line with the other imports near the top of the file:

```
import CoreML
```

In order to keep your code tidy and more easily maintainable, you'll store numeric configuration values as constants in the Config struct at the top of the class, just like you did in the GestureDataRecorder project. To start, add the following three constants to that struct:

```
static let samplesPerSecond = 25.0
static let numberOfFeatures = 6
static let windowSize = 20
```

These values **must match** those of the model you trained. You'll use samplesPerSecond to ensure the app processes motion data at the same rate your model saw it during training. The dataset provided in this chapter's resources was collected at 25 samples per second, so that's the value used here. However, change this value if you train your own model using data fed to it at a different rate.

> **Note**: In case it's not clear why the app's samplesPerSecond must match that of the dataset used to train your model, consider this example: Imagine you trained your model using a prediction window of 200 samples, on data collected at 100 samples per second. That means the model would learn to recognize actions seen in highly detailed, two-second chunks. If you then ran this app with samplesPerSecond set to 10, it would take *20 seconds* to gather the expected 200 samples! Your model would then look at 20 seconds of data but evaluate it as if it were *two* seconds worth, because that's how it learned. This would almost certainly make the patterns in these sequences appear different from what the model saw during training. Remember, machine learning models only work well with data that is similar to what they saw during training, so getting the sampling rate wrong here could make a perfectly good model seem completely broken.

Likewise, the model discussed in this chapter expects data in blocks of 20 samples at a time, with six features for each sample. The windowSize and numFeatures constants capture those expectations.

> **Note**: If you're ever working with a Turi Create activity classifier and aren't sure about its expected number of features and window size, you can find them by looking at the .mlmodel file in Xcode's Project Navigator. However, this does not include information about the rate at which motion data needs to be processed, so that you'll just need to know.

Now that you've added those constants, you can complete the starter code's implementation of enableMotionUpdates by setting the CMMotionManager's update interval. To do so, add the following line inside enableMotionUpdates, just before the call to startDeviceMotionUpdates:

```
motionManager.deviceMotionUpdateInterval = 1.0 /
  Config.samplesPerSecond
```

Just like you did in GestureDataRecorder, this tells `motionManager` to deliver motion updates to your app 25 times per second — once every 0.04 seconds.

Core ML models, such as `GestureClassifier`, expect their input in the form of `MLMultiArray` objects. Unfortunately, working with these objects involves quite a bit of type casting. Swift's type safety is great, and explicit type casting forces developers to be more thoughtful about their code — but I think we can all agree code gets pretty ugly when there's *too* much casting going on. To keep that ugliness — and the extra typing it requires — to a minimum, you'll be isolating any `MLMultiArray`-specific code within convenience methods. Add the first of these methods below the `MARK: - Core ML methods` comment in `GameViewController`:

```
static private func makeMLMultiArray(numberOfSamples: Int) ->
MLMultiArray? {
  try? MLMultiArray(
    shape: [1, numberOfSamples, Config.numberOfFeatures] as
[NSNumber],
    dataType: .double)
}
```

This function takes as input the number of samples the array should contain. It then attempts to make an `MLMultiArray` with a shape and data type that will work with our model: `[1, numSamples, Config.numFeatures]` and `double`, respectively. Notice how the shape needs to be cast as an array of `NSNumber`s — you'll see a lot of those types of casts when dealing with `MLMultiArray`s.

Attempting to create an `MLMultiArray` can fail by throwing an exception. If that occurs here, the `try?` causes this function to return `nil`. This might occur in situations such as when there is insufficient memory to create the requested array. Hopefully it doesn't ever happen, but you'll add some code to deal with that possibility a bit later.

Now that you have that handy function, you'll use it to create space to store motion data to use as input to your model. Add the following property, this time to the area under the `// MARK: - Core ML properties` comment:

```
let modelInput: MLMultiArray! =
  GameViewController.makeMLMultiArray(numberOfSamples:
Config.windowSize)
```

This creates the `modelInput` array, appropriately sized for the model you trained. Later you'll populate this array with motion data prior to passing it to your model for classification.

Note: You may have noticed that `modelInput` is declared as an implicitly unwrapped optional, but `makeMLMultiArray` can return `nil`. Doesn't that mean you run the risk of crashing your app elsewhere if you try to unwrap `modelInput` when it's `nil`? Normally, that would be a problem, but later you'll add some code that ensures this can never happen.

Overlapping prediction windows

Now, you *could* work with just a single `MLMultiArray` like `modelInput`, repeatedly filling it up over time and passing it to the model.

The diagram below shows what it would look like making two predictions with a window size of 20:

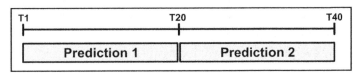

Reusing a single array to make predictions

As the diagram above shows, the array would fill up between times **T1** and **T20**, then you'd pass it to your model to make your first prediction. After that you'd reuse the array between times **T21** and **T40**, before passing it to your model again to make your second prediction.

This technique is the simplest to code and is fine for many apps. However, there are times when doing this would cause some problems. Consider the situation shown in the following diagram, where an activity you want to recognize spans across prediction boundaries:

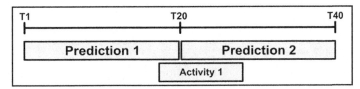

What if an activity spans across predictions?

In this case, a few things might happen. If the amount of data in the first prediction window is sufficient for the model to recognize the activity, then no problem — it returns the correct classification. But if the model needs to see more activity data than is available in the first window, it won't be able to classify it correctly until its *second* prediction.

In that case it takes longer than necessary to report the result, which makes your app feel sluggish. Or worse yet, all the non-activity data in the second window might make the second prediction fail to recognize the activity, too.

Delayed responses or inaccurate predictions — take your pick, but neither is a great option.

Now consider another problematic scenario, shown in the following diagram:

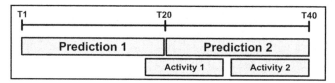

What if one prediction sees data for multiple activities?

Here there's one activity that spans across two predictions, just like before. But now a second activity occurs only within the second prediction window. In this case, assume the first prediction did not recognize anything, so now it's up to the second window to handle everything. How will it classify the two activities?

It can only make one prediction, so it will either correctly predict *one* of the activities, *or* it will become so confused that it fails to predict *either* of them. This isn't necessarily incorrect — it really depends on the app — but it's something you need to consider carefully.

In many cases it would be better if you could make predictions more often. You might try smaller prediction windows, but that isn't always an option because your model might need to see larger chunks of data to successfully recognize activities — that depends entirely on your specific data, model, and use case. But it turns out you *can* make predictions more often *without* changing the window size if you *overlap* your prediction windows, as shown in the following diagram:

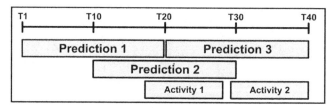

Overlapping predictions

In this case, the first prediction sees data from times **T1** to **T20**, and the *third* prediction sees the data from times **T21** to **T40**. But now a *second* prediction window overlaps each of those, spanning the data from times **T11** through **T30**.

Because this is like sliding the prediction window along the data (using offsets of 10 in this case), many people call these "sliding" windows.

An app using this design responds more quickly because it makes more predictions, and it's more accurate because it considers individual samples as part of multiple possible sequences. The first prediction window still might not recognize anything, but the second prediction would see the first activity — and predict it at **T30** instead of waiting until **T40**. And then the third prediction would recognize the second activity only 10 samples later. The app ends up feeling more responsive *and* it doesn't miss either activity.

Overlapping predictions *mostly* solves all of the problems mentioned earlier. But depending on how much data your model needs to see in order to make a prediction, and how much you overlap your windows, you still might run into missed or erroneous classifications. It's a matter of finding the best amount of overlap for your app.

You'll be implementing overlapping predictions in Gesture It, because you'll want fast response times to quickly evaluate the player's gestures.

But if you were making an app that tracks the amount of time you spend jogging, for example, you would probably be fine with non-overlapping predictions made over longer periods of time (maybe even once every several seconds).

> **Note**: How much you overlap your predictions directly affects more than just accuracy and response time. More overlap means running inference with your model more often, and that extra processing could increase battery drain. And depending on how long it takes your model to make predictions, it might not even keep up with the pace of requests, causing your app to exhibit other performance problems. So test various options and settle on making predictions only as often as is necessary to achieve your goals.

To help define your prediction windows, add the following constants to the `Config` struct at the top of the file:

```
static let windowOffset = 5
static let numberOfWindows = windowSize / windowOffset
```

Here you define `windowOffset` as five. This is not how much the window overlaps, but rather how far to offset the start of the window from the start of the previous window.

With the `windowSize` of 20 you defined earlier, this makes `numberOfWindows` equal four. That's how many prediction windows you'll have before you essentially wrap back around to the first one again.

This should be clearer if you refer to the the following diagram, which shows how your predictions would overlap for the first 40 samples:

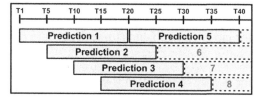

Gesture It's overlapping predictions — windowSize=20, windowOffset=5

With the settings you've made so far, Gesture It will take 0.8 seconds to respond with its first prediction, but then each successive prediction will occur every 0.2 seconds after that. That's because `samplesPerSecond` is 25, so each sample takes 0.04 seconds to arrive. A `windowSize` of 20 looks at 20 x 0.04s = 0.8 seconds of data, and a `windowOffset` of 5 means each prediction occurs 5 x 0.04s = 0.2 seconds after the last one.

Notice how different prediction windows overlap with various different combinations of other predictions. For example, Prediction Two sees the last 15 samples in Prediction One, and the first five samples in Prediction Five, along with 15 and 10 samples seen by Predictions Three and Four, respectively. And starting from Prediction Five, each window will process varying numbers of samples from *six* other prediction windows! All this overlap should help your model classify gestures quickly and accurately.

> **Note**: The integer division used to calculate `numWindows` means you'll never have a partial window. For example, if `windowOffset` were 20 with a `windowSize` of 50, you'd have two windows, one from **T1** to **T50** and another from **T21** to **T70**. The code you write in this app will handle that situation fine, but keep in mind that the predictions will not occur at a steady rate unless `windowSize` is evenly divisible by `windowOffset`. In this example, an offset of 20 would result in 20 samples between predictions one and two but 30 samples between predictions two and three.

The previous diagrams show what samples each prediction window should use, but how do you implement it? At the moment you've got a single `MLMultiArray` the size of *one* window, but now you need four.

While you *could* create four different arrays to store this data, that would waste memory. Instead, you'll make one slightly larger array that will act as a buffer area for the most recent motion data, and each prediction window will look at the appropriate subset of that larger buffer when necessary.

Add the following constant to the Config struct, which defines the size of the buffer you'll create:

```
static let bufferSize =
  windowSize + windowOffset * (numberOfWindows - 1)
```

You define a buffer size large enough to hold one full window plus the space taken up by the offsets for the other windows. So for the settings you've used so far, Gesture It's buffer will hold 35 samples. Don't worry if it's not yet clear *why* this is the right size — you'll see soon.

Now add the following properties to manage the buffer. Put them with the other ML-related properties in GameViewController:

```
let dataBuffer: MLMultiArray! =
  GameViewController.makeMLMultiArray(numberOfSamples:
  Config.bufferSize)
var bufferIndex = 0
var isDataAvailable = false
```

You create dataBuffer using the convenience method you wrote earlier. As new motion data arrives from the device, you'll use bufferIndex to determine where to store that data within the buffer. You'll set the isDataAvailable flag to true once the buffer contains enough data to perform its first prediction.

For the remainder of this discussion, please refer to the following diagram, which shows the buffer's contents at each prediction over the first 40 time steps:

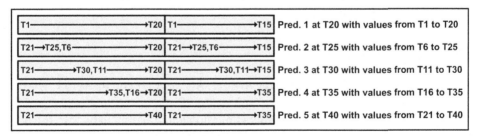

Buffer contents over time

Think of the buffer as having two halves, with a full prediction window on the left and auxiliary storage on the right. The second "half" isn't a true half in this case, because it's smaller than the first, but that won't be a problem.

You'll increment bufferIndex as new data arrives, moving it across the first half of the buffer, and you'll reset it to the beginning whenever it reaches the buffer's midpoint. That is, bufferIndex will always point to the next location to fill *within the first prediction window*. But whenever you store an item in the left half of the buffer, you'll also store it in the equivalent location in the right half. (You'll skip updates on the right side that would be out of bounds due to the size mismatch. You *could* make both sides the same size and then always store values in both places, but the approach used here saves some memory — usually a good thing for mobile apps.)

The top row of the diagram shows what the buffer looks like after 20 timesteps. The left side contains data from times **T1** to **T20**, and the right side contains copies of times **T1** to **T15**. It's at this point that you'll reset bufferIndex to zero, set isDataAvailable to true and perform the first prediction using times **T1** to **T20**.

As data continues to arrive, you'll keep filling the left and right sides of the buffer simultaneously. After five more timesteps, you'll be ready to make the second prediction. As you can see in the second row of the diagram, the first five items of the buffer contain data from times **T21** to **T25**, but the next 15 items still contain data from times **T6** to **T20**. And because you've been updating both sides of the buffer, the first five items on the *right* contain data from times **T21** to **T25**, too.

So you can now make your second prediction using times **T6** to **T25** by looking at a window that crosses into the second half of the buffer.

This process continues indefinitely, but the diagram shows the contents of the buffer when making each of the first five predictions. The key point to realize is that after the first time bufferIndex reaches the midpoint of the buffer and resets to the start, it is always the case that the the *next* 20 items starting at bufferIndex contain data from the *previous* 20 time steps.

Phew. That was a lot of discussion about such a small bit of code, so hopefully you're still here. Now back to the app!

Buffering motion data

Now you're going to add code to handle MLMultiArrays that end up as nil. Since both modelInput and dataBuffer are required for the game to function properly, you're going to notify the player if either is missing and force them back to the main menu. However, you may want to make your own apps more robust. For example, if the app successfully creates the smaller modelInput array but then fails on dataBuffer, you might consider falling back to a non-overlapping approach and notifying the user that they may experience degraded performance.

Add the following code inside `viewDidLoad`, immediately *above* the call to `enableMotionUpdates`:

```
guard modelInput != nil, dataBuffer != nil else {
  displayFatalError("Failed to create required memory storage")
  return
}
```

Here you check to ensure that the app was able to create each of its required `MLMultiArray` properties. If not, you call `displayFatalError`, a method in the starter code that alerts the player with the given error message and then dismisses the `GameViewController`.

> **Note**: The starter code enables motion updates when it loads the game view and stops them when the game is over. However, your production apps should be more robust than that. Be sure your apps are good iOS citizens and have them properly handle situations such as getting paused for incoming phone calls, etc.

The app will receive motion updates `Config.samplesPerSecond` times each second. For each update, you'll need to store the appropriate features in `dataBuffer`, the `MLMultiArray` you created earlier. You'll wrap this logic in helper methods to keep things easier to read. Add the first helper method to the class:

```
@inline(__always) func addToBuffer(
  _ sample: Int, _ feature: Int, _ value: Double) {
  dataBuffer[[0, sample, feature] as [NSNumber]] =
    value as NSNumber
}
```

The `addToBuffer` function isolates the `NSNumber` casts to one line, which keeps the code you'll add later easier to read. Declaring it with `@inline(__always)` tells the Swift compiler to replace any calls to this function with the contents of the function itself, ensuring your code executes as quickly as possible.

Swift is good about inlining these one-line functions on its own, but including this tag makes your intention clear.

This method sets a single value inside `dataBuffer`. That `MLMultiArray` is arranged as a 3-dimensional tensor, indexed as [batch, sample, feature]. The model's batch size is always one, so the first index value here is always 0. The `sample` and `feature` indices are passed as arguments to this method.

Next, add the following helper method:

```
// 1
func buffer(motionData: CMDeviceMotion) {
  // 2
  for offset in [0, Config.windowSize] {
    let index = bufferIndex + offset
    if index >= Config.bufferSize {
      continue
    }
    // 3
    addToBuffer(index, 0, motionData.rotationRate.x)
    addToBuffer(index, 1, motionData.rotationRate.y)
    addToBuffer(index, 2, motionData.rotationRate.z)
    addToBuffer(index, 3, motionData.userAcceleration.x)
    addToBuffer(index, 4, motionData.userAcceleration.y)
    addToBuffer(index, 5, motionData.userAcceleration.z)
  }
}
```

While this methods are essentially just updating an array, there are some important things to note:

1. You'll call `buffer` from within `process(motionData:)`, which you'll write next. It copies motion data into the correct locations in the large buffer backing the overlapping prediction windows described earlier.

2. This `for` loop ensures each value is stored at the position indexed by `bufferIndex`, as well as a position that is one window-span *later* in the buffer. The `continue` statement ensures that second write attempt is not outside the buffer's bounds, which would crash the app. For more details about how the overlapping windows work, refer to the discussion earlier in this chapter.

3. Here you call `addToBuffer` repeatedly to save the relevant data from the `CMDeviceMotion` object passed to this method. It's **extremely important** to store only the features your model expects, and in exactly the order it expects them. This was all determined when you trained the model, but you can verify the information by inspecting the .mlmodel file in Xcode's Project Navigator.

   Be sure to double check this step, because mistakes here will make your model function incorrectly — sometimes failing with a crash, sometimes by underperforming, and even sometimes by *appearing* to work! That last one might sound ok, but it just means you've got some lucky input and it's unlikely to work well for long.

Your code so far only adds data to dataBuffer, but you'll eventually need to pass modelInput to your ML model. That's because your model expects to see an MLMultiArray with modelInput's specific shape, not the larger buffer you created to implement overlapping windows. So, you'll need to copy data between these structures.

To make those copies as fast as possible, you'll be using low level pointers to copy chunks of memory directly. To do that, you need to know the exact number of bytes you want to access, so add the following constants to the Config struct:

```
static let windowSizeAsBytes = doubleSize * numberOfFeatures *
windowSize
static let windowOffsetAsBytes = doubleSize * numberOfFeatures *
windowOffset
```

Here you calculate the number of bytes it takes to represent a prediction window within an MLMultiArray, as well as the number of bytes necessary to represent the offset between prediction windows. The constant doubleSize referenced in these calculations already exists in the starter code — it stores how many bytes are used by one double. You'll use these constants soon.

You're now all set to fill in the placeholder process(motionData:) method. Insert the following code into that method:

```
// 1
guard expectedGesture != nil else {
  return
}
// 2
buffer(motionData: motionData)
// 3
bufferIndex = (bufferIndex + 1) % Config.windowSize
// 4
if bufferIndex == 0 {
  isDataAvailable = true
}
// 5
if isDataAvailable &&
    bufferIndex % Config.windowOffset == 0 &&
    bufferIndex + Config.windowOffset <= Config.windowSize {
  // 6
  let window = bufferIndex / Config.windowOffset
  // 7
  memcpy(modelInput.dataPointer,
         dataBuffer.dataPointer.advanced(
           by: window * Config.windowOffsetAsBytes),
         Config.windowSizeAsBytes)
  // 8
```

```
    // TODO: predict the gesture
  }
```

This is the meat of your data pipeline, so look carefully at what's going on here:

1. The starter project uses `expectedGesture` to keep track of what gesture the player should be making. This value will be `nil` whenever the game is not expecting a gesture, and this `guard` statement ensures this method doesn't process motion data in those cases.

2. Here's where you call the method you recently added, `buffer`. You pass it the `CMDeviceMotion` object given to this method, and it stores the motion data in the appropriate locations within `dataBuffer`.

3. Next, you update `bufferIndex` to keep track of the next available space in the buffer. You're incrementing it by one, and looping it back around to zero when it reaches the end of the first window.

4. Here you check to see if `bufferIndex` is zero. Because `bufferIndex` is updated *before* this line, it can only ever be zero *after* it has exceeded `Config.windowSize` and wrapped back around at least once. At that point, you update `isDataAvailable` to indicate you have at least one full window's worth of data.

5. This `if`-statement ensures you make predictions at the correct times. It first checks `isDataAvailable` to make sure at least one window is full. Then, it checks to see if `bufferIndex` is at the boundary of a window. Because `bufferIndex` resets when it reaches the end of the first window, you can only reliably check when it's at the *start* of most windows, not the end.

   This line determines that by checking to see if `bufferIndex` is some multiple of the window offset. It also verifies that there is a full `windowOffset` worth of space after this position in the window. That final check is just a precaution in case you ever use a window size that is not evenly divisible by the offset size. Without that check, the code at 7 would crash your app when it tried to access invalid memory. If all these checks pass, then the function knows it's OK to make a prediction.

6. Here you determine which prediction window you're working with so you'll know which data to access from the buffer.

7. Now you need to copy the samples for `window` from `dataBuffer` into `modelInput`. Conveniently, `MLMultiArray` objects expose a pointer for low level access to their backing memory via their `dataPointer` property, so here you take advantage of that fact and use `memcpy` to copy a window-sized chunk of memory directly from `dataBuffer` into `modelInput`.

   To locate the start of the window, you use the pointer's `advanced(by:)` method and some math to move it the appropriate number of bytes from the start of the buffer. Be extremely careful with `memcpy`: Getting anything wrong here will at best give you the wrong results, and at worst will crash your app.

8. Here is where you will eventually attempt to make your prediction. But you'll need to write just a bit more code before you do.

Making predictions with your model

At long last, your project is ready to start recognizing gestures. Almost. So far the app contains a lot of data processing and business logic — it still needs the machine learning bit!

Add your gesture recognition model into the app by initializing the following property with the other ML-related properties in `GameViewController`:

```
let gestureClassifier = GestureClassifier()
```

Xcode autogenerated the `GestureClassifier` class when you first dragged the .mlmodel file into the project, so all you have to do is instantiate it like this and then later call its `prediction` method with the appropriate inputs. It's almost *too* easy, right?

Well, it *would* be if that's all it took. Recall from the previous chapter's discussion about the model's inputs and outputs, the LSTM portion of the network requires you to provide it with the internal memory and output from its previous prediction. That means you'll need to store that information each time you make a prediction and then pass it back to the model when making the next one. To help with that, Xcode generated the `GestureClassifierOutput` class at the same time it made `GestureClassifier`. This class conveniently encapsulates all four of the model's outputs so you can save them for later use.

However, you've implemented your predictions using four overlapping windows, which means consecutive predictions aren't actually continuations of each other. That is, the first sensor reading in a prediction window is *not* the reading immediately after the last one in the previous window. Instead, it's a value *within* the previous window, offset from its start by `Config.windowOffset` samples. Because of that fact, it wouldn't make sense for the LSTM's internal state to carry over from the *previous* prediction — it needs to use the state from *four* predictions ago instead. To keep track of all these outputs, you'll maintain an array of `GestureClassifierOutputs`, so add the following property for that:

```
var modelOutputs = [GestureClassifierOutput?](
  repeating: nil,
  count: Config.numberOfWindows)
```

This array will hold one `GestureClassifierOutput` for each prediction window. The values are optional and will be `nil` for any window before you've used it. You can see the code for `GestureClassifierOutput` by selecting **GestureClassifier.mlmodel** in the Project Navigator, and then clicking the small arrow icon next to **GestureClassifier** in the **Model Class** section. It basically just provides properties to access the model's various outputs.

One last thing before you actually use your model. Earlier in the book, you read about how Core ML predictions come with probabilities which are essentially the model's confidence in the prediction. And, you saw how the model will always produce *some* prediction, but not necessarily with much confidence.

To avoid reacting to low probability predictions, you'll define a threshold that the probability must exceed to be considered sure enough to act upon. Add the following constant to `Config` at the top of the file:

```
static let predictionThreshold = 0.9
```

This basically means the model needs to be over 90% sure of a prediction before the app responds. This threshold was chosen after some playtesting, but it's mostly personal preference beyond a certain threshold. Values too low will make the app hallucinate gestures where there are none, so definitely avoid that, but other than that it's a matter of how touchy or picky you want the app to feel. Later, when you're done writing the app, try out different values here to see how they affect the gameplay.

With those small additions in place, it's now time to write the method that uses your trained model to recognize gestures. Add the following code to the end of `GameViewController`:

```swift
func predictGesture(window: Int) {
  // 1
  let previousOutput = modelOutputs[window]
  let modelOutput = try?
    gestureClassifier.prediction(
      features: modelInput,
      hiddenIn: previousOutput?.hiddenOut,
      cellIn: previousOutput?.cellOut)
  // 2
  modelOutputs[window] = modelOutput

  guard
    // 3
    let prediction = modelOutput?.activity,
    let probability =
  modelOutput?.activityProbability[prediction],
    // 4
    prediction != Config.restItValue,
    // 5
    probability > Config.predictionThreshold
  else {
      return
  }

  // 6
  if prediction == expectedGesture {
    updateScore()
  } else {
    gameOver(incorrectPrediction: prediction)
  }
  // 7
  expectedGesture = nil
}
```

You've written quite a bit of code already, but this method is really the only part of the app that actually uses machine learning. Here's what it does:

1. First it calls `prediction` on `gestureClassifier` to try to classify the motion data, and stores the result as `modelOutput`. Notice that you provide both `modelInput`, which you populated in `processMotionData`, as well as the LSTM's ouput and internal cell state from the previous prediction *for this window*. These values will be `nil` for each window's first prediction, and that's fine — this tells the classifier there is no history and it should initialize itself accordingly.

2. Then, it stores the model's response in `modelOutputs` so you can access it next time you make a prediction for this window.

3. Next, it grabs the predicted activity, along with the probability assigned to that prediction, from the model's output.

4. It checks for predictions of non-gestures — i.e. resting — and just ignores them.

5. For non-rest predictions, it checks to see if the probability exceeds the threshold you previously defined. If so, it considers it a real prediction; otherwise it does nothing and the app will continue processing motion events.

6. The next bit of code is game logic, but any app you write with a classification model will have something similar — a spot where you actually *use* the predicted value. If the model thinks the player made the correct gesture (i.e. the predicted gesture matches `expectedGesture`), then it calls `updateScore` to add a point; otherwise, the app thinks the player messed up and it calls `gameOver`.

7. Regardless of the prediction, the method resets `expectedGesture` to `nil` so that the app stops processing motion data for a while. The starter project's existing game logic will set this to a new gesture when appropriate.

> **Note:** The model class Xcode generates includes three different `prediction` methods, as well as a `predictions` (with an "s") method that batches multiple predictions in one call. This code uses the version that takes `MLMultiArrays` directly, but you might find situations where you'd prefer to use one of the other versions in your own apps, so be sure to check the generated code for options.

Now go back to that comment you added earlier — // TODO predict the gesture
— and replace it with a call to the method you just wrote:

```
predictGesture(window: window)
```

You already calculated the correct prediction window inside process, and here you pass that to predictGesture to perform inference.

Now build the app and run it on your iPhone. (Sorry, no motion data in the simulator!) You might succeed with the first gesture, but it won't take long before the app calls out a gesture and then immediately complains that you got it wrong. What gives?

Remember those fancy overlapping prediction windows? Well, that backing storage buffer you made still contains data from the previous sequences you were processing. So when the app asks for a new gesture, there's already a prediction window's worth of data just sitting there ready to be recognized — collected while you were making the *previous* gesture. And don't forget, recurrent models use state from previous predictions to help them make new predictions, because they assume the data is related. But when this app asks for a new gesture, it no longer wants the model to consider the prior data. Each new gesture needs a clean slate.

To correct this, you need to reset the buffer *and* the model's previous output states. Add the following method to GameViewController:

```
func resetPredictionWindows() {
  // 1
  bufferIndex = 0
  // 2
  isDataAvailable = false
  // 3
  for i in 0..<modelOutputs.count {
    modelOutputs[i] = nil
  }
}
```

It's not much code, but it's vital in order for your app to function properly. Here's what it does:

1. Reset `bufferIndex` to zero to start filling the buffer from the beginning again. This ensures new predictions are based on relevant sequence data, rather than data in the buffer left over from prior sequences.

2. Reset `isDataAvailable` to `false` to keep the app from trying to perform another prediction before it has at least one full window.

3. Set everything in `modelOutputs` to `nil` to clear out any internal model state built up from previous predictions. This ensures the underlying LSTM cells in your `GestureClassifier` model don't remember anything from sequences related to earlier gestures and then try to use that information when making new predictions.

Now that you've defined that method, call it at the top of `startTimer(forGesture:)`:

```
resetPredictionWindows()
```

The existing game logic already calls `startTimerForGesture` whenever it notifies the player to perform a new gesture. With this addition, you ensure the predictions made for new gestures are not using any data that arrived while the app was processing earlier gestures.

That's it! Build and run again, and have fun Gesturing It! If the game times out too quickly for you to respond, increase the value of `Config.gestureTimeout`. Or, if you want to increase the challenge, see how low you can decrease it. How many correctly recognized gestures can you get in a row?

Challenges

Challenge 1: Expanding Gesture

It would be a good way to get some practice with activity recognition. Adding new gesture types to the GestureDataRecorder project is a straightforward process, so start there, and then collect some data. Next, add your new data to the provided dataset and train a new model. Replace the model in the GestureIt project with your newly trained model, and make the few modifications necessary to add your new gesture to the game.

Challenge 2: Recognizing activites

After that, you could try recognizing activities other than gestures. For example, you could make an app that automatically tracks the time a user spends doing different types of exercises. Building a dataset for something like that will be more difficult, because you have less control over the position of the device and more variation in what each activity looks like. In those cases, you'll need to collect a more varied dataset from many different people to train a model that will generalize well.

Challenge 3: Using other devices

Keep in mind, these models work on other devices, too. The Apple Watch is a particularly fitting choice — a device containing multiple useful sensors, that remains in a known position on the user and is worn for all or most of the day. If you have access to one, give it a try!

Key points

- Use overlapping prediction windows to provide faster, more accurate responses.

- Call your model's `prediction` method to classify data.

- Pass multi-feature inputs to your models via `MLMultiArray` objects.

- Arrange input feature values in the same order you used during training. The model will produce invalid results if you arrange them in any other order.

- When processing sequences over multiple calls to `prediction`, pass the hidden and cell state outputs from one timestep as additional inputs to the next timestep.

- Ignore predictions made with probabilities lower than some reasonable threshold. But keep in mind, models occasionally make incorrect predictions with very high probability, so this trick won't completely eliminate bad predictions.

Section III: Natural Language Processing

In this section, you'll focus on a specific type of sequential data — natural language text. You'll learn how to use Apple-provided APIs to perform common language processing tasks. You'll also learn how to use text with neural networks, and you'll create a model with Keras that translates text from Spanish to English. Finally, you'll read about advanced techniques that you can experiment with to improve your model.

Chapter 14: Natural Language Classification

By Alexis Gallagher

Earlier in the book, you learned how to classify images — for example, judging whether they were of cats or dogs. You've also classified sequences of sensor data as device motions. Text is just another kind of data, and you can classify *it* as well. But what does a class of text look like?

Is this email legitimate or spam? Are customer messages praising your great work or demanding action to address complaints? What's the topic of an article, patent or court document? These are just a few examples of text classification tasks.

There are a wide variety of techniques for extracting useful information from text, all falling under the general term **natural language processing (NLP)**. This chapter focuses on using NLP for classification, specifically using the methods Apple provides as part of its operating systems. You may be familiar with NSLinguisticTagger, which has been available since iOS 5. It supports several NLP tasks and was covered in the "Natural Language Processing" chapter of our *iOS 11 by Tutorials* book, when Apple rewrote the class to take advantage of Core ML. This chapter does *not* use that class.

Apple introduced the new Natural Language framework in iOS 12 — and in each of its other device OS revisions that same year — which is meant to improve upon and replace NSLinguisticTagger. That's the framework you'll use here, along with Create ML to train your own models.

In this chapter, you'll build an app to read movie reviews. Along the way, you'll perform several NLP tasks:

- Language identification

- Named entity recognition

- Lemmatization

- Sentiment analysis

Don't worry if any of those terms are unfamiliar to you — you'll get to know them all soon.

A special thanks to Michael Katz and the editorial team of *iOS 11 by Tutorials*. Michael wrote that book's "Natural Language Processing" chapter, on which this chapter is heavily based. Specifically, we reuse much of the starter project and general structure from that chapter, but we implement things differently, here. This chapter does cover some additional topics, such as training custom models, so we recommend going through it even if you've already read that book.

Getting started

Open the **SMDB** starter project in Xcode. Build and run to check out the app, which starts out looking like this (pull down on the list to reveal the Search bar):

The SMDB app

The Search feature doesn't work yet, but you'll fix that soon. The app contains the following four tabs:

- **All**: Shows a list of every movie review loaded from the "server." (To keep things simple, SMDB actually loads from a JSON file included with the project.) You'll add "heart-eyes" and "sad-face" emojis to the positive and negative reviews, respectively.

- **By Movie**: Lists movie names where users can tap a name to only see reviews for that movie. You'll eventually include tomato ratings showing each movie's average review sentiment.

- **By Actor**: Currently empty, you'll make it show a list of names automatically discovered from the reviews, along with emoji showing the average sentiment for reviews mentioning each name. Users will be able to tap a name and see all the reviews that mention it.

- **By Language**: Currently empty, it will soon list languages detected in the reviews. Users will then be able to tap a language to read all the reviews written in it.

You'll add these missing features inside **NLPHelper.swift**, so open it now. It includes empty stubs for the functions that you'll implement. Notice that it also imports the Natural Language framework, giving you access to well-trained machine-learning models for several NLP tasks. The first one you'll take a look at is language identification.

Language identification

Your first classification task will be identifying the language of a piece of text. This is a common first step with NLP because different languages often need to be handled differently. For example, English and Chinese sentences are not tokenized in the same way.

This is important enough that classes in the Natural Language framework attempt to automatically identify the language of whatever text they encounter before moving forward with their own work, so in many cases you won't have to bother with this step. However, detecting languages is also a useful task on its own. For example, to direct support requests to the appropriate staff members, or perhaps — as in this app — to organize documents by language. For times like these, Apple provides `NLLanguageRecognizer`.

Replace getLanguage(text:) in **NLPHelper.swift** with the following code:

```
func getLanguage(text: String) -> NLLanguage? {
  NLLanguageRecognizer.dominantLanguage(for: text)
}
```

This function is only a single line — it takes a String and passes it to NLLanguageRecognizer's dominantLanguage(for:) function. That call returns an optional NLLanguage object for the language it thinks is most likely in use by the given text. The values are enums with names that match the language they represent, such as .english, .spanish and .german.

In situations wherein portions of the text are in different languages, it returns the language that makes up most of the text. This function returns nil when it can't determine the language.

> **Note**: You may be aware that many language names can be abbreviated by a two-character ISO 639-1 code. For example, "en", "es" and "de" for English, Spanish and German, respectively. You can access the two-character code for the language represented by an NLLanguage object via the object's rawValue property.

Build and run the app. Switch to the **By Language** tab, which should look like this:

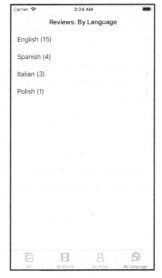

Languages identified in reviews

The table lists each language identified in the reviews, along with how many reviews use it. Tapping a row shows a list of reviews written in that language. Using the Natural Language framework, you've improved the app's user experience, because now users only have to scroll through reviews they can actually read.

Additional language identification options

The NLLanguageRecognizer performs just one task: **identifying languages** used in text. If you need it, then you'll most often use it as you did here, via its convenience function dominantLanguage(for:). However, there are situations that call for more control, and, in those cases, you'll need to create an NLLanguageRecognizer object and call some of its other methods.

You can pass it text via its processString function, which has no return value but stores the most likely dominant language in its dominantLanguage property. If you want more fine-grained information, you can get specific probabilities for multiple possible languages via its languageHypotheses(withMaximum:) function. The withMaximum parameter lets you specify how many probabilities you want to see — for example, the top five. Prior to processing a string, you can provide hints in the form of a dictionary containing the likelihood of encountering specific languages via the languageHints property. You can also restrict what language responses are possible via the languageConstraints property.

Finding named entities

Sometimes, you'll want to find names mentioned in a piece of text. Maybe you want to sort articles based on who they are about, organize restaurant reviews based on the cities they mention, or extract important information from a document, which often includes names of people, places and organizations. This is called named entity recognition (NER), and it's a common NLP task with many use cases. It's also a form of text classification.

When you're looking for a specific word, a simple search is often enough. However, when there are many such words, and especially when you aren't sure in advance what those words will be, that's when machine learning can help. The Natural Language framework provides well-trained models capable of finding names of people, places and organizations.

In this section, you'll give SMDB the ability to sort reviews based on the people's names they contain. The app doesn't know in advance what names might exist, so it has to examine the text and classify words as either names or not names. Apple provides a class that can handle this task — and more — called `NLTagger`.

Replace `getPeopleNames` in **NLPHelper.swift** with the following implementation:

```
func getPeopleNames(text: String, block: (String) -> Void) {
  // 1
  let tagger = NLTagger(tagSchemes: [.nameType])
  tagger.string = text
  // 2
  let options: NLTagger.Options = [
    .omitWhitespace, .omitPunctuation, .omitOther, .joinNames]
  // 3
  tagger.enumerateTags(
    in: text.startIndex..<text.endIndex, unit: .word,
    scheme: .nameType, options: options) { tag, tokenRange in
    // 4
    if tag == .personalName {
      block(String(text[tokenRange]))
    }
    return true
  }
}
```

The body of this function shows the general pattern that you'll follow for many NLP tasks. It goes as follows:

1. Create an `NLTagger` and pass in an array of `NLTagScheme` objects telling it what to look for in the text. (More on this later.) Then, you set the text for it to parse via its `string` property.

2. Fine-tune what the tagger returns with an array of `NLTagger.Options` values. In this case, you're going to skip whitespace, punctuation and non-linguistic tokens such as symbols. You also pass `.joinNames`, which tells the tagger to combine multi-part names into a single token. For example, "Jane Smith" instead of "Jane" and "Smith."

3. Call the tagger's `enumerateTags` method to iterate over whatever tokens it can find within the specified range of the text you set earlier, potentially assigning an `NLTag` to each one. (More on this later.)

4. Provide `enumerateTags` a code block to call for each token the tagger processes. In this case, you check that the tag is the name of a person — rather than a place or organization — and, if it is, you pass the identified token as a `String` into the block passed into `getPeopleNames`.

You'll use that pattern often: Create an `NLTagger`, use it to assign classes to tokens, and then process important tokens in some application-specific way.

Here are some more details about `NLTagger` and the code you just added:

- `NLTagger` operates on tokens, but what a "token" means depends on the value you pass to `enumerateTag`'s `unit` parameter. It can be any of `.word`, `.sentence`, `.paragraph` or `.document`. The tagger will consider text in these unit-sized chunks, broken up using the rules it understands for the text's language. Some tagging schemes only work with specific units — for example, the `.nameType` you used here only works with words.

- When `NLTagger` labels a token, it calls the code block you specify with an `NLTag` object and the range of the tagged token within the source text. The actual value of the `NLTag` object is based on the tagging scheme — in the case of names, it can be `.personalName`, `.placeName` or `.organizationName`, but there are other possibilities when using different tagging schemes.

- You used the `.nameType` tagging scheme to initialize the tagger to classify names, but Apple provides several different built-in options. You'll take a look at another one in the next section.

- `NLTagger` doesn't actually do all the work involved with classifying tokens. It's mostly a wrapper that uses different models based on the particular combination of tagging scheme and token unit you provide. Later in this chapter, you'll see how to provide custom models to add new types of tagging.

- You can initialize a tagger with more than one scheme to support multiple tasks, but `enumerateTags` only handles one scheme at time so you'll need to call it separately for each one you want to apply.

- Apple doesn't support every tagging scheme for every language. Call `NLTagger.availableTagSchemes(for: language:)` to get a list of supported schemes.

- Check out `NLTagger`'s `tag(at:unit:scheme:)` and `tags(in:unit:scheme:options:)` functions. They return a tag or tags directly rather than making you iterate over all the tokens with a block.

- Pro tip: Don't forget to set the `string` property before calling `enumerateTags`! The tagger won't complain if you don't, but it won't produce any results, either.

Build and run, again, and take a look at the **By Actor** tab.

Names identified in reviews

You'll see a list of names NSTagger thinks it has identified in the reviews. Tapping one leads to a list of reviews containing that name. The results aren't perfect, though. For example, it misses the name "Faire Playe," which appears in two reviews, and it identifies "O" as a name even though it was just part of the term "I/O." The tagger uses a model that has learned what names generally look like and how they are used in sentences, but in the end it still has to guess about each token it encounters. It will give you good results, but it will never be 100% correct.

Adding a search feature

In this next section, you'll use NLTagger for another task: **lemmatization**. That's the process of identifying the root version of a word. For example, consider the sentences, "I am running" and "I was running." Reducing each term to its root, both sentences become the same: "I be run." Sure, it no longer reads as correct, but it encapsulates *most* of the information contained in both sentences.

Historically, it's been common to preprocess text by lemmatizing it because it reduces the size of the vocabulary necessary to consider. You'll learn more about vocabulary sizes in the next chapter, but, intuitively, the larger they are the more difficult they are to support. So rather than needing to understand "run," "runs," "running" and "ran," you would just need to handle "run." However, as you can see in this example, some important contextual information, such as tense, gets lost in the translation. For some tasks, like machine translation, it is now common to use text without first lemmatizing it in order to get more accurate results.

> **Note: Stemming versus lemmatization.** You'll probably encounter both of these terms, often used seemingly interchangeably. In the case of stemming, the root is called a stem; in the case of lemmatization, it's called a lemma. These are essentially the same thing, but the process for generating them is different. Stemming involves basic rules like remove "ing" and "s" from the ends of words, which is fast and easy to implement but doesn't always produce the best results. On the other hand, lemmatization involves using a specific vocabulary for a language and applying more complex rules. It's more involved but usually gives better results.

You'll use lemmas in the SMDB app to support more sophisticated searches. When the user types search terms, the app will find all reviews containing those terms. But rather than only supporting exact matches, you'll broaden the results by using lemmas. When a user enters a word like "run," you'll make sure the app finds reviews using other forms of the word, like "running," too. Convenient!

Replace the empty `getSearchTerms` inside **NLPHelper.swift** with the following:

```
// 1
func getSearchTerms(text: String, language: String? = nil,
                    block: (String) -> Void) {
  // 2
  let tagger = NLTagger(tagSchemes: [.lemma])
  tagger.string = text
  let options: NLTagger.Options = [
    .omitWhitespace, .omitPunctuation, .omitOther, .joinNames]
  tagger.enumerateTags(
    in: text.startIndex..<text.endIndex, unit: .word,
    scheme: .lemma, options: options) { tag, tokenRange in
    if let tag = tag {
      // 3
      let lemma = tag.rawValue.lowercased()
      block(lemma)
    }
    return true
```

```
    }
  }
}
```

This code looks a lot like `getPeopleNames` that you added earlier. That's because it follows the same pattern. Here's what's different:

1. The function accepts an additional parameter — an optional language character code. You can ignore this for now.

2. You're using the `.lemma` tagging scheme, which tells the tagger you want it to return the lemma for each token it encounters. Just like when searching for names, the `.lemma` scheme only works for `.word` token units.

3. If the tagger identifies a lemma — it won't always be able to — then it's contained in the `NLTag`'s `rawValue` property. You extract it, ensure it's lowercased — this app won't support case-sensitive search — and then pass it to the block that was passed into `getSearchTerms`.

The app's starter code already calls `getSearchTerms` for each review, mapping the review to each term generated by this function. Therefore, you only have to build and run the app to try some searches. With the app open, pull down on the table to reveal a search bar where you can enter terms to find within reviews.

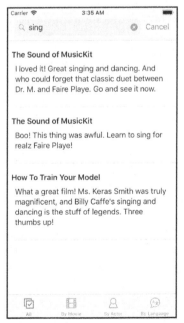

Search results for 'sing'

> **Note**: If you're curious to see how the app maps reviews to search terms, check out populateSearch in **ReviewsManager.swift**.

Throughout this section, you'll search for a few specific examples to see how the app performs and what motivates each specific code choice. These also serve to demonstrate a few of the difficulties involved when working with text. Try the following:

- Type **sing**, and you'll see three search results, all of which actually contain the word "singing." However, actually type **singing** and you get *zero* results. That's unsettling.

- Type **dance** and you'll get one result, which actually contains the word "dancing." However, type **dancing** and you'll get two *different* results, each of which seems to contain the same word. Suspicious, no?

- Type **bueno** and you'll get one result, which contains the word "buena." That's good — it shows lemmatization works for more than just English. However, type the actual word used in that review — **buena** — and you'll get no result. What gives?

The problem here *stems* from how you generated the search terms via their lemmas. See what I did there?

Remember the app maps reviews to terms generated by getSearchTerms. But this function returns **lemmas**, which may not match the original text in the review. For example, in these reviews the lemma of the word "singing" is "sing," so that's the only version of that word users can find via search. That's not very convenient, but it's something you should be able to fix. Instead of searching for exactly what the user types, you could search for the lemma of whatever the user types instead.

> **Note**: If you run the app on a hardware device, as opposed to the simulator, you may not get any results for terms in languages other than the device's native language. For example, if your phone has always been set to use English, you probably won't get results for the term **bueno** above. If you temporarily switch your device to another language — Spanish, for this tutorial — and then switch it back (hopefully, you won't get lost trying to return!), then the app should start finding search results for that language, too. However, the simulator should work fine for all languages iOS supports without you needing to do any extra work.

Switch over to **ReviewsTableViewController.swift** and replace findMatches with this new version:

```
func findMatches(_ searchText: String) {
  var matches: Set<Review> = []
  // 1
  getSearchTerms(
    text: searchText,
    language: Locale.current.languageCode) { word in
    // 2
    if let founds = ReviewsManager.instance.searchTerms[word] {
        matches.formUnion(founds)
    }
  }
  reviews = matches.filter { baseReviews.contains($0) }
}
```

This bit is more application-specific than the other functions you've added, but it shows one way to actually *use* the results of the tagging process.

1. You pass searchText — what the user entered in the search bar — to getSearchTerms in order to reuse the lemmatization code you added earlier. Now, the app lemmatizes the words users search *for* instead of just the words in the reviews that the app looks *at*.

2. For each lemma identified by getSearchTerms, you check inside the ReviewsManager's searchTerms dictionary. If it finds any reviews, it adds them to the results the user gets.

Build and run, and you'll see the search behavior has changed, but is it for the better? Try those three examples again.

- Typing **sing** and **singing** now both give the same results: *nothing*! Seems like a downgrade.

- Type **dance** and you'll now get zero results, while **dancing** gives you the one result that "dance" *used* to give you. Downgrade number two.

- Type **bueno** and you'll find the same review as before, but now typing **buena** *also* gives you that result. Finally, something got better!

These new errors occur because NLTagger sometimes has trouble lemmatizing short texts. You can test this out by typing just the letter "I", which will produce no results. Now continue typing so you search for "I sing". You'll find as soon as you start typing the second word, regardless of what you type, you'll get all the results that have the word "I" in them.

That's because now `NLTagger` sees it as a sentence and has a better guess about "I" being a word. Once you get to "I sing," you'll get all the reviews that contain "singing" — even if they do not contain the word "I."

The primary cause of this difficulty is that `NLTagger` can't always determine the *language* of shorter texts, and lemmatization requires language-specific knowledge. With longer samples, it's usually no problem, which you saw when you identified the languages for the reviews. But with shorter texts it's a good idea to help it if you can.

So how do you do that? By telling the tagger what language you're using prior to asking it to lemmatize the text. Remember that unused `language` parameter in `getSearchTerms`? Well, now it's time to use it.

Back in **NLPHelper.swift**, add the following lines inside `getSearchTerms`, just before the `let options: ...` line:

```
if let language = language {
  tagger.setLanguage(NLLanguage(rawValue: language),
                     range: text.startIndex..<text.endIndex)
}
```

This code sets the language on the tagger when a language is available, telling the tagger how to interpret the text stored in its `string` property. In this case, you'll have a language's two-character code, like "en" for English, and you'll create an `NLLanguage` object from it. You assign the language for the full range of the text, but you could assign different languages for different sections if necessary.

`NLTagger` offers another function named `setOrthography`, which sets even more information about the language, such as its script, but Apple recommends not using it unless you are sure of the value. The tagger will determine the orthography itself from the text, and setting the language — if set *correctly* — essentially guarantees you'll end up with the correct orthography anyway.

> **Note**: If your device's language is not set to English, then your results for the rest of this section may not exactly match what is described in the chapter. If this makes it difficult to follow along, go back to **ReviewsTableViewController.swift** and change `Locale.current.languageCode` in `findMatches` to be just the string `"en"`. This will force the tagger to assume all search terms are English.

Build and run the app, then try out those test searches again. How well do they work?

- Typing either **sing** or **singing** produces the same set of all three reviews that include "singing." Nice!

- Searching for **dance** or **dancing** gives the same *single* result, but we know there are two *other* reviews that contain the word "dancing." Better, but not quite right yet.

- Now, typing **bueno** or **buena** each give *zero* results. Uh oh, things are going in the wrong direction again. Coding is hard!

These errors are caused by two different issues, but solving one will solve the other well enough for this chapter's purposes.

The first problem — the one you won't fix here — is with the code you wrote earlier in findMatches. It passes the language code for the language *currently set on the device*. This will not always be correct — for example, when the user's iPhone is set to use English but they try searching for a Spanish term like "bueno." Now that we are setting the language directly, the NLTagger no longer determines it automatically, so it doesn't recognize this as Spanish and can't lemmatize it correctly.

A better approach would be first letting the NLTagger *try* to determine the language and only resorting to the user's default language when that fails. We won't show that here, but it's a small addition that readers should be able to make on their own after going through this chapter.

The second problem — the one you're about to fix — can be demonstrated more clearly with some other searches. Try searching for **Kotlin** or **realz**. Those terms appear in reviews, but they produce no search results. Why not?

It's because the tagger can't find lemmas for unknown terms like "Kotlin," but getSearchTerms currently only processes the lemmas it finds. Terms like these are considered out-of-vocabulary, but that doesn't mean users won't want to search for them.

In this case, you can fix the problem with a couple lines of code, but you'll see later in the book that out-of-vocabulary words cause other, more difficult, problems for NLP tasks, too.

Still in getSearchTerms, find the if statement inside the enumerateTags block, and add the following line right above it:

```
let token = String(text[tokenRange]).lowercased()
```

This line gets the token from the original text, and ensures it's lowercase just like how you handled the lemmas earlier.

Next, add an else block to the if:

```
if let tag = tag {
  ...
} else {
  block(token)
}
```

This the token to the block that the app passed into getSearchTerms. That means now all lemmas *and* any words that have no lemmas will get added as search terms.

Build and run with these changes. Repeating those searches gives the following results:

- Both **sing** and **singing** still work properly. That's a good sign!

- There is no change for **dance** or **dancing**. OK, at least they aren't worse, right?

- Now **bueno** works, but **buena** still finds nothing. That's at least *some* improvement.

- And what about words where the NLTagger could find no lemmas? Searching for these out-of-vocabulary words, like "realz" or "Kotlin," works properly and returns the appropriate reviews.

At this point, searching for either "dance" or "dancing" finds only one review containing "dancing" — the one when it's used as a verb. Here's why: When you search for the word "dancing," it gets lemmatized as "dance." But when the reviews were processed for search terms, the noun usages of "dancing" did *not* produce lemmas because "dancing" is a valid root when used as a noun. So NLTagger lemmatizes some terms differently when it encounters them in the reviews versus when it sees them as user-entered search terms. It's being clever by trying to give you the most appropriate lemmas for the context, which is *usually* a good thing. But you want users to be able to find both sets of reviews, so what can you do?

Go back to that same `if` statement inside the `enumerateTags` block, and add the following code just after the call to `block(lemma)`:

```
if lemma != token {
  block(token)
}
```

This new `if` statement checks to see when a token and its lemma are not the same word. In that case, it passes the token to the block that the app passed into `getSearchTerms`. So, in cases where you search for "dancing," it will process both "dance" and "dancing."

Build and run and try those test searches one last time. They mostly all work fine, but there's still a difference between the results for typing **dance** and **dancing** — the former finds the one review that uses "dancing" as a verb but misses the two reviews where it's used as a noun, while the latter finds all three of those reviews.

This is the best you're going to do without additional preprocessing. One option would be to lemmatize a sentence *and* attempt to break it up into tokens and lemmatize each token individually. That would give you more possible search terms because it would lemmatize each term both in and out of context. While it would fix the "dancing"-used-as-a-noun issue, you'd still have other problems. For example, spelling mistakes would still break the search, and out-of-vocabulary words still won't support even basic stemming, so searching for the singular of an unknown word does not find reviews containing usages of that word's plural.

One last thing: Remember earlier in `findMatches` when you passed `getSearchTerms` the device's current language along with the search term and that broke foreign-language searches? Now typing either **bueno** or **buena** works fine, but why? It's for a subtle reason: When the app lemmatizes the reviews, it correctly lemmatizes "buena" as "bueno" because it recognizes the language as Spanish. But now this new code you just added associates the review with *both* of those terms rather than just the lemma. Then later, when you try to search for one of them, even if the default language causes `NLTagger` to fail its lemmatization, it just goes down your other code branch that handles out-of-vocabulary words by looking for exact matches. And sure enough, the search finds what you typed — regardless of whether it was "bueno" or "buena."

At this point, you've got a pretty good search feature. It isn't industrial strength, for sure, but it's still surprisingly powerful for writing so little code. And along the way you've seen some of the problems you might encounter when tying to work with text in your own apps. Now, it's time to move away from the Natural Language framework's built-in support and train some custom models.

Sentiment analysis

Could we really cover machine learning for natural language without mentioning sentiment analysis? Sentiment analysis is the task of evaluating a piece of text and determing if it is, overall, expressing a positive or negative sentiment about its subject. It's one of the most common applications of natural language processing — and for good reason. Companies, politicians, market analysts — everyone with money at stake wants to know how the public feels about... *something.*

For this reason it's no surprise that Apple ships a built-in sentiment analysis model (as of iOS 13). Apple does not reveal how their model works and you cannot configure it or fine tune it for your problem domain, but it is certainly easy to use. You can feed this any piece of text and it will return a score from -1.0 to +1.0, indicating if the text is very negative or very positive.

It relies on a type that will be familiar to you by now, NLTagger, using a new dedicated tag scheme .sentimentScore. The .sentimentScore tag scheme configures a tagger that will return a tag containing a numerical sentiment score. The one quirk in this API is that, although it returns a numerical value, it returns this value as a String, requiring some trivial conversion on your part. Also, while you previously used tag schemes that return tag values at the level of a single word unit, the sentiment scheme returns a value at the level of a sentence or paragraph.

To write a function that does basic sentiment analysis add the following to **NLPHelper.swift**, just below your definition of getSearchTerms:

```
// 1
func analyzeSentiment(text: String) -> Double? {
  // 2
  let tagger = NLTagger(tagSchemes: [.sentimentScore])
  tagger.string = text
  // 3
  let (tag, _) = tagger.tag(at: text.startIndex,
                            unit: .paragraph,
                            scheme: .sentimentScore)
  // 4
  guard let sentiment = tag,
    let score = Double(sentiment.rawValue)
    else { return nil }
  return score
}
```

This is only slightly different from our previous functions:

1. The function is synchronous, taking a `String` and returning an optional `Double`.

2. You're using the `.sentimentScore` tagging scheme with your tagger, and handing it the text.

3. You're calling the synchronous `NLTagger.tag(at:unit:scheme:)` function, which returns an optional `NLTag` immediately rather than taking a callback.

4. Finally, you unwrap the optional and parse the `String` in `sentiment.rawValue` to return a `Double`, measuring the sentiment.

Later in this chapter we will show how to integrate this function's output into the user interface. But for now, just print the score to the console, by adding the following line to `tableView(_:cellForRowAt:)` in **ReviewsTableViewController.swift**, immediately before the `return` statement:

```
print("review text: \(review.text)\nscore: \(String(describing:
analyzeSentiment(text: review.text)))\n\n")
```

If you open the console as you scroll the app, you'll see reviews rolling by with their associated sentiment scores. "The Sound of MusicKit" rates a solid 1.0, but "The Swift and the Dead" only clocks in at -6.0.

Not bad a for just a few lines of code! But what if you want a bit more control?

Building a sentiment classifier

While it is convenient that Apple provides their own sentiment analysis API, it is instructive to build your own sentiment classifier. Why? Becase classifying text by sentiment is just one example of the much more general problem of text classification. Spam detection, prioritizing support requests, and identifying document topics are all variations of that same problem. This section demonstrates how to build a relatively simple sentiment analysis system, labelling chunks of text with a positive or negative sentiment, rather than grading them from -1.0 to +1.0. Remember, you can use these techniques for all sorts of classification tasks.

Training a text classifier with Create ML

You'll use Create ML to train an `MLTextClassifier` model. This class is meant to classify larger chunks of text rather than individual words, although it is technically capable of doing both. You'll see a different model later in this chapter that is better suited to classifying word tokens.

In previous chapters you've used the Create ML GUI application to train models. In this one you'll train your model in an Xcode playground. With the default model types, training the model in this section shouldn't take long and we recommend you go through the steps. However, if you'd prefer you can use the pre-trained model found at **projects/starter/models/SentimentClassifier.mlmodel** in the chapter resources.

> **Note**: As you may have seen, the Create ML GUI app provides a drag and drop interface to Create ML, allowing you to select your training data with a file picker, choose your model type by selecting a radio button, and kick off training by pushing a big "Train" button with the same familiar icon which the Music app uses for playing a tune. When this approach works, it's great! But it is also worth being familiar with playgrounds. For one thing, training on a playground will work on macOS Mojave (10.14) or macOS Catalina (10.15). In addition, playgrounds are closer to the typical machine learning workflow, since they support easier iteration, experimentation, and tracking of past results, like Jupyter notebooks.

Before dealing with Xcode, you'll need a dataset. Xcode playgrounds have special access to a specific folder on your Mac, where you'll store your dataset and output your trained model. If it doesn't already exist, create a folder named **Shared Playground Data** inside your **Documents** folder. This folder *must* have that exact name and be in that location for your playgrounds to access it.

> **Note**: You *can* add files directly to your playground's bundle resources — and you'll see that done later in this chapter. But when I tried that with the large dataset involved here, Xcode struggled and I spent way too much time staring at spinning beachballs and force-quitting the app. Things performed much better with the data stored outside of the bundle.

Next, create a folder named **TextClassification** inside **Shared Playground Data**.

You'll keep everything for this chapter organized there.

Find **projects/starter/datasets/MovieReviews.zip** in the chapter resources and unzip it into the **Shared Playground Data/TextClassification** folder you just created. You should now have a subfolder named **MovieReviews**.

This new folder contains subfolders with 50 thousand movie reviews, half labeled as positive and the other half negative. It's a slightly paired-down version of the Large Movie Review Dataset, from the 2011 paper, "Learning Word Vectors for Sentiment Analysis," by Andrew L. Maas et al., published by the Association for Computational Linguistics.

Interested readers can find the paper at www.aclweb.org/anthology/P11-1015. There's a **README** file describing the changes we made, primarily to save space by eliminating files which were unrelated to this chapter.

Create a new playground file using any template for **macOS**. The specific template doesn't matter, but the operating system does because Create ML is only available on macOS. Or if you'd rather follow along with a completed playground, you can find one at **projects/final/playgrounds/MovieSentiment.playground**.

If you started from a template, delete whatever starter code Xcode provided and add the following imports:

```
import CreateML
import PlaygroundSupport
```

You'll train your text classifier with Create ML, so you import it here. And you import the Playground Support framework to access the **Shared Playground Data** folder you set up earlier.

Now, add this next bit of code to access your training and test data:

```
// 1
let projectDir = "TextClassification/"
let dataDir = "MovieReviews/"
let trainUrl =
  playgroundSharedDataDirectory.appendingPathComponent(
    projectDir + dataDir + "train", isDirectory: true)
let testUrl =
  playgroundSharedDataDirectory.appendingPathComponent(
    projectDir + dataDir + "test", isDirectory: true)
// 2
let trainData =
  MLTextClassifier.DataSource.labeledDirectories(at: trainUrl)
let testData =
  MLTextClassifier.DataSource.labeledDirectories(at: testUrl)
```

This code creates the datasets that you'll use for training and testing your model. Here's what you did:

1. Create URLs pointing to the **MovieReviews/train** and **MovieReviews/test** folders containing your dataset.

2. Create `MLTextClassifier.DataSources` backed by those folders. This lets the model access data samples stored on disk as separate files, one subfolder per label you want your classifier to handle.

As you can see in the following image, your dataset includes two folders: "test" and "train," and each of those contains two more folders: "neg" and "pos."

Dataset folder structure

Each of the files stored in these subfolders contains a single review, and the name of its folder is its classification label. So all the reviews in a "pos" folder are classified with positive sentiment, and the ones in a "neg" folder are classified with negative sentiment.

> **Note**: This way of loading data works well when your dataset is spread across files like this. However, you can also train your model with an `MLDataTable`, which you can create from a JSON or CSV file, or from a Swift dictionary. You can even populate one programmatically if you need to. Use whatever method works best for your dataset. You'll see an example of loading a JSON file a bit later.

Now, create an `MLTextClassifier` with the following code:

```
let sentimentClassifier = try!
  MLTextClassifier(
    trainingData: trainData,
    parameters:
      MLTextClassifier.ModelParameters(language: .english))
```

This single line not only creates your model, it trains it, too! It even separates a portion of the training data to act as a validation set to ensure the model doesn't overfit.

Note the `ModelParameters` object which you pass to initialize the classifier. This object lets you specify what kind of classifier model to use, how to define your validation data, and the language of the text.

In the code above you you've only told it to train for English. This is a good idea because later you can query its supported language to ensure you only use it in the proper context. By default, the system will use a *maximum entropy classifier* with a validation set built from randomly picking less than 10% of the training dataset.

You can consider other settings later. For now, run the playground. Depending on the speed of your machine, this may take a few seconds to a few minutes, but you should get results similar to the following:

```
Automatically generating validation set from 5% of the data.
Tokenizing data and extracting features
10% complete
20% complete
30% complete
40% complete
50% complete
60% complete
70% complete
80% complete
90% complete
100% complete
Starting MaxEnt training with 23727 samples
Iteration 1 training accuracy 0.500611
Iteration 2 training accuracy 0.851182
Iteration 3 training accuracy 0.876976
Iteration 4 training accuracy 0.935053
Iteration 5 training accuracy 0.980276
Iteration 6 training accuracy 0.995153
Iteration 7 training accuracy 0.999579
Iteration 8 training accuracy 0.999958
Finished MaxEnt training in 9.81 seconds
```

Text classifier training output

You didn't specify a separate validation set as part of the ModelParameters, so the classifier reserves 5% of the training data for that purpose. It then spends a good bit of time tokenizing the reviews and converting them to training features. After that process completes, it starts training a MaxEnt model (more on that later), performing multiple training iterations until it reports a training accuracy close to 100%.

That's great performance on the *training* data, but what really matters is how it performs on data it hasn't ever seen. Add the following code to your playground to evaluate your model against a real test dataset:

```
// 1
let metrics = sentimentClassifier.evaluation(on: testData)
// 2
if metrics.isValid {
  print("Error rate (lower is better): \
(metrics.classificationError)")
} else if let error = metrics.error {
  print("Error evaluating model: \(error)")
} else {
  print("Unknown error evaluating model")
}
```

This looks like more code than it really is. Here's what you've added:

1. You pass a data source to the model's evaluation(on:) function. This compares the model's predictions for each item in the given test dataset against the correct labels.

2. Then you display the classification error if the model successfully calculated one, and print out any errors otherwise.

Here's the output for the model supplied in the resources for the finished project:

```
Error rate (lower is better): 0.12436000000000003
```

Error rate on test set

Notice that this reports the **error rate**, not accuracy. People commonly report the percentage of *incorrect* responses rather than the percentage of correct ones. It's important to keep track of which metric you're dealing with, otherwise you might not properly compare the performance claims of different models.

Also keep in mind these values are related to each other: Subtract either value from 1.0 to get the other value. So an error rate of 0.1244 is an accuracy of 0.8756 — or 87.56%.

Beyond error rate, the metrics returned by evaluation(on:) also include precision, recall and a confusion matrix describing how the model predicted values for each class. It's not shown here, but the confusion matrix for this model shows it handles each class equally well with no obvious bias toward one or the other.

While your model's accuracy of almost 88% is not state-of-the-art on this dataset, it's still quite reasonable for something you created with essentially a single line of code and no tinkering with parameters. If you really needed better results, you could create a model with one of the many other libraries that support conversion to Core ML.

Now that you have a trained model, add the following code to your playground to save it for use in your app:

```
// 1 (Optional)
let metadata = MLModelMetadata(
  author: "Your Name:",
  shortDescription:
    "A model trained to classify movie review sentiment",
  version: "1.0")
// 2
try! sentimentClassifier.write(
  to: playgroundSharedDataDirectory.appendingPathComponent(
    projectDir + "SentimentClassifier.mlmodel"),
  metadata: metadata)
```

These two lines do the following:

1. Specify your model's metadata. This isn't a requirement, but here's how to do it if you want to.

2. Export a Core ML version of your model. Here, you write it out to the playground's data folder.

Save this final version of your playground in case you ever want to come back to it. Then run it and you'll end up with a trained model file named **SentimentClassifier.mlmodel** stored in your **Shared Playground Data/ TextClassification** folder.

Now you can put this model to use. But before doing that, it's worth experimenting to determine if this is the best model you can make.

Exploring other model types

You initialized MLTextclassifier with default parameters, specifying only that the language was English. But you can and should explore other configurations.

In particular, setting the algorithm property determines what kind of what kind of classifier model is used. The basic choice of model architecture can be regarded as one of the *hyperparameters* chosen while exploring a problem. Just as the training process searches for the best parameter weights to fit a model to your data, you yourself are searching for the best hyperparameters guided by trial and error and intuition.

In this case, CreateML offers you four possible kinds of classifier models — either a maximum entropy classifier, a conditional random field classifier, or a classifier based on transfer learning. The transfer learning classifier builds on top of a pretrained model shipped with iOS, which knows statistical relationships of words in your language. This is the knowledge that is being "transferred" to your problem. With a transfer learning-based model, you can additionally choose to use either a static or dynamic embedding of words, the latter being more a sophisticated kind of model which takes into account the context rather than just the identity of every word. (We will discuss embeddings in more detail in two chapters.)

Which type of model should you use? Apple does not in fact publish description of the detailed models underlying these choices. And even if they did, it would be hard to anticipate the best one for your data. So you should simply try a few and see which works best. The more sophisticated models, such as the transfer learning-based classifier, will take longer to train. But the more sophisticated models are not guaranteed to perform better.

For instance, using this dataset on a MacBook Pro (a 15-inch from 2016, with a 2.9 GHz Quad-Core Intel Core i7, 16 GB memory, and an Intel HD Graphics 530 graphics card), training the maximum entropy classifier takes about 3 minutes, the conditional random field classifier takes almost four hours, a transfer learning model with static embedding takes almost two hours and forty-five minutes, and, finally, a transfer learning model with a dynamic embedding takes over four hours. However, test accuracy of the the simplest classifier is the best, around 87%, while the accuracy of the fancier transfer learning classifiers is only around 75%. In short, when in doubt, experiment!

For now, proceed withe the model trained using the maximum entropy classifier. It's time to put it in an app.

Use your text classifier in an app

Open your **SMDB** project in Xcode. Drag **SentimentClassifier.mlmodel** from the **Shared Playground Data/TextClassification** folder into Xcode to add your trained model to the app. Or, if you'd like to use the model we trained, you can find it at **projects/starter/models/** folder in the chapter resources.

Then select **SentimentClassifier.mlmodel** in the Project Navigator to see what Xcode tells you about the model:

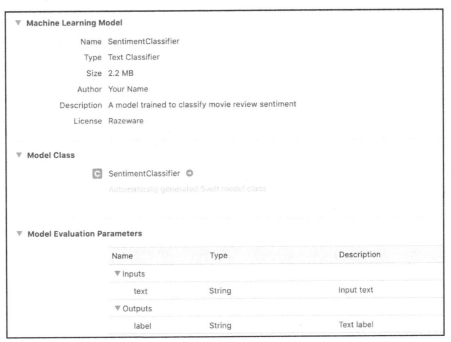

Looking at the mlmodel file

You've seen quite a few model summaries in Xcode at this point, and this one isn't much different. Here are some highlights:

- Its type is **Text Classifier,** which tells you more about what the model is *for* than what it *is*. It's actually a maximum entropy (MaxEnt) classifier, which is a probabilistic model that essentially determines how likely is it for a piece of text to represent a specific class. It generates numerical features from the text and performs a multinomial logistic regression over them. There are many possibilities for what features it could use — word counts, n-gram statistics, syntactical information, to name a few — but Apple doesn't expose what features Create ML uses.

- The model's not huge by machine learning standards, but at over 2MB, it's larger than some you've made in this book. Still, it should be fine for use on mobile.

- Both its inputs and outputs are listed as single `String` values — the input `text` and the output `label`, respectively. You'll give the model some text and it will return one of the labels — "pos" or "neg" — that you trained the model to predict.

Now that you've got your model in the project, open **NLPHelper.swift** and replace `getSentimentClassifier` with the following:

```
func getSentimentClassifier() -> NLModel? {
  try! NLModel(mlModel: SentimentClassifier().model)
}
```

This creates an instance of your model, but it does so a bit differently from other models you've created. Here you instantiate a `SentimentClassifier`, then use its `model` property to create an `NLModel`.

`NLModel` wraps Core ML models for use with the Natural Language framework. Xcode *will* let you use `MLTextClassifier` objects directly, like you've used models in earlier chapters, but it is **essential** to wrap them in `NLModel` first. This ensures the model preprocesses inputs the same way Create ML did during the training process. And as you've learned, it's vital for preprocessing steps to match between training and inference, otherwise your models won't produce the correct results.

Now replace `predictSentiment` inside **NLPHelper.swift** with the following code:

```
func predictSentiment(
  text: String, sentimentClassifier: NLModel) -> String? {
  sentimentClassifier.predictedLabel(for: text)
}
```

The SMDB app calls `getSentimentClassifier` once at startup and then passes the model it returns to `predictSentiment` for each review whose language matches the one supported by the model. To get a prediction, you call `predictedLabel(for:)`, which classifies the given text and returns the label it predicts with the highest probability. Remember the folders for your data were named "neg" and "pos", so those are the two possible return values here.

The `MLTextClassifier` — whether or not it's wrapped in an `NLModel` — does not provide access to the actual prediction probabilities it calculates. That makes it different from some other models you've worked with elsewhere in this book. It's a bit less flexible than some models, but what it lacks in flexibility it makes up for with ease of use.

Build and run one last time. You should now see happy faces on the positive reviews and sad faces on the negative ones.

Reviews with emoji showing sentiment

Notice the faces only appear on the English-language reviews. That's because the app only analyzes the sentiment of reviews whose language matches the one supported by your model. It accomplishes this with the following `guard` statement inside `findSentiment` in **ReviewsManager.swift**:

```
private func findSentiment(_ review: Review,
                           sentimentClassifier: NLModel?) {
  guard let sentimentClassifier = sentimentClassifier,
    review.language ==
      sentimentClassifier.configuration.language else {
    return
  }
  ...
}
```

NLModels have a `configuration` property that gives you access to an
`NLModelConfiguration` object that contains some information about the model.
Here, you access its `language` property to ensure it supports the review's language.

> **Note**: It's important that you always verify your model supports an input
> *before* using it, like this function does. If you don't, the model will still return a
> prediction, but it will be nothing more than a random guess.

The emoji feature uses a single sentiment prediction, but the app also shows how to
aggregate sentiment. It converts the predicted labels into numerical values of 1 and 0
for positive and negative reviews, respectively. It then uses those numbers to
calculate sentiment across multiple reviews. To see the *fruits* of that calculation, tap
the **By Movie** tab. Each movie now includes a tomato rating indicating the average
sentiment of its (English-language) reviews.

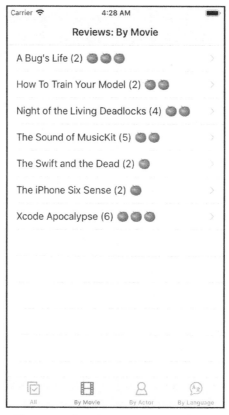

Tomatoes showing average sentiment

Finally, tap the **By Actors** tab. The list now lets you find the actors in the most-liked movies by showing an emoji indicating the prevailing sentiment of all the reviews mentioning that actor's name.

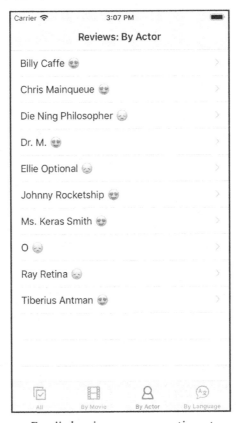

Emoji showing average sentiment

For readers who went through the "Natural Language Processing" chapter in *iOS 11 by Tutorials*, you've now had the experience of using a pre-trained model as well as training one on your own. The one you trained even outperforms the pre-trained model from that book. For example, here's a review that was scored with a negative sentiment in the original project: "What a great film! Ms. Keras Smith was truly magnificent, and Billy Caffe's singing and dancing is the stuff of legends. Three thumbs up!" If you check that same review in your app here, which you can find easily by choosing **Ms. Keras Smith** or **Billy Caffe** in the **By Actor** tab, you'll see it now correctly displays a happy face.

The `MLTextClassifier` you used in this section works well for larger chunks of text. In the next section, you'll create a model used to classify individual words *within* chunks of text instead.

Comparing the analyzers

Before we finish, let's make one more enhancement to the UI: update it to show the sentiment analysis from Apple's built-in analyzer, so we can compare the result to our own classifier and provide the user more information.

First, delete the `print` statement that you temporarily introduced to `tableView(_:cellForRowAt:)` **ReviewsTableViewController.swift**.

Instead of that line, update the call to `setSentiment` to this new form, where you also pass in the numerical sentiment from Apple's analyzer:

```
cell.setSentiment(sentiment: review.sentiment, score:
analyzeSentiment(text: review.text))
```

Now, in **ReviewTableViewCell.swift**, update the function `setSentiment(sentiment:)` as follows:

```
func setSentiment(sentiment: Int?, score: Double? = nil) {
  // 1
  let classified: String
  if let sentiment = sentiment {
    classified = sentimentMapping[sentiment] ?? ""
  } else {
    classified = ""
  }
  // 2
  let scored: String
  if let score = score {
    scored = "(: \(String(score)))"
  } else {
    scored = ""
  }
  // 3
  sentimentLabel.text = classified + " " + scored
}
```

This is fairly straightforward:

1. The first `if` statement takes your zero or one score and maps it to an emoji or an empty string.

2. The second `if` statement takes the numerical score, and yields a string with an Apple icon and the number, or else an empty string.

3. Then you save a concatenated string in the cell for display.

Run the app now, and when you browse reviews you will see both ratings.

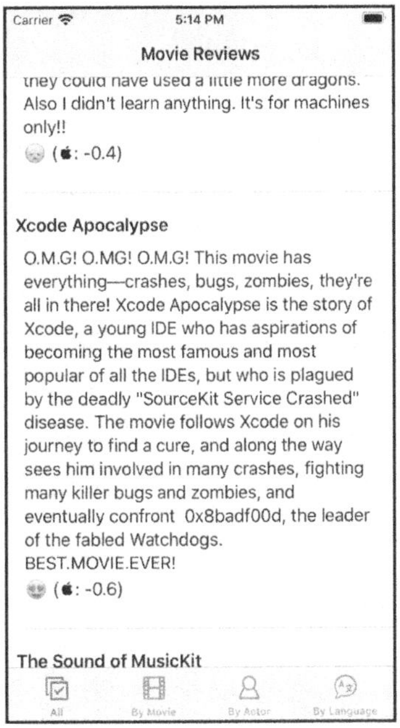

Emoji vs Apple sentiment

It's interesting to notice that in some places, such as is pictured below, your classifier clearly does a better job than the built-in sentiment analysis API, such as some of the reviews of "Xcode Apocalypse" shown above. Not bad!

Custom word classifiers

You're done with the SMDB app for now, but you'll come back to it again in the next chapter. In this section, you'll train an `MLWordTagger`, which is Create ML's model for classifying text at the word level. You'll use it to create a custom tagging scheme for `NLTagger`.

The model you make here attempts to identify names of Apple products mentioned in text, but you can train a model like this to tag individual words of any type. For example, imagine creating a profanity filter or automatically adding links to domain-specific jargon like legal or medical terms.

Create a new **macOS** playground and delete any code included from the template. Or, if you'd prefer, you can follow along with the completed playground at **projects/ final/playgrounds/CustomTokenTagging.playground**.

There's a tiny dataset stored in the chapter resources at **projects/starter/datasets/custom_tags.json**. Drag that file into the **Resources** folder in the playground's Project navigator to add it to the playground.

> **Note**: You could also use the **Shared Playground Data** folder like you did for the sentiment classifier, but this JSON file is quite small and Xcode should have no problem handling it as part of the playground bundle.

Select **custom_tags.json** in the Project Navigator to view the training examples. Here is a snippet from that file:

```
[
  ...
  {
    "tokens": ["The", "Apple", "TV", "is", "great", "for",
               "watching", "TV", "and", "movies", ",",
               "and", "you", "can", "play", "games",
               "on", "it", ",", "too", "!"],
    "tags": ["_", "AppleProduct", "AppleProduct", "_", "_", "_",
             "_", "_", "_", "_", "_",
             "_", "_", "_", "_", "_",
             "_", "_", "_", "_", "_"]
  },
```

```
  {
    "tokens": ["Apple", "adding", "Windows", "support", "for",
               "iTunes", "helped", "the", "iPod",
               "succeed", "."],
    "tags": ["_", "_", "_", "_", "_",
             "AppleProduct", "_", "_", "AppleProduct",
             "_", "_"]
  },
  ...
]
```

This JSON file contains a list, where each element is a dictionary with two keys: tokens and tags. Each dictionary in the list defines a single training example. The tokens key maps to a list of strings for a tokenized text sample, and the tags key maps to the list of tags that correspond to items in the tokens list.

The specific tags used here were chosen somewhat arbitrarily. Each word you're interested in — the ones that name Apple products — is tagged with "AppleProduct," whereas the other tokens are all tagged with a simple underscore. You could use a descriptive term if you'd prefer, but I chose this to help the product tags stand out in the list.

Notice the second example includes the word "TV" twice, tagged once with "AppleProduct" and once with an underscore. Learning to assign tags properly involves more than memorizing words; the model has to learn to evaluate tokens in context, otherwise it would not be able to handle cases like this one.

A few notes about the training data:

- The actual key names `tokens` and `tags` don't matter. You can name them anything you want as long as it's consistent across samples.

- Models are allowed to produce more than one tag. This example happens to assign everything either "AppleProduct" or an underscore, but feel free to include as many tags as necessary for your task.

- The formatting shown here is adjusted slightly from what you'll see in the actual file to make it easier to read in the book. Specifically, you don't actually need to split the tokens and tags into multiple lines like this.

Now that you've looked at the data, you'll train a model. To get started, add the following to your playground:

```
import Foundation
import PlaygroundSupport
import CreateML
import CoreML
import NaturalLanguage
```

You're importing several frameworks here because you're going to train a model *and* use this playground to simulate the model's usage in an app. However, they should all appear familiar to you now.

Next, prepare your training data with the following:

```
let trainUrl =
  Bundle.main.url(
    forResource: "custom_tags", withExtension: "json")!
let trainData = try MLDataTable(contentsOf: trainUrl)
```

You access the **custom_tags.json** file from the playground's resource bundle, and use it to create an `MLDataTable`. This class stores tabular data for use with Create ML. It populates itself with a new row for each item in the JSON file's list. It uses the keys it finds in each dictionary as column names, and maps the dictionary values to the corresponding row-column cell.

So for the file you just loaded, the `MLDataTable` will have 11 rows, each with two columns named `tokens` and `tags`.

Next, add the following line to create your model:

```
let model = try MLWordTagger(
  trainingData: trainData,
  tokenColumn: "tokens", labelColumn: "tags",
  parameters: MLWordTagger.ModelParameters(language: .english))
```

Here, you create an `MLWordTagger`, passing in the training data and the names of the columns, which define the tokens and labels. Regardless of how much data your table contains, the model only ever looks at the two columns you specify here. This is why it doesn't matter how you name the keys in your JSON file — pick whatever you like and then tell `MLWordTagger` what to look for when you create it.

Once again, you specify the language this model supports as English, to match the training data. You'll see how `NLTagger` uses this information a bit later.

In classic Create ML fashion, just creating your model object also handles training it. You could test this model like you would any other Create ML model, but for now just save it out with the following code:

```
let projectDir = "TextClassification/"

// Optionally add metadata before saving model
```

```
let savedModelUrl =
  playgroundSharedDataDirectory.appendingPathComponent(
    projectDir + "AppleProductTagger.mlmodel")

try model.write(to: savedModelUrl)
```

Here, you export your model in Core ML format to the same **Shared Playground Data/TextClassifier** folder you used to train your sentiment analysis model.

Next, you'll need to know how to use a custom word classifier like this one inside an app. But rather than pigeon hole this functionality into the SMDB project, you'll just use the model right here in the playground. However, to do that you do need to do one special step. Add the following line:

```
let compiledModelUrl =
  try MLModel.compileModel(at: savedModelUrl)
```

When you add a Core ML model to Xcode, it actually compiles it into a format that can be used by your app. However, this does not happen automatically in playgrounds. This line loads the model file at the specified URL, compiles it, and writes the results to a temporary folder on your device. It returns the URL of the compiled model.

The rest of this section shows code that you could use inside an app just like you do here. Add the following line to instantiate your model:

```
let appleProductModel =
  try NLModel(contentsOf: compiledModelUrl)
```

This is similar to what you did with the sentiment classifier. Here, you wrap your MLWordTagger inside an NLModel to ensure your app tokenizes inputs the same way as Create ML did when you trained the model. You create it with the URL of your compiled model, but in an app you could also create the model directly like you did earlier with SentimentClassifier.

Next, add the following code to configure an NLTagger to use your new model:

```
// 1
let appleProductTagScheme = NLTagScheme("AppleProducts")
// 2
let appleProductTagger = NLTagger(tagSchemes:
[appleProductTagScheme])
// 3
appleProductTagger.setModels(
  [appleProductModel], forTagScheme: appleProductTagScheme)
```

Here's how you configure the tagger:

1. Create a new NLTagScheme object to represent your word classifier. You can name it anything you like; it doesn't need to match the name of your model or the names of any tags it produces.

2. Create an NLTagger like you did before, but give it your new tag scheme. You can provide multiple schemes here, including built-in options and other custom ones.

3. Call setModels on appleProductTagger, passing it your custom model and tag scheme. This tells the tagger to use your custom model when asked to tag with that scheme on a language supported by the model. You can provide more than one model in this list if you've trained different ones for different languages, and the tagger will use the correct one based on the language of the text it processes.

And, finally, you'll this code to test out your model on some sample inputs. First, create some test strings to simulate inputs.

```
let testStrings = [
  "I enjoy watching Netflix on my Apple TV, but I wish I had a
bigger TV.",
  "The Face ID on my new iPhone works really fast!",
  "What's up with the keyboard on my MacBook Pro?",
  "Do you prefer the iPhone or the Pixel?"
]
```

These include a mix of Apple products that were in your training set, Apple products that were not in the training set, and non-Apple products.

Next, follow follows the same pattern you've seen before when using NLTagger to enumerate all Apple products:

```
let appleProductTag = NLTag("AppleProduct")
let options: NLTagger.Options = [
  .omitWhitespace, .omitPunctuation, .omitOther]

for str in testStrings {
  print("Checking \(str)")
  appleProductTagger.string = str
  appleProductTagger.enumerateTags(
    in: str.startIndex..<str.endIndex,
    unit: .word,
    scheme: appleProductTagScheme,
    options: options) { tag, tokenRange in

    if tag == appleProductTag {
      print("Found Apple product: \(str[tokenRange])")
    }
    return true
  }
}
```

The only difference here is you create a new NLTag for your custom tag name and check for that while processing the tokens.

Run the playground to train your model and see how it performs on your test cases:

```
Skipping automatic creation of validation set; training set has fewer than 50 points.
Holding out 2 samples for validation

Tokenizing data and extracting features
Starting CRF training with 9 samples
Iteration 1 validation accuracy 1.000000
Finished CRF training in 0.01 seconds
```

Word classifier training output

Here's what you see while training the model, line by line:

- According to the first message, the model doesn't create a validation set because your dataset has fewer than 50 items. Seems reasonable, but the very next message claims it's using two samples for validation. These two statements seem to contradict each other, but rest assured — you'll probably never see this message in real life because you would never train a real model with fewer than 50 samples, right? *Right?*

- Next, it tokenizes the data just like when you trained your sentiment analysis model. It goes much faster this time, though, mostly because you're working with a tiny dataset but also because the JSON file already defines each input as a list of tokens.

- It claims to start "CRF training," but what's that? It's just talking about training the model. CRF stands for "conditional random field," which is the algorithm `MLWordTagger` uses to classify words. This is another probabilistic model, but one that usually does better than MaxEnt when predicting labels on individual words — MaxEnt works better when classifying larger chunks of text. Its primary advantage is that it considers the tokens as **sequences**, which MaxEnt does not *necessarily* do. (It can use *some* sequential data, like n-gram statistics, but CRF relies on it more heavily.) Once again, Apple does not provide the details of Create ML's implementation.

- It trains for only one iteration over the dataset. It would likely train more if you ran with more data, but it achieves perfect accuracy on (all two of) the validation samples so it stops training.

And here's what its output from the tests looks like:

```
Checking "I wish I had a bigger TV to watch Netflix on with my Apple TV."
Found Apple product: Apple
Found Apple product: TV

Checking "The Face ID on my new iPhone works really fast!"
Found Apple product: Face
Found Apple product: ID
Found Apple product: iPhone

Checking "What's up with the keyboard on my MacBook Pro?"
Found Apple product: MacBook
Found Apple product: Pro

Checking "Do you prefer the iPhone or the Pixel?"
Found Apple product: iPhone
Found Apple product: Pixel
```

Word classifier test results

The model does really well, especially considering your dataset only had 11 samples — and the model only trained on nine of them! It managed to correctly label the different versions of "TV" in the first example, and even labeled "Face" and "ID" as Apple products, even though those tokens never appear in the training set.

However, it wasn't all good. Notice it also attributes "Pixel" to Apple, which I'm sure would surprise Google.

These examples prove the model learns something about the **context** where these tokens appear, rather than just memorizing the words. Training with a larger dataset will give better results, but just like everything else based on machine learning, it won't ever be perfect.

One last thing: Notice your model tags multi-word names like "Face ID" and "MacBook Pro" as multiple words. That's because the `NLTagger` first tokenizes the input based on its rules for the text's language, and it doesn't already know that these words are meant to go together. There's no way to avoid this, so you'll need to label them as separate words in your training data, and then write your own logic for recombining them later.

The remaining bits

The Natural Language framework supports a few other things not specifically covered in this chapter. The three you'll most likely use are **gazetteers**, **part-of-speech tagging**, and **tokenization**.

A gazetteer is a simple concept. It's essentially just a dictionary: It maps a predefined list of entities to a single tag for each entity. For example, in the last section, you trained a tagger that could consume a text string and tag which words were Apple products. Great! But in order to train that tagger, you needed to provide it training data – a collection of many sentences where you had already tagged the words representing Apple products.

But what if, starting out, you didn't have a large list of tagged sentences but you did have a plain old list of Apple products? This is exactly where you would need a `NLGazetteer`, also known by Apple as a **text catalog**. It holds a fixed list of entities and their tags in a highly efficient representation. Once you've set your `NLTagger` to use a gazetteer, then it can identify the entities you named. So you could define a gazetteer which mapped every known Apple product to a single tag, and use a tagger to find the Apple products. A gazetteer is not a machine learning model at all but it is worth keeping in mind in case it's what you really need.

Part-of-speech tagging refers to analyzing text for grammatical structure. In code, it requires nothing more than using an NLTagger just like you've done elsewhere in this chapter. In this case, you iterate over tokens using either the .lexicalClass or .nameTypeOrLexicalClass tag schemes and the tagger assigns NLTag values indicating how those tokens are used in the text. For example, .noun, .verb or .adjective. Consult the documentation for the possible values.

Tokenization is the process of splitting a piece of text into smaller units. It most often means dividing strings into individual words and punctuation, but it could mean breaking it into other units, like sentences or characters.

The classes you've used throughout this chapter all tokenize their inputs automatically, so you haven't needed to worry about it. However, if you ever need to do it yourself, the Natural Language framework provides NLTokenizer to chunk text by word, sentence, paragraph or document. It uses language-specific rules which are generally good but might not always be exactly what you want. Still, it's a nice option so you should at least try it the next time you need to tokenize some text.

You'll use NLTokenizer as a preprocessing step when you implement language translation in the next chapter. In the meantime, you can check out **NLExtras.playground** in the **projects/final/playgrounds** folder to see sample code for both part-of-speech tagging and tokenization.

Key points

- Use Apple's new Natural Language framework to take advantage of fast, well trained machine-learning models for NLP.

- `NLLanguageRecognizer` can identify the language used in a piece of text.

- `NLTagger` and `NLTagScheme` allow you to chunk text into specific, labeled types. There are several built-in tagging schemes available, and you can specify your own.

- `NLTokenizer` can break up text into documents, paragraphs, sentences or words.

- Use Create ML and `MLTextClassifier` to train your own models to classify larger chunks of text, like sentences, paragraphs or documents.

- Use Create ML and `MLWordTagger` to train models to classify text at the word level.

- `NLModel` wraps Create ML models like `MLTextClassifier` and `MLWordTagger` in a way that ensures inputs are preprocessed in your app the same way they were during training. It's also the required type for custom tagging schemes used with `NLTagger`.

Where to go from here?

This chapter covered most of what Apple makes easy via the Natural Language framework. You can find a completed version of the project in the chapter resources at **projects/final/SMDB**. When you're ready, go on to the next chapter, where you'll learn how to implement more advanced NLP features that involve creating custom models in Keras. You'll continue working with this app, adding the ability to translate Spanish-language reviews into English.

Chapter 15: Natural Language Transformation, Part 1

By Alexis Gallagher

The previous chapter showed you how to use Apple's Natural Language framework to perform some useful NLP tasks. But Apple only covers the basics — there are many other things you might like to do with natural language. For example, you might answer questions, summarize documents or translate between languages.

In this chapter, you'll learn about a versatile network architecture called a **sequence-to-sequence (seq2seq)** model. You'll add one to the SMDB app you already built, using it to translate movie reviews from Spanish to English, but the same network design has been used for many types of problems, from question answering to generating image captions. Don't worry if you didn't already make SMDB — we provide a starter project if you need it. But you can forget about Xcode for a while — seq2seq models require a lower-level framework, so you'll work with Python and Keras for most of this chapter.

Getting started

Some of the Keras code in this project was initially based on the example found in the file **examples/lstm_seq2seq.py** inside the Keras GitHub repository github.com/keras-team/keras. This chapter makes stylistic modifications, explains and expands on the code, and shows how to convert the models you build to Core ML and use them in an app.

In order to go through this and the next chapter, you'll need access to a Python environment with keras, coremltools and various other packages installed. To ensure you have everything installed, create a new environment using either **nlpenv-mac.yml** or **nlpenv-linux.yml**, which you'll find in **projects/notebooks**. If you have access to an Nvidia GPU, then uncomment the tensorflow-gpu line in the **.yml** file to greatly increase training speed.

Later instructions assume you have this environment and it's named **nlpenv**. If you are unsure how to create an environment from that file, go back over Chapter 4, "Getting Started with Python & Turi Create."

Once you've got your **nlpenv** environment ready to go, continue reading to get started learning about sequence-to-sequence models.

The sequence-to-sequence model

Inside the chapter resources, you'll find a text file named **spa.txt** in **projects/notebooks/data/**. This file comes originally from manythings.org at http://www.manythings.org/anki/, which provides sentence pairs for many different languages. These pairs were culled from an even larger dataset provided by the Tatoeba Project at www.tatoeba.org.

The file contains lines that look like this:

```
Go.     Ve.
Go.     Vete.
Go.     Vaya.
Go.     Váyase.
Hi.     Hola.
Run!    ¡Corre!
Run.    Corred.
```

The first seven lines of spa.txt

Each line has an English sentence — they aren't all one-word long like in the image — followed by one possible Spanish translation of that sentence. You're going to use this data to train a neural network to ingest Spanish text, like "¡Corre!", and translate it into English text, like "Run!"

> **Note:** As you can see in the image of samples from the data file, the same phrase may appear multiple times with different translations. If you were training a model to translate from English to Spanish, then this would likely confuse it, possibly forcing it to learn only one of the translations. However, your model will translate from Spanish to English, and there are far fewer duplicate Spanish phrases in the file, so it shouldn't be an issue.

Encoder-decoder models

There are multiple ways to accomplish this task. The network architecture you'll use here is called a sequence-to-sequence, or seq2seq, model. At it's most basic level, it works like this:

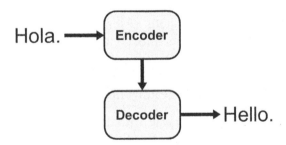

Text translation with seq2seq model

The seq2seq model consists of two networks operating together; these are called the **encoder** and the **decoder**.

The encoder processes some input — in this case, Spanish text — and produces some vector of output values that captures the essence of the input. The decoder then processes the encoder's output and produces its own output — here, English text — which represents its interpretation of the information captured by the encoder.

In other words, a lot of the magic happens in that intermediate vector of values that passes from the encoder to decoder. What's the right way to think about it? One intuition you can use is to think of that intermediate vector of values as the *meaning* of the text, independent of language.

While this intuition may be helpful, it is also wise not to take it too literally. A word like "meaning" suggests your model is doing more than it is. Does it understand meaning in the way that, say, a person does? And when you "train" a model and it "learns" to predict, has it done anything like what we mean when we say a person has learned? Of course not. The trap is that these words are evocative because they suggest analogies to what people do. But they are merely analogies.

Such evocative analogies are like friends: it is a good idea to have many of them, so that you always have a few different, competing perspectives on an issue.

So, more prosaically, you might also think of this encoder-decoder model as acting like a file compression algorithm. You start with an original file — the encoder's input — and compress it into some new format, which is the encoder's output. Later, you can uncompress that formatted data to recover the contents of the original file; this is essentially what the decoder does. But, this is a "lossy" compression scheme, like JPEG. Just as a low quality JPEG image compression will lose details of the image and keep the gross features, here we are losing the the details of the input text, such as the exact wording, and keeping the meaning. We are also decoding it into a different language along the way.

Finally, from a deep-learning perspective, you can think of this as a bit like the transfer learning you used in the computer vision chapters. There, you started with a pre-trained network and passed inputs through it to extract some set of features as output. Those features are really just the output activations from a specific layer in the network. Then you trained a new model to accept those output values as inputs and produce some new output, like a healthy/unhealthy label prediction.

The seq2seq model works in a similar way, with the encoder acting as the feature extractor and the decoder acting as the classification model. The difference here is that you're going to build and train the encoder and decoder together from scratch.

Seq2seq in depth

Digging a little deeper, the seq2seq model works with sequences both for inputs and outputs. That's where it gets its name — it transforms a sequence to another sequence. To accomplish this, the encoder and decoder usually both rely on recurrent layers — specifically, this chapter uses the LSTM layer introduced in the sequence classification chapter.

These LSTMs aren't shown in these diagrams, but keep in mind that the boxes labeled Encoder and Decoder each represent neural networks that include such layers.

The following image gives some more details about how your model will work, showing how it will predict its first output character "H" when translating "Hola." to "Hello.":

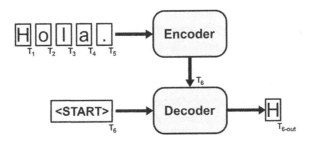

Inference with seq2seq, through the first output token

As you can see, the encoder will process its input as a sequence of individual characters. Each character is labeled in the image with its timestep so it's clear what order the model sees the input. After ingesting the entire sequence, only then will it pass its output on to the decoder. In other words, the encoder and the decoder each work one sequence at a time, rather than one token a time.

But how is the information actually passed from the encoder to the decoder? You learned in the sequence classification project how LSTMs maintain state that lets them keep track of information between timesteps within a sequence. The decoder will take advantage of that fact and use the final state from the encoder's LSTM layer as the initial state for its own LSTM layer. In other words, not only does the decoder never see the input sequence fed into the encoder; it also never sees how the encoder responded to early tokens in that input sequence. It only sees the final state of the encoder. Along with that state, the decoder will also take as input a special START token.

The decoder will then produce a single character as output. That is its first output character.

> **Note:** This chapter's model uses individual characters as inputs and outputs, and as such may use the terms "character" and "token" interchangeably. However, seq2seq models do not need to work at the character level. You'll see how to use full-word tokens in the next chapter, and find out about some other options, too. So keep in mind: The images of characters in this chapter apply to any size tokens.

The encoder is no longer involved after predicting the first character. As you can see in the following image, the decoder continues predicting the rest of its output sequence by passing its own output character back into itself as its next input character, in what is effectively a loop:

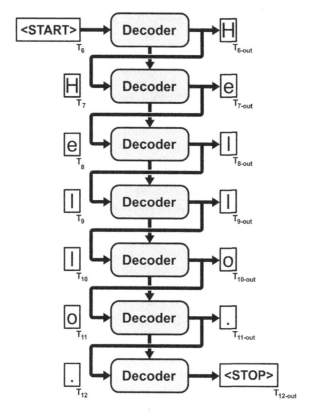

Decoder portion of seq2seq model during inference

The arrows pointing down in the above image, going directly from Decoder block to Decoder block, represent the output state from the decoder's LSTM layer. At each timestep after the first, the decoder uses the output state from the previous timestep as its new initial state. Not shown here is the initial state used to process the START token, which comes from the encoder. Likewise, each timestep after the first takes as input the previous timestep's output token. This process continues until the decoder produces a special STOP token, or until you stop it yourself if you want to limit the length of its output sequences.

Teacher forcing

That is how inference works. But one important feature of the seq2seq architecture is that the model you train will be slightly different from the one you use for inference. During training, your model will actually process each sample like this:

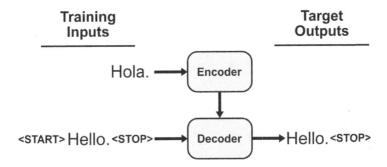

Training a seq2seq model

Individual timesteps aren't shown in order to simplify the diagram, but these sequences are still processed one token at a time. The important thing to notice is how, in training, the decoder pictured above receives as input the encoder's output *and* the full English translation of the encoder's input surrounded by START and STOP tokens.

At each timestep, the decoder takes a single input token and produces a single output token. As you saw earlier, the *trained* decoder uses its own output from one timestep as its input for the next one, but during training you'll always input to each timestep what the output *should* have been at the previous timestep.

The decoder learns to produce a specific character as output when it sees the START token in conjunction with a specific encoder state. From there, it learns to associate its own internal LSTM states with each new character to produce the next one, eventually learning to produce the entire sequence. Ensuring each timestep starts with the correct values — rather than what the decoder actually outputs while training — greatly increases the speed at which a recurrent network trains. This technique is known as **teacher forcing**.

There's one last subtlety visible in the diagram above: there's no START token in the target output. Why not? The target outputs you use to calculate the loss during training don't include the START token, because the decoder should only ever learn to produce what *follows* it in the sequence.

Phew! That was a lot of preliminary information, but hopefully getting the idea down first will make the rest of the chapter easier to follow. There are still quite a few details left to discuss, so let's get started.

Prepare your dataset

First, you need to load your dataset. Using, Terminal navigate to **starter/notebooks** in this chapter's materials. Activate your **nlpenv** environment and launch a new Jupyter notebook. Then run a cell with the following code to load the Spanish-English sequence pairs:

```
# 1
start_token = "\t"
stop_token = "\n"
# 2
with open("data/spa.txt", "r", encoding="utf-8") as f:
    samples = f.read().split("\n")
samples = [sample.strip().split("\t")
           for sample in samples if len(sample.strip()) > 0]
# 3
samples = [(es, start_token + en + stop_token)
           for en, es in samples if len(es) < 45]
```

Now, samples contains almost 100,000 sequence pairs. Here's how you set it up:

1. You define constants here indicating the tab and newline characters will act as the decoder's START and STOP tokens, respectively. You can assign anything as the START and STOP tokens, but they *must not appear elsewhere* in any output sequences.

2. You read each line of the data file, then split them around the tab character to create a list of English-Spanish sentence pairs. Notice how it only processes rows that include more than whitespace — this avoids accidentally adding bad entries for empty rows in **spa.txt**, but it's certainly not robust file processing. For example, this would still add bad entries for rows that don't include exactly one tab.

3. This line loops over the list you just created and swaps the order of the elements, creating a list of tuples with the Spanish phrases first. It also adds a START token at the beginning of each English phrase and a STOP token at the end.

Notice you only kept pairs where the Spanish sentence is less than 45 characters long. You'll read more about how sequence length affects things in the section on training your model, but for now just know we chose 45 based on the length of the Spanish sentences in the SMDB app.

You can display some of the list to be sure things look as expected:

```
print(samples[:2])

  [('Ve.', '\tGo.\n'), ('Vete.', '\tGo.\n')]
```

The first two samples after loading the dataset

Note: The two lines you wrote to create `samples` use a Python construct called list comprehension. If you aren't familiar with this syntax, it's an optimized way to create a list by iterating over a collection. The anatomy of a comprehension is `[a for b in c]`. It creates a new list filled with items made by calling the expression a with each item b from the collection c. Optionally, you can add a condition to limit which items from c you process, like this: `[a for b in c if d]` where d is some conditional expression involving b. You should get comfortable with this syntax if you plan on using Python since it's extremely common — plus the Python interpreter runs these more efficiently than `for` loops that build lists with append.

In and out of vocabulary

If you've followed along with the book thus far, then you already know it's best to have separate training, validation, and test sets when building machine learning models. Keras can randomly select samples from your training data to use for validation when you train your model, but you won't rely on that here.

That's because you will need to do some special processing on the validation set in order to setup your **vocabulary**. As you might guess, a sequence model's vocabulary is simply the model's set of allowed tokens, which in your case means the set of possible characters.

If you picked the validation set at random, then it might contain characters that never appeared in your training set. To avoid this, and to handle this situation in general, you are going to find the vocabulary and use it to preprocess sequences fed to our model, replacing any unsupported characters with **out-of-vocabulary** (OOV) tokens.

So for this model, you must separate the data into training and validation sets yourself. Run a cell with the following code to do so:

```
from sklearn.model_selection import train_test_split

train_samples, valid_samples = train_test_split(
    samples, train_size=.8, random_state=42)
```

This uses scikit-learn's `train_test_split` to randomly assign samples from your dataset into training and validation sets, with 80 percent going towards training. Providing a `random_state` is optional, but specifying 42 here generates the same datasets we used when training our models.

Before you can deal with OOV tokens, you need to know what's in the vocabulary. You'll train your model to recognize a specific set of input tokens (the input vocabulary) and to produce values from a specific set of output tokens (the output vocabulary). But don't worry: Even with a limited set of tokens, it can ingest and produce an infinite number of different sequences.

Run the following code in your notebook to gather the unique tokens in your dataset to act as your model's vocabulary:

```
# 1
in_vocab = set()
out_vocab = set()

for in_seq, out_seq in train_samples:
    in_vocab.update(in_seq)
    out_vocab.update(out_seq)
# 2
in_vocab_size = len(in_vocab)
out_vocab_size = len(out_vocab)
```

Here's how you built the input and output vocabularies for your model:

1. You loop over every sample in the training data and store each Spanish or English character in its corresponding vocabulary `set`. You call `update` instead of `add` on the `set`s so that it adds the individual characters rather than the entire strings. `update` identifies a string argument as iterable, and iterates over the characters, treating them as individual elements to be added to the set.

2. When you define your Keras model, you'll need to specify how many tokens each vocabulary contains — you'll learn why later when you read the discussion about one-hot encoding — so you grab those sizes, here. If you check you'll see `in_vocab_size` is 101 and `out_vocab_size` is 87.

Now, in_vocab contains every character present in the Spanish sequences from your training set, while out_vocab includes every character from the English sequences. If you're curious to see what you're working with, you can display the vocabulary by running a line like the following:

```
print(sorted(in_vocab))
```

Using sorted isn't necessary but it makes the list more readable. You'll see the input vocabulary consists of the following characters:

```
[' ', '!', '"', '$', '%', '"', '(', ')', '+', ',', '-', '.',
 '/', '0', '1', '2', '3', '4', '5', '6', '7', '8', '9', ':', ';',
 '?', 'A', 'B', 'C', 'D', 'E', 'F', 'G', 'H', 'I', 'J', 'K', 'L',
 'M', 'N', 'O', 'P', 'Q', 'R', 'S', 'T', 'U', 'V', 'W', 'X', 'Y',
 'Z', 'a', 'b', 'c', 'd', 'e', 'f', 'g', 'h', 'i', 'j', 'k', 'l',
 'm', 'n', 'o', 'p', 'q', 'r', 's', 't', 'u', 'v', 'w', 'x', 'y',
 'z', '¡', '«', '°', 'º', '»', '¿', 'Á', 'É', 'Ó', 'Ú', 'á', 'è',
 'é', 'í', 'ñ', 'ó', 'ö', 'ú', 'ü', 'Ş', 'с', '–', '€']
```

And running a similar line for out_vocab displays these characters:

```
['\t', '\n', ' ', '!', '"', '$', '%', '"', ',', '-', '.', '/',
 '0', '1', '2', '3', '4', '5', '6', '7', '8', '9', ':', ';', '?',
 'A', 'B', 'C', 'D', 'E', 'F', 'G', 'H', 'I', 'J', 'K', 'L', 'M',
 'N', 'O', 'P', 'Q', 'R', 'S', 'T', 'U', 'V', 'W', 'X', 'Y', 'Z',
 'a', 'b', 'c', 'd', 'e', 'f', 'g', 'h', 'i', 'j', 'k', 'l', 'm',
 'n', 'o', 'p', 'q', 'r', 's', 't', 'u', 'v', 'w', 'x', 'y', 'z',
 '°', 'á', 'ã', 'è', 'é', 'ö', '"', '"', '₂', '€']
```

It looks like the training data includes a good selection of characters, but notice how there are differences between the input and output vocabularies. This isn't surprising; after all, these are vocabularies for two different languages.

However, it's important to understand: *This vocabulary defines every character your model will* ever *handle.* That means it will never know what to do with an input character not found in in_vocab, and will never produce a sentence using a character not in out_vocab.

For example, notice the Spanish set contains parenthesis but the English one does not. You know parenthesis *should* be valid characters in English, but your model will *never* produce an output that includes them, no matter how many might appear in a given input sequence.

Now that you know which tokens your model can handle, any *other* tokens are considered OOV. There are different ways to handle OOV tokens, but none work perfectly and it's an open area of research. For this model, you'll take the most basic approach and remove OOV tokens from any inputs before processing them. For the validation set — and test set, if you had one — you'll need to remove them from both the inputs and target outputs.

> **Note**: This chapter's model processes sequences at the character level, so removing OOV tokens should not remove much information from a sequence. In the next chapter, where you'll learn about working with full word tokens, dealing with OOV tokens becomes much more difficult.

When you use your model in iOS, you'll preprocess each sequence before passing it to the model. But you'll test against your entire validation set every epoch while training, so it's more efficient to preprocess all of them at once beforehand. Run a cell with the following code to remove OOV tokens from the validation set:

```
tmp_samples = []
for in_seq, out_seq in valid_samples:
  tmp_in_seq = [c for c in in_seq if c in in_vocab]
  tmp_out_seq = [c for c in out_seq if c in out_vocab]
  tmp_samples.append(
    ("".join(tmp_in_seq), "".join(tmp_out_seq)))
valid_samples = tmp_samples
```

Here, you iterated over all the validation samples and created new sequences that only include characters that are found in the appropriate vocabulary set — in_vocab for the Spanish inputs and out_vocab for the English outputs.

> **Note**: If you compare your validation samples before and after removing the OOV tokens, you might find little or no difference. That's just happenstance based on what random split you got earlier from train_test_split, but the premise here still holds true; your model cannot handle tokens it doesn't see while training, so you need to do some preprocessing when working with sequences containing OOV tokens. This is true while testing and at runtime in your iOS app.

You aren't quite ready to train a model yet, but you've prepared enough to at least define the architecture. The next section walks you through that process.

Build your model

In this section, you'll use Keras to define a seq2seq model that translates Spanish text into English, one character at a time. Get started by importing the Keras functions you'll need with the following code:

```
import keras
from keras.layers import Dense, Input, LSTM, Masking
from keras.models import Model
```

You'll read more about these as you use them in the upcoming cells. But to summarize, you are importing Keras, the high-level machine learning library, and then some basic buildings blocks which Keras provides for defining a model.

> **Note**: When you execute this cell and the following one, you may see a small parade of warnings in your notebook, such as "FutureWarning: Passing (type, 1) or '1type' as a synonym of type is deprecated; in a future version of numpy, it will be understood as (type, (1,)) / '(1,)type'" or "The name tf.placeholder is deprecated. Please use tf.compat.v1.placeholder instead". Never fear. These are warnings, not errors, and they are safe to ignore. They are coming not from your code but from inside the TensorFlow machine learning library, as Tensorflow (which is developed by Google) complains that Keras (which is also developed by Google) is not using TensorFlow in the newest possible way. Google develops so fast, it cannot even keep up with itself. Remarkable.

Building the encoder

Now, let's start building the model. Run the following code in your notebook to define the encoder portion of the seq2seq model:

```
# 1
latent_dim = 256
# 2
encoder_in = Input(
  shape=(None, in_vocab_size), name="encoder_in")
# 3
encoder_mask = Masking(name="encoder_mask")(encoder_in)
# 4
encoder_lstm = LSTM(
  latent_dim, return_state=True, recurrent_dropout=0.3,
  name="encoder_lstm")
# 5
_, encoder_h, encoder_c = encoder_lstm(encoder_mask)
```

It takes only these five lines to define your encoder, but there's a lot to say about them:

1. The `latent_dim` variable defines how many nodes your LSTM uses to represent each recurrent step internally. This, in turn, defines the size of the feature vectors used to store the encoding produced by the encoder. In machine learning, we refer to the process of converting an input into a set of features as mapping it into latent space. So `latent_dim` defines the number of dimensions in the encoder's latent space as 256. This value directly affects the size and speed of your model: Larger values produce larger, slower models. However, models with more dimensions can technically learn more complicated relationships so they might produce better results. That is, *if* you can train them — the larger your model, the more data you need to train it. There are a lot of things involved with finding the right value here, but we chose this value arbitrarily. We encourage you to experiment with other values after you've finished the chapter.

2. Here, you make an `Input` layer, to which you'll pass batches of sequences during training. You specify two dimensions — `None` and `in_vocab_size`. The `None` tells Keras that you want it to support variable length inputs. That is, you'll be able to pass sequences of *any* length, which is good because sentences can come in any length. The `in_vocab_size` tells it how large the vectors are that hold each character — the same size as how many different possible tokens exist in the vocabulary. Essentially, these two dimensions tell Keras that each input sequence will consist of *any* number of characters, where *each* character is represented by a vector of length `in_vocab_size`. This will be more clear after you read about one-hot encoding later.

3. You pass the input layer through a `Masking` layer. This layer tells the network to ignore any timesteps in the sequence that are filled with zeros. It's common to train on **batches** of samples rather than one sample at a time, mainly to take advantage of the parallelism of the GPU. Batches are stored as tensors, and tensors have specific dimensions. But your model can handle variable length sequences, right? So how do you store variable length sequences in a fixed dimension tensor? You'll see the details later, but you'll end up padding the end of shorter sequences with zeros — essentially meaningless timesteps added to make all the sequences in a batch the same size. The `Masking` layer tells Keras not to train on those padding timesteps. This layer isn't absolutely necessary, but see the upcoming **Note** explaining a bit more about the choice to use a `Masking` layer here.

4. You create an LSTM layer to process the input sequence, passing `latent_dim` to define the size of its output. Setting `return_state` to `True` makes the LSTM layer output its hidden and cell states along with its regular output; you'll use these as the initial state for the decoder. Refer back to the discussion of the seq2seq model if you don't recall the role of the encoder's output states. You also use the `recurrent_dropout` parameter to add some dropout between timesteps in the LSTM. This can help your model generalize better to unseen data later. There are *many* parameters available to the LSTM initializer, so you should explore the Keras documentation as you dig deeper into the subject.

5. Here, you actually connect the masking layer as the input to the LSTM. Keras's functional API allows you to create the function `encoder_lstm` as an object in the previous line and then call it here with `encoder_mask` as its input. It will return three values: The first is the actual output from the LSTM layer, but you don't actually need that for a seq2seq model so you ignore it by assigning it to an underscore. The others are the LSTM's hidden and cell states, which you store in `encoder_h` and `encoder_c`, respectively. These two outputs will each hold vectors of length `latent_dim` containing whatever information the encoder extracts from its input. (Go back over the model description in the sequence classification chapter if you need a reminder about LSTMs and their hidden and cell states.)

If you look around online, you'll likely come across examples of networks that do not use `Masking` layers but still pad sequences to store them in batches. These still work, but there's a subtle issue with them: These networks consider the padding tokens to be just as important as the real tokens. This causes three problems.

First, they *appear* to have lower loss values when training, but that's only because such a large percentage of the tokens they test against are the same padding token and it learns to output a lot of them. The second, more important issue, is that it dilutes the information stored by the encoder because the weights are modified by essentially meaningless tokens. This reduces the power of your encoder. If that isn't clear now, don't worry, it will be by the end of the chapter. Finally, for these networks to produce their expected results, they require the same padding at inference time. For example, if you trained a model to translate "Hola." as part of a batch with 10-character-long sequences, you'd have five padding tokens. Your model would likely then only produce the correct result during inference if you tried to translate it with those same five padding tokens, because the same letters *without* the padding tokens would get encoded differently and likely translate to something else.

> **Note**: One drawback of using `Masking` layers is that, although Core ML 3.0 *does* support them (meaning they are available for iOS 13), the latest version of Apple's Core ML conversion tool (release 3.3) does *not* support them when converting from all Keras models. It won't be a problem for this project — you'll see why later — but it means you won't be able to perform batched translations in iOS because it's unlikely that you can create a batch of sequences of equal length without padding.

Building the decoder

Your decoder definition will look quite similar to that of your encoder, with a few minor but important differences. Run a cell with the following code now:

```python
# 1
decoder_in = Input(
    shape=(None, out_vocab_size), name="decoder_in")
decoder_mask = Masking(name="decoder_mask")(decoder_in)
# 2
decoder_lstm = LSTM(
    latent_dim, return_sequences=True, return_state=True,
    dropout=0.2, recurrent_dropout=0.3, name="decoder_lstm")
# 3
decoder_lstm_out, _, _ = decoder_lstm(
    decoder_mask, initial_state=[encoder_h, encoder_c])
# 4
decoder_dense = Dense(
    out_vocab_size, activation="softmax", name="decoder_out")
decoder_out = decoder_dense(decoder_lstm_out)
```

Here are the differences from what you wrote for the encoder:

1. The decoder starts with an `Input` layer passed through a `Masking` layer, just like the encoder did. The only difference is that it's sized for the output vocabulary.

2. It uses an LSTM layer just like the encoder, but it adds an additional `dropout` parameter. Unlike recurrent dropout, which works only on values passed between timesteps, this dropout value affects the original input passed in from the encoder. It's just an additional bit of regularization that might improve your model's ability to generalize to unseen data.

3. You connect the masking layer as the input to the LSTM, and set the LSTM's initial state to the output states from the *encoder's* LSTM. The decoder won't need to access its hidden or cell states while training — it already has access to them internally – so you ingore them by assigning them to underscore variables. You grab the rest of the outputs in decoder_lstm_out.

4. You pass the output from the LSTM into the decoder's final, fully connected layer. It has a node for each token in the output vocabulary and uses a softmax activation to produce a probability distribution over them. You'll use this to predict the next character in the output sequence.

Connecting the encoder and decoder

With the encoder and decoder defined, run the following code to combine them into a seq2seq model:

```
# 1
seq2seq_model = Model([encoder_in, decoder_in], decoder_out)
# 2
seq2seq_model.compile(
    optimizer="rmsprop", loss="categorical_crossentropy")
```

Here's how you combine the encoder and decoder to prepare them for training:

1. You construct a Keras Model with the input layers for both the encoder and decoder, as well as the decoder's output layer. Since you have more than one input layer, you combine them in a list.

2. The RMSProp optimizer uses an adaptive, per-parameter learning rate. We won't go into details about it here; it's enough to know that it's a good choice for training recurrent neural networks. And as you've seen with the various other classification models you've created throughout this book, categorical cross entropy is a good loss function when your outputs represent probability distributions across classes; in this case, the classes are the tokens in the output vocabulary.

Run the following line to display a summary of how the layers in your model connect:

```
seq2seq_model.summary()
```

Here's what you'll see:

```
Layer (type)                 Output Shape          Param #      Connected to
=================================================================================
encoder_in (InputLayer)      (None, None, 101)     0

decoder_in (InputLayer)      (None, None, 87)      0

encoder_mask (Masking)       (None, None, 101)     0            encoder_in[0][0]

decoder_mask (Masking)       (None, None, 87)      0            decoder_in[0][0]

encoder_lstm (LSTM)          [(None, 256), (None,  366592       encoder_mask[0][0]

decoder_lstm (LSTM)          [(None, None, 256),   352256       decoder_mask[0][0]
                                                                encoder_lstm[0][1]
                                                                encoder_lstm[0][2]

decoder_out (Dense)          (None, None, 87)      22359        decoder_lstm[0][0]
=================================================================================
Total params: 741,207
Trainable params: 741,207
Non-trainable params: 0
```

Keras seq2seq model for training

This is one reason it's a good idea to name your layers: It makes it easier to read summaries like this one. You can see which layers are connected and how data flows through the network —encoder_in connects to encoder_mask which connects to encoder_lstm, and decoder_in connects to decoder_mask, which connects to decoder_in, along with the second two outputs from encoder_lstm. Then decoder_lstm's output connects to decoder_out, which produces the model's output.

The summary's a bit misleading because it doesn't display the details of all the outputs for the LSTMs. Notice the Output Shape column for encoder_lstm shows the tuple (None, 256) with an opening bracket "[" before it and a comma "," after it, followed by the start of a second tuple showing (None,. You can see a similarly incomplete tuple for decoder_lstm. These were meant to show *lists* of outputs, but there's a glitch with the output displayed for the summary function.

Train your model

So far, you've defined your model's architecture in Keras and loaded a dataset. But before you can train with that data, you need to do a bit more preparation.

Numericalization

OK, full disclosure: Neural networks can't process text. It might seem like a bad time to bring this up, well into a chapter about natural language processing with neural networks, but there it is. Remember from what you learned elsewhere in this book: Neural networks are really just a bunch of math, and that means they only work with numbers. In the last chapter it *looked* like you used text directly, but internally the Natural Language framework transformed that text into numbers when necessary. This process is sometimes called **numericalization**. Now you'll learn one way to perform such conversions yourself.

Run the following code in your notebook in order to create dictionaries that map text to or from integers:

```
# 1
in_token2int = {token : i
                for i, token in enumerate(sorted(in_vocab))}
# 2
out_token2int = {token : i
                 for i, token in enumerate(sorted(out_vocab))}
out_int2token = {i : token
                 for token, i in out_token2int.items()}
```

Here's how you created your conversion maps:

1. This dictionary comprehension — like list comprehensions, but they create `dict` objects — maps each character in `in_vocab` to a unique integer. Sorting the vocabulary before assigning the integer values makes the values easier for you to reason about — "A" comes before "B", etc. — but it isn't actually necessary for the mapping to work.

2. Here, you create *two* dictionaries, one that maps each character in `out_vocab` to a unique integer, and one that maps back from integers to characters. You only needed one mapping for the Spanish characters because the model only translates *from* Spanish, not *to* it. But remember, you defined the model to use teacher forcing, which requires you to feed the target English phrases into the decoder along with the output from the encoder. That means you need to convert English characters to and from integers.

Now you've got Python dictionaries you can use to easily convert Spanish characters into integers, as well as convert English characters both to and from integers. For example, calling `out_token2int['A']` returns the value 25, and calling `out_int2token[25]` gets you back `'A'`.

You've got a way to turn text into numbers — so far, so good. But here's some *more* full disclosure: You won't want to use those numbers for machine learning, either.

One-hot encoding

While neural networks require numeric input, they don't want just *any* numbers. In this case, the numbers are stand-ins for text. But if you use these values as is, it will confuse the network because it appears as though some ordinal relationship exists that doesn't. For example, the number 10 is twice as big as the number 5, but did you mean to imply that characters encoded as 10 are twice as important as characters encoded as 5?

No, you didn't, but there's no way for a machine learning algorithm to know that. Larger values for a given feature affect the model's calculations more than smaller ones. The essential problem is that you want the numerical value to *indicate* a particular token, not to *measure* the magnitude of a token. At worst this will ruin your model, but at best it will slow down the training process as the model attempts to undo those implied relationships.

There are a couple ways to resolve this encoding problem. You'll see a different option in the next chapter, but here you'll convert each token's integer value into what's called a **one-hot encoding**.

One-hot encoding a feature involves replacing each value with a vector the same length as the number of all possible values. These vectors are filled with zeros in all but one position, which contains a one. Imagine you wanted to use just the days Monday through Friday as possible inputs to a model.

The following image shows what it looks like to one-hot encode those values:

Monday	1	0	0	0	0
Tuesday	0	1	0	0	0
Wednesday	0	0	1	0	0
Thursday	0	0	0	1	0
Friday	0	0	0	0	1

One-hot encoded values

As you can see, each vector is has a length of five — the same length as the number of possible values. And each of these vectors is filled with zeros except for a single one in a unique location. This essentially turns one feature — the day of the week — into five mutually exclusive features representing boolean flags indicating their absence or presence.

For your seq2seq model, there are `in_vocab_size` possible input values, and `out_vocab_size` possible output values. Rather than pass a sequence of integers to the model, you'll pass a matrix wherein each row represents a single character, one-hot encoded as a vector the same size as the corresponding vocabulary.

Batching and padding

To keep things in more manageable chunks, you'll split the logic to one-hot encode training batches into two functions. The first will create appropriately sized NumPy arrays filled with zeros, and the second will place ones into those arrays at the correct locations to encode the sequences.

Run the following code to import NumPy and define the first of those two functions:

```python
import numpy as np

def make_batch_storage(batch_size, in_seq_len, out_seq_len):
    enc_in_seqs = np.zeros(
        (batch_size, in_seq_len, in_vocab_size),
        dtype=np.float32)
    dec_in_seqs = np.zeros(
        (batch_size, out_seq_len, out_vocab_size),
        dtype=np.float32)
    dec_out_seqs = np.zeros(
        (batch_size, out_seq_len, out_vocab_size),
        dtype=np.float32)

    return enc_in_seqs, dec_in_seqs, dec_out_seqs
```

You declare `make_batch_storage` to take three parameters, which — along with the vocabulary sizes — define the dimensions of the storage tensors it creates. It returns three NumPy arrays, sized to hold `batch_size` sequences that are each in/out_seq_len characters long, with each character being in/out_vocab_size wide. Specifying `dtype=np.float32` keeps NumPy from defaulting to 64-bit floats.

The `in_seq_len` and `out_seq_len` parameters to `make_batch_storage` deserve more explanation. Consider this: If you create a batch with random samples from your training set, are all their sentences guaranteed to have the same length?

The answer is no, but consider trying to store the following input sequences together in a batch:

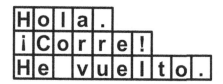

Mixed-length sequences without padding

Each sequence has a different length, but tensors need fixed dimensions. That means each item in a batch needs to fill the same amount of space in the tensor, regardless of how many tokens are in the actual sequences. To accomplish this, you'll use special **padding tokens** at the end of each input sequence shorter than in_seq_len, and at the end of each output sequence shorter than out_seq_len. So those same examples would look more like this in a batch:

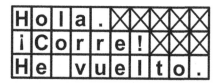

Mixed-length sequences with padding

This image shows padding as crossed-out boxes, but you could use anything that isn't already in the vocabulary. These padding tokens are the ones that the masking layer will instruct the network not to weight too excessively while learning. For this project, you'll pad sequences with zero-filled vectors. Since make_batch_storage returns a batch filled with zeros, that means it's basically pre-padded and there's no need to add new padding-specific tokens to the vocabularies.

However, while the figure shows a batch as a two-dimensional array (a matrix) to clarifying padding, recall that because of one-hot encoding every batch will in fact be a three-dimensional array. One dimension's length is batch_size since its index specifies the batch. Another dimension's length is the maximum sequence length, since its index specifies position in a sequence. And the third dimension's length is the size of the vocabulary (the set of possible characters), since this is the one-hot encoding vector and its index specifies which character is represented. So every batch is a three-dimensional array, a cube of ones and zeroes.

Now, run the following code to define the second of the two functions for one-hot encoding — the one that actually encodes the batch:

```python
def encode_batch(samples):
  # 1
  batch_size = len(samples)
  max_in_length = max([len(seq) for seq, _ in samples])
  max_out_length = max([len(seq) for _, seq in samples])

  enc_in_seqs, dec_in_seqs, dec_out_seqs = \
    make_batch_storage(
      batch_size, max_in_length, max_out_length)
  # 2
  for i, (in_seq, out_seq) in enumerate(samples):
    for time_step, token in enumerate(in_seq):
      enc_in_seqs[i, time_step, in_token2int[token]] = 1

    for time_step, token in enumerate(out_seq):
      dec_in_seqs[i, time_step, out_token2int[token]] = 1
    # 3
    for time_step, token in enumerate(out_seq[1:]):
      dec_out_seqs[i, time_step, out_token2int[token]] = 1

  return enc_in_seqs, dec_in_seqs, dec_out_seqs
```

Here's how this function one-hot encodes a list of samples as a training batch:

1. You find the batch size and the lengths of the longest input and output sequences in the batch, then use those values to create empty tensors to store the batch data.

2. You loop over the samples and one-hot encode each of their sequences into enc_in_seqs, dec_in_seqs and dec_out_seqs as appropriate. That is, for each token in a sequence, you place a 1 in its corresponding location within a vector of zeros.

3. Notice how when you populate dec_out_seqs, you use out_seq[1:] to skip the START token in the sequence. That's because this tensor contains the outputs your model learns to **predict**. It will never predict the START token because it's always *given* that as its first input, and it learns to predict the *next* token.

The only thing left to do is one-hot encode your datasets, then you're ready to train. You *could* encode them all at once and then let Keras randomly sample batches — that works and it's how many people do it. However, if you ensure batches contain only sequences of similar lengths, you can minimize the amount of padding necessary.

Why does that matter? The Masking layers you added to seq2seq_model ensure the padding doesn't affect your training results, but it still takes time to process those steps in the sequences. With this model and dataset, minimizing padding makes training go nearly *twice* as fast.

The chapter resources include a file called **seq2seq_util.py** in the **notebooks** folder. It defines a class called Seq2SeqBatchGenerator that you'll use to generate properly randomized batches while minimizing necessary padding. We won't go over the details of its code here; read through the code and comments in the file if you're interested. Run the following code in a new cell to import the Seq2SeqBatchGenerator class and create instances of it for your training and validation datasets:

```
from seq2seq_util import Seq2SeqBatchGenerator

batch_size = 64
train_generator = Seq2SeqBatchGenerator(
  train_samples, batch_size, encode_batch)
valid_generator = Seq2SeqBatchGenerator(
  valid_samples, batch_size, encode_batch)
```

You'll use these objects while training your model to create batches with the given batch size. Seq2SeqBatchGenerator needs a way to one-hot encode each batch of samples, so you pass it the encode_batch function.

Training with early stopping

Warning: Running the following cell will take considerable time. Expect it to run for multiple hours even with a GPU. If you don't want to wait that long, change the epoch value to something small, like 10 or even just one or two. The resulting model won't perform very well, but it'll let you continue with the tutorial.

Now, run a cell with the following code to train your model:

```
# 1
from keras.callbacks import EarlyStopping
early_stopping = EarlyStopping(
  monitor="val_loss", patience=5, restore_best_weights=True)
# 2
seq2seq_model.fit_generator(
  train_generator, validation_data=valid_generator,
  epochs=500, callbacks=[early_stopping])
```

There are many parameters available to control training models. Here's how you trained this one:

1. Keras lets you add callbacks to monitor and modify the training process between epochs. You create an `EarlyStopping` callback that will stop training if the validation loss stops improving. The `patience` parameter tells it to keep training for that number of epochs even if the loss isn't improving, and `restore_best_weights` tells it to use the model weights from the epoch with the best value rather than the last epoch.

2. You call `fit_generator` on the `seq2seq_model` object you created earlier, passing it the two `Seq2SeqBatchGenerator` objects you just made. This function trains the model, using those objects to create batches for training and validation. You told it to train for 500 epochs, but the `early_stopping` callback should stop it long before it reaches that number.

The model provided with the chapter had its best validation loss of `0.5905` at epoch 179. If you try training your own model, you'll get different results, but probably not *too* different. The specific values aren't really important, here, just that you understand the architecture so you can apply it to your own problems in the future.

Now that you have a trained model, continue on to the next section to learn how to perform inference with seq2seq models, which requires some changes from what you did for training.

Inference with sequence-to-sequence models

The model you've trained so far isn't actually useful for inference — at least, not in its current form. Why is that? Because the decoder portion of the model requires the correctly translated text as one of its inputs! What good is a translation model that needs *you* to do the translations?

But don't worry: You won't have to throw out all your hard work. The model has learned something useful, you just have to access it a different way.

Assembling an inference model

First, separate the encoder and decoder into two models. Keras makes this easy. You declare a new Model and pass it the input and output layers you want to use, like this:

```
inf_encoder = Model(encoder_in, [encoder_h, encoder_c])
```

Running a cell with the above code creates a new encoder model called inf_encoder, short for "inference encoder". It uses the same input layer and encoder state output layers that you created earlier: encoder_in, encoder_h and encoder_c. Keras maintains a graph of layer connections, so it automatically adds to this Model any existing layers necessary to connect these inputs and outputs. This means you're actually using the same LSTM and Masking layers that you trained as part of seq2seq_model, too. In essense, inf_encoder accesses *only* the encoder portion of your original trained model.

You can run the summary function to see what Keras actually built:

```
inf_encoder.summary()
```

Which produces the following output:

```
Layer (type)                  Output Shape            Param #
=================================================================
encoder_in (InputLayer)       (None, None, 101)       0
_____
encoder_mask (Masking)        (None, None, 101)       0
_____
encoder_lstm (LSTM)           [(None, 256), (None, 256) 366592
=================================================================
Total params: 366,592
Trainable params: 366,592
Non-trainable params: 0
```

Keras encoder model for inference

It shows encoder_in feeds into encoder_mask, which feeds into encoder_lstm, and the final layer outputs two length 256 vectors. These are all layers you created earlier to train seq2seq_model, just repurposed in a new Model object.

You've isolated the encoder, so now do the same for the decoder. Run the following code:

```
# 1
inf_dec_h_in = Input(shape=(latent_dim,), name="decoder_h_in")
inf_dec_c_in = Input(shape=(latent_dim,), name="decoder_c_in")
# 2
inf_dec_lstm_out, inf_dec_h_out, inf_dec_c_out = decoder_lstm(
    decoder_in, initial_state=[inf_dec_h_in, inf_dec_c_in])
# 3
inf_dec_out = decoder_dense(inf_dec_lstm_out)
# 4
inf_decoder = Model(
    [decoder_in, inf_dec_h_in, inf_dec_c_in],
    [inf_dec_out, inf_dec_h_out, inf_dec_c_out])
```

This looks a lot more complicated than what you did for the encoder, but it's really only a *little* more complicated. Let's go through it step by step:

1. You create two new Input layers with the same shapes as the encoder's two outputs — inf_dec_h_in and inf_dec_c_in. (The names are getting longer so we're abbreviating more heavily now.) Remember how in the full seq2seq model, the decoder's initial state came directly from the encoder. For this new model, you'll provide the initial state programmatically, and you'll use these inputs to do it.

2. Here, you connect the new inputs as the initial state for your trained LSTM layer, along with the original decoder_in that lets you give the decoder a one-hot encoded sequence. You passed entire sequences to decoder_in while training seq2seq_model, but during inference you'll only give it the most recently predicted character for each new prediction. You also grab the LSTM's state outputs as inf_dec_h_out and inf_dec_c_out, rather than discard them like you did in seq2seq_model. You'll pass these outputs from one prediction as inputs for the next one.

3. This line connects the new output from the LSTM layer to the dense layer you trained earlier, giving you a new output layer for the decoder model.

4. Finally, you build the new decoder Model. Notice it includes outputs from different layers in the network — the dense layer's character probabilities and the LSTM's output states. There's nothing about neural networks that says the outputs can only come from the last layer!

Once again, the `summary` function shows you how Keras connected the model's layers:

```
inf_decoder.summary()
```

Which outputs this:

```
Layer (type)                 Output Shape          Param #    Connected to
================================================================================
decoder_in (InputLayer)      (None, None, 87)      0

_____
decoder_h_in (InputLayer)    (None, 256)           0

_____
decoder_c_in (InputLayer)    (None, 256)           0

_____
decoder_lstm (LSTM)          [(None, None, 256),   352256     decoder_in[0][0]
                                                              decoder_h_in[0][0]
                                                              decoder_c_in[0][0]

_____
decoder_out (Dense)          (None, None, 87)      22359      decoder_lstm[1][0]
================================================================================
Total params: 374,615
Trainable params: 374,615
Non-trainable params: 0
```

Keras decoder model for inference

As you can see, `decoder_in`, `decoder_h_in` and `decoder_c_in` all flow into `decoder_lstm`, which in turn leads to `decoder_out`. Once again, the summary doesn't display all the values in the Output Shape column, but you get the idea.

You're going to write a function that translates sequences using the separate encoder and decoder models you just created. But before you do, run the following code to define a few useful constants:

```
max_out_seq_len = max(len(seq) for _, seq in samples)
start_token_idx = out_token2int[start_token]
stop_token_idx = out_token2int[stop_token]
```

The values for these three constants are all specific to this project, but you'll need to think about them in your own projects as well. Here's what they're for:

- `max_out_seq_len`: This value defines the maximum length of a translation. Ideally, your decoder will predict a STOP token at some point, but this specifies how long you're willing to wait for one before giving up. You could choose any value here — the model has no limit to the length of sequence it can process — but this line uses the length of the longest English sentence in the training set. Why? Because you know the model never got any practice creating sequences longer than this, so it seems like as good a place as any to call it quits.

- start_token_idx: This is the integer encoding of the START token. You'll need to know this to signal the decoder to start translating a new sequence.

- stop_token_idx: This is the integer encoding of the STOP token. You'll need to know this because it's how the decoder signals to you that it's done translating a sequence.

Running inference

With those constants defined, you're ready to actually use your models to translate text. Define the following function in your notebook. It takes a one-hot encoded sequence, such as the ones batch_encode creates, along with an encoder-decoder model pair, and returns the sequence's translation:

```
def translate_sequence(one_hot_seq, encoder, decoder):
  # 1
  encoding = encoder.predict(one_hot_seq)
  # 2
  decoder_in = np.zeros(
    (1, 1, out_vocab_size), dtype=np.float32)
  # 3
  translated_text = ""
  done_decoding = False
  decoded_idx = start_token_idx
  while not done_decoding:
    # 4
    decoder_in[0, 0, decoded_idx] = 1
    # 5
    decoding, h, c = decoder.predict([decoder_in] + encoding)
    # 6
    encoding = [h, c]
    # 7
    decoder_in[0, 0, decoded_idx] = 0
    # 8
    decoded_idx = np.argmax(decoding[0, -1, :])
    # 9
    if decoded_idx == stop_token_idx:
      done_decoding = True
    else:
      translated_text += out_int2token[decoded_idx]
    # 10
    if len(translated_text) >= max_out_seq_len:
      done_decoding = True

  return translated_text
```

This logic drives the translation process, so let's go over it carefully:

1. The function receives a NumPy array containing a one-hot encoded sequence — one_hot_seq — and passes it to encoder's predict function to process it. The encoder model passed to this function should output its LSTM's h and c states as a list, which you save as encoding.

2. Next, you create a NumPy array to store a one-hot encoded character you'll give the decoder. Remember from the diagrams earlier in the chapter, you'll call the decoder repeatedly with the most recently predicted character as input.

3. These variables keep track of the translation so far and control the decoding loop. You'll set decoded_idx to the one-hot encoding index of the decoder's most recently predicted character. However, you **initialize** it to the START token's index, because you trained the decoder to start decoding sequences using the encoder's output and START as the initial token.

4. The loop starts by one-hot encoding the current character, indicated by decoded_idx. **Important**: This *must* initially equal the index of the START token.

5. It calls predict on the decoder, passing in the most recently predicted character and the most recent cell state. Remember, the first time through this loop, decoder_in contains the START token and encoding contains the outputs from the encoder.

6. Next, you save the decoder's output h and c states as encoding. You'll pass these back to the decoder as inputs to predict when predicting the next character.

7. Finally, you clear out the one-hot encoded index, so now decoder_in contains all zeros once again.

8. The decoder doesn't return a character. Instead, it returns a **probability distribution** over all *possible* characters. So which one do you choose? Here you take a greedy approach and always choose the character predicted with the highest probability. This isn't necessarily the best approach, which you'll read about later.

9. Given the index of the predicted character, you check to see if it's the STOP token. If so, the translation is complete and you stop the loop. Otherwise, you convert the index to text and add it to the translation.

10. The final check ensures the loop doesn't go on forever by stopping it if the translation length reaches its limit.

Now you're ready to see what your model can do. The **notebook** folder's **seq2seq_util.py** includes a function that loops over a list of sample tuples and displays the predictions along with the correct translations for comparison. It takes as arguments the encoder and decoder models, along with a function to one-hot encode sequences and a decoding function like the one you just wrote.

To see how your model performs, use code like the following, which displays your model's output for the first 100 samples in the validation set:

```
from seq2seq_util import test_predictions

test_predictions(valid_samples[:100],
                 inf_encoder, inf_decoder,
                 encode_batch, translate_sequence)
```

Let's look at some of the results *we* got on the validation set when training the model included with the chapter resources. Yours will likely be different but should be in the same quality range, provided you trained for roughly the same number of epochs.

First, there are several like the following which produced the expected results perfectly. Who needs Google Translate, amirite?

| Yo jugaré contigo. | I'll play with you. | I'll play with you. |
| ¿Quieres ir primero? | Do you want to go first? | Do you want to go first? |

Great results on validation samples: Source, Target, Model Output

Then there are several like the following, which seem like reasonable translations even if they aren't exactly what the human translators wrote:

| Nadie me dijo nada. | No one said anything to me. | No one told me anything. |
| Hagamos lo que dijo Tom. | Let's do what Tom said. | Let's do what Tom wanted. |

Good results on validation samples: Source, Target, Model Output

Sadly, there are quite a few where our model basically spit out nonsense, like these:

| ¡Mira! Hay un avión despegando. | Look! There's a plane taking off. | Look at a picture of Sunday, Tom. |
| Até a mi perro a un árbol del jardín. | I tied my dog to a tree in the garden. | I attend my author on the train to the bank. |

Bad results on validation samples: Source, Target, Model Output

And, finally, there are some translations like these, that start off looking great and then take horrible turns:

¿Alguna vez has comido insectos?	Have you ever eaten insects?	Have you ever eaten some children?
Tom se rió de todos los chistes de Mary.	Tom laughed at all of Mary's jokes.	Tom laughed at Mary's eyes every morning.

Almost-right-but-horribly-wrong results on validation samples: Source, Target, Model Output

Considering eating children? Laughing at poor Mary's eyes day in and day out? We've created an AI monster!

In all seriousness, it's pretty amazing that with so little effort you've created a piece of software that learned to look at Spanish text — one character at a time — and generate English — again, *one character at a time* — that consists of properly spelled words, mostly arranged in grammatically correct sentences complete with proper punctuation!

And the fact that it generates text that also sometimes translates between languages *correctly*? That's a bit mind blowing.

Let's save the discussion about model quality until the end of the chapter. For now, go on to the next section to learn how to convert your seq2seq model for use in iOS.

Converting your model to Core ML

So far, you've used teacher forcing to train a Keras seq2seq model to translate Spanish text to English, then you used those trained layers to create separate encoder and decoder models that work without you needing to provide them with the correct translation. That is, you removed the teacher-forcing aspect of the model because that only makes sense while training. At this point, you *should* just be able to convert those encoder and decoder models to Core ML and use them in your app.

But is it ever that easy?

Currently, there are issues with Core ML and/or `coremltools` (the Python package that converts models into Core ML format), preventing you from exporting the models you've made. Don't worry — this section shows you how to work around each of them and convert your models to Core ML.

Start with the encoder: Run the following code to do a bunch of stuff you shouldn't have to do, which is all explained after the code block:

```
# 1
coreml_enc_in = Input(
   shape=(None, in_vocab_size), name="encoder_in")
coreml_enc_lstm = LSTM(
   latent_dim, return_state=True, name="encoder_lstm")
coreml_enc_out, _, _ = coreml_enc_lstm(coreml_enc_in)
coreml_encoder_model = Model(coreml_enc_in, coreml_enc_out)
# 2
coreml_encoder_model.output_layers = \
   coreml_encoder_model._output_layers
# 3
inf_encoder.save_weights("Es2EnCharEncoderWeights.h5")
coreml_encoder_model.load_weights("Es2EnCharEncoderWeights.h5")
```

Everything you just wrote is to work around a conversion problem you'd otherwise have if you didn't do these things. Here's what's going on:

1. This bit creates a new, untrained encoder model, completely separate from the one you trained. This is necessary to work around *two* issues you would encounter without it. First, Core ML does not currently support Masking layers, so you need to create a new connection from the Input layer directly to the LSTM to remove the Masking layer from the network. The second issue is a bug that causes the converter to crash when exporting models that contain shared layers. That is, layers used by more than one model. Currently, you're sharing several layers between your seq2seq model and the encoder and decoder models you made for inference. By creating new Input and LSTM layers, this encoder now contains no shared layers.

2. This line is a bit ridiculous, but when using the versions of Keras and coremltools that we used for this book, the Core ML converter looks for the layers using the name output_layers instead of its actual name, _output_layers. This super-hacky line just adds a new property on the model, using the name the converter expects. Hopefully, this bug will get fixed soon and this will no longer be necessary.

3. Finally, you extract the weights from your original, trained encoder and apply them to the new, untrained one. The load_weights function attempts to match weights by layer names, like "encoder_lstm", but if the layers don't have identical names then it will try its best to match them based on the architecture. In the end, your new coreml_encoder_model is separate from the models you trained earlier, but contains the same trained weights so it will produce the same results for a given input.

The `coremltools` Python package provides converters and other utilities to help get models from various machine learning frameworks into Core ML's format. Run the following code to use the Keras converter to export your encoder model:

```
import coremltools

coreml_encoder = coremltools.converters.keras.convert(
  coreml_encoder_model,
  input_names="encodedSeq", output_names="ignored")
coreml_encoder.save("Es2EnCharEncoder.mlmodel")
```

After importing the `coremltools` package, you use the Keras converter to create a Core ML definition of your model and save it to disk. Notice the `input_names` and `output_names` parameters: These are used by Xcode to name the inputs and outputs in the classes it generates, so it's a good idea to put something descriptive here. You named them "encodedSeq" and "ignored", respectively, to indicate the input is a one-hot encoded sequence and the output is unused by the app.

> **Note**: You do *not* mention the LSTM's h and c states that you intend to pass from your encoder to your decoder — the converter adds those automatically and currently doesn't let you change their names. You'll see the final set of names later in Xcode.

With your encoder exported, it's time to turn to the decoder. Run the following code to perform the same workarounds to prepare your decoder for export to Core ML:

```
coreml_dec_in = Input(shape=(None, out_vocab_size))
coreml_dec_lstm = LSTM(
  latent_dim, return_sequences=True, return_state=True,
  name="decoder_lstm")
coreml_dec_lstm_out, _, _ = coreml_dec_lstm(coreml_dec_in)
coreml_dec_dense = Dense(out_vocab_size, activation="softmax")
coreml_dec_out = coreml_dec_dense(coreml_dec_lstm_out)
coreml_decoder_model = Model(coreml_dec_in, coreml_dec_out)

coreml_decoder_model.output_layers = \
  coreml_decoder_model._output_layers

inf_decoder.save_weights("Es2EnCharDecoderWeights.h5")
coreml_decoder_model.load_weights("Es2EnCharDecoderWeights.h5")
```

This code does for the decoder all the same things you did for the encoder. It makes a new model that mirrors the one you trained but without any `Masking` or shared layers, performs the `output_layers` hack, and copies the weights from the trained decoder onto the new one.

Then export the decoder like you did for the encoder:

```
coreml_decoder = coremltools.converters.keras.convert(
    coreml_decoder_model,
    input_names="encodedChar", output_names="nextCharProbs")
coreml_decoder.save("Es2EnCharDecoder.mlmodel")
```

Here, you convert the decoder model to Core ML and save it to disk, the same way you did for the encoder. The descriptive names for the input and output will make your iOS code more readable later; they remind you that the model takes as input a single one-hot encoded character, and outputs a probability distribution for a single character.

Quantization

The models you've saved are fine for use in an iOS app, but there's one more simple step you should always consider. With apps, download size matters. Your model stores its weights and biases as 32-bit floats. But you could use 16-bit floats instead. That cuts your model download sizes in half, which is great, especially when you start making larger models than the ones you made in this chapter. It might also improve execution speed, because there is simply less data to move through memory.

This process of reducing the floating point accuracy of parts of a model in order to improve its size and performance is called **quantizing** a model, and the result is called a quantized model. You might expect that simply throwing away half your numerical precision would ruin the accuracy of the model. But this generally turns out not to be the case. Some have even experimented with quantizing models to 8- or 4-bit floats. The limits of such quantization are still an active research topic. For now, let us stick to 16 bits.

In order to quantize your model, run a cell with the following code to define a function you can use to convert existing Core ML models from 32 to 16-bit floating point weights:

```
def convert_to_fp16(mlmodel_filename):
  basename = mlmodel_filename[:-len(".mlmodel")]
  spec = coremltools.utils.load_spec(mlmodel_filename)

  spec_16bit = coremltools.utils.\
    convert_neural_network_spec_weights_to_fp16(spec)

  coremltools.utils.save_spec(
    spec_16bit, f"{basename}16Bit.mlmodel")
```

This takes advantage of functions from `coremltools` to load an existing Core ML model, convert its weights into 16-bit floats, and then save a new version back to disk. It derives a new filename so it won't overwrite the original model.

Now, call that function for each of your models to create 16-bit versions:

```
convert_to_fp16("Es2EnCharEncoder.mlmodel")
convert_to_fp16("Es2EnCharDecoder.mlmodel")
```

The conversion tools will tell you that it is quantizing the layers. If everything worked, you should now have four model files saved in your **notebooks** folder: **Es2EnCharEncoder.mlmodel**, **Es2EnCharDecoder.mlmodel**, **Es2EnCharEncoder16Bit.mlmodel** and **Es2EnCharDecoder16Bit.mlmodel**. It's nice to keep both versions in case you want to compare their performance, but the rest of this chapter will use the models with 16-bit weights.

Numericalization dictionaries

One last thing: When you use your models in your iOS app, you'll need to do the same one-hot encoding you did here to convert input sequences from Spanish characters into the integers your encoder expects, and then convert your decoder's numerical output into English characters.

To ensure you use the correct values, run the following code to save out the numericalization dictionaries you've been using:

```
import json

with open("esCharToInt.json", "w") as f:
    json.dump(in_token2int, f)
with open("intToEnChar.json", "w") as f:
    json.dump(out_int2token, f)
```

Using Python's `json` package, you save `in_token2int` and `out_int2token` as JSON files. You'll use these files, along with the Core ML versions of your encoder and decoder models, in an iOS app in the next section.

Using your model in iOS

Most of this chapter has been about understanding and building sequence-to-sequence models for translating natural language. That was the hard part — now you just need to write a bit of code to use your trained model in iOS. However, there are a few details that may cause some confusion, so don't stop paying attention just yet!

You'll continue working on your finished project from the previous chapter, so open it now in Xcode. If you skipped that chapter, you can use the **SMDB** starter project in this chapter's resources.

Drag your trained Core ML model files — **Es2EnCharEncoder16Bit.mlmodel** and **Es2EnCharDecoder16Bit.mlmodel** — into Xcode to add them to the **SMDB** project. Or, if you'd prefer to use the larger versions, use the models with the same name minus the "16Bit". Keep in mind that if you choose not to use the 16-bit versions, you'll need to remove `16Bit` from any code instructions that include it.

> **Note**: If you didn't train your own models, you can find all the necessary files in the **pre-trained** folder of this chapter's materials.

Select **Es2EnCharEncoder16Bit.mlmodel** in the Project Navigator to view details about the encoder. You'll see the following, which should remind you a bit of the model you saw in the sequence classification chapters.

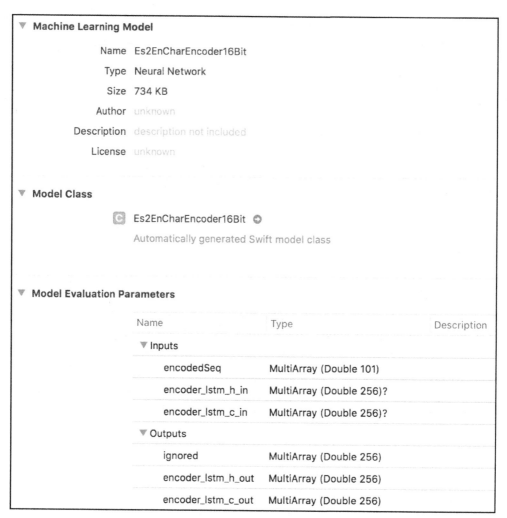

▼ **Machine Learning Model**

Name	Es2EnCharEncoder16Bit
Type	Neural Network
Size	734 KB
Author	unknown
Description	description not included
License	unknown

▼ **Model Class**

Es2EnCharEncoder16Bit ◯

Automatically generated Swift model class

▼ **Model Evaluation Parameters**

Name	Type	Description
▼ Inputs		
encodedSeq	MultiArray (Double 101)	
encoder_lstm_h_in	MultiArray (Double 256)?	
encoder_lstm_c_in	MultiArray (Double 256)?	
▼ Outputs		
ignored	MultiArray (Double 256)	
encoder_lstm_h_out	MultiArray (Double 256)	
encoder_lstm_c_out	MultiArray (Double 256)	

Looking at the encoder mlmodel file

As you can see, the summary includes the input value `encoderSeq`, and the output value `ignored`, which you specified when you exported the encoder as Core ML. But notice it also includes h and c state vectors for the LSTM; you didn't specify these but Core ML always adds them automatically for recurrent networks.

The most important thing to point out here is the misleading size shown for `encodedSeq`. According to this report, it expects an `MLMultiArray` of 101 Doubles. That's not entirely untrue; it *can* accept such an input. However, recall from the one-hot encoding section that you're storing each character in a sequence as a length 101 vector, so this makes it appear as though your model can only take a single character as input. This is *not* the case.

The encoder can take a one-dimensional array *or* a three-dimensional array. You'll use the second option to provide the entire sequence at once rather than feeding it one character at a time. You'll go over more details about this when you get to the code.

To be thorough, select **Es2EnCharDecoder16Bit.mlmodel** in the Project navigator to view the decoder model:

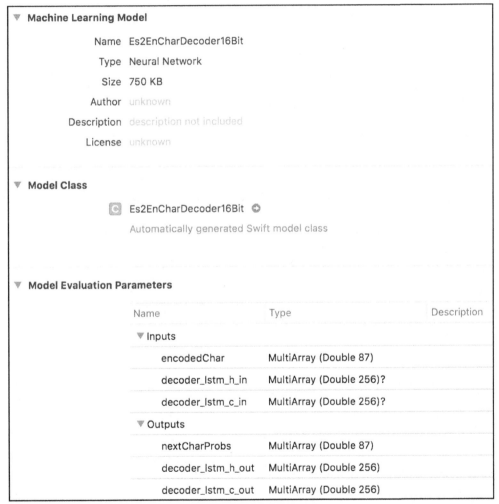

Looking at the decoder mlmodel file

This summary shouldn't hold any surprises for you. Notice again the `encodedChar` input claims to be an `MLMultiArray` with a single dimension. In this case, it's telling you the truth: You actually will provide inputs to the decoder one character at a time.

With your models in Xcode, you can finally write some code to use them. The first problem you need to solve: How to one-hot encode your inputs?

When you one-hot encode characters in iOS, you'll need to ensure each character maps to the same integer you used when you trained your model. Fortunately, you saved your conversion mappings as JSON files — **esCharToInt.json** and **intToEnChar.json**. Add those files to your Xcode project now.

> **Note**: In the following step, you'll add some globals to **NLPHelper.swift**, along with all the global functions you've been writing in this and the previous chapter. Rest assured, we aren't proposing you forget everything you've probably learned about avoiding globals. You should continue to organize and encapsulate your own code well, but we chose to structure SMDB this way so that you could see working results quickly without dealing with details of app architecture.

Add the following code to load the mapping files as Swift dictionaries to the top of **NLPHelper.swift**:

```
let esCharToInt = loadCharToIntJsonMap(from: "esCharToInt")
let intToEnChar = loadIntToCharJsonMap(from: "intToEnChar")
```

The two functions you call here are provided in **Util.swift**. They load the JSON files and convert their contents to the expected data types.

Next, add the following import to the file:

```
import CoreML
```

With the conversion maps loaded, add the following function that builds inputs for your encoder model:

```
func getEncoderInput(_ text: String) -> MLMultiArray? {
  // 1
  let cleanedText = text
    .filter { esCharToInt.keys.contains($0) }

  if cleanedText.isEmpty {
    return nil
  }

  // 2
  let vocabSize = esCharToInt.count
  let encoderIn = initMultiArray(
```

```
    shape: [NSNumber(value: cleanedText.count),
            1,
            NSNumber(value: vocabSize)])

  // 3
  for (i, c) in cleanedText.enumerated() {
    encoderIn[i * vocabSize + esCharToInt[c]!] = 1
  }

  return encoderIn
}
```

Here's how the function one-hot encodes text for use with your encoder:

1. First, you remove any OOV tokens from the text, and return `nil` if you end up removing everything.

2. Then you use `initMultiArray`, a helper function provided in **Util.swift**, to create an `MLMultiArray` filled with zeros. Notice the number of dimensions of the array. You might expect two but it's three because of a quirk of Core ML. The first dimension's length is the length of the sequence because this dimension represents the sequence itself. The second dimension always has a length of one. This dimension exists only as a side effect of Core ML's computer-vision-focused design; it doesn't affect how much space you allocate, but your app will crash without it. The third dimension's length is the input vocabulary size, since each character needs to be one-hot encoded into a vector of that length.

3. Finally, you loop over the characters in the cleaned text and set the appropriate item in the array to one. You index the multi-dimensional `MLMultiArray` as if it's a standard flat array, because that's how its memory is arranged. And remember it's filled with zeros, so you only have to worry about where to put the ones and you'll end up with properly one-hot encoded vectors.

That does it for the encoder's input. Now add another function, this time to process encoded inputs and produce the initial input for your decoder model:

```
func getDecoderInput(encoderInput: MLMultiArray) ->
  Es2EnCharDecoder16BitInput {
  // 1
  let encoder = Es2EnCharEncoder16Bit()
  let encoderOut = try! encoder.prediction(
    encodedSeq: encoderInput,
    encoder_lstm_h_in: nil,
    encoder_lstm_c_in: nil)
  // 2
  let decoderIn = initMultiArray(
    shape: [NSNumber(value: intToEnChar.count)])
```

```
// 3
return Es2EnCharDecoder16BitInput(
  encodedChar: decoderIn,
  decoder_lstm_h_in: encoderOut.encoder_lstm_h_out,
  decoder_lstm_c_in: encoderOut.encoder_lstm_c_out)
}
```

Here's how this function produces the input you'll pass to your decoder model:

1. First, you create your encoder model and pass encoderInput to its prediction function. This call returns an Es2EnCharEncoder16BitOutput object that contains the encoder's latent state after processing the input sequence.

2. You create a zero-filled MLMultiArray just large enough for a single, one-hot encoded character. Notice you use intToEnChar.count because the decoder has a different vocabulary from the encoder. You leave it as all zeros for now.

3. Finally, you create and return an Es2EnCharDecoder16BitInput object, using the empty MLMultiArray you just built as storage for the encodedChar field. You'll reuse this object for each character you pass to the decoder, but for now you set its initial state inputs to the states from encoderOut. Remember this is what you did earlier in the Jupyter notebook, passing the input text to the encoder and then using the encoder's output as the initial h and c states for the decoder.

Before writing the guts of the translation logic, add the following constants in **NLPHelper.swift**:

```
let maxOutSequenceLength = 87
let startTokenIndex = 0
let stopTokenIndex = 1
```

These are the values you found for the similarly named constants in the Jupyter notebook. A quick refresher:

- maxOutSequenceLength: Defines the maximum length of a translation. If the decoder produces this many tokens without predicting a STOP token, you'll stop translating to avoid an infinite loop.

- startTokenIndex: Int value of START token in intToEnChar. Used for one-hot encoding.

- stopTokenIndex: Int value of STOP token in intToEnChar. Used for one-hot encoding.

The starter project already includes an empty function called spanishToEnglish in **NLPHelper.swift**, and that's where you'll put together everything you've added so far to translate reviews. This logic essentially duplicates the translate_sequence function you wrote in Python earlier, but we'll go over the details again.

Start by adding the following code at the beginning of the function:

```
// 1
guard let encoderIn = getEncoderInput(text) else {
  return nil
}
// 2
let decoderIn = getDecoderInput(encoderInput: encoderIn)
// 3
let decoder = Es2EnCharDecoder16Bit()
var translatedText: [Character] = []
var doneDecoding = false
var decodedIndex = startTokenIndex
```

Here's what you've done so far:

1. First, you call getEncoderInput to one-hot encode the input text, and exit the function if that fails.

2. Using getDecoderInput and encoderIn, you create the initial input for the decoder.

3. Then you create the decoder model, along with some variables you'll use to keep track of the translation's progress. Notice you initialize decodedIndex to the index of the START token.

Now add the following code, still inside spanishToEnglish but *after* what you just added and *before* the return statement:

```
while !doneDecoding {
  // 1
  decoderIn.encodedChar[decodedIndex] = 1
  // 2
  let decoderOut = try! decoder.prediction(input: decoderIn)
  // 3
  decoderIn.decoder_lstm_h_in = decoderOut.decoder_lstm_h_out
  decoderIn.decoder_lstm_c_in = decoderOut.decoder_lstm_c_out
  // 4
  decoderIn.encodedChar[decodedIndex] = 0
}
```

You aren't done writing this `while` loop yet, so don't worry about the fact that it currently has no way to stop. Here's what it *does* do, so far:

1. The loop starts by one-hot encoding the most recently predicted character, indicated by `decodedIndex`, and storing it in `decoderIn`.

2. It calls `prediction` on the decoder model. Remember, the first time through this loop, `decoderIn` contains the output state from the encoder that was set in `getDecoderInput` and its `encodedChar` is the `START` token.

3. Next, `decoderIn`'s `h` and `c` states are set to the `h` and `c` output states from the call to `prediction`. These will serve as the initial state when the loop repeats to predict the next character in the translation.

4. Finally, you clear out the one-hot encoded index to ensure `decoderIn`'s `encodedChar` contains only zeros.

Now, add the following code, at the end — but still *inside* — of the `while` loop you were just writing:

```
// 1
decodedIndex = argmax(array: decoderOut.nextCharProbs)
// 2
if decodedIndex == stopTokenIndex {
  doneDecoding = true
} else {
  translatedText.append(intToEnChar[decodedIndex]!)
}
// 3
if translatedText.count >= maxOutSequenceLength {
  doneDecoding = true
}
```

This code extracts the predicted character, as well as stops the `while` loop when appropriate. Here are some details:

1. Here you use `argmax`, provided in **Util.swift**, to find the index of the highest value in the probability distribution returned by the decoder. Remember we mentioned earlier that this greedy approach does not necessarily produce the best results.

2. Check to see if the decoder predicted the `STOP` token. If so, stop the loop; otherwise, add the token to the translation.

3. This check stops the loop if the translation length reaches its limit. Without this, you run the risk of an infinite loop.

Finally, replace the `return nil` statement included with the starter code with the following line. It converts the list of `Character` predictions into a `String`:

```
return String(translatedText)
```

The final version of `spanishToEnglish` should look like this:

```
func spanishToEnglish(text: String) -> String? {
  guard let encoderIn = getEncoderInput(text) else {
    return nil
  }

  let decoderIn = getDecoderInput(encoderInput: encoderIn)

  let decoder = Es2EnCharDecoder16Bit()
  var translatedText: [Character] = []
  var doneDecoding = false
  var decodedIndex = startTokenIndex

  while !doneDecoding {
    decoderIn.encodedChar[decodedIndex] = 1

    let decoderOut = try! decoder.prediction(input: decoderIn)
    decoderIn.decoder_lstm_h_in = decoderOut.decoder_lstm_h_out
    decoderIn.decoder_lstm_c_in = decoderOut.decoder_lstm_c_out
    decoderIn.encodedChar[decodedIndex] = 0

    decodedIndex = argmax(array: decoderOut.nextCharProbs)
    if decodedIndex == stopTokenIndex {
      doneDecoding = true
    } else {
      translatedText.append(intToEnChar[decodedIndex]!)
    }

    if translatedText.count >= maxOutSequenceLength {
      doneDecoding = true
    }
  }

  return String(translatedText)
}
```

With that function done, there's just one final bit of code you need to write — a helper function to break reviews into sentences. Replace `getSentences` in **NLPHelper.swift** with the following:

```
func getSentences(text: String) -> [String] {
  let tokenizer = NLTokenizer(unit: .sentence)
  tokenizer.string = text
  let sentenceRanges = tokenizer.tokens(
```

```
    for: text.startIndex..<text.endIndex)
  return sentenceRanges.map { String(text[$0]) }
}
```

This uses `NLTokenizer` from the Natural Language framework, which you explored in the previous chapter. It attempts to divide the given text into sentences and returns them as a list. You're going to translate reviews one sentence at a time for two reasons: First, you only trained your model on single sentence examples, so it's unlikely it will ever produce anything other than a `STOP` token after a sentence-ending punctuation mark. And secondly, your model's performance degrades as its input sequences get longer. By giving it only one sentence at a time, your model has a better chance to produce reasonable results. More discussion on this later.

> **Note**: While it's fine for this project, and might be good enough in many other situations, translating sentences individually without maintaining any context between them is unlikely to produce state of the art results. There are many cases where information in one sentence might influence the translation of another one. Still, reduced performance in exchange for simpler models that are easier to train is a reasonable concession, here.

The project's starter code uses the `getSentences` and `spanishToEnglish` functions you just wrote to translate reviews when possible. For each review, code inside **ReviewsManager.swift** calls `translateReview`, which does the following:

1. Ensures it's a Spanish-language review, because that's all it currently knows how to handle. You could modify it to handle other languages if you train a model that supports them.

2. Calls `getSentences` to tokenize the review into sentences. This gives the model shorter text chunks to translate, which should improve the results because you only trained the model on short sentences.

3. Trims whitespace from the ends of the tokenized sentences. This is important because your model didn't train with any extra whitespace and you *will* get different translations for a sentence if it includes even a single extra space at the end.

4. Translates each sentence with `spanishToEnglish`, then stores the translation as part of the `Review`. The logic in **ReviewsTableViewController.swift** ensures table cells display the translation, along with the original text, for reviews that have one.

So how well does your model actually perform? Build and run the app, go to the **By Language** tab and choose **Spanish** from the list.

You should see something like the following results, though they likely won't be exactly the same unless you are running with the pre-trained model we provided.

SMDB app with translated reviews

Yikes! Even if you don't know Spanish, it's pretty clear these translations aren't very good. Does that mean there's no hope for this model?

Let's talk translation quality

Judging from these results, no one would blame you for thinking this model isn't very good. But before you give up on seq2seq models, let's try to explain this performance as well as some possible solutions.

First, this chapter described the most basic version of a seq2seq model — the encoder and decoder each consist of just a single LSTM layer. LSTMs don't stack as well as convolutional layers do, but you can still see improvement using more than one. In the next chapter, you'll try a slightly different encoder that should improve things a bit.

Secondly, we performed absolutely **no** hyperparameter tuning. How would it perform if the LSTMs had more units, like 512 instead of 256? What about a different optimizer or learning rate? Tuning the model's hyperparameters would almost certainly lead to at least slightly better results, even training with this same dataset.

And that brings us to the dataset. There are several reasons why this particular dataset likely won't lead to great results:

- It's *way* too small. To create a reasonable Spanish-to-English translator, you'd need a dataset with many millions — or better yet, billions — of words, which would make training far too resource intensive for this book. Why? Because the possibilities of language are infinite and each individual sample is extremely sparse. That is, each sample sentence you train with covers such a small portion of all the sentences that *could* exist, so your model learns very little from each sample. Or it learns *too much* and overfits your training data, which is just as bad. However, remember that if you have a more restricted use case — translating words you might find on common street signs, for example — then you can get away with a small dataset.

- It's biased toward certain types of phrases, so it likely won't translate just *any* sentence. For example, Tom and Mary are the only two names used — they each appear thousands of times, with Tom appearing five times more than Mary. Your model learns what letters are likely to follow other letters, so seeing just these names so many times biases it, especially when dealing with proper nouns. Notice in the image, the model's translation for the review of the Sound of MusicKit ends up mentioning Tom, and the one for Night of the Living Deadlocks mentions Mary! Those two are everywhere!

Note: To be fair, please keep in mind the dataset you used here was *not* created for machine learning. It's actually made up of flashcards meant to help people learning English as a foreign language. However, it's well formatted and easy to work with so it serves as a good starting point for exploring machine translation.

So what if you had a huge dataset, and you performed rigorous hyperparameter tuning to create the best version of this model possible? Would it be good enough to translate any Spanish text to English? Not exactly, due to some other important issues.

First, there's one major drawback to encoder-decoder models implemented the way we do here: The encoder processes the *entire* input sequence, and then outputs a *fixed size* vector meant to encode it. Why's that a problem? If you consider that longer sequences contain more information, it means as sequences get longer it gets more difficult to include all their information into that fixed-size vector. You can increase the size of this vector to improve performance to a point, but there will always be some limit to how much information you can store in any fixed-sized space. The best current solution to this problem involves something called attention. We won't implement it in this book, but we'll explain the concept in the next chapter.

The second issue with your current implementation involves the greedy algorithm for choosing each character. If you always take the next token with the highest probability, you force the results down well-trodden paths. For example, imagine an English sentence that starts with the letters "Th." If you just go by probability, the next letter is likely "e" because "The" is such a common word, but maybe this sentence starts with "Though." Hopefully, the encoder signals to the decoder something about this sentence to make it predict "o" instead of "e", but there will always be times when the correct result doesn't end up being the top prediction. The next chapter will discuss a method called beam search that can help improve this situation.

Finally, there's one more detail about this model that warrants discussion: It tokenizes text at the character level. Is that a good idea? Don't we lose all sorts of information about words when we look at them as individual letters? Yes we do, but it's a good way to introduce the topic because it simplifies some details like how we deal with OOV tokens. There are other benefits of character-level models, too, but we'll save that discussion for the next chapter, where we'll also point out the changes necessary to work on word-level tokens.

Key points

- **Encoder-decoder** pairs are powerful and versatile; they've been used for many tasks, including translation, image captioning and question answering.

- Encoders map their inputs into a latent space. Decoders map an encoder's latent space to a desired output. You train them together in an end-to-end process, passing inputs to the encoder and minimizing a loss function against the decoder's outputs.

- The **sequence-to-sequence model** architecture is an instance of the encoder-decoder architecture. It takes a sequence as input and produces one as output.

- Use padding tokens to make all sequences in one batch the same length.

- The Keras `Masking` layer ensures models ignore padding tokens. Without this layer, models will assume the padding tokens are just as significant as all the others.

- Speed up training by using batches of similarly-sized sequences to reduce padding.

- When translating languages, you'll always need *some* way to deal with OOV tokens. In this chapter, you dropped them, but the next chapter considers other options.

- You can one-hot encode nominal categorical features, like characters in text, to represent them as numbers without implying any ordinal relationships.

- Greedy algorithms for choosing the decoder's predicted token do not alway produce the best results. The next chapter briefly describes an alternative.

- Core ML and the `coremltools` Python package are actively evolving and using them sometimes requires workarounds. For example, `coremltools` currently cannot convert Keras models based on TensorFlow 1 that include shared layers or masking layers, requiring you to build new encoder and decoder models and set their weights from your trained seq2seq model.

- Reduce your app's download size by converting your model weights from 32-bit floats down to 16-bit instead.

- In model summaries, Xcode displays sequential inputs as an `MLMultiArray` big enough for *one* element in a sequence, but models can actually accept sequences of any length. To pass a *sequence* to a model, use a three-dimensional `MLMultiArray` with shape SEQUENCE_LENGTH x 1 x ITEM_SIZE. When one-hot encoding, ITEM_SIZE is the number of possible values, such as the vocabulary sizes used in this chapter.

Where to go from here?

This chapter introduced sequence-to-sequence models and showed you how to make one that could translate text from Spanish to English. Sometimes. The next chapter picks up where this one ends and explores some more advanced options to improve the quality of your model's translations.

Chapter 16: Natural Language Transformation, Part 2

By Alexis Gallagher

The previous chapter introduced **sequence-to-sequence models**, and you built one that (sort of) translated Spanish text to English. This chapter introduces other techniques that can improve performance for such tasks. It picks up where you left off, so continue using the same **nlpenv** environment and SMDB project you already made. It's inadvisable to read this chapter without first completing that one, but if you'd like a clean starter project, use the final version of SMDB found in Chapter 15's resources.

Bidirectional RNNs

Your original model predicts the next character using only the characters that appear *before* it in the sentence. But is that really how people read? Consider the following two English sentences and their Spanish translations (according to *Google Translate*):

English	Spanish
She waited by the bank of the river.	Ella esperó a la orilla del río.
She waited by the bank until he came out with the money.	Ella esperó junto al banco hasta que él salió con el dinero.

Examples where context after a word matters

The first five words are the same in the English versions of both sentences, but only the first two words end up the same in the Spanish translations. That's because the meaning of the word "bank" is different in each sentence, but you cannot know that until you've read *past* that word in the sentence. That is, its meaning comes from its context, including the words both before *and* after it.

In order to consider the full context surrounding each token, you can use what's called a **bidirectional recurrent neural network (BRNN),** which processes sequences in both directions, like this:

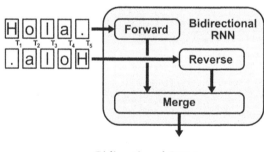

Bidirectional RNN

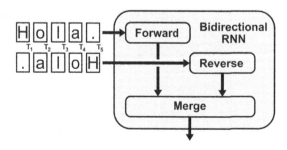

Bidirectional RNN

The forward and reverse layers themselves can be any recurrent type, such as the LSTMs you've worked with elsewhere in this book. However, in this chapter, you'll use a new type called a **gated recurrent unit**, or GRU.

GRUs were invented after LSTMs and were meant to serve the same purpose of learning longer-term relationships while training more easily than standard recurrent layers. Internally, they are implemented differently from LSTMs, but, from a user's standpoint, the main difference is that they do not have separate hidden and cell states. Instead, they only have hidden states, which makes them a bit less complicated to work with when you have to manage state directly — like you do with the decoder in a seq2seq model.

So now you'll try a new version of the model you trained in the previous chapter — one that includes a bidirectional encoder. The Python code for this section is nearly identical to what you wrote for your first seq2seq model. As such, the chapter's resources include a pre-filled Jupyter notebook for you to run at **notebooks/Bidir-Char-Seq2Seq-Starter.ipynb**. Or, you can just review the contents of **notebooks/Bidir-Char-Seq2Seq-Complete.ipynb**, which shows the output from the run used to build the pre-trained bidirectional model included in the **notebooks/pre-trained/BidirCharModel/** folder.

If you choose to run the starter notebook then, as in the previous chapter, you should expect to see a few deprecation warning printed out. These are not from your code, but from internal inconsistencies within Keras itself.

The rest of this section goes over the important differences between this and the previous model you built.

The first difference isn't out of necessity, but this model uses a larger latent_dim value:

```
latent_dims = 512
```

The previous model used 256 dimensions, which meant you passed 512 features from your encoder to your decoder — the LSTM produced two 256-length vectors, one for the hidden state and one for the cell state. GRU layers don't have a cell state, so they return only a single vector of length latent_dim. Rather than send only half the amount of information to the decoder, the author chose to double the size of the GRUs.

The biggest differences for this model are in the encoder, so let's go over its definition:

```
# 1
encoder_in = Input(
    shape=(None, in_vocab_size), name="encoder_in")
encoder_mask = Masking(name="encoder_mask")(encoder_in)
# 2
fwd_enc_gru = GRU(
    latent_dim, recurrent_dropout=0.3, name="fwd_enc_gru")
rev_enc_gru = GRU(
    latent_dim, go_backwards=True, recurrent_dropout=0.3,
    name="rev_enc_gru")
fwd_enc_out = fwd_enc_gru(encoder_mask)
rev_enc_out = rev_enc_gru(encoder_mask)
# 3
encoder_out = Concatenate(name="encoder_out")(
    [fwd_enc_out, rev_enc_out])
```

This encoder uses a bidirectional RNN with GRU layers. Here's how you set it up:

1. The `Input` and `Masking` layers are identical to the previous chapter's encoder.

2. Rather than creating one recurrent layer, you create two — one that processes the sequence normally and one that processes it in reverse because you set `go_backwards=True`. You feed the same masking layer into both of these layers.

3. Finally, you concatenate the outputs from the two GRU layers so the encoder can output them together in a single vector. Notice that, unlike in the previous chapter, here you don't use the h states and instead use the layer outputs. This wasn't mentioned before, but that works because the hidden states *are* the outputs. The reason you used the states for the LSTM was to get at the **cell** states, which are *not* returned as outputs like the hidden states are.

As far as the decoder goes, one important difference is in the size of the inputs it expects. We define a new variable called `decoder_latent_dim`, like this:

```
decoder_latent_dim = latent_dim * 2
```

The decoder's recurrent layer needs twice as many units as the encoder's did because it accepts a vector that contains the concatenated outputs from two of them — forward *and* reverse.

The only other differences with the decoder are in the following lines:

```
decoder_gru = GRU(
    decoder_latent_dim, return_sequences=True,
    return_state=True, dropout=0.2, recurrent_dropout=0.3,
    name="decoder_gru")
decoder_gru_out, _ = decoder_gru(
    decoder_mask, initial_state=encoder_out)
```

Once again, you use a GRU layer instead of an LSTM, but use `decoder_latent_dim` instead of `latent_dim` to account for the forward and reverse states coming from the encoder. Notice the GRU only returns hidden states, which you ignore for now by assigning them to an underscore variable. This differs from the LSTM you used in the previous chapter, which returned both hidden and cell states.

> **Note**: One important detail is that the decoder does *not* implement a bidirectional network like the encoder does. That's because the decoder doesn't actually process whole sequences — it just takes a single character along with state information.

If you run this notebook, or look through the completed one provided, you'll see a few things. First, this model is much larger than the last one you built — about 5.4 million parameters versus 741 thousand. Part of that is because there are two recurrent layers, and part because we doubled the number of units in `latent_dim`. Still, each epoch only takes a bit longer to train.

The other thing that stands out is the performance. This model trained to a validation loss of 0.3533 by epoch 128 (before automatically stopping training at epoch 133). Compare that to the previous model, which only achieved a 0.5905 validation loss, and it took 179 epochs to do it. So this model achieved lower loss in fewer epochs, thanks mostly to the additional information gleaned from the bidirectional encoder.

For inference, the only difference is with the encoder's output. Instead of outputting the encoder's latent state, you use the concatenated layer `encoder_out`, like this:

```
inf_encoder = Model(encoder_in, encoder_out)
```

The notebook includes code to export your encoder and decoder models to Core ML. There are slight differences to match the new model architecture, but nothing should look unfamiliar to you. It includes the same workarounds you used in the last chapter.

Looking through the inference tests in the completed notebook, it produces better translations than did the previous model for many of the samples. For example:

Target Translation	Original Model's Output	Bidirectional Model's Output
I saw him just now.	I just told it.	I just saw him.
Let me think this over.	Let me tell this one of that.	Let me think about this again.
They enjoy playing together.	They like to play tennis.	They like to play together.

It does about as well on most — but not all — of the other tests, too. Some of the most interesting are those it gets wrong, but less wrong than the last model did. Such as:

Target Translation	Original Model's Output	Bidirectional Model's Output
I like listening to good music.	I like to get much business.	I like to hear music very much.
I will take you for a swim.	I'll tell you again.	I'll take you a swim.
I've done questionable things.	I've done the songs.	I've done so much things.

Notice that, in each of these examples, the bidirectional model does better then the previous chapter's model when translating words that appear near the *end* of the sentences. That makes sense, since it looks at the sequence in both directions, letting it encode more context for the decoder.

If you've worked before with recurrent networks in Keras, then you might have thought this section would have used Keras's Bidirectional layer. Before trying out your new model in Xcode, take a look at this brief discussion of why we didn't use that class, here.

Why not use Keras's Bidirectional layer?

Keras includes a Bidirectional layer that simplifies the creation of bidirectional RNNs. You initialize it with a single recurrent layer, like an LSTM or GRU layer, and it handles duplicating that as a reversed layer for you. To use it, you'd write something like this for a bidirectional LSTM:

```
encoder_lstm = Bidirectional(
  LSTM(latent_dim, return_state=True, recurrent_dropout=0.3),
  name="encoder_lstm")
encoder_out, fwd_enc_h, fwd_enc_c, rev_enc_h, rev_enc_c = \
  encoder_lstm(encoder_mask)
```

Or like this for a bidirectional GRU:

```
encoder_gru = Bidirectional(
  GRU(latent_dim, return_state=True, recurrent_dropout=0.3),
  name="encoder_gru")
encoder_out, fwd_enc_h, rev_enc_h = encoder_gru(encoder_mask)
```

Each of these examples sets return_state=True so the layers return their hidden and cell states (for LSTMs, which have cell states). So when you connect the Bidirectional layer to a network, it returns the output along with the forward and reverse states. Then you would concatenate the states like this:

```
encoder_h = Concatenate(name="encoder_out")(
  [fwd_enc_h, rev_enc_h])
encoder_c = Concatenate(name="encoder_out")(
  [fwd_enc_c, rev_enc_c])
```

Finally, you'd pass those concatenated states to the decoder as its initial state. And in Keras all of that works great.

Unfortunately, just like with masking layers, here you encounter a major roadblock to using the Bidirectional class: coremltools. If you try to setup a bidirectional GRU layer, coremltools will emit a helpful error message that "Keras bi-directional wrapper conversion supports only LSTM layer at this time". This is true for coremltools version 3.3, which is the latest releases at the time of this writing.

Until this issue is resolved, it's a better idea to create bidirectional models like you did here, using multiple recurrent layers explicitly.

Using your bidirectional model in Xcode

Open the SMDB project you've been working with for the past couple chapters in Xcode, or use the starter project found in this chapter's resources. Then, add the **Es2EnBidirGruCharEncoder16Bit.mlmodel** and **Es2EnBidirGruCharDecoder16Bit.mlmodel** models to SMDB like you've done before. If you didn't train your own, you can find the ones we trained in the **notebooks/pre-trained/BidirCharModel** folder.

Here's the encoder's model summary, minus the unimportant bits to conserve space:

▼ **Machine Learning Model**

Name	Es2EnBidirGruCharEncoder16Bit
Type	Neural Network
Size	3.8 MB

▼ **Model Evaluation Parameters**

Name	Type	Description
▼ Inputs		
oneHotEncodedSeq	MultiArray (Double 101)	
fwd_enc_gru_h_in	MultiArray (Double 512)?	
rev_enc_gru_h_in	MultiArray (Double 512)?	
▼ Outputs		
decodersIntialState	MultiArray (Double 1024)	
fwd_enc_gru_h_out	MultiArray (Double 512)	
rev_enc_gru_h_out	MultiArray (Double 512)	

Looking at the encoder mlmodel file

One big difference is just how big the encoder is — 3.8MB versus the 734KB encoder from the previous chapter. The other thing to notice are the input and output names, which are different from what you used in your first encoder.

The decoder's summary (not shown) is similar to the decoder in the previous chapter, but it's 7MB instead of 750KB. That's nearly 10 times larger!

Note: If you've followed along building this and the previous model, or are using the provided resources, then there is no need to add the vocabulary JSON files **esCharToInt.json** and **intToEnChar.json** to the project. That's because the files from the previous chapter are exactly the same. But if you split your training data differently, then there's a chance your JSON files are different, too. In that case, add your new JSON files to the project with different names and then modify the declarations of esCharToInt and intToEnChar in **NLPHelper.swift** to load them.

Now to actually use the new models. Rather than remove the code you wrote in the previous chapter, you'll create a separate function that creates the decoder input suitable for your bidirectional model. Add the following function inside **NLPHelper.swift**:

```
func getBidirDecoderInput(encoderInput: MLMultiArray) ->
  Es2EnBidirGruCharDecoder16BitInput {
  let encoder = Es2EnBidirGruCharEncoder16Bit()
  let encoderOut = try! encoder.prediction(
    oneHotEncodedSeq: encoderInput,
    fwd_enc_gru_h_in: nil,
    rev_enc_gru_h_in: nil)

  let decoderIn = initMultiArray(
    shape: [NSNumber(value: intToEnChar.count)])

  return Es2EnBidirGruCharDecoder16BitInput(
    encodedChar: decoderIn,
    decoder_gru_h_in: encoderOut.decodersIntialState)
}
```

This is almost identical to what you wrote in `getDecoderInput` in the previous chapter. This version only changes class and parameter names to match the ones Xcode created for your new models. Notice you set `decoder_gru_h_in` to the encoder output's `decodersInitialState` value — that's the name of the output that concatenates the outputs of the forward and reverse GRUs.

Now, you need to call this new function and pass its output to the decoder model that pairs with your bidirectional encoder. To do that, find the following two lines inside `spanishToEnglish`:

```
let decoderIn = getDecoderInput(encoderInput: encoderIn)
let decoder = Es2EnCharDecoder16Bit()
```

And replace them with these two:

```
let decoderIn = getBidirDecoderInput(encoderInput: encoderIn)
let decoder = Es2EnBidirGruCharDecoder16Bit()
```

Nothing new, here: You're just calling a different function to get the decoder's input and using your new bidirectional decoder model.

Finally, you need to modify the parameters on the decoder's input. Find these two lines:

```
decoderIn.decoder_lstm_h_in = decoderOut.decoder_lstm_h_out
decoderIn.decoder_lstm_c_in = decoderOut.decoder_lstm_c_out
```

And replace them with this one:

```
decoderIn.decoder_gru_h_in = decoderOut.decoder_gru_h_out
```

That's it. Build and run the app, then choose **Spanish** in the **By Languages** tab to see your model in action!

SMDB app with reviews translated by bidirectional character-level model

Better than the model from last chapter? Um, *kind of*, in places, but not much. It got close on some sentences, such as, "I don't usually like music," instead of the expected translation, "I don't usually like musicals," and "How boring!" which is close to the correct "Very boring!" It also included additional correct words within translations, such as "worst" and "movie" in its translation of, "Es mi peor pesadilla hecha película," and "bad" when translating, "Muy mala película."

While this doesn't seem like much of an improvement, keep in mind that you haven't addressed most of the problems mentioned at the end of the last chapter. For example, the dataset is still too small, and you're still predicting characters with a greedy algorithm. But bidirectional models generally produce better results for tasks like translation, where useful context can appear before *and* after an item in a sequence.

The rest of this chapter shows some other techniques that might lead to better performance. In the next section, you'll learn about a popular alternative to greedy decoding called **beam search**. In the process, you'll find out this model wasn't as far off as it seems with many of its translations.

Beam search

This and the previous chapter have both implied there's a better option than greedily choosing the token predicted with the highest probability at each timestep. The solution most commonly used is called beam search, and you should strongly consider implementing it if you want to improve the quality of a model's generated sequences.

Beam search is a heuristic-based searching method that considers many possible sequences, and it ranks them based on the total probability of the **sequence**, regardless of the probability of individual choices at any particular timestep.

What's that mean? Consider the following contrived example, wherein a model attempting to predict the first word of a sequence tries *both* choices for the first character instead of just the most probable one:

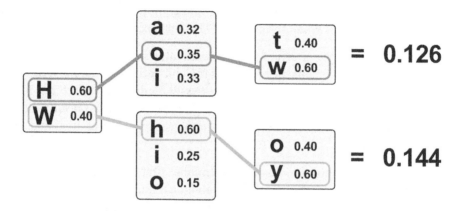

The numbers in the above image have all been fabricated, and they make the unrealistic assumption that all the unlisted characters have zero probability, but it demonstrates the issue. As you can see, choosing the highest probability character for the first choice — "H" — does *not* lead to the highest probability sequence: "Why."

Each prediction the model makes affects all its future predictions in that sequence, so any single bad choice can ruin the rest of the translation. That's why using the greedy approach doesn't usually lead to the best results. There's no perfect neural network, so do you really want to count on a prediction with probability `0.0134` being *definitely* the right choice over one with probability `0.0133`?

Beam search attempts to work around this issue by not committing to any one sequence. Instead, it maintains multiple possible search paths, and it expands the most promising sequences, eventually returning the one it finds with the best overall probability score. So in the above example, beam search would predict "Who" instead of "How," even though it *seemed* like the correct first character should have been "H" when the model first started translating the sequence.

The basic algorithm goes like this:

1. Define the number of sequences you'll maintain, called the beam width, B.

2. Make a prediction with the model, then take the values with the top B probabilities and store them as the start of B different sequences.

3. For each of the current B sequences, make another prediction with the model and extend the sequence with the top B prediction results, giving you BxB sequences.

4. Store the top B sequences from this set.

5. Repeat steps 3–4 until you have B sequences that have all predicted STOP tokens or reached their maximum length.

6. Return the top sequence from the final B sequences.

There are variations you can make to this basic algorithm, such as sometimes sampling randomly to include lower probability sequences (in case they surprise you and improve later), or storing previously discarded sequences in case you want to return to them if they look better after exploring other search paths.

> **Note**: It's important to realize that beam search is not guaranteed to find the best result. It does not try every possible sequence — that would be too computationally expensive — so it returns the best result if can find using its heuristics and available resources.

Implementing beam search isn't really related to machine learning; it's just a useful algorithm for dealing with joint probabilities. As such, we won't provide code for it, here. However, we do want to point out a few potential gotchas that you should be aware of for when you try to implement it yourself.

The probability of a *sequence* is the joint probability of *all* the predictions used to create the sequence. You calculate it by multiplying these probabilities together. For example, there's a 0.5 probability of getting heads when flipping a coin once, so the probability of getting three heads in a row is 0.5 x 0.5 x 0.5 = 0.125.

The trouble is, probabilities are small numbers between 0 and 1, and multiplying them produces even smaller numbers. It doesn't take long before the limited precision available on computers for floating point arithmetic introduces errors, and eventually underflows and ruins everything by multiplying by zero.

You can avoid this by adding the logarithms of the probabilities instead of multiplying the probabilities directly. So in the earlier example, taking the log probabilities and adding them together gives you these values:

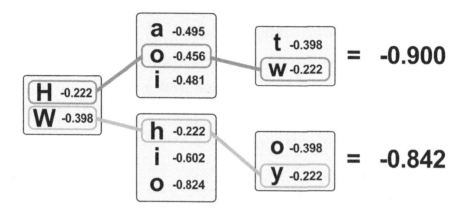

The logs are all negative, but notice they still work out so that higher values correspond to higher probabilities. Maximizing the sum of log probabilities — or minimizing the sum of the negatives of the log probabilities, if you prefer to implement it that way — produces the same sequences as multipyling the probabilities, but the math is stable.

The next issue relates to sequence length. Each additional token lowers the total probability for the sequence, so comparing these totals directly would penalize longer sequences. You'll need to normalize them before making any comparisons.

One way to do that is to divide each of the sums by the length of its sequence. However, according to Andrew Ng, it's common to divide by the length raised to some power between zero and one; using zero turns off normalization completely, and using one normalizes by the length directly, but any value between those normalizes by the length while still preferring shorter sequences to some degree.

Ng claims there is no good mathematically rigorous way to choose this value; it's just something you experiment with until you find a value you like, but he says 0.7 seems to work well.

Finally, you'll need to decide how many resources you can dedicate to running the beam search. The more sequences you try, the longer it will take. And, depending on your design, wider beams could lead to a great deal more memory use, too. You'll have to experiment and make performance tradeoffs, especially to run it on mobile.

So if you implemented beam search and used it with the bidirectional model you trained earlier in the chapter, without training with more data or making any other changes, would it help?

Consider when it translates this sentence: "Entonces esta película te sorprenderá." By choosing the character with the highest prediction probability at each step, it currently outputs, "So what this movie will surprise you." This sentence has a normalized sum of log probabilities of -0.341630.

However, the correct translation — according to *Google Translate* — is, "This movie will surprise you." And *this* sentence has a normalized sum of log probabilities of -0.300456.

Producing this better translation requires making three choices that are not the highest probability character for those steps — the fourth highest for the first character, and the second highest for two others. Depending on how you implement it and the beam width you use, beam search could find this correct translation. That means the current model can produce better translations just with the help of some smarter decoding processing.

> **Note**: This chapter's bidirectional model can translate quite a few of the review and test sentences correctly if we occasionally choose lower-probability characters. For example, choosing "u" instead of "o" when translating, "Hay un gato debajo de la mesa," correctly outputs, "There is a cat under the table," instead of, "There is a cat on the table." Just adding beam search doesn't mean you'll get these translations. That's because they still end up with lower total probabilities than what the model finds using greedy search.
>
> However, that's because of the training data more than the model or the search algorithm; training with larger datasets means gathering better language usage statistics, so once you have a model trained with a lot of data, coupling it with beam search gives you the best chance of producing high quality results.

Attention

The previous chapter mentioned an important problem with the encoder portion of your seq2seq model: It needs to encode the entire sequence into a single, fixed-length vector. That limits the length of the input sequences it can successfully handle, because each new token essentially dilutes the stored information.

To combat this issue, you can use a technique called **attention**. The most basic implementation of attention works like this: Instead of using one vector to represent the entire sequence, the encoder uses a vector *per input token*. Then the decoder learns to apply different weights to each vector at each *output* timestep, essentially *paying attention* to specific combinations of words. The weights are often visualized as attention maps, like in the following image:

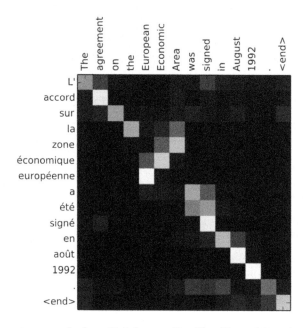

Attention alignments example from Bahdanau, D., Cho, K., and Bengio, Y. (2015). Neural machine translation by jointly learning to align and translate. International Conference on Learning Representations (ICLR 2015)

There's a column for each token in the input sequence — in this case, the tokens are words, not characters — and a row for each output token. The colors in the rows indicate how much each column's input token was considered for that timestep, from black (zero) to white (one).

Notice how it doesn't necessarily focus on the word aligned with the same timestep. For example, it needs to look at terms out of order when translating "the European Economic Area" to "la zone économique européenne." Using attention, models learn to relate specific parts of their output with specific parts of their input, which produces much better results than the basic seq2seq models you've built here, especially on longer sequences. It has proven so powerful that it's now used in most state-of-the-art models for NLP, as well as for other tasks like some computer vision problems.

There's a variation of attention called **self-attention** that gives even better results. Whereas regular attention works between the encoder and decoder, self-attention gains additional information by allowing the encoder to apply attention between the input tokens, and it lets the decoder apply attention between its output tokens. That is, regular attention only relates the inputs to output tokens, but self-attention relates tokens within each sequence to other tokens in the *same* sequence, as well.

Self-attention performs even better than regular attention because it lets the encoder fine tune its encodings based on relationships it finds between input tokens, such as noun-verb agreement or to whom a pronoun refers in a sentence. In fact, self-attention is *so* good that current state-of-the-art models, often based on a network architecture called a Transformer, do away with the recurrent portions of the encoder and decoder and rely *entirely* on self-attention. Not only do they perform better, but they train faster, too!

These state-of-the-art models are quite large, so they usually run in the cloud. However, you can take advantage of these techniques in smaller models, too, depending on the task and the details of your implementation. If you decide to explore adding attention to your own networks, you may want to look at some of the important papers related to it:

- "Neural Machine Translation by Jointly Learning to Align and Translate" arxiv.org/abs/1409.0473

- "A Structured Self-attentive Sentence Embedding", arxiv.org/abs/1703.03130

- "Attention Is All You Need", arxiv.org/abs/1706.03762

We glossed over how the previous image showed whole word tokens, not characters like what you've used in your models. The next section discusses the choice to work with characters instead of words in these chapters.

Why use characters at all?

The seq2seq models you've made in this book work with sequences at the character level, but why? How much information does a model get from each token when it views sequences this way? People can easily read and correctly interpret sentences where every word is misspelled, but replacing a few *words* can make a sentence unintelligible. It seems like most individual characters don't add much information to a sentence, whereas most words do, so shouldn't translation models consider words instead?

The answer to that is yes — and also maybe not.

Researchers are always exploring different options, e.g., combining words into phrases or going the other way and breaking them into subwords. There are hybrid approaches that look at tokens in multiple ways, e.g., as words *and* as characters, which can help when dealing with OOV tokens. They've even made models that work with text as sequences of *bytes*! Working with whole words is probably the most common approach, but there are some difficulties involved that you should be aware of before attempting to build such models.

First, there's vocabulary size. It may not be obvious if you haven't dealt much with these models, but vocabulary size matters quite a bit, for these three reasons:

1. The model's output layer performs a softmax calculation across the entire vocabulary to produce the probabilities for each token — the more tokens, the longer that calculation takes. A byte-level model has a vocabulary of just 256 values and is capable of representing anything; a character-level model for a *restricted* character set, like ASCII, will vary but likely will be in the hundreds or low thousands; full Unicode support would include over 1.1 million characters; and using word level tokens means a potential vocabulary size of many millions.

    In fact, working with words basically *requires* limiting the vocabulary to some subset of common words, and then you need to add in ways to deal with OOV tokens. There are some tricks you can implement to reduce the computations required at this softmax level to speed up training — look up terms like "adaptive softmax" and "hierarchical softmax" for some ideas — but it's still easier to deal with fewer items.

2. The larger the vocabulary, the larger the model. That's because it increases the width of your input and output layers (at least), and those layers end up contributing most of your model's trainable parameters. Mobile devices don't have the resources to deal with very large models, so it may not be feasible to support very large vocabularies on them.

3. The dreaded **curse of dimensionality**. You'll hear this term a lot in machine learning. It refers to the fact that, as you increase the number of input features, the possible combinations of inputs can grow exponentially. (See the upcoming **Note** for an example.) As the possible combinations grow, each specific training sample covers a smaller percentage of those possibilities. The primary result: As you add features, you need to increase the size of your training set — possibly exponentially. Now consider that each token in the vocabulary is a unique input dimension, and you'll see you need ever more training data as the size of your vocabulary grows.

> **Note**: Here's an example of the curse of dimensionality. Consider a model that takes only one input feature — an integer from 1 to 10. There are only 10 possible inputs, so each training sample essentially covers 10% of all possible inputs this model can ever see.
>
> Adding a second input feature — again an integer from 1 to 10 — gives you a two-dimensional input with 100 possible combinations, so each training sample now only covers 1% of the possible inputs. And adding a similar third dimension brings the possible combinations up to 1,000, which would mean each sample then covers only one tenth of 1%.
>
> As the number of dimensions goes up, a model must train on drastically more data in order to learn an accurate representation of the input space.

Secondly, working with subword tokens makes it easier to deal with OOV tokens. At the byte level, you can remove the problem entirely — there will only ever be 256 possible values; with characters you can delete OOV tokens and rarely lose much information. But with words, it becomes a difficult problem that's still an open area of research. You'll read more about it in the next section.

Even with those things going against it, using words still has one overwhelming advantage: Words convey *meaning*. Computers can't really *understand* what they read — not yet, anyway — but they can definitely learn to identify important things like semantic relationships between words. The next section points out a few things you'll need to do differently when dealing with word tokens instead of characters, and it introduces a popular way to represent them: **embeddings**.

Words as tokens and word embedding

Recall that neural networks require numerical inputs. So far, you've been one-hot encoding text prior to using it, but that essentially means your network sees mostly just zeros. What if you could provide more useful information?

It turns out, you can, with something called word **embeddings**, or word vectors; you'll see these terms used interchangeably. These are vectors that represent words in some abstract n-dimensional space, and in the process, capture meaningful information about them. You can then use these vectors as inputs to your networks instead of one-hot encodings.

This essentially lets you provide information *about* a word instead of just a Boolean flag indicating the *presence* of a word. All that information makes the work easier for the rest of your model, and results in a better accuracy for your model as a whole.

This can all sound rather abstract. It's easiest to understand by analogy.

For instance, to make a 2D map of Earth, you need to project 3D geographic positions into a 2D coordinate system. While that isn't hard to imagine for positions, you can actually project any set of values into a different coordinate system. Consider the following graph, which projects Marvel characters onto the two alignment axes from Dungeons & Dragons — one represents their morality from good to evil, and one represents their behavior from lawful to chaotic:

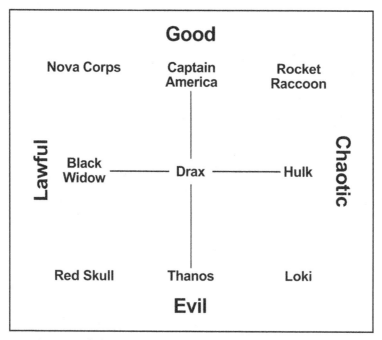

Marvel characters projected onto D&D alignments

The specific alignments given for each character are from the *ComicsVerse* blog post, "Good? Evil? The Alignment of MCU Characters" https://comicsverse.com/good-evil-mcu-alignment/.

Check it out if you're curious about the arguments behind each assignment. It's not important if you don't know these characters or the details of D&D's alignment system. What *is* important is how this shows words plotted in 2D space, where each axis represents a qualitative feature and the word's position along that axis gives you a quantitative measure of how much that word represents or manifests that quality.

> **Note**: This example uses discrete values of good-neutral-evil and lawful-neutral-chaotic, but there's no reason we couldn't plot these values in a continuous feature space instead. For example, it's not difficult to imagine a character that is not *totally* good, but still leans toward being mostly good.

While this example was a bit contrived, it demonstrates a couple things. First, it show you can plot **qualities** along axes just like you plot **quantities**. That's the essential idea behind word embeddings: Take a word and plot it into a n-dimensional space that describes how it relates to various qualities. This example only had two dimensions, but using a higher number lets you capture more features. In practice, word embeddings often use between 50 and several hundred dimensions, and we don't specify what they represent. It may be that no single dimension represents any specific quality, but rather combinations of dimensions end up representing useful things.

The second thing shown is how embeddings are a matter of choice. The good vs evil and lawful vs chaotic word embedding is, obviously, fanciful. But you could, if you wanted, use this embedding to map out the relationships of all the world's heads of state. However, you could also do it in more predictable ways. You could, for instance, map every head of state to the longitude and latitude coordinates of their country's capital city.

From this perspective, even the one-hot encoding can be seen as a kind of embedding, a degenerate one. It's the embedding you get when you don't reduce the number of dimensions at all, and every single entity gets its own dimension, and the meaning of a dimension is just to identify that entity. The reason this is not particularly useful is that, because it does not make any choices about how it reduces the number of dimensions, it does not express relationships between the entities.

So what embedding should you choose? In general, you don't do the choosing. In machine learning, you let a model learn the embedding from the data, rather than hand designing it based on prior insights.

There are several ways to learn such embeddings and we won't go into the details here, but they all revolve around the same basic premise: Words are given random positions in some n-dimensional vector space, and their positions are adjusted a bit each time the word is used in the dataset. After processing a large text corpus, words that are used in similar ways end up closer to each other in vector space.

Because this process learns the embedding from the data, the embedding ends up discovering relationships between words that were implied by the data. For example, the following chart shows one such discovered relationship — that of gender — between the words "man" and "woman." Other words that have a similar gender relationship, such as "king" and "queen" or "uncle" and "aunt," display a similar mathematical up vs down relationship in the vector space:

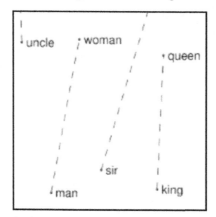

Word relationship example from Pennington, J., Socher, R., and Manning, C. D. (2014)
GloVe: Global Vectors for Word Representation.

You can learn more about word embeddings and the algorithms used to make them, as well as find many pre-trained vectors, by searching online for "word embeddings" or "word vectors." Word2Vec, GloVe and fastText are common embedding options. You could train your own, but learning high-quality embeddings requires lots of data. For example, one set of GloVe embeddings you can download was trained on a corpus of 840 *billion* tokens.

Using word embeddings instead of one-hot encodings greatly increases performance on most NLP tasks. They are one of unsupervised learning's greatest success stories.

Word embeddings in iOS

Apple provides support for word embeddings via the `MLWordEmbedding` and `NLEmbedding` types. That support makes certain uses of word embeddings straightforward.

For starters you don't need to train your own embedding at all. `NLEmbedding` comes with built in word embedding for seven major languages. Apple does not say how these embeddings are trained except that they are trained over bodies of text with "billions of words." This makes them good for general purposes uses.

However, if you do want to provide your own embedding then you can do that too. You can create an MLWordEmbedding by providing a dictionary mapping every word to its numerical vector, save the compiled embedding to disk, and then use that file to create a NLEmbedding. This would be a good idea if you want to experiment with other general purpose pretrained embeddings (like the GloVe embedding depicted in the figure above), to use a pretrained embedding targeted at a specific vocabulary domain, or to import an embedding that you trained yourself.

The saving to disk is not just a piece of busy work in the middle. As with text catalogs (mentioned in Chapter 14), with that step you are compiling the data into a highly efficient storage format. This will be critical if you are defining an embedding over a large vocabulary and do not want embedding data to increase your app's download size unnecessarily.

Experimenting with this now will show you the benefits and the limits of the system. Open the starter playground **projects/starter/playgrounds/ WordEmbeddings.playground** in the chapter resources. The code already in the playground imports modules and defines a URL for saving and loading the uncompiled embedding.

Now add the following code to define the Marvel character entities via an embedding:

```
let vectors = [
  "Captain America": [0.0, 1], "Rocket Raccoon": [1, 1],
  "Hulk": [1, 0],  "Loki": [1, -1],
  "Thanos": [0, -1], "Red Skull": [-1, -1],
  "Black Widow": [-1, 0], "Nova Corps": [-1, 1],
]
```

This defines vectors representing the characters exactly as depicted in the figure, using a positive x for chaotic and a positive y for good. Now add the following:

```
// 1
let embedding1 = try MLWordEmbedding(dictionary: vectors)
try embedding1.write(to: marvelModelUrl)
// 2
let compiledUrl = try MLModel.compileModel(at: marvelModelUrl)
// 3
let embedding2 = try NLEmbedding(contentsOf: compiledUrl)
```

This does the following:

1. Initializes an `MLWordEmbedding` and writes it to disk.

2. Compiles it as a Core ML model, for efficiency gains.

3. Load the compiled model as an `NLEmbedding` which can be used by the Natural Language framework.

So what can you do with this? Apple's API makes it easy to use the embedding vectors to provide *direct information* about the relationships between entities.

For instance, since the embedding positions your entities into an embedding space, it becomes possible to talk about the "distance" between entities in that space. Suppose you asked a Marvel fan, "What's the distance between Captain America and the Rocket Raccoon?" They might look at you funny, since if you're not talking about where they are standing it's not quite clear what the question means. But if then you asked, "Are they closer to each other than, say, Captain America and Loki?" you would probably get a quickly reply. Of course the captain and the raccoon are closer. They're both good guys, they're both trying to save the world, they seem to get along, while Loki is a chaotic god of disorder.

The point is, an embedding lets you take this intuitive notion of "distance" between entities and make it concrete. Add the following code to see this in action:

```
embedding2.distance(between: "Captain America",
                    and: "Rocket Raccoon",
                    distanceType: .cosine)
// => 1.414
embedding2.distance(between: "Captain America",
                    and: "Loki",
                    distanceType: .cosine)
// => 1.847
```

This asks the embedding object to calculate the distance between the two entities. It returns distances of 1.414 and 1.847, consistent with intuition (as of Xcode 11.3.1). The embedding object also provides API for efficiently searching for other entities within a given distance, or listing the entities nearest to another entity.

The parameter `distanceType` specifies how the distance is calculated; at present, cosine distance is the only available option. Let's look at some other distances. Try the following:

```
embedding2.distance(between: "Captain America",
                    and: "Thanos",
                    distanceType: .cosine)
```

```
// => 1.414
```

Wait, what? That's the same value we got for Captain America and Rocket Raccoon! Is Captain America as similar to Rocket Raccoon (another good guy) as he is to Thanos, who wants to destroy half the life in the universe? Thanos certainly looks farther away on the chart using the vectors that we ourselves defined. Something is puzzling here.

Apple's documentation says that the `.cosine` represents cosine distance. But you can write your own definition of cosine distance as follows (following the definition offered in Mathematica and in Wikipedia):

```
func cosineDistance(v: [Double], w: [Double]) -> Double {
  let innerProduct = zip(v, w)
    .map { $0 * $1 }
    .reduce(0, +)

  func magnitude(_ x: [Double]) -> Double {
    sqrt(x
      .map { $0 * $0}
      .reduce(0,+))
  }

  let cos =  innerProduct / (magnitude(v) * magnitude(w))
  return 1 - cos
}
```

This computes one minus the cosine of the angle between two vectors. And if you calculate cosine distance directly, you get the following:

```
cosineDistance(v: vectors["Captain America"]!,
               w: vectors["Rocket Raccoon"]!)
// => 0.29
cosineDistance(v: vectors["Captain America"]!,
               w: vectors["Loki"]!)
// => 1.707
cosineDistance(v: vectors["Captain America"]!,
               w: vectors["Thanos"]!)
// => 2
```

These numbers are different from Apple's not only in the magnitude of distances but even in their *ordering.*

So what is going on here? Hard to say. But one reasonable conclusion is that Apple's embedding API is very new, not yet well documented, and may not behave in the way you expect. If you do want to use a custom embedding in order to use functionality like measuring distances or fast search for neighboring entities, you should take care to validate that the API is defining distance in the way you expect.

Whatever the explanation for these surprising values, the fact is that most of the time in machine learning models embeddings are *not* used in order to directly access information about entities, but as an early layer in a larger model, used in order to prepare an enriched representation of input values so that the rest of the model can do a better job.

The next section will discuss how this might work for our sequence to sequence translation model.

Building models with word embeddings

This section points out some changes you'd need to make to your existing seq2seq models in order to have them use word tokens instead of characters. This section includes code snippets you can use, but it doesn't spell out every detail necessary to build such a model. Don't worry! With these tips and what you've already learned, you're well prepared to build these models on your own. Consider it a challenge!

We'll assume you're starting with pre-trained word embeddings. The first thing you'll need to decide is how many words you want to include in your vocabulary. Just because you have an embedding for a word doesn't mean you'll want to use it in your model. Remember, vocabulary size affects model size, so you'll need to keep things manageable. But there's another reason you might not want to use all the embeddings you download: some of them may be garbage.

Word embeddings are trained in an unsupervised manner with huge datasets often scraped from the internet, so it's not uncommon for bad tokens to slip through. For example, there are two million tokens in the Spanish embeddings you can download at https://fasttext.cc/docs/en/crawl-vectors.html. However, these include thousands of tokens like "11234567891011121314151617 3" and "PaísEnglishEspañolPortuguêsCanadaUnited" that would just take up space in your model without serving any useful purpose.

Important: The more embeddings you include, the larger your model will be. It's common to choose a few tens of thousands of the most commonly used words, but whatever you do, try to limit it to a reasonable set for your task.

An important step when dealing with word tokens is... tokenizing your text into words. You've got different choices for how to do this. For example, the English contraction "don't" could become the tokens don't, do and n't, don and 't, or don, ' and t.

The first two options are the ones you're most likely to come across, but whatever you choose, you need to make sure of a couple things:

1. If you're using pre-trained word embeddings, make sure you create tokens in the same way as the creators of the embeddings did, otherwise you'll end up with more OOV tokens than you should because you won't have embeddings for some of your tokens that you otherwise would have. For example, if you parse the word "don't" as the token don't, but the pre-trained embeddings contain the two tokens do and n't, you'll end up having to treat every "don't" you encounter as an OOV token.

2. Tokenize text in your iOS code the same way you do in Python. The Natural Language framework's NLTokenizer doesn't let you configure its tokenization settings like you can with Python packages like nltk, so you may have to write your own tokenization logic to produce the tokens your model expects.

For your special START and STOP tokens, you should add some word to your vocabulary you know *never* appears in the data, e.g., <START> and <STOP>. You'll need to deal with OOV tokens quite differently, too. You can't just remove them like you did with the characters, so you'll replace them with a special token, such as <UNK>.

Note: You learned in the first NLP chapter that it's possible to tag text with its parts of speech. Instead of using a single <UNK> token for all OOV tokens, you may get better performance if you replace words with part-of-speech-specific tokens, such as <UNK_NOUN>, <UNK_VERB>, etc. This gives the model additional context that might help when translating sequences that contain OOV tokens.

Once you've loaded your vocabulary of pre-trained embeddings, you'll need to add embeddings for the OOV token(s) you defined, too. Assuming your embeddings are in a NumPy array called es_token_vectors, and you have an OOV token in the variable unk_token, you could add a random embedding like this:

```
es_token_vectors[unk_token] =
    2 * np.random.rand(embedding_dim).astype(np.float32) - 1
```

This assigns an <UNK> token an embedding filled with embedding_dim random values in the range [-1,1]. That's not necessarily the best range to use — you might want to check the pre-trained embeddings you've got to see the range of values you're already dealing with — but the point of using random values is to hopefully keep your OOV tokens from being too similar to any other words in the vocabulary.

> **Note**: You could try various options for the embeddings for your unknown token(s). For example, take an average of all or some set of noun embeddings for an UNK_NOUN token, an average of verb embeddings for an UNK_VERB token, etc. It's unclear whether that would be helpful, but trying out different ideas is part of the fun of machine learning, right?

You'd identify which tokens are OOV by checking the tokens in your training set against your word embeddings. That is, if your training set contains a token that does not exist in your pre-trained embeddings, you'd remove that term from your vocabulary.

> **Note**: If you're training your own embeddings, you would define your vocabulary differently. You'd most likely start by counting the uses of each token in your training data, and then choosing some number of most commonly used terms. Those terms then define the vocabulary for which you'd train embeddings.

Once you've settled on the vocabulary you'll support — let's assume it's a set of tokens stored in in_vocab — you need to go through all your training, validation and test data and replace any OOV tokens with the appropriate <UNK> token(s). This is different from how you removed OOV from your datasets when you work with characters.

At this point your embeddings are likely in a dictionary keyed off of tokens, and it may contain more embeddings than you actually plan to use in your vocabulary. You'll need to put the embeddings for these individual vocabulary words into a single NumPy array to use with your network, like this:

```
# 1
num_enc_embeddings = in_vocab_size + 1
# 2
pretrained_embeddings = np.zeros(
    (num_enc_embeddings, embedding_dim), dtype=np.float32)
# 3
for i, t in enumerate(in_vocab):
    pretrained_embeddings[i+1] = es_token_vectors[t]
```

Here's how you'd grab the embeddings for the words in your vocabulary:

1. Your encoder will need to embed each token in your vocabulary, plus an *additional* embedding to act as a padding token during training.

2. Create a NumPy array of all zeros, shaped to hold the correct number of embeddings of size `embedding_dim`. You can find pre-trained embeddings in various dimensions, especially for English, but it seems 300 is the most common. Embeddings of that size for a reasonably sized vocabulary may give you models that are too big for mobile devices, so you may need to train your own if you cannot find smaller embeddings for the language you need.

3. Notice how each embedding is stored with the index `i+1`. This leaves index zero unassigned, which is the value reserved by Keras's `Embedding` layer for the padding token. You'll read about the `Embedding` layer next.

Next, you'd replace the `Masking` layers you were using in your earlier seq2seq models with `Embedding` layers. These can perform the same masking, but additionally they map scalar integers into higher dimensional vector coordinates. Here's how you would define your encoder's embedding layer:

```
# 1
enc_embeddings = Embedding(
    num_enc_embeddings, embedding_dim,
    weights=[pretrained_embeddings], trainable=False,
    mask_zero=True, name="encoder_embeddings")
# 2
enc_embedded_in = enc_embeddings(encoder_in)
```

Embedding layers usually go at the start of a network, like this:

1. When creating an Embedding layer, you specify the number of possible input tokens — defined here as num_enc_embeddings — and the number of dimensions to map those values into, defined here as embedding_dim. When using pre-trained embeddings, you provide them using the weights parameter and then set trainable=False so the model doesn't modify their values while training.

2. Then you pass your Input layer into the Embedding layer, just like what you did before with the Masking layers. The Embedding layer will still perform masking because you created it with mask_zero=True. That tells it to treat the input value zero as a padding token, but you *must* include that extra token in your input token count. That's why you had to add one to the size of the vocabulary when you declared num_enc_embeddings.

You could declare the decoder's Embedding layer the same way, using pre-trained embeddings for your target language. However, Keras can also learn its own embedding values during training. To do that in your decoder, for example, you'd declare your Embedding layer like this:

```
num_dec_embeddings = out_vocab_size + 1
dec_embeddings = Embedding(
  num_dec_embeddings, embedding_dim,
  mask_zero=True, name="decoder_embeddings")
```

The difference here is that you don't supply an argument for the weights parameter, and you rely on the default value of True for the trainable parameter. This Embedding layer will initialize its embeddings to random values and modifying them during training, just like it modifies the weights of other layers in the network.

> **Note:** Another option for your Embedding layers is to start with pre-trained embeddings but set trainable=True. Or even train for a while with it set to False before training for additional epochs with it set to True. In either case, the idea is to take advantage of the information the embeddings contain while fine-tuning them to be more appropriate for your model's specific task.

The `Embedding` layers reserve zero for the padding token, so you'll need to avoid that ID for your real tokens. One option is to shift all your token IDs by one when making your conversion maps, like this:

```
in_token2int = {token : i + 1
                for i, token in enumerate(in_vocab)}
out_token2int = {token : i + 1
                 for i, token in enumerate(out_vocab)}
```

You'd need to make minor differences in `make_batch_storage` and `encode_batch`, too, because the input sequences are no longer one-hot encoded. For example, you would set tokens like this:

```
enc_in_seqs[i, time_step] = in_token2int[token]
```

Instead of:

```
enc_in_seqs[i, time_step, in_token2int[token]] = 1
```

You still one-hot encode the target sequence, since the decoder still outputs a probability distribution over the vocabulary. However, make sure the decoder's output layer has the correct size.

You can use `num_dec_embeddings`, but that includes an extra padding token that your model should never output. Or you can use `out_vocab_size`, but then you'll need to subtract 1 from its training output targets so it doesn't try one-hot encoding values larger than its max.

Using word embeddings in iOS

When it comes to using your trained model in an app, it's similar to what you did in the SMDB project. However, there are a few important caveats:

- You'll have to include mappings for your tokens, just like you did with the character-based models. However, these will be quite a bit larger due to the larger vocabulary and the fact that the tokens aren't single characters. You'll also need to know the indices of any special tokens, like <START>, <STOP> and <UNK>.

- Pre-trained word embeddings are often produced for lower-case tokens. That means that you'll need to convert your input sequences to lower case prior to translating them, then figure out what to capitalize in the output. You can use specific rules or heuristic-based approaches, or you might try training a separate neural network to capitalize text.

- As mentioned earlier, tokenize the input text the same way you did when training. You didn't have to worry about that when working with characters, because there's no ambiguity about what constitutes a token in that case.

- Be sure to replace any OOV tokens with the proper <UNK> token(s). You just dropped OOV tokens when working with characters, but you'll lose too much information if you do that with whole words.

- After running your model — maybe with a nice beam search — you'll be left with a list of tokens that might look like this: `['i', 'do', "n't", 'like', '<UNK>', 'or', 'bugs', '.']`. You'll need to perform post-processing to properly capitalize words, insert spaces appropriately and connect contractions. You'll also need a plan for dealing with any <UNK> tokens. One option is to align the sentence in some way and copy over words that seem to match. For example, if there is one <UNK> token in each of the input and output sequences, just copy the original unknown input token directly into the output. Translating between some language pairs requires a reordering of terms, and sometimes the numbers of missing terms won't match up. Even when things seem to line up, that won't always produce a good result. Dealing with OOV tokens is an open area of research and there isn't any easy answer that always works. When in doubt, you always have the option of leaving them unknown.

To conclude this introduction to using word tokens, keep these tips in mind:

- Pre-trained embeddings learn the biases of the data they are trained on. For example, embeddings trained on internet data usually place the word "apple" closer to tech companies, like Microsoft, than to fruits, like banana.

- Each embedding represents the average of all uses for that word. That means words used in multiple different ways have diluted embeddings that don't always represent any of their uses well. There have been attempts to deal with this issue using context-sensitive embeddings. These are more complex but may be worth looking into for some projects.

- Try running a spell checker on your sequences prior to looking for OOV tokens. That should help reduce the number of tokens you can't find in your vocabulary.

- When you encounter an OOV token during preprocessing, you might want to consider lemmatizing or stemming it and checking for that instead. Sometimes, vocabularies only contain other variations of a word, but that may give you better results than using an <UNK> token.

- Similar words should have similar embeddings. That means you *may* get reasonable results for words in your vocabulary even if they weren't present in your training data, as long as they are similar in usage to other words that were in the data. However, training with more data that fully covers your vocabulary is still preferred.

- There have been attempts to create vectors for OOV tokens on the fly, or to use hybrid models that treat OOV tokens at the character level instead of as whole words. You should research ideas like these if you have a project that needs to handle many rare or unknown words.

Key points

- **Bidirectional recurrent networks** produce better encodings in cases wherein context appears both before and after an item in a sequence.

- Use **beam search** with your decoder to produce better translations.

- Seq2seq models that include **attention** mechanisms generally outperform those that do not, because they learn to focus on the most relevant parts of sequences.

- Word **embeddings** encode information about the contexts in which words are used, capturing relationships between words in an unsupervised manner. Using them improves performance on most NLP tasks.

- OOV tokens are more difficult to handle when using word tokens, but you'll need a plan for dealing with them because it's much less likely that you'll be able to fully support your source or target languages at the word level.

Where to go from here?

These past three chapters have only scratched the surface of the field of NLP. Hopefully, they've shown you how to accomplish some useful things in your apps, while sparking your interest to research other topics. So what's next?

The past year has brought an important advance in the field of NLP that we didn't cover: language models. While word embeddings are essentially a type of transfer learning for NLP, the latest state-of-the-art techniques extend this concept to use neural networks to create pre-trained **language models**. These essentially learn to predict the next word in a sentence, and in doing so they seem to learn useful, transferable knowledge about the language. Building models on top of them greatly improves performance on most NLP tasks, beyond what has been achieved with word embeddings, and is the basis for exciting efforts in language generation tasks, too.

The pre-trained language models currently available are still quite large, but they'll make their way into smaller packages more suitable for mobile soon. They're certainly a good candidate for inclusion as part of Core ML, the way Apple currently supplies common computer vision models, so who knows? Either way, I recommend reading up on the subject if NLP interests you.

Finally, rather than list specific projects to consider or topics to learn, here's a great GitHub repo that tracks the current state-of-the-art solutions and useful datasets for various NLP tasks: nlpprogress.com. These aren't necessarily all feasible on mobile devices, but it shows you the types of things people are doing with natural language — and how they do it. If you're at all interested in the field and what's currently possible, I recommend spending some time exploring it.

Conclusion

Congratulations! You've completed your journey into Machine Learning. The knowledge and skills you've gained throughout these chapters will help you in all your future machine learning projects.

The world of machine learning is constantly evolving, we hope that this book has been useful to you as a guide for your first steps into this amazing tech and will prove to be a valuable resource in your pursuit of deeper knowledge.

If you have any questions or comments as you work through this book, please stop by our forums at http://forums.raywenderlich.com and look for the particular forum category for this book.

Thank you again for purchasing this book. Your continued support is what makes the tutorials, books, videos, conferences and other things we do at raywenderlich.com possible, and we truly appreciate it!

Wishing you all the best in your continued adventures,

– Matthijs, Chris, Audrey, Alexis, Marin, Phil, Vijay and Manda

The Machine Learning by Tutorials team

Photo Credits

Snacks Dataset

The images used for training the snacks models are taken from the Google Open Images dataset at https://storage.googleapis.com/openimages/web/index.html

See the file credits.csv for the names of the authors, the original image URLs, and the licensing terms for each photo.

App Icons

The camera icon was made by Daniel Bruce and is licensed under Creative Commons CC BY 3.0. Downloaded from https://www.flaticon.com/authors/daniel-bruce

The picture frame icon was made by Dave Gandy and is licensed under Creative Commons, CC BY 3.0. Downloaded from https://www.flaticon.com/authors/dave-gandy

- http://creativecommons.org/licenses/by/3.0/

Chapter 1

Pineapple photo by rrei320

- URL: https://www.flickr.com/photos/27673266@N05/14553029897

- License: https://creativecommons.org/licenses/by/2.0/

Muffins photo by vania

- URL: https://www.flickr.com/photos/v-recipes/578020399
- License: https://creativecommons.org/licenses/by/2.0/

I'm a good dog photo by Greg Heo

- URL: https://www.instagram.com/p/BLZTFnQAhwv

Waffles photo by Shanna S

- URL: https://www.flickr.com/photos/pineappleandcoconut/15933599971
- License: https://creativecommons.org/licenses/by/2.0/

The boy is holding a baseball bat

- URL: https://blog.keras.io/the-limitations-of-deep-learning.html

Chapter 2

Cat photo by Alan Loda

- URL: https://www.flickr.com/photos/144036100@N03/27791840904
- License: public domain

Dog photo by Patrick Vince

- URL: https://www.flickr.com/photos/atwistedpoet/23169235843
- License: public domain

Peeled banana photo by Slipp D. Thompson

- URL: https://www.flickr.com/photos/slippyd/8277559220
- License: https://creativecommons.org/licenses/by/2.0/

Hotdog photo by Alexis Lamster

- URL: https://www.flickr.com/photos/amlamster/7316391958
- License: https://creativecommons.org/licenses/by/2.0/

Ambiguous salad photo by Joselu Blanco

- URL: https://www.flickr.com/photos/silverman68/5623882552
- License: https://creativecommons.org/licenses/by/2.0/

M&M KitKat cake photo by Janet

- URL: https://www.flickr.com/photos/13698839@N00/8618561269
- License: https://creativecommons.org/licenses/by/2.0/

Oranges photo by bizmac

- URL: https://www.flickr.com/photos/bizmac/14712610901
- License: https://creativecommons.org/licenses/by/2.0/

Pretzels photo by Allagash Brewing

- URL: https://www.flickr.com/photos/allagashbrewing/16874642802
- License: https://creativecommons.org/licenses/by/2.0/

Apples photo by Jitze Couperus

- URL: https://www.flickr.com/photos/jitze1942/20471969212
- License: https://creativecommons.org/licenses/by/2.0/

Waffles photo by Arnold Gatilao

- URL: https://www.flickr.com/photos/arndog/5608469721
- License: https://creativecommons.org/licenses/by/2.0/

Castle photo by Tyler Brenot

- URL: https://www.flickr.com/photos/152474924@N02/36728130146/
- License: public domain

Hotdogs and apples photo by Neeta Lind

- URL: https://www.flickr.com/photos/neeta_lind/11369529674
- License: https://creativecommons.org/licenses/by/2.0/

Pineapple photo by rrei320

- URL: https://www.flickr.com/photos/27673266@N05/14553029897
- License: https://creativecommons.org/licenses/by/2.0/

Cookie photo by Stacy Spensley

- URL: https://www.flickr.com/photos/notahipster/4054380865
- License: https://creativecommons.org/licenses/by/2.0/

Apples and carrots photo by Breville USA

- URL: https://www.flickr.com/photos/breville/8734805221
- License: https://creativecommons.org/licenses/by/2.0/

Chapter 3

Doughnut photo by Jessica Spengler

- URL: https://www.flickr.com/photos/wordridden/9049507338
- License: https://creativecommons.org/licenses/by/2.0/

Ice cream photo by The MisAdventures of Maja

- URL: https://www.flickr.com/photos/misadventuresofmaja/18314540852
- License: https://creativecommons.org/licenses/by/2.0/

Pineapple pieces photo by leighklotz

- URL: https://www.flickr.com/photos/leighklotz/19572186218
- License: https://creativecommons.org/licenses/by/2.0/

Salad photo by rusvaplauke

- URL: https://www.flickr.com/photos/rusvaplauke/1115667258
- License: https://creativecommons.org/licenses/by/2.0/

Waffles photo by Shanna S

- URL: https://www.flickr.com/photos/pineappleandcoconut/15933599971
- License: https://creativecommons.org/licenses/by/2.0/

Pineapple photo by rrei320

- URL: https://www.flickr.com/photos/27673266@N05/14553029897
- License: https://creativecommons.org/licenses/by/2.0/

Ice cream guy photo by Michelle Tribe

- URL: https://www.flickr.com/photos/greencolander/7273153472
- License: https://creativecommons.org/licenses/by/2.0/

Muffins photo by vania

- URL: https://www.flickr.com/photos/v-recipes/578020399
- License: https://creativecommons.org/licenses/by/2.0/

Chapter 4

(All the photos in this chapter are part of the dataset.)

Chapter 5

Green apples photo by Alan Levine

- URL: https://www.flickr.com/photos/cogdog/21315932745
- License: https://creativecommons.org/licenses/by/2.0/

Chapter 6

Muffins photo by N i c o l a

- URL: https://www.flickr.com/photos/15216811@N06/8694455448
- License: https://creativecommons.org/licenses/by/2.0/

Apples photo by Kirinohana

- URL: https://www.flickr.com/photos/kiri_no_hana/9558521857
- License: https://creativecommons.org/licenses/by/2.0/

Chapter 7

(All the photos in this chapter are part of the dataset.)

Chapter 8

Banana guy photo by zeevveez

- URL: https://www.flickr.com/photos/zeevveez/5932888099
- License: https://creativecommons.org/licenses/by/2.0/

Salad or strawberries image photo by Steven Depolo

- URL: https://www.flickr.com/photos/stevendepolo/6023062188
- License: https://creativecommons.org/licenses/by/2.0/

Chapter 9

Cat and dog photo

- This is 2007_002597.jpg from the Pascal VOC dataset.
- http://host.robots.ox.ac.uk/pascal/VOC/voc2012/index.html

Chocolate cake photo by Calgary Reviews

- URL: https://www.flickr.com/photos/calgaryreviews/6674880811
- License: https://creativecommons.org/licenses/by/2.0/

Orange photo by Emiliano Horcada

- URL: https://www.flickr.com/photos/emilianohorcada/4667500048
- License: https://creativecommons.org/licenses/by/2.0/

Salad photo by Tatsuo Yamashita

- URL: https://www.flickr.com/photos/yto/4196836777
- License: https://creativecommons.org/licenses/by/2.0/

Hot dog photo by scott feldstein

- URL: https://www.flickr.com/photos/scottfeldstein/177839329
- License: https://creativecommons.org/licenses/by/2.0/

Green apples photo by Alan Levine

- URL: https://www.flickr.com/photos/cogdog/21315932745
- License: https://creativecommons.org/licenses/by/2.0/

Banana and salad photo by Maurina Rara

- URL: https://www.flickr.com/photos/maurina/7162799390
- License: https://creativecommons.org/licenses/by/2.0/

Chapter 10

Muffins photo by N i c o l a

- URL: https://www.flickr.com/photos/15216811@N06/8694455448
- License: https://creativecommons.org/licenses/by/2.0/

Cat and dog photo

- This is 2007_002597.jpg from the Pascal VOC dataset.
- http://host.robots.ox.ac.uk/pascal/VOC/voc2012/index.html

Fruit photo by Robert Scoble

- URL: https://www.flickr.com/photos/scobleizer/3373156563
- License: https://creativecommons.org/licenses/by/2.0/

Motorcycle photo

- This is 2007_005989.jpg from the Pascal VOC dataset.
- http://host.robots.ox.ac.uk/pascal/VOC/voc2012/index.html

Tropical island image by Ky0n Cheng

- URL: https://flic.kr/p/XfwbHy
- License: public domain